W9-BIO-607

CHICAGO ACCESS®

Orientation

Rising up brazen and brilliant from the plains of America's heartland, Chicago astonishes. The nation's third-largest city covers 227 square miles and stretches 33 miles along the shores of **Lake Michigan**, a Great Lake that looks more like an infinite sea. Suburbs in six counties expand the metropolitan area to 3,721 square miles, collectively known as "Chicagoland." European explorers first came upon this part of the world in 1680, and were followed a century later by fur trappers and soldiers. The settlement of 340 people was incorporated as a town in 1833, and its name was derived from the Illini word *che-cau-gou,* meaning either "wild onion" or "strong and great." Today, more than three million people reside here in a colorful mosaic, from the old guard to recent émigrés from Korea, Poland, India, and Iran.

The city's complex character and raucous history are legendary. Chicago is the city that rebuilt itself from the ground up in no time flat after the devastating Great Fire of 1871. And this is the city where Al Capone celebrated St. Valentine's Day in 1929 with a machine-gun massacre of rival gangsters. From the formation of labor unions to antiwar marches during the 1968 Democratic National Convention, great social events have unfolded here too.

Chicago is a virtual textbook of architectural styles. The spectacular skyline stretches from the Gothic **Tribune Tower** to the Art Deco **333 North Michigan Avenue** to the sleek Modernism of **Mies van der Rohe**'s steel-and-glass skyscrapers, then reaches up to America's tallest building—the **Sears Tower.** Closer to ground level, the city boasts elegant turn-of-the century mansions in the **Gold Coast,** which is studded

Map labels

- 19 W Irving Park Rd.
- 41
- WRIGLEYVILLE
- W Addison St.
- Belmont Harbor
- LAKE VIEW
- N Halsted St.
- N Lake Shore Dr.
- W Belmont Ave.
- N Lincoln Ave.
- N Clark St.
- Diversey Harbor
- W Diversey Pkwy.
- N Branch Chicago River
- W Fullerton Ave.
- Lake Michigan
- to O'Hare International Airport
- 90
- 94
- DEPAUL
- John F. Kennedy Expwy.
- LINCOLN PARK
- Lincoln Park
- N Milwaukee Ave.
- 64 W North Ave.
- OLD TOWN
- GOLD COAST
- BUCKTOWN/ WICKER PARK
- NEAR NORTH
- MAGNIFICENT MILE
- W Augusta Blvd.
- W Chicago Ave.
- RIVER NORTH
- STREETERVILLE
- W Grand Ave.
- N Western Ave.
- N Ogden Ave.
- RIVER WEST
- Chicago River
- E Wacker Dr.
- W Washington Blvd.
- W Randolph St.
- W Warren Blvd.
- W Washington Blvd.
- Grant Park Garage
- W Madison St.
- W Jackson Blvd.
- Chicago Harbor
- 290 Eisenhower Expwy.
- LOOP
- Congress Pkwy.
- Grant Park
- 90
- 94
- S Canal St.
- S Clark St.
- W Taylor St.
- W Roosevelt Rd.
- S Branch Chicago River
- Chicago Meigs Field
- W 18th St.
- S Indiana Ave.
- SOUTH LOOP
- W Cermak Rd. (22nd St.)
- Burnham Park
- to Midway Airport
- 55
- Stevenson Expwy.
- S Archer Ave.
- W 31st St.
- W 35th St.
- S Dr. Martin Luther King Jr. Dr.
- W Pershing Rd.
- S Ashland Ave.
- S Halsted St.
- Dan Ryan Expwy.
- 90
- 94
- S State St.
- S Michigan Ave.
- S Drexel Blvd.
- W 47 St.
- HYDE PARK/ KENWOOD
- Washington Park
- N
- km 1 2
- mi 1 2

with literally hundreds of historic buildings, and **Frank Lloyd Wright's** groundbreaking Prairie School designs, which live on throughout **Oak Park** and at his masterful **Robie House** in **Hyde Park.**

Visitors are dazzled by the array of stores and glitzy shopping malls preening along **Magnificent Mile**, fascinating **Shedd Aquarium**, and the treasures of the **Art Institute of Chicago**, including one of the country's most extensive collections of Impressionist paintings. Baseball fans won't want to miss a pilgrimage to historic **Wrigley Field**, home of the **Cubs. Lake Shore Drive** is another must-see, a stunningly scenic route skirting the city and lake.

In 1893, during the World's Columbian Exposition, a visiting reporter dubbed Chicago the "Windy City" because of all the bragging residents did about the place. Boastfulness can still be discerned here. Even an insult—as when New York essayist A.J. Liebling called Chicago the "Second City"—is proudly flaunted like a scar from a hard-won battle. Chicago is, after all, birthplace of the Chicago blues as well as home to an internationally acclaimed symphony orchestra, a renowned theater scene, a bustling financial district, miles of public beaches, acres of parks, world-class cuisine, and the ever-popular deep-dish pizza—a diversity of riches that begs exploration and enjoyment.

How To Read This Guide

CHICAGO ACCESS® is arranged by neighborhood so you can see at a glance where you are and what is around you. The numbers next to the entries in the following chapters correspond to the numbers on the maps. The type is color-coded according to the kind of place described:

Restaurants/Clubs: Red   **Hotels:** Blue

Shops/ ☂ Outdoors: Green   **Sights/Culture:** Black

♿ **Wheelchair accessible**

Wheelchair Accessibility
An establishment (except a restaurant) is considered wheelchair accessible when a person in a wheelchair can easily enter a building (i.e., no steps, a ramp, a wide-enough door) without assistance. Restaurants are deemed wheelchair accessible *only* if the above applies, *and* if the rest rooms are on the same floor as the dining area and their entrances and stalls are wide enough to accommodate a wheelchair.

Rating the Restaurants and Hotels
The restaurant ratings take into account the quality, service, atmosphere, and uniqueness of the restaurant. An expensive restaurant doesn't necessarily ensure an enjoyable evening; however, a small, relatively unknown spot could have good food, professional service, and a lovely atmosphere. Therefore, on a purely subjective basis, stars are used to judge the overall dining value (see the star ratings at right). Keep in mind that chefs and owners often change, which sometimes drastically affects the quality of a restaurant. The ratings in this guidebook are based on information available at press time.

The price ratings, as categorized at right, apply to restaurants and hotels. These figures describe general price-range relationships among other restaurants and hotels in the area. The restaurant price ratings are based on the average cost of an entrée for one person, excluding tax and tip. Hotel price ratings reflect the base price of a standard room for two people for one night during the peak season.

Restaurants
★	Good
★★	Very Good
★★★	Excellent
★★★★	An Extraordinary Experience
$	The Price Is Right (less than $10)
$$	Reasonable ($10-$15)
$$$	Expensive ($15-$20)
$$$$	Big Bucks ($20 and up)

Hotels
$	The Price Is Right (less than $100)
$$	Reasonable ($100-$175)
$$$	Expensive ($175-$250)
$$$$	Big Bucks ($250 and up)

Map Key

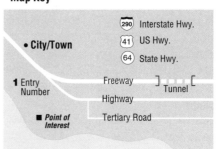

(290)	Interstate Hwy.
• City/Town (41)	US Hwy.
(64)	State Hwy.
1 Entry Number	Freeway / Tunnel
	Highway
■ *Point of Interest*	Tertiary Road

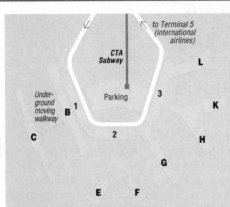

Baggage claim areas and free shuttle-bus service to all terminals and the parking lot are located on the lower level.

O'HARE INTERNATIONAL AIRPORT

Terminal Locations for Airlines

1 United
United Express
Lufthansa (departures only)

2 America West
Continental
Northwest
United
USAir

3 Air Canada
American
American Eagle
Delta
Qantas
Sun Country
TWA

Terminal 5
Location of international airlines including Aeroflot, Air France, Air Ukraine, Alitalia, American Trans Air, Austrian, Aviateca, British Airways, China Eastern, Czechoslovak, El Al Israel, JAL, KLM, Korean Air, LOT Polish, Lufthansa, Mexicana, Royal Jordanian, Sabena, SAS, Swissair, Taesa, Tarom, and Varig Brazilian.

Area code 312 unless otherwise noted.

Getting to Chicago

Airports

O'Hare International Airport (ORD)

O'Hare International Airport (ORD) is 17 miles northwest of the **Loop** on the **Kennedy Expressway (I-90/94).** The nation's busiest airport, it covers a vast area (the distance between two concourses can stretch more than a mile); the terminals are connected by pedestrian passageways, moving sidewalks, and a free "people mover" shuttle that circulates every 7.5 minutes among the three domestic terminals, the international terminal (Terminal 5), and the long-term parking facility. To make connections, allow at least 30 to 50 minutes between flights, and 1.5 hours for international flights. The airport is fully accessible to people with disabilities.

Airport Services

Airport Emergencies	686.2236
Business Service Center	686.0400
Currency Exchange	686.7965
Customs and Immigration	894.2900
First Aid	686.2288/9
Ground Transportation	686.2200
Information	686.2200, Terminal 5 894.2000
Lost and Found	686.2385
Paging	686.2200, Terminal 5 894.2000
Parking	800/547.5673
Police	686.2230
Traveler's Aid	686.7562

Airlines

Air Canada	800/776.3000
America West	800/235.9292
American	800/433.7300
American Eagle	800/433.7300
British Airways	800/247.9297
Continental	800/525.0280
Delta	800/221.1212
Northwest	800/225.2525
TWA	800/221.2000
United	800/241.6522
United Express	800/241.6522
USAir	800/428.4322

Getting to and from O'Hare

By Bus

Continental Air Transport (454.7800) offers door-to-door bus service to about 30 downtown and suburban hotels. Service is offered daily, at 15-minute intervals, from 6AM to 11:30PM. Departures are from the lower level of each terminal.

The **Regional Transit Authority** (836.7000, 800/972.7000) provides public bus service to several suburbs. The bus departs from Door 1G of Terminal 1 and outside the **Rotunda Building** between Terminals 2 and 3. Buses to more distant suburbs and neighboring cities run from the lower levels of Terminals 1, 2, and 3.

By Car

From the airport to the Loop, head east on the Kennedy Expressway and follow the signs. Exit at either **Ohio Street** (north downtown area) or **Congress Parkway** (South Loop). The trip takes 30 to 90 minutes, depending on traffic.

From the Loop to the airport, follow signs on the Kennedy Expressway (I-90/94) west to **O'Hare.** A free, elevated people mover runs every 7.5 minutes from the remote, long-term parking lot to all terminals.

The following car-rental agencies staff 24-hour counters in the baggage-claim areas of Terminals 1, 2, and 3; in Terminal 5, consult the Information oard in the main lobby. All provide courtesy buses etween the terminals and their lots.

Rental Cars

Alamo	800/327.9633
Avis	694.5680, 800/331.1212
Budget	686.6800, 800/527.0700
Dollar	694.2200, 800/800.4000
Hertz	686.7272, 800/654.3131
National	694.4640, 800/328.4567

By Limousine

Car service to the city, suburbs, and far-flung towns is offered by several companies. Counters are located in the baggage claim areas, or call 686.2200 for information.

By Taxi

Taxis line up at the lower level of each terminal. Share-a-Ride drivers take several passengers to separate downtown locations for a per-person fare. **American United** (248.7600), **Checker** (243.2537), **Flash** (561.1444), and **Yellow** (829.4222) have 24-hour service.

By Train

The **Chicago Transit Authority** (**CTA**; 836.7000) operates 24-hour train service to and from the airport on the **O'Hare/Congress/Douglas** line. This mode is frequently the fastest, and is convenient if you're traveling light (getting to the station requires some walking and stair climbing). Trains depart every 10 minutes from the lower level under the main parking lot; the trip to the Loop takes 40 minutes.

MIDWAY AIRPORT

to I-55 →

Terminal Locations for Airlines

A Southwest

B Air South
Chicago Express
Comair
Frontier
KIWI
Myrtle Beach Jet Express
Vanguard
Western Pacific

C American
Trans Air
Northwest

S Cicero Ave.

Parking

S Cicero Ave.

N

Midway Airport (MDW)

Smaller (and often saner) than **O'Hare, Midway Airport** serves 14 domestic airlines. It is located 10 miles southwest of the Loop off the **Stevenson Expressway (I-55)** at 5500 to 6300 South Cicero Avenue.

Airport Services

Airport Emergencies	767.0500, ext 360
First Aid	767.0500, ext 291
Ground Transportation	767.0500, ext 320
Information	767.0500
Lost and Found	767.0500, ext 360
Paging	767.0500
Parking	767.0500, ext 302
Police	735.7773
Traveler's Aid	686.7562

Airlines

America West	800/235.9292
American Trans Air	800/225.2995
Chicago Express	800/264.3929
Comair	800/354.9822
Continental	800/525.0280
Frontier	800/432.1359
KIWI	800/538.5494
Myrtle Beach Jet Express	800/386.2786
Northwest Airlines	800/225.2525
Southwest Airlines	800/435.9792
TWA	800/221.2000
Valujet	800/825.8538
Vanguard	800/826.4827
Western Pacific	800/930.3030

Getting to and from Midway

By Bus

Continental Air Transport (454.7800) provides door-to-door bus service between the airport and a dozen downtown hotels. Service is daily, with departures every 30 minutes from 6AM to 10PM.

By Car

Driving from the Loop, take Lake Shore Drive or the **Dan Ryan Expressway (I-90/94)** south to the Stevenson Expressway, exit at **Cicero Avenue,** and continue three miles south. The trip takes 30 to 60 minutes, depending on traffic.

The following car-rental agencies, located in the baggage-claim areas, provide 24-hour service.

Rental Cars

Avis	800/331.1212
Budget	686.6800, 800/527.0700
Dollar	735.7200, 800/800.4000
Hertz	735.7272, 800/654.3131
National	471.3450, 800/227.7368

By Limousine

Information on limo service to Chicago and its suburbs is available at the main terminal information booth, or by calling 767.0500.

By Taxi

Taxis line up outside the main terminal. A trip to the Loop can take anywhere from 30 minutes to one hour, depending on traffic.

By Train

The **Chicago Transit Authority**'s (836.7000) **Orange Line** runs between **Midway** and the Loop daily every 10 minutes between 5AM and 11PM; the trip takes 25 minutes and the view (it's all aboveground) is striking.

Meigs Field

This small airport (744.4787), located at the lakefront and **15th Street,** is used by private planes and charters.

Bus Station (Long-Distance)

The **Greyhound Bus Terminal** is located in the Loop (630 W Harrison St, at N Desplaines St). For local information, call 408.5930; national, 800/231.2222.

Train Station (Long-Distance)

Chicago is a major hub for **Amtrak** service, with approximately 50 trains arriving and departing daily. **Union Station** is located in the Loop, at West Adams and Canal Streets. For local information, call 655.2385; national, 800/USA.RAIL.

Getting Around Chicago

Bicycles

While cycling is not a practical means of transportation around the city, cyclists enjoy mile after mile of paths meandering along Lake Michigan and through Chicago's many parks. **Lincoln Park** is particularly pretty for cycling and has bikes available for rent.

Boats

Chicago's position at the junction of lake and river makes it an ideal city to tour by water. For details see "Tours," below.

Buses

The **CTA**'s (836.7000, 836.4949 for the hearing impaired) comprehensive system of buses provides a convenient way to get around the city—or to the suburbs via **PACE** buses. Buses run daily; schedules vary, but exact times and routes are given at bus stops and on **CTA** maps. Use your judgment in taking a bus after dark.

Exact change or tokens are accepted on buses. Tokens are sold in packs of 10, and can be used on the subway or el trains (buy them at banks, currency exchanges, some el stations, and **Jewel** and **Dominick's** supermarkets). Transfers, sold at a nominal charge, allow you to switch to two other connecting routes within a two-hour period. Children under seven ride free; children ages 7 to 11, seniors, and people with disabilities pay discounted fares.

Driving

While gridlock doesn't paralyze Chicago's busiest streets, driving in the Loop, Magnificent Mile, or **River North** areas on weekdays can be slow and confusing. No traffic is allowed on **State Street** in the Loop, and other Loop streets run one way in alternate directions. A cavernous underpass—**Lower Michigan Avenue** and **Wacker Drive**—runs from Congress Parkway to **Grand Avenue,** bypassing heavy traffic. Enter on Grand Avenue heading toward Michigan Avenue, or exit Congress Parkway onto **Lower Wacker Drive.** Also note: During rush hour, the direction of some lanes on Lake Shore Drive is reversed to handle heavy traffic—but the switch isn't always well marked.

Chicago's expressways are good routes for long hauls, though they're no fun during rush hour. Major expressways include the Stevenson (I-55) to the **Southwest Side** and beyond; the Dan Ryan (I-90/94) running south of the Loop; the Kennedy (I-90/94), running north and northwest of the Loop and breaking off into the **Edens Expressway** to the northern suburbs; and the **Eisenhower (I-290),** which heads due west of the Loop.

Finding a parking spot in or even near the Loop takes time, money, or both. Most curbside spots have meters, usually with 30-minute limits. Watch out for signs that prohibit parking or designate a tow zone, as the cops are dead serious about handing out tickets. If your car gets towed, the ransom will be at least $100 cash. Relatively cheap parking is available in the **Grant Park Garage** (294.4598, 294.4593) off Michigan Avenue. Access is off **Randolph, Monroe,** and **Van Buren Streets.** Next best are **Self-Park** garages; one always seems to be right around the corner. Avoid leaving valuables in your car or trunk, wherever you park.

Subways and Elevated Trains

What's collectively known as "the el" includes subways as well as elevated trains and crisscrosses the entire city (see the **CTA/METRA** map on the inside back cover of this book). Continual but inconsistent upgrading has left some parts of the system looking seedy and others sleek. For the most part, it's clean and dependable, with routes that take you directly to or within a few blocks of your destination.

The **CTA** is an especially good choice in lieu of driving in the jam-packed Loop, Magnificent Mile, or River North areas, though the system gets crowded during weekday rush hours. Most trains run 24 hours; for safety's sake, don't take them after the evening rush hour.

Money-saving tokens sold in packs of 10 can be used on all conveyances (buy them at banks, currency exchanges, some el stations, and **Jewel** and **Dominick's** supermarkets). Transfers, sold at a nominal charge, allow you to switch to two other connecting routes within a two-hour period. Some lines of the el require no transfers between them; ask a fare-taker for information. Children under seven ride free; children ages 7 to 11, seniors, and people with disabilities pay discounted fares.

Taxis

Cabs may be hailed in the street; they are unoccupied if the top light is on. In some downtown areas—around the **Fulton Street** dance clubs, for instance—you'll need to call one for a pickup. Companies include

American United...248.7600

AMMS Limos 792.1126

Checker 243.2537

Flash 561.1444

Yellow 829.4222

Tours

By Air

For a bird's-eye view, contact **Chicago by Air** (708/524.1172). Cessna airplanes take you (by advance reservation only) from **Meigs Field** downtown (15th St at the lakefront) for 30-minute-long narrated tours.

By Boat

The city of Chicago exists because it is here that Lake Michigan meets the Chicago River, forming a link between the Great Lakes and the Mississippi River, or, by extension, between the Atlantic Ocean and the Caribbean. Native Americans used this link for hundreds of years. One of the best ways to see Chicago is still from the water, and there are several sightseeing boats from which to choose.

The **Chicago Architecture Foundation** (922.3432) conducts tours along the Chicago River that focus on the city's remarkable architectural wealth. **Wendella** (337.1446) and **Mercury Cruises** (332.1353) both have tour boats that go out into the lake, leaving from the **Michigan Avenue Bridge** by the **Wrigley Building. Chicago's First Lady** (708/358.1330) offers architecture tours from the lake and river, leaving from **North Pier** (E Illinois St at N McClurg Ct), as does **Chicago from the Lake**

(527.2002). The latter offers mealtime cruises, as do the **Spirit of Chicago** (836.7888) and **Odyssey** (708/990.0800); both depart from **Navy Pier.** Most boat tours are available from May through October, but the **Spirit of Chicago** offers several Christmastime cruises.

By Bus

Bus tours are offered by **American Sightseeing** (427.3100) and **Gray Line of Chicago** (427.3107). The **Chicago Motor Coach Company** (922.8919) runs double-decker tours of the Loop and **North Michigan Avenue. Untouchable Tours** (881.1195) does a lighthearted tour of gangster sites. Occasionally, the **Chicago Architecture Foundation** (922.3432) conducts well-informed bus tours.

By Foot

Chicago is a great city for walkers (it's flat, like most of the Midwest). Ask about walking tours at your hotel desk or call any of the following organizations:

Chicago Architecture Foundation................922.3432

Chicago Historical Society...........................642.4600

Friends of the Chicago River........................939.0490

My Kind of Town 708/432.6060

Trains

There are 11 commuter lines offering daily service to the suburbs and **Southeast Side,** departing from four different stations in the Loop. For information on services of all lines, call 836.7000.

Walking

Chicago is easily—perhaps best—explored on foot. For self-guided walking tours, a number of titles are available at local bookstores. A particularly good one is *Walking with Women Through Chicago History*, available at the bookstores of the **Chicago Architecture Foundation** (224 S Michigan Ave, at E Jackson Blvd, 922.3432) or the **Chicago Historical Society** (1601 N Clark St, between W North Ave and W Eugenie St, 642.4600).

FYI

Accommodations

Like most big cities, it's best to make hotel reservations in advance of a visit. In Chicago, you must have reservations during the 4th of July holiday and during the prime convention months of May, June, September, and October. In addition to hotels, there are a variety of bed-and-breakfasts in the area; for more information, call the **Bed and Breakfast Association** (951.0085).

Climate

Chicago is notorious for its unseasonable climate, especially in the winter months when subzero temperatures and icy winds challenge even the most hardy travelers. In spring, expect a combination of lingering winter and balmy summer previews—often in the same day. Summer is very pleasant, although the thermometer can top 100 degrees at times. The prolonged autumn season, when it's sunny yet cool, is the ideal time for a visit. But whenever you visit, be prepared for rapid changes in temperature.

Months	Temperature Range (°F)
January	15-31
February	18-34
March	27-45
April	38-59
May	47-70
June	57-79
July	61-83
August	60-82
September	52-75
October	42-66
November	30-48
December	19-35

Drinking

The drinking age is 21. No store may sell liquor on Sunday before noon.

Hours

Opening and closing times for shops, attractions, coffeehouses, etc. are listed only by day(s) if normal hours apply (opening between 8 and 11AM and closing between 4 and 7PM). In unusual cases, specific hours are given.

Money

At **O'Hare International Airport,** international currencies can be converted at the **Foreign Currency Exchange** (686.7965), which has two branches in the international terminal (Terminal 5); one branch in Terminal 3; and mobile carts that service international departures for one hour prior to boarding time. In town, there are two offices of **Thomas Cook Foreign Exchange** (111 W Washington St, between N Clark and N La Salle Sts, 807.4940; 100 E Walton St, at N Michigan Ave, 649.0288). Banks, many stores, and restaurants accept traveler's checks, generally requiring a photo ID. You can purchase them at **American Express** (625 N Michigan Ave, at E Ontario St, 435.2570), **Thomas Cook** (see above), and most major banks. Banks are generally open Monday through Friday from 8:30AM to 5:30PM.

Personal Safety

As in any city, use common sense: If an area looks questionable, stay out of it. Much of the **South Side** and **West Side** are anything but hospitable. Exceptions are **Little Italy, Chinatown,** Hyde Park, and **Pullman,** which are reachable by cab or car. On the **North Side,** even the nicest areas can be next to trouble spots, so stay within the neighborhood boundaries as defined in this book. Sometimes safety is a matter of day and night. The lakefront, public parks, the Loop, and the **South Loop** are active during the day, but are often deserted after dark; take a cab or car directly to nighttime destinations in these areas. On the other hand, the Magnificent Mile and **Oak, Rush,** and **Division Streets** in the Gold Coast are active well into the night. Just stay within well-lighted areas and watch out for seedy characters who might have an eye on your wallet or purse. Pickpockets are especially active in downtown shopping crowds during the winter holidays.

Publications

The city's largest daily newspaper, the *Chicago Tribune,* concentrates on national news and features; the smaller tabloid *Chicago Sun-Times* does a good job with local news, politics, and sports. The *Chicago Daily Defender* serves the city's African-American population. The *Reader* is a free, liberal weekly with reviews and extensive entertainment listings; *New City,* another weekly freebie, also has helpful listings, especially for art galleries (both are distributed throughout the downtown area on Thursday afternoons). *Chicago* magazine is a glossy monthly with numerous event and restaurant listings and an upscale audience. A notch higher on the snob scale is *North Shore,* a monthly magazine; *Crain's Chicago Business,* a weekly, provides in-depth coverage of local business; and the free weekly *Windy City Times* caters to the gay and lesbian community. Chicago's ethnic population is served by a number of foreign-language newspapers, among them the Polish *Daily Zgoda; La Raza,* a Spanish weekly; and *Hankook Ilbo* or *Korea Times,* which is published every day except Sundays.

Restaurants

Reservations are essential at most trendy or expensive restaurants, and it's best to book far in advance at such dining spots as **Charlie Trotter's, Everest Room, Ambria,** or **Le Francais.** If you want to avoid crowds, ask about late seatings. In general, jackets and ties are not required, except at the posh and popular places, and most establishments accept credit cards.

Shopping

North Michigan Avenue has become one of the leading shopping streets in the world; from **Armani** to **Escada, Tiffany** to **Barneys,** branches of international retailers are located here and on adjacent Oak Street. State Street, long the nation's leading retail street, has lost its former glamour. However, it's reviving as a center for off-price retailing, with stores like **Filene's, T.J. Maxx,** and **Toys R Us.** Adjacent **Wabash Avenue** has branches of **Ann Taylor, Eddie Bauer,** and the **Gap,** as well as local specialists like **Otto Pomper,** a purveyor of cutlery and gadgets. For funkier, offbeat items, visit the numerous stores along **Halsted Street,** particularly either side of **Armitage** (2000 North). To see how city-dwelling Chicagoans shop for basic necessities, visit the sprawling shopping area just west of the intersection of **West North** and **North Clybourn Avenues.**

Smoking

City laws require all restaurants to have nonsmoking sections, and prohibit smoking in theaters, public buildings, and on public transportation.

Street Plan

One 19th-century visitor described Chicago as "the most right-angle town" he'd ever seen—a characteristic that proves helpful in finding your way around. Except for the rare diagonal, streets are arranged on a grid, with the zero point for addresses at the intersection of State and **Madison Streets** in the Loop. The city's North Side is north of Madison Street and the South Side is south of it. The West Side is west of State Street. In the Loop and north of it, most of the **East Side** stretches along Lake Michigan; in Hyde Park, though, the lake is nearly two miles east of State Street. Street numbers generally run in increments of 100 per block, with eight blocks to a mile. North Side streets and north-south streets on the South Side generally have names, while east-west streets on the South Side for the most part go by numbers. Hence, you'll find **Wellington Avenue** at 3000 North, and **30th Street** at 3000 South. When discussing street directions with Chicagoans, by the way, they will say "30 hundred," not "three thousand."

Taxes

The local sales tax is 8.75 percent; none is imposed on groceries.

Tickets

The main ticket sources are **Ticketmaster** (559.1212) and **Hot Tix** (977.1755). **Hot Tix** booths are located at 108 North State Street, near West Washington Street; the sixth level of **Chicago Place** at 700 North Michigan Avenue; and 1616 Sherman Avenue, between Davis and Church Streets, **Evanston.** The two Chicago booths are open Monday through Saturday from 10AM to 6PM and Sundays from 12 to 5 PM; The Evanston booth is open Wednesdays and Thursdays from 11AM to 3PM; Friday and Saturday, 10AM to 4PM and Sundays from 12 to 4PM.

Tipping

Leave a 15- to 20-percent gratuity in restaurants and for personal services. Taxi drivers expect a 15-percent tip.

Time Zone

Chicago is on Central Standard Time, one hour behind New York and two hours ahead of California.

Visitors' Information Offices

Chicago Office of Tourism information centers are located in the **Old Water Tower** (806 N Michigan Ave, at Chicago Ave; open Monday to Friday from 9:30AM to 6PM, Saturday from 10AM to 6PM, and Sunday from 11AM to 5PM); the **Chicago Cultural Center** (77 E Randolph St, between N Michigan and N Wabash Aves; open Monday to Friday from 10AM to 6PM, Saturday from 10AM to 5PM, and Sunday from noon to 5PM); and Navy Pier (700 E Grand Ave, off N Lake Shore Dr; open Monday through Thursday from 10AM to 9PM, Friday and Saturday from 10AM to 10PM, and Sunday from 10AM to 7PM). The general information number is 744.2400.

Phone Book

Emergencies

Ambulance/Fire/Police	911
AAA Emergency Service	800/262.6327
Dental Referral	726.4321
Medical Referral (nonemergency)	670.2550
Northwestern Memorial Hospital, Streeterville	908.2000
Poison Control	942.5969
Rape Crisis Hotline	372.6600
Rush Presbyterian St. Luke's, Northwest Side	942.5000
24-hour Pharmacy	664.8686

Sports and Recreation

Chicago Bears	708/615.2327
Chicago Cubs	404.2827
Chicago Blackhawks	455.7000
Chicago Bulls	455.4000
Chicago Fine Arts Hotline	346.3278
Chicago Live Concert Line (popular music)	666.6667
Chicago Music Alliance	987.9296
Chicago White Sox	924.1000
Dance Hotline (performances)	419.8383
Illinois Lottery Winning Numbers	976.6060
Special Events Hotline	744.3370

Visitors' Information

American Youth Hostels	327.8114
Amtrak	558.1075
Chicago Transit Authority/Regional Transit Authority	836.7000
Greyhound/Trailways Bus Lines	800/231.2222
Handicapped Services Information	744.4016
Legal Assistance Foundation	341.1070
Passport Information	353.7155
Time and Weather	976.8367
Western Union	800/325.6000

Chicago Celebrations

From Latin music concerts and funny film festivals to Venetian boat parties and the annual singing of Christmas carols to the inhabitants of the **Lincoln Park Zoo,** Chicago offers festivities for folks of all ages every month of the year. For more information on the following activities, call the **Chicago Office of Tourism** (744.2400).

January

Navy Pier Art Fair (throughout January) showcases the work of local artists amid the palm trees and water fountains of the Crystal Gardens at **Navy Pier.**

Heartland Fishing, Hunting & Boat Show/RV and Camping Show (mid-January) is where exhibitors from all over the US and Canada strut their stuff at **Illinois State University.**

February

Black History Month celebrates the cultural heritage of African-Americans through various events and displays at **Navy Pier.**

Chicago Chinese New Year Parade (last weekend in February) kicks off the new year in Chinatown.

March

St. Patrick's Day Parade (17 March) unleashes Irish pride and carousing. The politicians are out in full force and the river is dyed green.

April

Lincoln Park Conservatory Spring and Easter Flower Show (throughout April) displays a stunning array of springtime flora.

Earth Day (23 April) teaches families about the earth's natural resources around the city.

Cinco de Mayo Festival (last weekend in April), an early celebration of Mexican independence held at **McCormick Place,** is the largest indoor Hispanic festival in the Midwest.

Ikenobo Ikebana Japanese Flower Arranging Show (last weekend of April) highlights traditional and unique Japanese flower arrangements and illustrates the fundamentals of Japanese flower arranging at the **Chicago Botanic Garden.**

May

Art Chicago at Navy Pier (mid-May) features work of emerging and famous artists represented by local, regional, national, and international galleries.

Viva! Chicago Latin Music Festival (last weekend in May) showcases international performers from Mexico, Latin America, South America, and the Caribbean, as well as national and local groups.

June

Chicago Blues Festival (first weekend in June) is the largest free blues festival in the world—three days of great blues performed by top blues artists at **Grant Park.**

57th Street Art Fair (first weekend in June), near the **University of Chicago** campus, celebrates its 50th anniversary (1997), attracting artists from throughout North America.

Chicago Gospel Festival (early June), held at **Grant Park,** is a joyous and free celebration of gospel music.

Old Town Art Fair (second weekend in June) features more than 225 invited artists at the oldest juried art fair in the US.

Printer's Row Book Fair (third weekend in June) means thousands of new, used, rare, and antiquarian books for sale, as well as events like author signings and readings.

July

Taste of Chicago (first week in July) serves up culinary delights from more than 70 restaurants, peppering the festivities with terrific live music.

Independence Day Concert and Fireworks (3 July) provides one of the summer's most spectacular events as the **Grant Park Symphony Orchestra**'s rousing rendition of the *1812 Overture* accompanies a huge fireworks display.

Chinatown Summer Fair (late July) features a sidewalk sale, farmer's market, art fair, stage show, and children's activities.

Chicago's Venetian Night (late July) is an evening aquatic parade along the downtown shoreline of **Lake Michigan.**

August

Gold Coast Art Fair (second weekend in August) is an outdoor art show exhibiting the works of artists from over 25 states and countries.

Chicago Air and Water Show (third

weekend in August) provides demonstrations of skill by teams of international aviation and aquatics experts.

Chicago International Concours d'Elegance (late August) is a showcase for vintage automobiles just south of **Buckingham Fountain.**

Chicago Jazz Festival (Labor Day weekend) brings together top international and local jazz musicians and millions of fans for this free concert in **Grant Park.**

September

African/Caribbean International Festival of Life (first weekend in September) rocks with reggae, calypso, samba, salsa, jazz, blues, and more at the **North Pier.**

Berghoff Oktoberfest (mid-September) lures about 100,000 revelers for a four-day street party. Hosted by **The Berghoff Restaurant,** the party takes over **West Adams Street** (between South State and South Dearborn Streets) for a celebration of bratwurst, beer, and German music.

October

Chicago International Children's Film Festival (early October) is the nation's oldest and largest competitive festival for children's films.

Chicago International Film Festival (mid-October) showcases films from around the world at various theaters throughout the city.

November

Chicago Humanities Festival (mid-November) hosts speeches, concerts, dramatic readings, and panel discussions at various cultural institutions.

Magnificent Mile Lights Festival (mid-November) kicks off the holiday season with a festive weekend as the stores unveil their Christmas windows and 150 trees along **Michigan Avenue** are lit with 600,000 lights.

December

In the Spirit is a month-long celebration of the different holiday traditions of Christmas, Hanukkah, and Kwanzaa. Events throughout the city include storytelling, films, music, dance, and theater.

Carol to the Animals (second Sunday in December) gives humans the gift of singing Christmas carols to their four-legged friends at the **Lincoln Park Zoo.**

Bests

Catherine Johns
Talk show host, WLS Talk Radio

Shopping: North Michigan Avenue. Start at the **Chicago River** and walk north. Check out the **Wrigley Building** on your left, **Tribune Tower** on the right. Then head on into shoppers' heaven: **Crate and Barrel, Saks, Bloomie's, Neiman Marcus, Water Tower Place.** And don't max out your credit cards before you hit the fabulous **Oak Street** boutiques.

Take a short trip north to the **Chicago Botanic Gardens** in Glencoe. Be sure to spend some time in the idyllic Japanese garden.

For a downtown take-out meal—fabulous fried shrimp at the **Fish House** at Wells and Grand.

Be sure to drive along **Lake Shore Drive,** as far south and north as you can.

Cruise **Sheridan Road,** from Chicago's northern edge, through the **North Shore** suburbs. Stately mansions, beautiful landscape, the spectacular **Baha'i House of Worship,** and our glorious lake.

Try the restaurants in the old Italian neighborhood, **Taylor Street.**

Take the kids to the **Chicago Children's Museum** at **Navy Pier,** and see the skyline from the huge Ferris wheel.

Chinatown is full of good restaurants, and bakeries, and shops peddling mysterious potions and lotions.

Walk, bike, or rollerblade the lake front path. Even in "bad" weather Chicago's lake shore is beautiful.

In nice weather, take one of the cruises offered along the river. They'll take you out into the lake, along the shore, and you won't want to get off the boat.

Don't miss the **Frank Lloyd Wright Home and Studio** in Oak Park.

Chicago's loaded with fabulous Mexican restaurants. One of the best is **Abril** at **Logan Square.**

Listen to **WLS Talk Radio 890 AM.** The day's hottest issues and lots of fun.

Kevin Butler
Kicker, Chicago Bears

Hotel Nikko's Sunday brunch: a great way to finish a weekend in the city.

A **Cubs** game: never been; a must.

Taste of Chicago: all the flavors of Chi-town in one place.

A **Bears** game in December: bring your earmufffs.

Second City: laughs and more.

Golf courses: so many . . . **Kemper Lakes** and **Cog Hill,** where the pros play.

Michigan Avenue: you need it, they have it.

The Loop

Commerce, culture, and City Hall politics coalesce and collide downtown in the Loop, where movers and shakers make the world of Chicago go 'round. All roads lead here: the expressways, **Lake Shore Drive** and other main thoroughfares, commuter and freight trains, boats, buses, subways, the el—and, in decades past, cable cars that converged in an embracing loop, giving the area its name. Since the 1970s, **State Street** has lost much of its retail cachet to the famous shopping strip known as the Magnificent Mile; but it is still home to **Marshall Field's**, located in a stately building designed a century ago by **Daniel Burnham**, and **Louis Sullivan**'s cast iron–adorned **Carson Pirie Scott & Company** and stores abound one block east on **Wabash Avenue**. Just another block farther east, the **Art Institute of Chicago**, **Orchestra Hall**, and the **Fine Arts Theater** line **Michigan Avenue**. Across this thoroughfare stretches **Grant Park**, site of the annual jazz, blues, and gospel festivals and the **Taste of Chicago** fair. West of State Street, concrete canyons exude money and might, from bank headquarters and stock exchanges to **Holabird & Roche**'s turn-of-the-century **City Hall** and **Skidmore, Owings & Merrill**'s **Sears Tower**, America's's tallest building. Enclosing it all in a quiet curve is **Wacker Drive**, parallel to the **Chicago River**, where it all began.

In 1837 the town, filled with log cabins and 4,170 people, was incorporated as a city; its first marketplace was already developing along a street called **South Water Market** (now Wacker Drive) on the south bank of the Chicago River. By 1840 the population had mushroomed to 30,000. Wealthy citizens built homes in the Loop, especially south of **Van Buren Street** in what is now the

South Loop, an easy commute from their business offices. Many working-class immigrants dwelled in shanty towns near the river or in slums hidden in alleys behind the business district. In the 1850s the city's first architect, **John Mills Van Osdel**, and his colleagues began designing buildings as tall as five stories along nearby **Lake Street.**

Meanwhile, entrepreneur Potter Palmer bought three-quarters of a mile of land along State Street. He knocked down a sorry strip of shanties, paved the street, and persuaded the **Field, Leiter, and Company** department store to rent a building he constructed, thus inspiring the birth of a new center of commerce. In 1870 Palmer opened his first **Palmer House Hotel** (today it's in its third building at Wabash Avenue and **Monroe Street**). A year later, everything went up in smoke when the Great Fire—believed to have started in a barn just to the southwest—reduced most of Chicago to rubble in three days. In a show of amazing resilience, the city quickly rebuilt itself, this time in accordance with a new law that permitted only brick or stone buildings in and near the Loop. Downtown became strictly business, as workers moved on to cheaper neighborhoods and the wealthy built mansions farther south on **Prairie Avenue.**

The 1880s marked the start of the Loop's heyday, which lasted for more than half a century. Train stations and shipping piers connected the city to the rest of the world. Corporations built their national headquarters here. The Chicago School of Architecture emerged, with such eminent names as **Adler & Sullivan** and **Burnham & Root.** The Loop became a center of culture, entertainment, and hospitality, with world-class theaters and hotels. But the 1940s brought the flight of business and industry to the suburbs, and it wasn't until the **Prudential Building** was constructed in 1955 that growth again seemed possible. In 1978 State Street was closed to vehicular traffic in an attempt to revive ailing businesses, but many failed anyway. Still—especially during the affluent 1980s—new offices, apartment buildings, and hotels sprang up throughout the Loop, perhaps most noticeably along Wacker Drive.

A stroll through the Loop is a must, whether to shop, immerse yourself in the culture, or simply gape at the tall buildings. Activity of every sort is at its frenzied height Monday through Friday from 8AM to 6PM. On evenings and weekends the area is far quieter, but not nearly so deserted as it was a decade ago. Stores on State Street are now open on Sunday, and people stroll along Michigan Avenue until late at night, particularly in the summer. For a perfect introduction to the Loop, start your visit with one of several guided tours offered by bus or boat; see the "Orientation" chapter for suggestions.

AGNIFICENT MILE/STREETERVILLE

Chicago River
E Wacker Dr.
7
6
E Randolph Dr.
U.S. Coast Guard Station
N Lake Shore Dr.
Columbia Yacht Club
Richard J. Daley Bicentennial Plaza
Monroe Harbor
Chicago Yacht Club
E Monroe Dr.
S Lake Shore Dr.
James C. Petrillo Music Shell
Breakwater
E Jackson Dr.
1 Grant Park
Chicago Harbor
Clarence Buckingham Fountain
E Balbo Dr.

1 Grant Park During the 1920s this park was built on landfill in accordance with **Daniel Burnham**'s Chicago Plan of 1909, a design blueprint that was influential in Chicago's development. The park occupies the northern edge of a miles-long strip of parks and beaches that stretches to the South Side. Designed in French Classical style, the park's 220 acres feature the country's largest remaining stand of elm trees, two symmetrical rose gardens, and vast grassy spaces that have invited promenades, picnics, and protests— the most famous one during the 1968 Democratic National Convention. Throughout the summer, the Grant Park Concerts Society invites classical music lovers to bring a blanket and a picnic to the **Petrillo Music Shell** for free concerts beneath the stars, with a startling view of the glistening Chicago skyline as a backdrop. A Fourth of July concert culminating in the *1812 Overture,* punctuated by an extraordinary fireworks display, is a tradition for the evening of July 3. The city's annual music galas, including the Jazz, Blues, and Gospel festivals, attract millions; an evening at any of these is a must. This is also where the annual **Taste of Chicago**, a 10-day-long feeding frenzy featuring food from many of Chicago's leading restaurants, starts the last week of June. ♦ Concerts: W, F-Su nights June through August. Bounded by E Roosevelt Rd and E Randolph Dr, and Lake Michigan and Michigan Ave. Concert information 819.0614

Within Grant Park:

The Bowman & The Spearman
Two statues of Indians on horseback in heroic poses, bow and spear drawn, mark the entrance to the park off Congress Parkway. They were designed in 1928 by Ivan Mestrovic. ♦ Inside the park at the intersection of Congress Plaza and Congress Plaza Dr

Balbo Drive in Grant Park was named after General Italo Balbo, an Italian aviator who visited the 1933 Century of Progress Exposition with his flying armada.

Beaubien Court (120 E, from 150 N to 186 N) was named after "Jolly Mark" Beaubien (1800-1881), fur trader, ferryman, innkeeper, and fiddle player. Mark and his brother, Jean Baptiste, fathered a total of 43 children, more than the entire population of the city in 1829.

Restaurants/Clubs: Red **Hotels:** Blue
Shops/ ♟ Outdoors: Green **Sights/Culture:** Black

Clarence Buckingham Fountain In 1927 Kate Buckingham presented this Beaux Arts fountain of Georgia pink marble to the city in honor of her brother Clarence, a trustee and benefactor of the **Art Institute.** Symbolizing Lake Michigan, **Bennett, Parsons & Frost**'s Rococo fountain (pictured above) sits in a pool containing four bronze sea horses (cast by Marcel Francois Loyau) representing the four states that border the lake: Illinois, Wisconsin, Minnesota, and Michigan. A million-and-a-half gallons of water circulate through the fountain; colored lights that play off the water are a favorite attraction on warm nights. Nearly 8,000 rosebushes planted in beds to resemble the gardens of Versailles surround the fountain. ♦ At the center of a rectangle bounded by E Balbo and E Jackson Drs, and S Lake Shore and S Columbus Drs

Chicago Yacht Club and Columbia Yacht Club
These private clubs (the **Columbia** is located in the formerly seafaring *Abegweit* docked in the harbor) welcome members of yacht clubs from around the world. Even if you lack such status, you can still enjoy a warm-weather stroll nearby, taking in the pretty view of Monroe Harbor and, to the south, Burnham Harbor, where anyone is entitled to launch a boat. Every August, boat owners throughout the city decorate their vessels with colored lights and parade them against a black backdrop of water and sky in the magical Venetian Night Boat Parade. ♦ Chicago: E Monroe Dr and Lake Michigan. 861.7777; Columbia: 111 N Lake Shore Dr (at E Randolph Dr). 938.3625

 Richard J. Daley Bicentennial Plaza
Several seasonal activities are offered at this public recreational facility. In winter an outdoor 80-by-135-foot ice-skating rink offers great views of the lake and the Loop; the same rink is used for roller skating in summer. Skates are available for rental. There are also 12 lighted tennis courts; call ahead to reserve time. Immediately south of the plaza is Chicago's largest garden of prairie

wildflowers. ♦ Admission for skating and tennis. Tennis: daily April through October. Skating: daily December through March, when weather permits. 337 E Randolph Dr (at N Columbus Dr). 747.2200

2 Amoco Building Holding the title of the tallest marble-clad structure in the world turned out to be more liability than asset for the owners of what was originally the **Standard Oil Building.** Designed by **Edward Durell Stone** with the **Perkins & Will,** and built in 1974, this monolith was clothed in white Carrara marble that proved unable to withstand Chicago's extreme temperatures and high winds. The gleaming white panels have been replaced with speckled granite. The reflecting pool in the lower level plaza contains *Sounding,* a 1975 sculpture designed by Harry Bertoia; its breeze-ruffled clusters of copper rods produce pleasant metallic sounds. ♦ 200 E Randolph Dr (between N Columbus Dr and N Stetson Ave)

3 Prudential Building Built in 1955 from a design by **Naess & Murphy,** this gray limestone and aluminum structure was the tallest building in the city for more than a decade. Look for sculptor Alfonso Iannelli's exterior relief of the *Rock of Gibraltar,* which is the company's trademark. ♦ 130 E Randolph St (between N Stetson Ave and N Beaubien Ct)

3 Two Prudential Plaza Since 1990, **Loebl Schlossman & Hackl**'s setback granite tower (pictured at right) punctuates the skyline at the north end of **Grant Park.** The various shades of gray granite and tinted glass were chosen to harmonize with the adjacent limestone and aluminum **Prudential Building.** The best feature of "Two Pru," as it is popularly called, is the one-acre **Beaubien Plaza** (named for the city's first innkeeper) on the northwest corner of the block, graced with waterfalls and terraces, and shielded from the summer sun by the original **Prudential Building.** ♦ N Stetson Ave (at E Lake St)

4 Fairmont Hotel $$$ This copper-roofed, pink granite Neo-Classical building stands in contrast to the giant glass boxes that make up most of the nearby **Illinois Center** (see below). Each of the 700 rooms is individually decorated in contemporary to period furniture, and all have wonderful views of **Grant Park** and Lake Michigan. The hotel is popular with business travelers who can take advantage of secretarial services, closed-circuit TV, telex, fax, and meeting facilities. Other perks include guest membership in a nearby health club, and valet and concierge service. There are three restaurants: **Entre Nous** offers French cuisine; **Primavera,** Italian; and **Metropole,** hearty sandwiches. Weekend packages are available. Frequent corporate travelers receive special discounts. ♦ 200 N Columbus Dr (between E Lake and E South Water Sts). 565.8000, 800/527.4727; fax 856.9020 ♿

5 Athletic Club Illinois Center Kisho Kurokawa designed this building in 1990. Six floors of white walls and glass, topped with Japanese wind sculptures, enclose luxury health facilities for people who don't mind taking out a second mortgage to pay the dues. The club boasts a 100-foot-high indoor rock-climbing wall, tons of fitness equipment, basketball and handball courts, a rooftop terrace with a sundeck, a pool, an alfresco restaurant, and a full-service European spa for massages and skin treatments. Open to members, as well as guests of the **Hyatt Regency** and **Fairmont** hotels, it's worth a look-see just for fun. ♦ Daily. 211 N Stetson Ave (at E Lake St). 616.9000

6 Illinois Center Golf Vacationers who want to take a break from sight-seeing can tee at off this nine-hole, par-three golf course located in the heart of downtown. The driving range features grass tees at both ends with target greens and sand bunkers to simulate an actual game experience. The complex's **David Leadbetter Academy** conducts a complete schedule of lessons and clinics. The clubhouse includes a fully stocked pro shop, men's and women's locker rooms, and a bar and grill. Equipped with heated and covered driving stalls, the center is open year-round. And with Chicago's business district just a swing away, a quick game can be played by executives on their lunch hour-and-a-half. ♦ Fee. Golf course: daily 7AM to sunset. Driving range: daily 7AM to 9PM. 221 N Columbus Dr (between E Randolph Dr and E Wacker Dr). 616.1234

Two Prudential Plaza

Courtesy of Loebl Schlossman & Hackl

7 Swiss Grand Hotel $$$ A dramatic glass triangle at the eastern edge of **Illinois Center** (see below), this luxury high-rise hotel with 630 rooms offers a quiet European ambience and fantastic views. Large guest rooms, writing desks, seating areas, and two-line phones are standard. Complimentary valet services include pressing and mending, and newspapers are delivered every morning. The **Penthouse Health Spa,** which overlooks the lake, has a heated pool, exercise equipment, whirlpool, sauna, and steam room, and offers Swedish massage. The executive business center provides secretarial services, computers, telex, and fax. Dining facilities include the **Cafe Suisse,** which serves Swiss, American, and Italian dishes; the more casual **Garden Cafe;** the **Americus Bar,** serving English pub fare; the **Konditorei** bakery; and a lobby bar. ◆ 323 E Wacker Dr (off N Columbus Dr). 565.0565, 800/635.GRAND; fax 565.0315 ♿

8 Hyatt Regency Chicago $$$ The 2,019 modestly furnished guest rooms in the two towers of this **Illinois Center** hotel are popular with conventioneers. The main public space is a multilevel glass-enclosed lobby complete with a pool and waterfall surrounded by lush greenery. Amenities include six restaurants, among them the **All-Seasons Cafe, Knuckles Sports Bar, Mrs. O'Leary's** deli, **Skyway,** and **Stetson's Chop House,** as well as the glassed-in **Big Bar** with its intoxicating city view. Slightly more expensive, the **Regency Club** section of the west tower has its own concierge and private lounge with complimentary continental breakfast and cocktails. VIP suites have fireplaces and saunas. Weekend rates are available. ◆ 151 E Wacker Dr (between N Columbus Dr and N Stetson Ave). 565.1234, 800/233.1234; fax 565.2966 ♿

9 Illinois Center The world's largest mixed-use project is built on more than 80 acres of obsolete rail yards once operated by the **Illinois Central Railroad. Mies van der Rohe** conceived the original design, which was begun in 1967; various architects have been involved since. **One Illinois Center** was the first building completed in this vast, rather sterile complex, and the addition of **Two** and **Three Illinois Center** and **Boulevard Towers** did nothing to humanize the scale. *Splash,* a colorful sculpture by Jerry Peart installed on the plaza in 1986, brought a spot of warmth to these dark, looming canyons. The underground level has a variety of shops that seem to go out of business and change owners frequently. ◆ Bounded by E Lake St and E Wacker Dr, and N Columbus Dr and N Michigan Ave

10 333 North Michigan Avenue Based on **Eliel Saarinen**'s second-prize design for the **Tribune Tower, Holabird & Root**'s 1928 structure was Chicago's first Art Deco skyscraper and the last of four buildings forming a gateway between the Loop and North Michigan Avenue. Its strong vertical tower, capped with clifflike setbacks, rises from a smooth, polished marble base. At the fifth floor, Fred Torrey's seven-foot-high limestone panels carved in low relief depict episodes of early Chicago history, including Father Jacques Marquette and the Fort Dearborn Massacre. ◆ At E Wacker Dr

10 Site of Old Fort Dearborn Bronze bricks embedded in the sidewalks just south of the Chicago River mark the outline of **Fort Dearborn,** located here from 1803 to 1812, when the outpost was abandoned and its fleeing inhabitants were massacred by angry Native Americans. ◆ N Michigan Ave (at E Wacker Dr)

11 360 North Michigan Avenue Crowned by an open, domed pavilion, **Alfred S. Alschuler**'s 1923 Neo-Classical skyscraper was angled on its irregular site to face the **Wrigley Building,** completed in 1922, and the 1920 Michigan Avenue Bridge. The griffins and coats of arms from the City of London that grace the lobby and concave exterior are reminders that this was originally the **London Guarantee Building** (it was later the **Stone Container Building**). Once majestic, the central arched entrance flanked by four Corinthian columns is not nearly as elegant today. ◆ At E Wacker Dr

12 Lincoln Tower Built in 1928, **Herbert H. Riddle**'s pencil-like tower carries the distinction of having the smallest floor space per floor of any building downtown. ◆ 75 E Wacker Dr (between N Michigan and N Wabash Aves)

12 Clarion Executive Plaza $$ This 1960s-style hotel features 415 unusually spacious guest rooms. Be sure to request a riverside room for a fantastic view. All rooms are equipped with voice mail, coffee makers, mini-bars, irons, hair dryers, and bathroom telephones. The three tower floors offer even more amenities, including daily newspapers and plush terry-cloth bathrobes. **Florio's** restaurant serves American cuisine and the **Midnight Star Saloon** serves typical bar offerings in a noisy setting of video games and TV sets. ◆ 71 E Wacker Dr (at N Wabash Ave). 346.7100, 800/621.4005; fax 346.1721 ♿

12 Seventeenth Church of Christ, Scientist, Chicago Designed in 1968 by **Harry Weese & Associates,** this travertine marble church was curved to fit the site, with a bronze-and-glass lobby recessed behind a sunken platform to shield it from the street. Notice the domed lantern centered over the reader's platform in the semicircular auditorium space. ◆ 55 E Wacker Dr (at N Wabash Ave). 236.4671

13 Heald Square The square was named for Captain Nathan Heald, ill-fated commandant of **Fort Dearborn** when in 1812, the fort was evacuated and its fleeing occupants massacred. In 1941, a bronze statue by sculptor Lorado Taft with Leonard Crunelle was dedicated here; it depicts George Washington flanked by two entrepreneurs: the English-born Robert Morris and Polish-born Haym Salomon. These successful American businessmen were the principal financiers of the Revolutionary War, and the monument is intended, as inscribed, to be a "Symbol of American tolerance and unity and of the cooperation of people of all races and creeds in the upbuilding of the United States." ♦ Traffic Island (off E Wacker Dr, between N Wabash Ave and N State St)

13 35 East Wacker Drive Thielbar & Fugard with **Giavar & Dinkelberg** designed this building, completed in 1926. The letters "JB," worked into the Neo-Baroque ornament throughout, are reminders that this was originally the **Jewelers Building.** The 17-story tower is crowned by a domed, column-encircled pavilion that contains the office of architect **Helmut Jahn.** Until 1940, tenants could drive into the building from lower Wacker Drive, go straight into an elevator, exit and park on their floor. ♦ At N Wabash Ave

14 Leo Burnett Building Roche/Dinkeloo Associates's 1989 design is related to **Robert A.M. Stern**'s 1975 Late Entry to the Chicago Tribune Tower Competition, which in turn translated **Adolf Loos**'s famous Ionic column entry of 1922 into a Postmodern form. Here a freestanding monumental column sheathed in a checkerboard pattern of granite has a giant order of abstract columns forming the base, a device that repeats at setback and crown. ♦ 35 W Wacker Dr (at N Dearborn St)

15 225 West Wacker Drive The architectural firm of **Kohn Pedersen Fox** designed this well-proportioned office building (pictured at right) in 1989. The structure has four corner towers linked in pairs like bedposts. These links are actually metal bridges, architecturally reminiscent of the many beautiful and graceful bridges spanning the Chicago River. ♦ At N Franklin St

Courtesy of Kohn Pedersen Fox Associates

16 333 West Wacker Drive In 1983 this building put **Kohn Pedersen Fox** on the Chicago map with a three-story marble-and-granite base relating to the street, and a sheer, green glass wall bowed to follow and reflect the Chicago River's curve. The **Chicago Athenaeum,** an independent three-branch museum, usually mounts an interesting architecture and design exhibit in the lobby here. ♦ Between N Franklin and W Lake Sts

17 Presidential Towers Solomon Cordwell Buenz & Associates's complex of four 49-story apartment towers with a 40-foot skylit atrium and an 80,000-square-foot mall is notable for several reasons, none of them architectural. Heralded as the hope of the blighted West Loop, it has been a financial headache since completion in 1986. Construction was subsidized with federal funds from the Department of Housing and Urban Development, obtained with the help of former US Representative Dan Rostenkowski, who arranged an exemption from public funding requirements. Despite that and its popularity with young Loop office workers, this may be the biggest HUD defaulter in the country. ♦ 555-625 W Madison St (bounded by W Monroe, N Clinton, and N Desplaines Sts)

18 Northwestern Atrium Center Architect **Helmut Jahn** successfully adapted 1930s streamlined forms to the building requirements of the 1980s in this impressive mixed-use building of green glass and aqua-tinted steel, constructed in 1987. Unlike many of his colleagues inspired by historical models, **Jahn** is an unabashed modernist in his use of materials. The north and south facades step back in a series of curves to create a striking profile (undoubtedly inspired by the cascading walls and light fixtures in the **Board of Trade** lobby—both the original and **Jahn**'s addition). An arched entrance on Madison Street leads to a dramatic multilevel lobby that serves the train station and office tower. The lobby's exposed steel structure is inspired by the great 19th-century iron-skeleton train sheds. Here and at **O'Hare Airport**'s **United Airlines Terminal, Jahn** has created dynamic spaces that recapture the excitement of travel for even the most jaded commuter. ♦ 500 W Madison St (at N Canal St)

Within Northwestern Atrium Center:

Chicago & Northwestern Station This grand dame among railway stations was here long before the modern edifice that surrounds it. Situated in the north section of the building on the second level, it's one of four stations serving commuter railroads from the suburbs and beyond. ♦ W Madison and N Canal Sts. 836.7000

Starting in the early 1900s and throughout most of this century the intersection of State and Madison Streets was often called the world's busiest corner. The truth of the statement was never tested but it did lure many tourists to the spot.

19 Riverside Plaza In 1929 this **Holabird & Root** design was built right over train tracks leading into **Union Station** (the train smoke is vented through the roof). The generous riverfront plaza, which provides the best view of the building, shows its vertical piers and deep setbacks. The relief carving on the base depicts great people in the history of journalism, from an ancient scribe to a Linotypist. The real treat is just inside the entrance: In the long tunnel-like concourse leading to **Northwestern Station** is a ceiling mural by John Warner Norton that uses jazzy semiabstract forms to depict the activities of the building's first owner, the *Chicago Daily News*. In the summer you can beat the traffic and reach Michigan Avenue by boat from the plaza. Vessels operated by the **Wendella** company dock here. ◆ 400 W Madison St (at N Canal St)

20 Civic Opera House Above the grand colonnade along Wacker Drive rises this 1920s tower typical of architects **Graham, Anderson, Probst & White.** The lavishly decorated Art Deco auditorium, home to the **Lyric Opera of Chicago** since the 1950s, has Egyptian-inspired details. Jules Guerin selected rich vermilion and orange accented with gold leaf as the interior color scheme; he also designed the stage's lovely fire-curtain mural. The masks of comedy and tragedy, and lyre, trumpet, palm leaf, and laurel wreath motifs appear in terra-cotta and bronze on the exterior and interior. This stage has also been host to ballet companies and other traveling troupes.

Renovations completed in 1996 created a new rehearsal space, an improved air-circulation system, and access for the disabled. Many Chicagoans consider it well worth making a cultural commitment to **Lyric** performances by buying season tickets—particularly now that it's under the supervision of general manager Ardis Krainik and artistic director Bruno Bartoletti. ◆ 20 N Wacker Dr (between W Madison and W Washington Sts). Lyric Opera box office 332.2244 ⅘

21 Corbetts $$ Except for office workers' fast food, this part of downtown doesn't offer much in the way of places to eat, which is why this rather ordinary spot is a find. The **Lyric** is right across the street, so it's popular with people on their way to the opera and celebrities such as Luciano Pavarotti, Placido Domingo, and Mikhail Baryshnikov. It's usually closed on Saturdays and Sundays, but when the opera's in town not only does the large dining room along Wacker stay open on weekends, but the staff put on their tuxes and lay out the white-linen tablecloths. The fare runs to hearty racks of lamb, strip steaks, and an assortment of salads. The best time to visit the bar on the Washington Street side is during Happy Hour when you can enjoy the warm, friendly atmosphere and free hors d'oeuvres. From the bar menu, you'll find light fare—steak sandwiches, club sandwiches, and salads. ◆ American ◆ M-F breakfast and lunch; dinner on opera nights. 333 W Washington St (at N Wacker Dr). 368.1591 ⅘

773-434-4225

22 Chicago Mercantile Exchange This is the most boisterous of the city's many trading exchanges. Futures and options on agricultural commodities (think pork bellies), foreign currencies, interest rates, stock market indices, and gold are traded on two separate floors via the open outcry system, wherein crowds of grown men and women shout loudly, make frantic hand signals, and jump up and down to get the seller's attention. This madness can be witnessed from galleries above each trading floor, where interactive videos further elucidate the goings-on. ◆ Free. M-F 7:30AM-3:15PM. 30 S Wacker Dr (between W Monroe and W Madison Sts). 930.8249 ⅘

23 Rand McNally Map and Travel Store An excellent selection of travel guides and maps, historic and topographic as well as the basic road variety, are offered. You will also find a great array of literature and video travelogues for the armchair traveler, geographic games and toys, and language guides. Whether or not you're planning a journey, a visit here will spark your imagination and might well give you wanderlust. ◆ Daily. 150 S Wacker Dr (at W Adams St). 332.2009. Also at: 444 N Michigan Ave (at E Illinois St). 321.1751

24 Union Station **Amtrak** trains as well as commuter lines from the suburbs use this station. Its vast restored lobby will transport you back to the time when trains were trains. ◆ W Adams and S Canal Sts. 655.2385, 800/USA.RAIL

25 Lou Mitchell's ★$ This hole-in-the-wall has been popular for breakfast since it opened in 1935, thanks to really good coffee with fresh cream, double-yolk eggs, omelettes and hash browns served in skillets, and homemade jams. On Saturday, expect a long wait for a seat at the cafeteria-style tables. ◆ American ◆ M-Sa breakfast and lunch. 565 W Jackson Blvd (between S Clinton and S Jefferson Sts). 939.3111

Stock Exchange Signals Used by the Traders

Buy

Full cent

One-half cent

Sell

Three-quarter cent

One-quarter cent

Chris Middour

26 Greyhound Bus Terminal The terminal handles **Greyhound** and **Trailways** long-distance bus services. ♦ 630 W Harrison St (at S Desplaines St). 800/231.2222

27 Main Post Office Straddling the Eisenhower Expressway ramp to Congress Street, this massive structure is headquarters for what government surveys indicate is the worst local postal system in the nation in terms of customer satisfaction. A self-service facility on the Van Buren Street side is open 24 hours a day, seven days a week. ♦ 433 W Van Buren St (at S Canal St). 765.3000 &

28 311 South Wacker Drive  **Kohn Pedersen Fox**'s largest—and least successful—Chicago endeavor was built in 1990. The 65-story structure is the tallest reinforced concrete building in the world, and its facade features a dizzying composition of granite and glass. The landscaping surrounding the building is impressive, and the barrel-vaulted winter garden (pictured above) is an attractive pass-through to the restaurant **Yvette Wintergarden.** ♦ Between W Van Buren St and W Jackson Blvd

Courtesy of Kohn Pedersen Fox Associates

Within 311 South Wacker Drive:

Yvette Wintergarden ★$$$ Bob Djahanguiri's (of **Yvette** on the Gold Coast) ambitious restaurant spills out onto the winter garden. The spacious plum and dark wood dining room serves bistro classics. Try salmon gravlax, chicken breast with pesto, or grilled striped bass with roasted tomatoes, artichokes, mushrooms, and wild green onions. The full menu is also served in the adjacent bar and winter garden. Live jazz and Latin music are played nightly. ♦ French ♦ M-F lunch and dinner; Sa dinner. 408.1242

29 Comic Relief Kids of all ages will enjoy the wide selection of comic books and games. At lunch hour, the store is crowded with businesspeople seeking comic relief from their jobs. ♦ Daily. 219 W Jackson Blvd (at S Wells St). 431.1515. Also at: 69 E Madison St (between N Michigan and N Wabash Aves). 332.0043

Restaurants/Clubs: Red   **Hotels:** Blue
Shops/ ♥ Outdoors: Green   **Sights/Culture:** Black

Sears Tower

Lunchtime waits are long, whether you want a black leather booth or favor the pale-green lunch counter. Signed photographs of celebrities who have eaten here line the walls, along with advertisements for Mrs. Levy's own brand of matzoh balls and other treats. Milk shakes are a specialty. ♦ Deli ♦ M-F breakfast and lunch. Street level, Franklin St side. 993.0530

31 AT&T Corporate Center Though built in 1989, this **Skidmore, Owings & Merrill** skyscraper (pictured at right) has polished granite curtain walls with strong vertical lines that recall the 1920s. Go into the luxuriant lobby of Italian marble, gold leaf, and rich wood trim, which also features a masterful trompe l'oeil mural by Richard Haas. Take the escalator to the second level

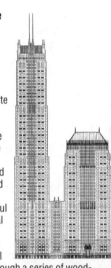

for great views through a series of wood-trimmed cutouts. The "bustle" addition to the south is the **US Gypsum Building,** designed by the same architects in 1991. The **Gallery Cafe** (332.1075) offers light fare for breakfast and lunch. ♦ 227 W Monroe St (at S Franklin St)

30 Sears Tower Built in 1974, this is America's tallest building. **Skidmore, Owings & Merrill**'s innovative structural system consists of nine square tubes that together form a larger square. The tubes rise to different levels—only two of them continue all the way to the top—and create a dramatic staggered profile. The 1,450-foot-tall structure (pictured above) was the highest allowed by the Federal Aeronautics Administration at the time it was built. More than a hundred elevators transport the 12,000 people who visit the building each day. Take a ride to the **Skydeck Observatory** on the 103rd floor for a spectacular panoramic view. In 1985 **SOM** added a four-story vaulted atrium on Wacker Drive to enlarge the lobby and make the retail space more appealing. The *Chicago Experience* at the visitors' center is a multi-image slide show. Also featured is a nine-foot working model of the tower. ♦ Skydeck: fee. Skydeck: October through February, daily until 10PM; March through September, daily until 11PM. Last ticket sold 30 minutes before closing. Bounded by W Jackson Blvd and W Adams St, and S Franklin St and S Wacker Dr. 875.9696 ᵴ

Within the Sears Tower:

Universe In 1974, sculptor Alexander Calder turned on the switch activating the motors powering the five primary-colored elements of his piece. A sun, a black pendulum, and three flowers are among the moving parts of this 33-foot-high construction. ♦ Calder level

Mrs. Levy's Deli $ This huge New York–style deli does a land office business.

32 303 West Madison Street Color and disciplined variety characterize **Skidmore, Owings & Merrill**'s finely detailed, modestly scaled 1988 office building (pictured above), geared to the smaller tenant. Leaded colored glass in the spirit of **Frank Lloyd Wright** enlivens the Franklin Street entrance. ♦ At S Franklin St

33 One South Wacker Drive Another of
Helmut Jahn's attempts to evoke 1930s
skyscrapers with a glass box, this 1982
building's huge floor areas defy efforts
at streamlining. ♦ At W Madison St

34 Dawn Shadows This black-painted
steel sculpture designed in 1983 by Louise
Nevelson was inspired by the configuration
of the elevated train tracks above Wells Street.
One of the best views of the piece is from the
station platform. ♦ Madison Plaza Bldg, 200
W Madison St (at N Wells St)

35 Bismarck Hotel $$ The ghosts of
backroom political wheeler-dealers and
the scent of cigar smoke seem to linger in
the corridors of this aging 520-room hotel.
For years, the hotel was the site of the Cook
County Democratic Party's meetings and
election-night victory parties. With rates well
below those of other hotels, it's a bargain for
visitors who want to stay in the Loop. It has
a bar, two eateries serving breakfast and
lunch, and one restaurant offering dinner, but
better options can be found nearby. Weekend
packages are available. ♦ 171 W Randolph St
(at N Wells St). 236.0123; fax 236.3177 &

36 James R. Thompson Center No one is
indifferent to **Murphy/Jahn**'s 1985 structure,
named for the governor who commissioned it.
Outside, gray- and salmon-colored piers rise
like a modern Stonehenge along Randolph
and Clark Streets, and Jean Dubuffet's
black-and-white sculpture, *Monument with
Standing Beast,* anchors the corner. Although
the red-and-blue–paneled exterior is not
wearing well, the interior is spectacular,
with offices ringing the skylit rotunda.
Two glass elevator shafts rise through the
space, and the top-floor view down into the
classically patterned marble and granite floor
is awesome—and dizzying. Chicagoans visit
the offices to get help with their taxes, renew
their driver's licenses, and obtain postal
service. Those with a more leisurely agenda
can enjoy a lunchtime concert played in a
resounding acoustical space, or have a snack
at the **Great State Fare** food court downstairs.
♦ Bounded by W Randolph and W Lake Sts,
and N Clark and N LaSalle Sts

Within the James R. Thompson Center:

Illinois Artisans Shop Works by some
of the state's finest craftspeople are for sale
here. ♦ M-F. Mezzanine. 814.5321

On 25 May 1981, "Spider" Dan Goodwin scaled
the Sears Tower while hundreds of astonished
spectators looked on. Later the same year, when
Goodwin attempted to climb the John Hancock
Center, Chicago firefighters doused him with
water, forcing him to turn back.

State of Illinois Gallery Frequently
changing exhibitions here showcase Illinois
artists' work in such media as painting,
sculpture, quilting, and performance art.
♦ M-F. Mezzanine. 814.5322

37 City Hall–County Building The mayor
hangs his (or her) hat on the fifth floor of this
massive Neo-Classical structure designed by
Holabird & Roche and built in 1911. Ongoing
melodramas and aldermanic turf battles are
acted out in the **City Council Chamber** on
the second floor. Council meetings are open
to the public, and when certain issues are
up for debate, it's great entertainment. There
is no set day for meetings, which are held
about every two weeks. ♦ Bounded by
W Washington and W Randolph Sts, and
N Clark and N LaSalle Sts. 744.3081 &

38 Richard J. Daley Center Civil courts, and
city and county offices are contained within
this building's triple bays of russet Cor-Ten
steel, which requires no maintenance and
becomes more handsome with the passing
years. Designed by **C.F. Murphy Associates,**
the center (pictured above) opened in 1965.
An eternal flame flickers in the adjacent plaza
in memoriam to the late Richard J. Daley,
mayor of Chicago for 21 years. The site of
many civic gatherings, both organized and
spontaneous, the plaza is perhaps best known
as home to the Cor-Ten steel *Chicago Picasso.*
Installed in 1967, the 50-foot-high Cubist
sculpture is an abstraction of a woman's head.

During the holidays, Chicago's official Christmas tree is set up on the plaza. The tree is created by lashing together as many as a hundred smaller evergreens in the form of one giant tree, which is trimmed with tens of thousands of ornaments and colored lights. ♦ Bounded by W Washington and W Randolph Sts, and N Dearborn and N Clark Sts

39 Chicago Temple (First United Methodist Church of Chicago) The "Chapel in the Sky," built in 1923 to plans by **Holabird & Roche,** rises 400 feet above ground, and its spire can be viewed only from a distance. At street level, a series of small stained-glass windows depicts the history of the church. Joan Miró's 93-foot-tall sculpture, *Miró's Chicago,* installed in 1981, sits in the adjacent narrow plaza. ♦ 77 W Washington St (at N Clark St)

40 Trattoria No. 10 ★★$$ This attractive subterranean restaurant, warmly decorated with stucco walls, a terra-cotta floor, and a beamed ceiling, serves very good basic and creative pasta dishes. It's popular with the lunchtime business crowd, and since the menu and prices are the same at lunch and dinner, it's an especially good deal in the evening. The hot appetizer buffet served at cocktail time, which includes all of the menu's appetizers plus pastas cooked and sauced before your eyes, is highly recommended. ♦ Italian ♦ M-Sa lunch and dinner. Reservations recommended. Valet parking after 5:30PM. 10 N Dearborn St (between W Madison and W Washington Sts). 984.1718 &

40 Sopraffina First Class Market ★$ Off-hours are likely best for a lunchtime visit to this popular cafeteria-style eatery—the line is long at noon, and you probably won't find a place to sit if you arrive five minutes later. Run by the same people who operate **Trattoria No. 10** (see above), it offers lighter and less-pricey fare—thin-crust pizza with spinach, asparagus, and goat cheese, along with a host of vegetable and pasta salads. Takeout is available, and Italian condiments, oils, and vinegars are sold in the market in the front of the restaurant. ♦ Italian ♦ M-F breakfast, lunch, and dinner; Sa lunch. 10 N Dearborn St (between W Madison and W Washington Sts) &. Also at: the AT&T Corporate Center. 984.0044

41 Chicago Loop Synagogue Look for *The Hands of Peace* metal sculpture by Israeli artist Henri Azaz stretching out from the facade, and the stained-glass window by Abraham Rattner illuminating the spacious interior of this 1958 building, which was designed by **Loebl Schlossman & Bennett.** ♦ 16 S Clark St (at W Madison St). 346.7370 &

42 181 West Madison Street Closely spaced columns of white granite with narrow mullions soar to nickel-plated finials at the parapets of this 1990 **Cesar Pelli & Associates** tower. The surface flattens on a gray day and shimmers when the sun shines. ♦ At S Wells St

43 Midland Hotel $$ This renovated 1920s hotel sits in the heart of the financial district. The lobby's gilded ceiling, with its Florentine-style relief, casts a warm glow. Decor in the 257 rooms and suites is ordinary—about what you would find at many other midrange hotels—but the furnishings are comfortable. Amenities include same-day laundry and dry cleaning, reduced rates at a nearby health club, 12 conference rooms, and fax and photocopying services. There are several restaurants, including the semiformal **Exchange** on the ornate balcony, and the **Ticker Tape Bistro,** which recreates the ambience of the 1920s Paris bistro where Hemingway and Fitzgerald met. Weekend packages are available. ♦ 172 W Adams St (between S LaSalle and S Wells Sts). 332.1200, 800/621.2360; fax 332.5909 &

44 190 South LaSalle Street John Burgee and **Philip Johnson**'s first building in Chicago went up in 1987. The five-story red granite base is similar to the **Rookery Building** across the street (see page 23), and the copper-clad gabled top recalls architect **John Wellborn Root**'s now-demolished Masonic Temple. The pink granite tower is an elegant addition to the LaSalle Street canyon, and the cathedral-scale lobby is its showpiece. Rich marble spans floors and walls, and the dazzling barrel-vaulted ceiling is covered in gold leaf. *Chicago Fugue,* a 28-foot-high welded bronze sculpture by Anthony Caro, fills a niche at the northern end; the south lobby is dominated by an iridescent weaving by Helena Hernmarck that pictures the Chicago Plan of 1909. ♦ At W Adams St

---

Animation genius Walt Disney was born in Chicago. Disney received 39 Oscars in his lifetime, the most ever received by one person.

Illinois has 13 nuclear power plants and ranks first in the US in number of nuclear power plants and nuclear-energy creating capacity.

In 1991 the renowned Chicago Symphony Orchestra's centennial gala concert was interrupted when souvenir alarm clocks presented to patrons went off during the program.

45 Sydel & Sydel Ltd. High-quality gems, beautifully designed jewelry, and outstanding service make this store a particular favorite of LaSalle Street businessmen with a romantic mission. Husband and wife Jeff and Mary Lou Sydel are among those who will attend to your needs with patience and excellent advice. ◆ M-F; Sa by appointment only. 208 S LaSalle St (at W Adams St). 332.4653

46 Rookery Building This well-known Chicago gem (pictured below), with its rusticated masonry base, Romanesque arches, and Moorish and Venetian details, has presided over South LaSalle Street since 1888, when it was built to plans by **Burnham & Root.** The building's name derives from the temporary **City Hall** that occupied the site after the 1871 fire; the dilapidated structure was a favorite pigeon roost. Two rooks at the LaSalle Street entrance playfully refer to these origins. In 1905 **Frank Lloyd Wright** was commissioned to remodel the lobby and light court, and this interior space retains his designed ornament. The building was restored in 1991 to its circa-1910 appearance by the **McClier Corporation** and **Hasbrouck Peterson Associates.** ◆ 209 S LaSalle St (at W Adams St)

47 Continental Illinois National Bank and Trust Company Building Its Classical exterior relatively unadorned, this 1924 building's striking feature is the grand, blocklong banking floor with majestic Ionic columns, painted friezes, and high coffered ceiling. **Graham, Anderson, Probst & White** were the architects. The smell of coffee (courtesy of **Starbucks**) greets visitors to the handsome lobby. Walls once lined with tellers' booths are now home to a collection of clothing stores, including **Baskin** (men's and women's), **Ann Taylor** (women's), and **Chiasso** (designer accessories). ◆ 231 S LaSalle St (at W Jackson Blvd)

Within the Continental Bank:

Caffè Baci ★$ Garlic, dried peppers, and herbs not only decorate the entrance to this Italian deli, but accent the food as well. There are American sandwiches (prime rib, turkey breast) as well as Italian *panini* sandwiches (try the eggplant with mozzarella), plus a variety of salads. The cafe serves *dolci* (sweets) and *bibite* (drinks), for midmorning or afternoon snacks, too. ◆ American/Italian ◆ M-F breakfast and lunch. 629.1818

Rookery Building

Postmoderns on Parade: Sculpture in the Loop

On 15 August 1967, Mayor Richard J. Daley pulled a cord and unveiled Pablo Picasso's sculpture in the **Civic Center Plaza.** Although onlookers expected to see a dazzling masterpiece, they were far from impressed. One alderman actually introduced a motion in the City Council that it be removed and replaced by a monument to **Cubs** baseball hero Ernie Banks. Yet since that time the sculpture has become an accepted, even beloved, part of the cityscape, visited as often as the **Art Institute** or the **John Hancock Center.** It also helped inspire architects to provide more space for public artwork around their new buildings, and as a result many sculptures in a variety of media by internationally recognized artists have sprung up all over the **Loop**—and beyond. Here's a 12-stop tour of some of the best:

1 *Ceres* (1930, John Storrs) **Chicago Board of Trade** (see page 25), 141 W Jackson Blvd (at S LaSalle St)

2 *Flamingo* (1974, Alexander Calder) **Federal Center** (see page 28), 219 S Dearborn St (between W Adams St and W Jackson Blvd)

3 *Untitled Light Sculpture* (1980, Chryssa Varda) Six identical translucent acrylic modules joined by slim polished aluminum rods are suspended into the eight-story atrium lobby. White neon tubing is electronically programmed for repeated patterns of lighting intensity. Lobby, 33 W Monroe St (at S Dearborn St)

4 *Radiant I* (1958, Richard Lippold) This delicate construction of gold, stainless steel, and enameled copper set above a reflecting pool was one of the first pieces of sculpture by a contemporary American artist placed on public view in Chicago. Lobby, **Inland Steel Building,** 30 W Monroe St (at S Dearborn St)

5 *The Four Seasons* (1975, Marc Chagall) **First National** plaza (see page 26), W Monroe St (between S Clark and S Dearborn Sts)

6 *Miró's Chicago* (1967, Joan Miró; installed 1981) **Chicago Temple** (see page 22), 69 W Washington St (at N Clark St)

7 *Untitled Picasso Sculpture* (1967, Pablo Picasso) **Richard J. Daley Center** (see page 21), W Washington St (between N Dearborn and N Clark Sts)

8 *Being Born* (1982, Virginio Ferrari) This stainless steel sculpture consists of two circular elements, one within the other, standing about 20 feet high and set within a marble reflecting pool. A gift of the Tool and Die Institute, it is a tribute to the precise skills of die-making. State Street Mall (at E Washington St) in front of **Marshall Field's**

9 *Monument with Standing Beast* (1985, Jean Dubuffet) **James R. Thompson Center** (see page 21), 100 W Randolph St (at N Clark St)

10 *Dawn Shadows* (1983, Louise Nevelson, see page 21) Madison Plaza, 200 W Madison St (at N Wells St)

11 *Batcolumn* (1977, Claes Oldenburg) To some, this 100-foot tall statue is simply an oversize baseball bat, to others a symbol of clout in Chicago; to still others, a breezy phallic symbol. You choose. Social Security Administration Building Plaza, 600 W Madison St (at N Clinton St)

12 *Universe* (1974, Alexander Calder, see page 20) Lobby, **Sears Tower,** W Adams St (at S Franklin St)

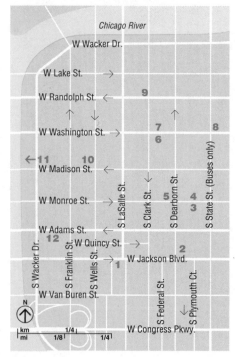

48 Chicago Board of Trade This Art Deco monument to commerce rises at the southern terminus of LaSalle Street, Chicago's equivalent to New York's Wall Street. The board was founded by 82 merchants in 1848 to stabilize grain prices and create a regulated marketplace. The world's oldest and largest futures and options-on-futures exchange was designed by **Holabird & Root** and built in 1930; **Murphy/Jahn** conceived the 1980 addition. The institution's agrarian focus is represented by relief sculptures flanking the huge clock over the entrance: A hooded figure holds a sheaf of wheat, and an Indian grasps a stalk of corn. The pyramidal roof is crowned by sculptor John Storrs's 30-foot statue of *Ceres*, the Roman goddess of grain. Cascading tiers of black-and-buff marble detail the striking three-story lobby. Trading can be viewed from the fifth-floor visitors' center. ♦ Free. M-F 9AM-2PM. A 30-minute tour is conducted every half-hour from 9:30AM-noon. 141 W Jackson Blvd (at S LaSalle St). 435.3590

49 Chicago Board Options Exchange The country's largest exchange for trading stock options is housed in a 1985 structure by **Skidmore, Owings & Merrill.** The pedestrian bridge that spans Van Buren Street is perhaps the only one to win an award from the American Institute of Architects. By linking the exchange to the **Board of Trade,** it creates the largest contiguous trading floor area in the US. The bridge has a raised floor that contains raceways for every conceivable electrical connection between exchanges. The steel-truss structure doesn't need any support where it joins the exchange, which was designed with the bridge in mind, but requires a giant pier where it meets the **Board of Trade** addition. Visitors may watch the action from the fourth-floor viewing gallery. Groups of 10 or more (college age or older) can take a more extensive tour. ♦ Free. M-F 8:30AM-3PM. 400 S LaSalle St (at W Van Buren St). 786.7492

50 Midwest Stock Exchange In this version of a marketplace, buyers and sellers—through their agents—gather to trade stocks of American and foreign businesses. Organized in 1882, it is the second-largest exchange in the US and ranks fifth in the world. It is electronically linked with the other major US stock exchanges. Visitors can watch from a fifth-floor gallery, but it's a tad dull as most trading is done by computer. ♦ Free. M-F 8:30AM-3PM. 440 S LaSalle St (between W Congress Pkwy and W Van Buren St). 663.2222

Within the Midwest Stock Exchange building:

Everest Room ★★★★$$$$ This stunning safari-style restaurant perched 40 stories above LaSalle Street and the financial heart of the Midwest is a must-visit for dedicated foodies. Dishes, all innovative and many prepared in the classic French tradition with a contemporary touch, are spectacularly presented on oversize dinnerware. Among the outstanding seafood and game specialties is salmon soufflé. Desserts are delectable, and the wine list is very good, with a strong selection of white wines from chef Jean Joho's native Alsace. Service is impeccable, and even the waiters' trays are graced with fresh flowers. While high-level wheeling and dealing certainly occurs here, it's a place for romance as well. For the best view, ask for a table on the lower level along the windows. An eight-course prix-fixe degustation menu is available for a minimum of two diners, and private business luncheons can be arranged for six or more. ♦ French ♦ Tu-Sa dinner. Reservations required. Free valet parking. 40th floor. 663.8920

Courtesy of Skidmore, Owings & Merrill

| Chicago Board of Trade | Board of Trade Addition | Pedestrian Bridge | Chicago Board Options Exchange | One Financial Place | Midwest Stock Exchange | LaSalle Street Station |

Savoy Bar and Grill ★$ Pick up your choice of soups, salads, deli sandwiches, burgers, or hot specials and head for one of five attractively decorated rooms where tables are set with napkins and silver. One of the bars has quotation screens for stock and futures exchanges so financial types who frequent this spot won't lose touch for a moment. ♦ American ♦ M-F lunch. Second floor. 663.8888

50 LaSalle Street Station This is one of four stations serving commuter railroads to the suburbs. Trains pull in right under the **Stock Exchange.** ♦ 414 S LaSalle St (between W Harrison and W Van Buren Sts). 836.7000

51 Metropolitan Correctional Center Few visitors to Chicago can gaze upon this triangulated monolith from outside without asking, "What's *that?*" Heaven forbid you should end up posing the question from inside—it's a federal prison. Somewhat innovative in design, the top 16 stories, which house 44 prisoners, have five-inch windows—the maximum width a federal corrections institution is allowed. The bottom 11 floors, which house administrative offices, have larger windows. ♦ S Clark St (at W Van Buren St)

52 Marquette Building This 1895 building's restrained decoration and pattern of large windows that express the steel structure within make this the archetypal Chicago School office building. Although the monumental cornice that originally terminated the base-shaft-capital composition was removed in the 1950s, the rest of the facade, including the original storefronts, was carefully restored by **Holabird & Roche** in 1980. Notice the superb entrance and lobby on Dearborn Street. Entrance door kickplates sport tomahawks, and pushplates are adorned with bronze panther heads designed by Edward Kemeys, a 19th-century animal sculptor whose best-loved beasts are the **Art Institute** lions (see below). Elaborate panels above the front door and in the lobby illustrate events in the life of Father Jacques Marquette, the French missionary who was one of the first Europeans to traverse the upper Mississippi in the 17th century. J.A. Holzer designed the lobby balcony's mosaic of Tiffany glass and mother-of-pearl; he later worked on the Tiffany mosaics at the **Chicago Cultural Center.** ♦ 140 S Dearborn St (at W Adams St)

53 Italian Village ★$$ Three restaurants are housed in one building. **La Cantina** is a clublike cafe that serves both American and Italian specialties. **The Village** is decorated with murals of villages, twinkling star lights, and booths like individual houses. It serves good, traditional, reasonably priced Italian food and is popular with the young business crowd. **Vivere** has a dramatic, Baroque decor courtesy of hotshot designer Jordan Mozer and features sophisticated regional Italian dishes along with an outstanding selection of about 1,500 wines. These restaurants are some of a handful in the Loop that keep late-night hours. ♦ Italian ♦ La Cantina: M-F lunch and dinner, Sa dinner; The Village: daily lunch and dinner; Vivere: M-Sa lunch and dinner. Valet parking. 71 W Monroe St (between S Dearborn and S Clark Sts). La Cantina and The Village 332.7005, Vivere 332.7005

54 First National Bank of Chicago C.F. **Murphy Associates** with the **Perkins & Will** designed this building, which was completed in 1969. Tapered and graceful, the sweeping curve of its sorth and south sides expresses its functional needs: the larger floor area is at the base, where commercial banking functions are located. The plaza is a popular summertime gathering place: Ledges offer comfortable perches for sun worshiping, chatting, munching, and enjoying summer lunchtime concerts, and Marc Chagall's massive five-sided architectural mosaic, *The Four Seasons* (1975), provides a focal point. The 70-foot-long piece depicts the artist's fantasy views of Chicago in all seasons. A mosaic bed of flowers "planted" on the top of the sculpture can be appreciated only from the windows of surrounding skyscrapers. ♦ 1 First National Plaza, W Monroe St (between S Dearborn and S Clark Sts)

54 Nick's Fishmarket ★$$$ Big, comfy booths, each with a phone jack and a dimmer switch, are conducive to privacy—whether for business or romance.  The fresh fish is fine, especially grilled, as are the hard-to-find seafood choices, such as Hawaiian opakapaka and abalone. Service is attentive, even obsequious; prices are steep and it's open late. ♦ Seafood ♦ M-Sa lunch and dinner. Reservations required. Jacket recommended. Valet parking after 6PM. 1 First National Plaza, W Monroe St (between S Dearborn and S Clark Sts). 621.0200 ⑇. Also at: 10275 W Higgins Rd (at Manheim Rd), Rosemont. 847/298.8200 ⑇

55 Delaware Building This High Victorian Italianate structure designed by **Wheelock & Thomas** was erected immediately following the Great Fire of 1871, and is the oldest building in the Loop. It was restored in 1988 by **Hasbrouck Peterson Associates,** and even the ground-floor **McDonald's** seems graceful here. ♦ 36 W Randolph St (at N Dearborn St)

56 Bart's Bar and Grill $$ Opened three decades ago as a German restaurant, this cozy spot doesn't have much of a menu, but the original leaded glass windows remain, and the walls are decorated with signed photos of the usual suspects, giving it an authentic Chicago ambience. The fare is limited primarily to bratwurst and hamburgers, but it's reasonably tasty. This is a perfect spot for the late-night crowd—the action often continues until after sunrise. ♦ American ♦ Daily dinner. 164 N State St (between W Randolph and W Lake Sts). 641.9550 &

57 Chicago Theater Celluloid illusion and architectural fantasy went hand in hand when this lavish movie palace designed by **Rapp & Rapp** first opened its doors in 1928. The grandeur of the interior's Baroque forms was restored in 1986 by **Daniel P. Coffey & Associates** after a period of neglect; and now concerts, touring companies of Broadway musicals, dance performances, and variety shows take the stage. A white terra-cotta triumphal arch hides behind the huge marquee. ♦ 175 N State St (at E Lake St). 443.1130

58 Marshall Field's With more than 450 departments and 73 acres of merchandise, it would take untold days to explore the riches of this Chicago legend. The story goes that Marshall Field said, "Give the lady what she wants," and the store has been doing just that since it opened (in a different location) in 1853. **D.H. Burnham & Co.** designed the present store between 1893 and 1907. Everything you could ever want in fashion, housewares, and furniture is arranged in departments around two galleried atriums, one of which is topped with a glass-mosaic dome designed by Louis Comfort Tiffany and unveiled in 1907. Specialty shops within the store feature designer boutiques, exotic foodstuffs, rare books, estate jewelry, and more. Melt-in-your-mouth Frango mints are Chicago's most popular take-home gift. A $110-million renovation has restored the gold leaf to main-floor columns, added a skylighted escalator atrium, and expanded the Men's Department to fill an entire city block along Wabash Avenue.

Among the augmentations is **Down Under,** a city of small shops on the lower level offering a dizzying array of housewares, hosiery, and more. In addition to gourmet wine and food shops, there is a bright, inviting food court where you can choose from taste treats at various counters and enjoy them at nearby tables. The seventh floor also has quite a few restaurants to choose from, including such old standbys as the **Walnut Room** (781.3697) and the **Crystal Palace** (781.3181), an ice-cream parlor. Personal shoppers are available to assist you, and the bridal registry is an excellent service. And be sure to see the intricately created Christmas windows. An annual tradition among Chicagoans is lunch at the **Walnut Room** overlooking the towering, sparkling Christmas tree. ♦ Daily. 111 N State St (between E Washington and E Randolph Sts). 781.1000 &. Also at: Water Tower Place, 835 N Michigan Ave (at E Chicago Ave). 335.7700 &

59 Block 37 One of the several edifices demolished at this site was the office building where **Louis Sullivan** reportedly met his future partner, **Dankmar Adler.** Another razed office building on the site housed Clarence Darrow's law office. **Helmut Jahn** was to design a shopping galleria on the spot, but the bottom fell out of the building boom before anything went up. In the 1980s a group of visionaries led by cultural affairs commissioner Lois Weisberg decided that the city-owned land ought to be dedicated to public use: It's now a giant outdoor skating rink in winter and the site of an art program for city high schoolers in the summer. A huge mural by Roger Brown decorates a Commonwealth Edison substation that couldn't be demolished. ♦ Across N State St from Marshall Field's (bounded by W Washington, W Randolph, and N Dearborn Sts)

Within Block 37:

Skate on State Not quite as elegant as New York City's Rockefeller Center, this outdoor rink isn't quite as cramped either. There's a warming room and skate-rental area. ♦ Admission. December through March: daily, when weather permits. 744.2893

Hot Tix Booth Run by the Chicago League of Theatres, this kiosk sells full-price, advance-sale tickets as well as half-price and discounted day-of-performance tickets for shows throughout the city. Half-price tickets for Sunday are available on Saturday. Come with cash only and be prepared to wait in line. ♦ 108 N State St (near W Washington St) (M noon-6PM; Tu-F 10AM-6PM; Sa 10AM-5PM). Also at: Chicago Place, 700 North Michigan Ave (M-Sa 10AM-6PM; Sun 12PM-5PM); 1616 Sherman Ave (between Davis and Church Sts), Evanston (Tu noon-3PM; W-Th 10AM-3PM; F-Sa 10AM-4PM)

60 Reliance Building After a hundred years, the most elegant of the Chicago School skyscrapers, with large expanses of glass and delicate Gothic ornament wrought in once-creamy terra-cotta, continues to fight a losing battle against the Loop's grime; years of neglect and a radically altered base have taken their toll. At press time, no tenant has been found who can afford the cost of the renovation. ♦ 32 N State St (at W Washington St)

61 International Importing Bead and Novelty Company Baubles, bangles, and beads of every size, shape, color, and material pack this shop. So do theater people, clothes designers, and ordinary folks awed by all the goodies, from sequined patches to feathered Las Vegas-style headdresses. ♦ M-Sa. 17 N State St (between E Madison and E Washington Sts; entrance also on N Wabash Ave), Eighth floor. 332.0061

62 One North State Though State Street hasn't yet fully regained its vitality as the nation's leading shopping street, some new stores indicate the direction a rejuvenation might take. Head up the escalator for **T.J. Maxx**'s often unruly collection of clothing, housewares, and decorative items; and down for **Filene's** extensive assortment of things to wear. Street-level shops include **The Body Shop, Ladies Foot Locker,** and **Contemporary Casuals.** ♦ Daily. At E Madison St

63 Carson Pirie Scott & Company This stunning building, **Louis Sullivan**'s last major commission in Chicago, was built between 1899 and 1904. Above the second story of what was originally the **Schlesinger & Meyer Company Store,** the steel frame is clad in terra-cotta. At street level, intricate cast-iron panels framing display windows are encrusted with **Sullivan**'s ornamentation that melds natural and geometric forms. His rounded corner entrance is spectacular. Additions by **D.H. Burnham & Co.** and **Holabird & Root** follow **Sullivan**'s design. In 1979 it was beautifully restored by **John Vinci.** As for the store, **Carson**'s doesn't carry the high-end merchandise you find at **Field's,** but the selection is wide and of good quality. **Level Six** is the spot for linens and housewares designed for the yuppie market. The **Corporate Level** caters to the needs of the stylish businesswoman, offering everything from beautiful suits to the shoes, belts, and scarves that make an ensemble. ♦ Daily. 1 S State St (at E Madison St). 641.7000 ♦

64 Toys R Us The arrival of this store distressed some purists, who don't like to think of State Street as a strip mall. The three-level store is one of the chain's few urban versions. ♦ Daily. 10 S State St (between W Monroe and W Madison Sts). 857.0669 ♦

Restaurants/Clubs: Red   Hotels: Blue

Shops/ ♀ Outdoors: Green   **Sights/Culture: Black**

65 Inland Steel Building In 1957 **Skidmore, Owings & Merrill** boldly turned this stainless-steel and glass-curtain–walled skyscraper design inside out. Supporting columns on the exterior allow for unbroken floor space inside; even the mechanical facilities (including elevators) are housed in a separate structure to the east. ♦ 30 W Monroe St (between S State and S Dearborn Sts)

65 Shubert Theater Touring Broadway musicals often land in this 1904 theater, designed by **Edmund C. Krause.** ♦ 22 W Monroe St (between S State and S Dearborn Sts). 977.1700 ♦

66 City Tavern $$ Booths and woodwork with Prairie School accents make for a handsome atmosphere. Breakfast is the best meal here; at lunchtime the volume goes up as crowds pour in for burgers and salads. It's also a popular after-work watering hole and convenient spot for dinner before a show at the nearby **Shubert Theater.** ♦ American ♦ M-F breakfast, lunch, and dinner; Sa dinner (when there's a show). Valet parking in the evening. 33 W Monroe St (between S State and S Dearborn Sts). 280.2740

The Berghoff

67 Berghoff Restaurant ★★$$ The bustling beer-hall atmosphere in this oak-paneled landmark dates back to 1893, when the enterprise was founded as an outdoor beer garden at the World's Columbian Exposition. Particularly favored by tourists, the huge dining room is usually full, so expect a wait at lunch and before 7PM. German classics such as Wiener schnitzel and sauerbraten are recommended, and the creamed spinach is a nice side order. Wash down your meal with a mug of Berghoff light or dark beer, on tap. The **Berghoff Cafe,** a stand-up bar on the east end of the main floor offering freshly carved roast beef, turkey, and corned beef sandwiches on fresh Berghoff's bread, is a fun and inexpensive spot for a quick lunch. ♦ German/American ♦ M-Sa lunch and dinner Reservations recommended for five or more. 17 W Adams St (at S State St). 427.3170 ♦

68 Federal Center Shortly before his death, **Mies van der Rohe** (with **Schmidt, Garden & Erikson, C.F. Murphy Associates,** and **A. Epstein & Sons**) designed these buildings, completed in 1975. Light-gray granite paves the plaza and building lobbies of the vast 4.5-acre site. The spare geometry and sleek sophistication of these three velvety black steel-and-glass structures—a single-story post office and two office buildings—are heightened by contrast to Alexander Calder's red *Flamingo* stabile (1974). Pedestrians can walk through the soaring curves of this 53-foot-tall sculpture, a favorite Chicago landmark. ♦ 219 S Dearborn St (between W Jackson Blvd and W Adams St)

69 Monadnock Building Boston developer Peter Brooks's demand that the exterior be without ornament was met by one of architect **John Wellborn Root**'s most powerful designs. The rhythm of gently projecting bays in this majestic structure (built in 1891) of deep purple-brown brick needs no frills. The north half has load-bearing walls, six feet thick at street level (one of the tallest buildings ever constructed that way), while the south half (added two years later by **Holabird & Roche**) has a skeletal steel frame. This is a must-see. ♦ 53 W Jackson Blvd (between S Dearborn and S Federal Sts)

Within the Monadnock Building:

B. Collins, Ltd. Brian Collins and his wife are the proprietors of this enticing pen shop with an 1890s feel. Nibs abound, and an array of fountain pens, ballpoints, and mechanical pencils from the quotidian to the extraordinary are proffered for prices ranging from $24 up to $8,000. Other merchandise includes sealing wax, stationery, greeting cards, and wrapping paper. ♦ M-Sa. 431.1888 &

Cavanaugh's Bar and Restaurant $$ Standard fare, including burgers, chicken, and a variety of salads, is served in a pleasant wood-paneled room. Plenty of booths, and tall, round bar tables are among the seating options. ♦ American ♦ M-F lunch and dinner. 939.3125

Jacobs Bros. Bagels $ An array of fresh bagels spread with a variety of cream cheeses or made into hearty sandwiches are served here, as are muffins, brownies, soups, and salads. ♦ Deli ♦ M-F breakfast, lunch, early dinner; Sa breakfast and lunch. 922.2245. Also at: 58 E Randolph St (at N Wabash Ave). 368.1180; 50 E Chicago Ave (between N Rush St and N Wabash Ave). 664.0026

70 Fisher Building A steel skeleton supports expanses of glass and pale salmon-colored terra-cotta, and flat and trapezoidal window bays alternate across the facade of this 1896 building by **D.H. Burnham & Co.** (with a 1907 north addition by **Peter J. Weber**). Elaborate Gothic arches share the upper level with carved eagles and salamanders, while, in a play on the building's name, lower stories are encrusted

with fish (see the Dearborn Street entrance), crabs, shells, and other aquatic forms. ♦ 343 S Dearborn St (at W Van Buren St)

71 Old Colony Building Holabird & Roche's projecting rounded-corner bays distinguish this office building, constructed in 1894 at a time when the south end of Dearborn Street was emerging as the center of the printing industry in the Midwest. Backing on Plymouth Court, the building is a tribute to the Plymouth colony, whose seal is located at the doorways. ♦ 407 S Dearborn St (at W Van Buren St)

72 Manhattan Building In 1890 this became the first tall office building to have a frame completely constructed of iron and steel. Also note **William Le Baron Jenney**'s terra-cotta ornament and variety of window treatments. ♦ 431 S Dearborn St (at W Congress Pkwy)

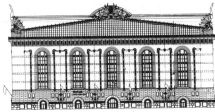

Courtesy of Hammond, Beeby & Babka

73 Harold Washington Library Center The opening of the world's second-largest public library (only the British Library in London is bigger) in 1991 ended almost two decades of frustration for Chicago's library users. During that period, the collection was split up and housed in several satellite locations while the City Council pondered where to build a central library and how to pay for it.

That's now history, thanks to this state-of-the-art facility—named after the city's first African-American mayor and a notorious bookworm—housing more than two million volumes. Features include an 18,000-square-foot children's library; a 400-seat auditorium/theater; a TV studio and film/video center; special collections on Chicago theater, the Civil War, and Harold Washington himself; materials in 90 foreign languages; and a language learning center. Artworks punctuate the interior; an intriguing tribute to Washington can be viewed from the lobby rotunda; the 9th-floor gallery atrium is lush and sun drenched.This 10-story, Neo-Classical structure (pictured above), designed by **Hammond, Beeby & Babka**, references numerous city landmarks: The red-granite base and brick walls are bows to the **Rookery** and **Monadnock Buildings**, both by **Burnham & Root;** the arched entrances recall **Adler & Sullivan**'s **Auditorium Building;** and the facade and roof pediments echo the **Art Institute.** The steel-and-glass-curtain wall along the Plymouth Court side is a Modernist touch. Free tours and a video overview are available in the **Orientation Theater** on the third floor. ◆ Tu-Sa. 400 S State St (between W Congress Pkwy and W Van Buren St). Public information 747.4050; catalog information 747.4340; newspapers and periodicals 747.4300 ও

74 Binyon's Restaurant ★$$ Judges, attorneys, and other political types have patronized this place since Prohibition days. The inconsistent menu ranges from basic prime rib to not-to-be-missed thick turtle soup. ◆ American ◆ M-F lunch and dinner, Sa dinner. Reservations recommended at lunch. 327 S Plymouth Ct (between W Van Buren St and W Jackson Blvd). 341.1155

74 Chicago Bar Association This 16-story granite and precast-concrete melding of Neo-Gothic and Miesian influences by **Tigerman, McCurry** went up in 1990. ◆ 321 S Plymouth Ct (between W Van Buren St and W Jackson Blvd)

75 DePaul University Loop Campus More than 10,000 students attend classes here at the colleges of law and business and the **School for New Learning** of this Catholic university (see the "Lincoln Park/ DePaul" chapter for information on the main campus). Until 15 years ago, the college's main building was the flagship store of the **Goldblatt Bros. Department Store,** and the "R" repeated throughout the exterior decoration is a reminder that this was originally built as a Rothschild store in 1912, designed by **Holabird & Roche.** A graceful, Prairie-style renovation created ground-floor retail space. While you're here, take a look at the nearby buildings on Jackson, which are vaguely Medieval in style. ◆ 1 E Jackson Blvd (between S Wabash Ave and S State St). 362.8300

76 Krystyna's Cafe ★$ Order croissants for breakfast or lunch, homemade soups, tasty muffins, omelettes, and pizzas. Try the vegetarian pizza or lasagna for a healthy and hearty lunch. Cappuccino and other coffee drinks are also served, and there are outdoor tables for summer dining. ◆ Cafe ◆ M-Sa breakfast, lunch, and early dinner. 8 E Jackson Blvd (between S Wabash Ave and S State St). 922.9225 ও. Also at: 203 N Wabash Ave (at E Lake St). 750.0553

77 Afrocenter Book Store This specialty bookshop stocks books and magazines about African-American history, culture, and lifestyle, as well as titles on African and Third World issues. ◆ M-Sa. 234 S Wabash Ave (at E Jackson Blvd). 939.1956 ও

78 Carl Fischer of Chicago Here you'll find a mind-boggling inventory of scores and sheet music for piano and guitar, other individual instruments, band and orchestra, and choral groups. Some music is stored in rows of dingy gray filing cabinets, but don't despair—staff members can find anything. ◆ M-Sa. 312 S Wabash Ave (between E Van Buren St and E Jackson Blvd). 427.6652

79 Hubbard Street Dance Company Founded in 1978, this popular troupe is considered by many to be Chicago's premier dance company, staging performances here and around the world. Artistic director Lou Conte leads his talented dancers through a uniquely American blend of styles, from ballet to jazz. More than 300 students a year take classes at Conte's studio, also located here. You might catch a glimpse of classes or rehearsals through the windows overlooking Wabash Avenue. ◆ 218 S Wabash Ave (between E Jackson Blvd and E Adams St), Third floor. 663.0853

80 Miller's Pub ★$$ Since 1935 this bustling watering hole and chophouse has been a popular haunt, particularly for night owls. The walls are festooned with autographed publicity shots of celebrities who have visited through the years. Go for the ambience, not the cuisine. ◆ American ◆ Daily lunch and dinner until 3AM. 134 S Wabash Ave (at E Adams St). 645.5377 ও

81 Fifty Yard Line Brought to you by W.H. Smith, the British company that has a near monopoly on airport and hotel outlets, this is a shop for sports fans. The carpeting includes a **Bears** football field and **Sox** park; sports videos play continually on several TV screens; and there's a wall lined with team caps from around the country. T-shirts, jackets, books, and other fan paraphernalia are also offered. Michael Jordan stuff is still the most popular; **Bulls** in general generate half the store's sales. ◆ Daily. 120 S Wabash Ave (between E Adams and E Monroe Sts). 917.1740 ও

82 Palmer House Hotel $$$ The original hotel, built by Potter Palmer, was reduced to ashes by the Great Chicago Fire only 13 days after it opened, and was rebuilt in 1875. The French Empire-style lobby of **Holabird & Roche**'s elegant 1927 replacement, complete with 12 ceiling paintings by Louis Rigal, is located on the second floor; the first is given over to an arcade of shops and restaurants. The 1,600 rooms and 88 suites are warmly residential with rich hues and walnut furnishings. Two rooms per floor are designed for guests with disabilities. The two-story, top-level **Towers** is an exclusive section with its own lobby, lounge, and concierge. There's a fitness center that has a pool, whirlpool, steam room, sauna, and exercise equipment; it also offers aerobics and massages. A business and conference center has computers and secretarial services. Restaurants include the once trendy **Trader Vic's,** the **French Quarter,** and **Palmer's**

Steak and Seafood House. Weekend packages are available. ♦ 17 E Monroe St (between S Wabash Ave and S State St). 726.7500, 800/445.8667; fax 263.2556 &

Within the Palmer House Hotel:

Pendleton Products Store An abundance of rich plaids fills this small arcade shop, which carries blankets, scarves, and apparel. It would be difficult to choose a favorite tartan. ♦ M-Sa. 119 S State St (between E Adams and E Monroe Sts). 372.1699 &

83 SuperCrown The first chain to discount best-sellers, **Crown** built its empire on a barebones philosophy—no carpeting, no upkeep, limited stock. But once superstores became a market force, a new approach was needed, so **Crown** created this considerably more elegant shop in 1993. Pluses include a bright, colorful decor, excellent selections of books on tape and of magazines, and well-stocked bookshelves. ♦ Daily. 105 S Wabash Ave (at E Monroe St). 782.7667 &

83 Nefertiti Jewelers For almost 30 years, this shop has sold, repaired, and appraised fine jewelry; they specialize in custom designs. ♦ M-F. 111 S Wabash Ave (between E Adams and E Monroe Sts). 236.0009

83 Otto Pomper This wonderful cutlery store—which has been in the Loop at one location or another since 1890—carries knives, scissors, and sharpeners, plus a diverse assortment of gadgets from kitchen items to opera glasses. ♦ M-Sa. 135 S Wabash Ave (between E Adams and E Monroe Sts). 372.0881 &

84 Charette One of the city's oldest art-supply stores is a favorite with students. Framing services are on the first level, and art supplies take over the other four floors. ♦ M-Sa. 23 S Wabash Ave (between E Monroe and E Madison Sts). 822.0900

84 Iwan Ries & Co. Since 1857, this tobacco store has been purveying pipes (it stocks more than 25,000), cigars (a refrigerated walk-in humidor holds a fine selection that can be warmed immediately in the store's microwave), tobacco, and smoking accessories directly and by mail to a vast number of aficionados. Don't miss the **Pipe Museum** within the store; it has many rare and elaborately carved pieces. ♦ M-Sa. 19 S Wabash Ave (between E Monroe and E Madison Sts), Second floor. 372.1306

85 Chicago Trunk & Leather Works, Inc. An extensive offering of fine luggage, handbags, business cases, trunks, and personal leather goods has been available here since 1911. Free monogramming on luggage by some makers gives a personal touch. ♦ M-Sa. 12 S Wabash Ave (at E Madison St). 372.0845

Mole's-Eye View of Chicago

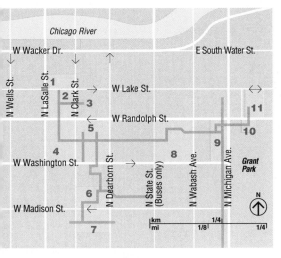

1 203 North LaSalle Street

2 State of Illinois Center

3 Chicago Title & Trust Center

4 City Hall/County Building

5 Richard J. Daley Center

6 3 First National Plaza

7 First National Bank of Chicago

8 Marshall Field's

9 Chicago Cultural Center

10 Illinois Central/Metra Station

11 Prudential Building

Neither rain nor sleet nor rush-hour pedestrian traffic jams can keep you from walking in relative ease in the **Pedway.** Chicago's still-growing underground walkway connects the major buildings listed here, offers entrances to **CTA** public transportation, and is lined with numerous shops, services, and cafes. The walkway is open Mondays through Fridays from 6:30AM to 6PM.

86 Mallers Coffee Shop & Deli ★$ This gem of a coffee shop is tucked away on the third floor of the Mallers Building along **Jewelers Row.** Fast service and arguably the best Reuben sandwich in the city keep those in the know coming back day after day. ♦ Deli ♦ M-Sa breakfast and lunch. 5 S Wabash Ave (at E Madison St). 263.7696

86 Jewelers Row For more than 150 years, the heart of Chicago's jewelry business has been located in a series of buildings along Wabash Avenue. Hundreds of businesses, many of which are still small family operations, are packed into the one-block stretch between Washington and Madison Streets. Within the street-level **Wabash Jewelers Mall,** 60 jewelers, separated only by their glass display cases, deal in every sort of jewelry imaginable, from birthstone rings to out-of-this-world diamond and ruby necklaces. Some are wholesalers, some retailers, and some make and repair jewelry at workbenches right in front of you. ♦ M-Sa. Jewelers Row: 55 E Washington St, 29 E Madison St, 5 N Wabash Ave, and 5 S Wabash Ave. Wabash Jewelers Mall: 21 N Wabash Ave (at E Madison St). 263.1757

87 Wolf Camera & Video A wide selection of photo equipment and supplies meets the needs of all shutterbugs, from professional photographers to serious hobbyists. ♦ M-Sa. 66 E Madison St (between N Michigan and N Wabash Aves). 346.2288. Also at: Numerous locations throughout the city

88 Brooks Shoe Service Inc. In addition to mending shoes, luggage, and other leather goods, this cobbler offers expert dyeing services. ♦ M-Sa. 55 E Washington St (at N Wabash Ave), Suite 335. 372.2504

89 Mallards This haberdashery sells custom-tailored men's suits. ♦ M-Sa. 50 E Washington St (at N Wabash Ave), Second floor. 444.9295

MALLARDS

89 Mothers Work Fashions that provide "a professional image for the pregnant woman" are the specialty of this chain maternity clothing store. ♦ M-Sa. 50 E Washington St (at N Wabash Ave), Second floor. 332.0022

89 Crate & Barrel It is unlikely that you will be able to pass through this housewares and home accessories store without making a purchase—quality is high and prices extremely reasonable. Outfit your entire kitchen and other parts of your home in style; even furniture, office accessories, and luggage are alluringly displayed. Salespeople are young, attractive, and energetic. The bridal registry is extremely popular. ♦ M-Sa. 101 N Wabash Ave (at E Washington St). 372.0100

&. Main store: 646 N Michigan Ave (at E Erie St). 787.5900 &; Bargain outlet: 800 W North Ave (at N Halstead St). 787.4775 &

89 Heaven on Seven ★$ While you'll find burgers and BLTs on the coffee shop menu, the cognoscenti come here for the Cajun food: gumbo, Cajun fried chicken, jambalaya, oyster-shrimp salad, and red beans and rice that will give you an itch for the Big Easy. Finish with an All-American chocolate-chip cookie. If you want a seat at lunch, arrive before 11:30AM; the obscure location doesn't deter enthusiastic regulars. Mardi Gras is celebrated here in style. ♦ Cajun/Creole/ Coffee shop ♦ M-Sa breakfast and lunch. 111 N Wabash Ave (between E Washington and E Randolph Sts), Seventh floor. 263.6443

90 Eddie Bauer, Inc. Their rugged men's and women's clothes are great to wear while chopping firewood—or heading out to a city lot for a Christmas tree. Serious campers, hunters, and anglers will find everything they need for a trip out of town. ♦ Daily. 123 N Wabash Ave (between E Washington and E Randolph Sts). 263.6005. Also at: Water Tower Place, 835 N Michigan Ave (at Chicago Ave). 337.4353 &

90 Hirk Company The unprepossessing buildings along this part of Wabash are chock-full of unique services and merchants. This is one. While monogramming furs and linens is their specialty, they will embroider even the lowliest bowling shirt. ♦ M-F. 125 N Wabash Ave (between E Washington and E Randolph Sts), Fourth floor. 346.0194

90 B. Dalton Bookseller A wide selection of books and magazines is available at this national chain. ♦ Daily. 129 N Wabash Ave (between E Washington and E Randolph Sts). 236.7615 &. Also at: 175 W Jackson Blvd (between S LaSalle and S Wells Sts). 922.5219; 645 N Michigan Ave (between E Ontario and E Erie Sts). 944.3702 &; Merchandise Mart (at the Chicago River, between N Wells and N Orleans Sts,). 329.1881

91 Self-Park Garage In 1986 **Tigerman, Fugman, McCurry** created the ultimate expression of building as billboard. The facade of this 10-level parking garage is painted to look like the front end of an antique car, complete with hood ornament, tire-tread awnings, and a vanity plate that reads "SELF PARK." ♦ 60 E Lake St (between N Michigan and N Wabash Aves). 269.9157

91 Cafe Angelo ★$$$ This plush, old-fashioned restaurant features authentic regional Italian cooking. Try the mixed grill, the low-fat variations of items more commonly loaded with cholesterol, such as *bruschetta* (grilled bread with oil, garlic, and olive pesto).

The pretheater prix-fixe dinner (served daily from 5PM to 6:30PM) is a good buy. ♦ Italian ♦ M-F breakfast, lunch, and dinner; Sa-Su dinner. Reservations recommended. 225 N Wabash Ave (at E Lake St). 332.3370

92 Carbide and Carbon Building From a base of black polished granite where the entrance is detailed in black marble and bronze, the **Burnham Brothers**' green terra-cotta–clad tower rises to fanciful finials trimmed in gold leaf. According to legend, this 1929 Art Deco skyscraper's dramatic color scheme was inspired by a green glass Champagne bottle capped in glittering foil. The lobby is a Deco masterpiece. ♦ 230 N Michigan Ave (at E South Water St)

That's Our Bag, Inc.

92 That's Our Bag, Inc. A huge inventory of handbags, carryalls, briefcases, and luggage is sold at discount prices. ♦ Daily. 230 N Michigan Ave (at E South Water St). 984.2628.

93 Pauline Book and Media Center The Daughters of St. Paul perform their mission of preaching through communication by selling Roman Catholic and inspirational books, tapes, and videos in shops like this throughout the US. A peaceful chapel in the back of the shop is open during store hours. Mail order is available. ♦ M-Sa. 172 N Michigan Ave (between E Randolph and E Lake Sts). 346.4228

94 150 North Michigan Avenue Turned on a 45-degree angle and bisected into two triangular towers, this 1984 office building by **A. Epstein & Sons** has a sloping glass roof that slices diagonally through the top 10 floors. At night this slanted diamond is outlined in a string of white lights. While its sail-like mirrored planes and distinctive top are generally admired by the public, architects and the press have criticized the prominently located building as disruptive of Michigan Avenue's architectural continuity. ♦ At E Randolph St

95 Randolph Street Station The **South Shore** and **Metra Electric** trains going to Chicago's South Side are served by this station, which is entirely undistinguished except for one brief piece of gangster lore. Jake Dingle, a reporter who covered Capone and friends, was assassinated here; after his death, it was discovered that he'd been getting huge payoffs from the boys for letting them know what the police and FBI knew about them.

♦ Underground at E Randolph St and N Michigan Ave. 836.7000

96 Chicago Cultural Center Shepley, **Rutan & Coolidge,** the Boston firm commissioned to design the **Art Institute of Chicago,** designed this 1897 building in the Neo-Classical style. Along Michigan Avenue, an Ionic colonnade supports a frieze bearing the names of historic authors. The main entrance, on the Washington Street side, opens to a grand staircase made of white Carrara marble inlaid with marble and glass mosaics. Head up these magnificent stairs to **Preston Bradley Hall,** lush with more marble and mosaics and topped by a spectacular illuminated Tiffany stained-glass dome. The **Grand Army of the Republic Exhibition Hall** (third floor on the Randolph Street side) was inspired by Italian Renaissance palaces. Once the main library, the building presents a wide variety of high-quality cultural offerings, from art exhibitions—historical and contemporary—to lectures, concerts (particularly every Wednesday at noon), films, and theatrical performances; all are free to the public. This building is a must-see. ♦ Daily. 78 E Washington St (at N Michigan Ave). General information 744.6630, events hotline 346.3278

Within the Chicago Cultural Center:

Museum of Broadcast Communications Highlights of national radio and television history, including an extensive library of rare tapes and kinescopes, are preserved at this lively museum. Exhibits showcase Chicago's significant role in early broadcasting ("Fibber McGee and Molly," for example) and the evolution of TV advertising. Visitors can anchor their own news show (and buy a tape to take home), listen as radio shows are broadcast, and shop in the **Commercial Break** store for anything from mugs and keychains to replicas of ventriloquist dummies Charlie McCarthy and Mortimer Snerd. ♦ Free. M-Sa. 629.6000

97 Gage Group In 1899 **Holabird & Roche** designed these three commercial buildings for the wholesale millinery trade. Then the tenant of the northernmost building commissioned **Louis Sullivan** to design a more elaborate facade. In 1902 four stories were added to the building, altering the original proportions, and in the early 1950s, the ground floor's cast-iron ornament was removed; a fragment of it is now on display across the street in the **Art Institute of Chicago** (see below). ♦ 18-30 S Michigan Ave (between E Monroe and E Madison Sts)

Chicago resident Frances E. Willard helped to found the Woman's Christian Temperance Union in 1874.

Restaurants/Clubs: Red   **Hotels:** Blue
Shops/♥ Outdoors: Green   **Sights/Culture:** Black

98 University Club In 1909 **Holabird & Roche** added Collegiate Gothic, appropriately enough, to the potpourri of building styles along the avenue. This is a private, members-only club, but visitors can wander into the lobby. ♦ 76 E Monroe St (at S Michigan Ave)

99 Beaux Arts Gallery This gallery offers a vast array of sculpture, pottery, and vases to satisfy the upscale tourist or the serious collector. ♦ M-Sa. 106 S Michigan Ave (at E Monroe St). 444.1991

99 Arts & Artisans, Ltd. Filled with handcrafted work by American designers, this shop is a good spot to find a souvenir for someone really special. Browse among the vases, lamps, paperweights, kaleidoscopes, and jewelry displayed here. ♦ Daily. 108 S Michigan Ave (between E Adams and E Monroe Sts). 641.0088

99 Mama Mia Pasta ★$$ Dependably good, freshly made pasta and sauces are served in a casual setting. In nice weather, grab a seat on the sidewalk patio overlooking the **Art Institute of Chicago** across the street. ♦ Italian ♦ Daily lunch and dinner. 116 S Michigan Ave (between E Adams and E Monroe Sts). 580.0788 ♿

100 Art Institute of Chicago Incorporated in 1879 for the purpose of maintaining a museum and a school of art, the institute grew steadily under the direction of Charles L. Hutchinson, first president of the Board of Trustees and president of the Corn Exchange National Bank. Chicago's leading businessmen and philanthropists, all trustees of the museum (among them Potter Palmer, John J. Glessner, and Martin A. Ryerson), agreed that the occasion of the **1893 World's Columbian Exposition** was an excellent time to build a grand museum to both represent and accommodate the city's cultural expansion. Chicago architects **Burnham & Root** were invited to submit a design for the building, which was to be located in the park. **John Wellborn Root**'s premature death and **Daniel Burnham**'s preoccupation as chief of construction for the Exposition led to the commission being given to the Boston firm of **Shepley, Rutan & Coolidge**, who completed this structure, designed in a traditional Classical-Renaissance style, in 1892.

Architects who contributed to the building's interior include **Coolidge & Hodgdon** (**McKinlock Court**, 1924); **Holabird & Root** (**North Wing**, 1956); **Shaw, Metz & Associates** (**Morton Wing**, 1962); **Skidmore, Owings & Merrill** (**East Wing**, 1976), and **Hammond, Beeby & Babka** (**Rice Wing**, 1988). The **Departments of Prints and Drawings** and **Photography** have study centers here, where members and students can examine objects that are not on display in the galleries. The **Ryerson** and **Burnham Libraries** have a fantastic collection of art and architectural publications.

Capped by a new skylight in 1987, the **Grand Staircase** rises elegantly from the main entrance, where there is a circular information center to get you started. The second-floor galleries of *European Art* are arranged chronologically (from Late Medieval to Postimpressionist), with paintings and sculpture in skylit chambers, and prints and drawings in the corridor galleries. This organization provides a rare opportunity to study the development of particular artists and their subjects in various media: In **Gallery 21** hangs Canaletto's *Portico with a Lantern* in oil; the etching is in the adjacent corridor. The Impressionist collection is renowned, and highlights include five of the paintings in Monet's *Haystack* series, and Caillebotte's *Paris Street, Rainy Day.* Seurat's *A Sunday on La Grande Jatte—1884*, which inspired Stephen Sondheim's Broadway musical *Sunday in the Park with George,* may be the museum's best-known painting.

Art Institute of Chicago

While it would be impossible to recount the treasures of each department, a not-to-be-missed tour would include the **Edward B. Butler Gallery,** an entire roomful of mesmerizing works by George Innes; the following 15 paintings: *Bathers by a River* by Matisse, *Nighthawks* by Edward Hopper, *Snowfield, Morning, Roxbury* by John La Farge, *Nocturne in Grey and Gold* by Whistler, *Croquet Scene* by Winslow Homer, *Mère Gregoire* by Courbet, *Still Life: Corner of a Table* by Henri Fantin-Latour, *House of Mère Bazot* by Daubigny, *The Millinery Shop* by Degas, *Bedroom at Arles* by Van Gogh, *Landscape: Window Overlooking the Woods* by Vuillard, *Mater Dolorosa* by Dieric Bouts, *The Nativity* by the Master of the Historia Friderici et Maximiliani, *American Gothic* by Grant Wood, and *The Adoration of the Christ Child* by Jacob Cornelisz van Oostsanen; and the reconstructed **Trading Room** of the **Chicago Stock Exchange.** Designed by **Adler & Sullivan**, the stock exchange building was demolished in 1972. In 1976, **Vinci-Kenny Architects** began their intricate reassembly of the trading room that had been salvaged from the razing, resulting in this remarkable display.

The two bronze lions standing guard at the Michigan Avenue entrance were unveiled in 1894 and were immediately adopted by Chicagoans as the symbol of the museum. Designed by American sculptor Edward L. Kemeys, these majestic animals don wreaths at Christmas and have even sported giant **Bears** helmets and **Cubs** caps.

Several construction projects have been completed in recent years. The new **Kraft Education Center** was the **Children's Museum** until Kraft endowed the museum with funds to overhaul and expand its special galleries and programs for children. Also restored (and installed in new galleries) were the extremely popular **Miniature Thorne Rooms,** 68 dollhouse-scale re-creations of period interiors. The elegant new **Rice Building** is home to *American Arts* and *20th-Century American Painting and Sculpture,* and has the vast **Regenstein Hall** for changing exhibitions.

The gardens are spectacular in spring, summer, and fall. Beautifully groomed, they are a favorite haven of museum employees and workers from nearby office buildings who come to read or people watch. The museum publishes *The Art Institute of Chicago: The Essential Guide,* which includes discussion of 256 favorite and notable objects. Free guided tours are offered each day; inquire at the information desk. ♦ Admission; free on Tuesday. Children 5 years and under free. Daily; Tu until 8PM. S Michigan Ave (at E Adams St). Wheelchair accessible entrance on Columbus Drive. General information

443.3600, museum information and events of the day 443.3600 ♿

Within the Art Institute of Chicago:

Museum Shop Along with a good selection of exhibition catalogs and art books, children's books, calendars, posters, postcards, lovely jewelry, and various gift items are sold at this store. Even if you don't go to the museum, come here for beautifully designed Christmas cards featuring pieces from the collection. ♦ First floor. 443.3583

Restaurant on the Park ★$$ This lovely room overlooking **Grant Park** to the east is a quiet and relaxing place to enjoy a leisurely and elegant lunch. The food is quite good and includes a nice selection of pasta, grilled chicken and fish, and salads. ♦ American ♦ M-F lunch. Reservations recommended. Second floor. 443.3543

Garden Restaurant ★$ During the summer this is a beautiful outdoor spot to enjoy a refreshing lunch of cold soup, a fresh fruit plate, or salad. It's enclosed on all four sides by museum galleries, and trees provide a shady respite from the sun. A jazz band plays on Tuesday evenings. ♦ American ♦ Daily lunch; Tu early dinner June through September (weather permitting). McKinlock Court. 443.3600

Court Cafeteria $ This is a cheerful and inexpensive place to eat; it uses the same kitchen as the **Garden Restaurant.** ♦ American ♦ Daily lunch; Tu early dinner. Lower level, S Columbus Dr side. 443.3600

101 Goodman Theatre Designed by **Howard Van Doren Shaw**, this theater was built in 1925 and donated to the **Art Institute** by the parents of Kenneth Sawyer Goodman, a dramatist-poet who died in World War I. Under artistic director Robert Falls, shows have ranged from innovative versions of Shakespeare to the latest from August Wilson, and each season usually ends with a musical, such as Stephen Sondheim's *A Little Night Music.* Excellent sightlines and ample legroom contribute to the pleasurable experience of attending productions here. The studio houses more experimental works. ♦ Box office open daily; on day of performance until 8PM. 200 S Columbus Dr (at E Monroe Dr). 443.3800 ♿

102 School of the Art Institute What began as the **Chicago Academy of Design** in 1866 became the **Chicago Academy of Fine Arts** in 1879, with academic and exhibiting functions. In 1882 the name was changed to the **Art Institute.** The first director of the school, William French, brother of sculptor Daniel Chester French, held the post until 1914. Georgia O'Keeffe, Thomas Hart Benton, Grant Wood, Claes Oldenburg, and Leon Golub are among the illustrious graduates. The school's **Film Center** offers a fascinating program of foreign, independent, experimental, and vintage films, sometimes supplemented with personal appearances by filmmakers. ♦ 280 S Columbus Dr (at E Jackson Dr). Public information 899.5100, Film Center 443.3733

103 Russian Tea Cafe ★★$$ Not too long ago, Klara and Vadim Muchnik were in their native Uzbekistan, but Chicagoans are fortunate they found their way here to open this charming spot around the corner from **Symphony Hall.** Ukrainian borscht is the house specialty; the marinated beets and Tashkent carrot salad are far better here than tourists in the Muchniks' homeland are likely to have; the gefilte fish and stuffed cabbage are also winners. ♦ Russian ♦ M lunch; Tu-Su lunch and dinner. Reservations recommended. 63 E Adams St (between S Michigan and S Wabash Aves). 360.0000

103 Posters Plus Chicago's largest collection of vintage posters, including spectacular selections of London Transport Board, **South Shore** line, and French advertising posters are sold here. Also offered are historic Chicago, fine art, and contemporary placards. ♦ Daily. 210 S Michigan Ave (at E Adams St). 461.9277 ♿

104 Orchestra Hall Daniel Burnham, an Orchestral Association trustee, donated his services to this project, a response to complaints about the vastness of the **Auditorium Theatre** lodged by Theodore Thomas, organizer and first conductor of the **Chicago Symphony Orchestra (CSO).** The redbrick Georgian Revival-style building with its more intimate hall was a significant addition to the prominent cultural institutions springing up along Michigan Avenue at the turn of the century. Daniel Barenboim is currently music director of this more-than-a-century-old orchestra. Tickets to a single performance of this internationally renowned orchestra can be difficult to come by, as subscribers tend to fill the house. But the concerts are well worth the perseverance. The hall is also home to **Chicago Symphony Chorus,** which presents, among other performances, the annual *Do-It-Yourself Messiah.* ♦ Box office M-Sa; Su varies according to concert schedule. 220 S Michigan Ave (between E Jackson Blvd and E Adams St). 435.6666 ♿

104 Santa Fe Building Originally the **Railway Exchange Building,** this was the location of **Daniel Burnham**'s architectural office. **Burnham** designed it himself; it was completed in 1904. On the exterior, bright white glazed terra-cotta is delicately molded in Classical details. Elegantly restored in 1985 by **Frye, Gillan & Molinaro,** the skylit lobby with its grand central staircase must be visited. The stenciled Pompeiian decoration on the skylight rafters and the marble floor pattern with a five-color border were part of the original design, but weren't added until the restoration. ♦ 224 Michigan Ave (at E Jackson Blvd)

Within the Santa Fe Building:

Chicago Architecture Foundation Shop and Tour Center (CAF) Visitors wishing to unravel the mysteries and histories of Chicago's buildings and neighborhoods should not pass up this shop. In addition to its huge selection of architecture books and periodicals, guidebooks and maps, children's books and toys, and unusual gifts with an architectural bent, the center has an exhibition gallery and offers lectures and more than 50 tours (by foot, bike, boat, and bus) that cover most of Chicago. ♦ Fee for tours. Daily. 922.3432, recorded tour information 922.8687; fax 922.0481 ♿

Sherry-Brener Ltd. Here's a music publisher that also sells fine handmade musical instruments, mainly strings, new and used (99 percent of good violins are over 300 years old, instructs the proprietor). The shop also repairs instruments and offers lessons for the serious student. ♦ M-Sa. 427.5611 ♿

105 Savvy Traveller All manner of travel guides, maps, travel-oriented literature, and travel accessories are sold here. The shop also offers a series of talks on subjects ranging from "How to Pack" to "Adventure Travel for Women over 30." ♦ M-Sa. 310 S Michigan Ave (between E Van Buren St and E Jackson Blvd). 913.9800 ♿

106 Booksellers Row In this browser's paradise, shelves are packed with a vast and eclectic assortment of secondhand books organized by subject, all in excellent condition and offered at reasonable prices. New Chicago guidebooks are also for sale here. ♦ Daily until 8:30PM. 408 S Michigan Ave (between E Congress Pkwy and E Van Buren St). 427.4242. Also at: 2445 N Lincoln Ave (at W Fullerton Ave and N Halsted St). 348.1170 ♿

106 Fine Arts Building Originally housing a showroom and factory for Studebaker carriages, the rosy Romanesque **Studebaker Building** (designed by **Solon Spencer Beman**

and built in 1885) was converted into two theaters on the first floor, and offices, artists' studios, and practice rooms on the upper floors in 1889. At that time, "All Passes— ART Alone Endures" was carved inside the entrance. Among the many whose creative endeavors found a haven in the "Carnegie Hall of Chicago," L. Frank Baum and illustrator William W. Denslow collaborated on *The Wizard of Oz*, architect **Frank Lloyd Wright** and sculptor Lorado Taft had studios here; and drama teacher Ann Morgan staged the first American performances of plays by George Bernard Shaw and Henrik Ibsen. Current residents include **Performing Arts Chicago,** the **Jazz Institute of Chicago,** the **Boitsov Classical Ballet Company,** and the **Hungarian Opera Workshop.** Numerous music teachers have their studios here, too. A walk through the hallways on many an evening is a stroll through a melody of voices and instruments from behind closed doors. ♦ 410 S Michigan Ave (between E Congress Pkwy and E Van Buren St)

Within the Fine Arts Building:

Fine Arts Theater In 1982 the two first-floor theaters were converted into a four-screen cinema. The theater features a good selection of independent and foreign films. Be forewarned: the seats are not plush. ♦ 939.3700

Artists Restaurant $ This is your basic Greek restaurant, serving spinach pie, as well as cheeseburgers, plus various coffees. The sidewalk patio is an excellent place for people watching in sunny weather. ♦ Greek ♦ Daily breakfast, lunch, and dinner. 939.7855 ♿

107 Auditorium Building President Grover Cleveland laid the cornerstone in 1887, and three years later this Romanesque Revival-style edifice designed by **Adler & Sullivan,** with its great rusticated granite arches, opened to rave reviews. Among other distinctions, it was the heaviest building in the world (110,000 tons). In its early days the now-defunct **Auditorium Hotel** was the first choice of Chicago's distinguished visitors, and **Adler & Sullivan** were among those who established offices at this address. The acoustics and sightlines of the **Auditorium Theatre** are renowned, as is its lavish interior, designed by **Louis Sullivan.** Mosaic floors, sinuously curved balconies, stained-glass windows, murals on side walls and the proscenium arch, gold stenciling, and encrusted ornament throughout are a feast for the eyes, thanks to the loving restoration work of architect **Harry Weese,** completed in 1967. The building has been subject to changing fortunes over the years and has served many purposes: In 1891 an indoor baseball game took place in the theater; the stage was used as a bowling alley for servicemen during World War II. After decades of neglect, **Roosevelt University** acquired the building in the 1940s and converted offices and hotel rooms into classrooms (its Michigan Avenue lobby is very much worth a stop, and make sure you see the building model on display there). Such recent hits as *Les Misérables, The Phantom of the Opera,* and *Miss Saigon* have put the theater back in the limelight. Inquire about tours. ♦ Box office: Daily. 50 E Congress Pkwy (between S Michigan and S Wabash Aves). 922.4046 ♿

Bests

Douglas Post
Playwright/Composer

Driving south down **Lake Shore Drive** into town.

Spending an afternoon at the **Lincoln Park Zoo.**

Attending new and old exhibits at the **Chicago Historical Society.**

Strolling down **Lincoln Avenue** between Belmont and Fullerton.

Browsing through the bargains at **Powell's Book Store** on Lincoln.

Eating at **La Creperie** on Clark, **Moti Mahal** on Belmont, **P.S. Bangkok** on Halsted, and the **Wild Union** on Lincoln.

Seeing a play at the **Goodman, Steppenwolf,** and **Victory Gardens** theaters.

Catching a film at the **Music Box Theater.**

Playing volleyball in **Waveland Park** and swimming in the lake.

Riding the **Ravenswood el train** around the **Loop.**

James Sherman
Playwright; President, Magic Time

See a new play at **Victory Gardens Theater**—the home of the most exciting world premieres in the US.

Watch a **Cubs** game at **Wrigley Field.** Yes, it is the best place to watch a game.

Before or after the game, have a hot dog at **Murphy's** on Belmont—the best hot dog in Chicago, the only Chicago hot dog chosen to be sold in Japan.

Walk around the **Lincoln Park Zoo.** Or if it's too cold outside, walk around the **Art Institute.**

Take an architectural boat tour on the **Chicago River.**

Go to **Highland Park.** Hear a concert at **Ravinia.**

Listen to the midnight special on **WFMT.**

Buy a box of Frango Mints at **Marshall Field's**— they're half off the day *after* Valentine's Day.

> The Great Chicago Fire burned at a rate of 65 acres per hour.

South Loop/ Burnham Park

A morning of shopping, an afternoon excursion to the **Field Museum of Natural History**, and an evening of fine dining at **Prairie** or **Printer's Row** are all in a day's walk in the South Loop. Chicago's founders put their soul into this part of town, as evidenced by the elegant Old World hotels and the fine architecture that remain. But with the area's continued development around the turn of the century, they lost heart, forsaking it for more pristine quarters to the north. Today the South Loop, bordered by **Congress Parkway Cermak Road, Lake Michigan,** and the **Chicago River,** is springing back to life. The historic **Printing House Row District,** just south of Congress Parkway, has been transformed into apartments, offices, restaurants, and shops. New residential complexes such as **Dearborn Park** are home to a middle-class populace that enjoys a short commute to work and a rich choice of urban entertainment, from jazz at some of the city's finest clubs to **Chicago Bears** games at **Soldier Field.** The South Loop also boasts the handsome **Prairie Avenue Historic District** south of **18th Street, Shedd Aquarium, Adler Planetarium,** and **McCormick Place-on-the-Lake,** one of the busiest convention centers in the nation.

The history of the South Loop dates to the early 1800s. In 1836, when Chicago was still a log cabin settlement clustered near the river, Henry and Caroline Clarke opened a general store here. With dreams of grandeur, they built a white frame Greek Revival house on what was then the shore of Lake Michigan. The **Clarke House,** still standing near its original location in the Prairie Avenue Historic District, is the city's oldest surviving building. Around the time of the city's incorporation in 1837, many wealthy merchants, wanting to live near their businesses in the Loop, settled south of **Van Buren Street.** Development here continued after the Great Fire of 1871 roared through the city's center. **Clarke House** and the surrounding environs survived unscathed, and prosperous merchants and captains of industry began to build elaborate mansions along **Prairie Avenue** between **16th** and **22nd Streets.** Entrepreneurs Potter Palmer, Philip Armour, Marshall Field, and John Glessner were among those who built the grand homes. They were members of the congregation of the **Second Presbyterian Church,** which they supported in great style, lavishly decorating it with stained-glass windows designed by Louis Comfort Tiffany.

But the area did not remain a wealthy enclave for long. Prostitutes, gamblers, and other denizens of Chicago's vice district relocated from downtown to **Dearborn Street** between **Polk** and 16th Streets, just a few blocks from Prairie Avenue. This new **Levee District,** presided over by politicians "Hinky Dink" Kenna and "Bathhouse John" Coughlin, flourished until 1915. The area took on an industrial grittiness when four of Chicago's six major train depots, including **Dearborn Railroad Station,** were constructed nearby, complete with clamoring freight yards and warehouses. The proximity of such unbecoming activities triggered the exodus of many families north to the Gold Coast around the turn of the century.

All was not lost, however. **Daniel Burnham**'s Chicago Plan of 1909 paved the way for the development of the city's exceptional lakefront park system, including the South Loop's **Burnham Park.** Between World War I and World War II, more than a billion dollars was spent on landfill for Lake Michigan's shoreline, which now supports an abundance of parks and recreational and cultural facilities.

Today, the South Loop is being revitalized by new construction of apartment complexes and adaptive reuse projects that combine the commercial and the residential. On Father's Day weekend each June, Printer's Row hosts the

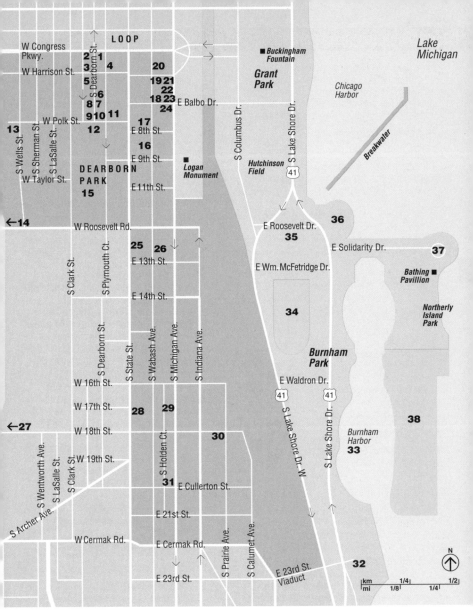

Midwest's largest outdoor book fair along **South Dearborn Street**. Hotels along **South Michigan Avenue**, which from the turn of the century attracted affluent society folk as well as colorful political and entertainment personalities, have been renovated—from a little spit and polish at the **Blackstone** to an overhaul costing millions at the **Chicago Hilton and Towers.**

1 Printing House Row District In the late 1880s Chicago's printing industry began locating in this area, which was convenient to the then-new **Dearborn Railroad Station.** This district is now included on the National Register of Historic Places, and many of the subtly detailed brick loft buildings have been renovated for new uses. ♦ S Dearborn St (between W Polk St and W Congress Pkwy)

1 Edwardo's ★$ This eatery is one of Chicago's several branches of a national chain that serves up healthful pizzas made from natural ingredients. Basil is grown on the premises, and fresh tomatoes, spinach, mushrooms, and sweet peppers are among the many topping choices. Stuffed spinach pizza is delicious. The open, high-ceilinged loft space with wood floors is bright and attractive and can accommodate large groups. ◆ Pizza ◆ Daily lunch and dinner. 521 S Dearborn St (between W Harrison St and W Congress Pkwy). 939.3366. Also at: Numerous locations throughout the city

2 Hyatt on Printer's Row $$$ In 1995 the architectural firm of **Booth/Hansen & Associates** joined the top floors of two 19th-century buildings to a new building, then standardized the rooms to create this hotel. The 1886 redbrick **Duplicator Building** (architect unknown) is plainer than the Neo-Classical, light brick **Morton Building** (an 1896 design by **Jenney & Mundie**). Each of the 161 rooms has 13-foot ceilings, large loft-style windows, an oversize bathroom of travertine marble, two phones and two color TVs (one of each in the bathroom), and a VCR. Weekend packages and special discounts are available. ◆ 500 S Dearborn St (at W Congress Pkwy). 986.1234, 800/233.1234; fax 939.2468 ♿

Within the Hyatt on Printer's Row:

Prairie ★★★$$$
Chef Stephen Langlois has developed a menu featuring Midwestern ingredients prepared in inventive combinations. Baby coho salmon with bacon, leeks, and walnuts is a mouthwatering delight, as is the perfect meal finale, homemade berry ice cream. With its oak furniture and traditional Arts and Crafts detailing and stenciled walls, the interior is pleasantly reminiscent of the Prairie School designs of **Frank Lloyd Wright.** ◆ American ◆ Daily breakfast, lunch, and dinner. Valet parking at dinner. Reservations required. 663.1143 ♿

3 Pontiac Building This is **Holabird & Roche**'s oldest remaining skyscraper. Built in 1891, the 14-story building, clad in dark brown brick, does not express its steel frame as clearly as later buildings do, such as the Loop's **Marquette,** but the four-window bays on the Dearborn Street side are graceful, and there is lovely terra-cotta detailing at the cornice and just above the second floor. Listed on the National Register of Historic Places, it was renovated in 1985 by **Booth/Hansen & Associates.** ◆ 542 S Dearborn St (between W Harrison St and W Congress Pkwy)

3 Printer's Row ★★★$$$ Owner and chef Michael Foley has been credited with developing a distinct Midwestern American cuisine that skillfully blends regional ingredients with international techniques. Foley, who opened this restaurant long before the neighborhood became fashionable, puts his own spin on traditional American comfort foods. Whether you opt for one of the

standard dishes such as four-grain risotto with sea scallops or fillet of pork tenderloin with onion, citrus, and mint, or one of the seasonal specials—ragout of wild mushrooms with Madeira and cream, for example—you're in for a culinary treat. Plan to spend a leisurely evening enjoying your meal and the clubby atmosphere. ◆ American ◆ M-F lunch and dinner, Sa dinner. Valet parking. Reservations recommended. 550 S Dearborn St (at W Harrison St). 461.0780 ♿

4 Mergenthaler Linotype Building Ken Schroeder's playful 1982 renovation is typical of his imaginative approach to adaptive reuse. Now an apartment building, the principal facade of the 1917 structure by **Schmidt, Garden & Martin** is left relatively unchanged, while the brick sidewall features bright red gridded window frames and full-story triangular pop-out bays. Part of an old building (**Tom's Grill,** a long-closed hamburger stand) remains on the corner, treated as an archaeological fragment. Residents drive into the parking lot through a freestanding roll-up door from an old loading dock. ◆ 531 S Plymouth Ct (between W Harrison St and W Congress Pkwy)

5 Trattoria Caterina ★$ If you're looking for a leisurely meal, this bustling cafe is not the place, but it wins awards for cheap eats and has an outdoor cafe in summer. The concept is Italian fast food; try the *pasta con pesce* (with fish). ◆ Italian ◆ Daily lunch and dinner. 616 S Dearborn St (between W Polk and W Harrison Sts). 939.7606

5 Taste of Siam $$ This airy dining spot is notable for serving a wide range of Thai food at reasonable prices. Its soups and salads are quite good. ◆ Thai ◆ Daily lunch and dinner. 618 S Dearborn St (between W Polk and W Harrison Sts). 939.1179 ♿

6 Grace Place A 1915 three-story printer's building is now an ecumenical house of worship, thanks to an award-winning 1985 conversion by **Booth/Hansen & Associates.** There's a meeting space at street level, a sanctuary for concerts and services on the second floor, and a worship area enclosed by a circular wall and arched windows in the third-floor loft, whose huge timber structure was left in place. The only overtly religious symbol—a metal cross—doubles as a structural support. In an unusual arrangement, the church is shared by **Grace Episcopal Church, Christ the King Lutheran Church,** and **Makom Shalom** synagogue.

♦ 637 S Dearborn St (between W Polk and W Harrison Sts). Grace Episcopal 922.1426, Christ the King Lutheran 939.3720, Makom Shalom 913.9030

7 Kasey's Tavern Located in an 1883 building that housed one of the first printers in the area, this has been a tavern ever since 1890. Until 1974, when the conversion of Printer's Row into a residential area began, the bar kept printers' hours of 8AM to 6PM. Now it's a neighborhood hangout, where patrons can watch sports, play pool, or listen to the jukebox. During the Printer's Row Book Fair each June, the Nelson Algren Society meets here to swap stories of the famed Chicago writer. No food, other than frozen pizza and the barkeep's fried eggs, but the beer's on tap and there's wine and espresso. ♦ Daily. 701 S Dearborn St (between W Polk and W Harrison Sts). 427.7992

8 Sandmeyer's Bookstore
Owners Ulrich and Ellen Sandmeyer have assembled an excellent selection of books for the traveler—from practical guidebooks to good reads for those who never leave their armchairs. Books both

SANDMEYER'S BOOKSTORE

by Chicagoans and about the city are well represented. They also carry wonderful titles for children and high-quality fiction for adults in this spacious and attractive shop. ♦ Daily; Th until 8PM. 714 S Dearborn St (between W Polk and W Harrison Sts). 922.2104

9 Franklin Building The highly decorated facade of **George C. Nimmons**'s 13-story brown brick building comes as a bit of a surprise in this utilitarian neighborhood. Abstract multicolor terra-cotta designs enliven the upper stories, and panels between the first and second floors pay homage to the printing trade. The detailing is masterful throughout. ♦ 720-36 S Dearborn St (at W Polk St)

Within the Franklin Building:

Gourmand Coffeehouse $ A variety of brewed gourmet coffees and baked goods are available, and you can also buy many varieties of coffee beans. Try the hot chocolate—rich Ghirardelli chocolate in steamed milk. ♦ Cafe ♦ Daily 7AM-11PM. 728 S Dearborn St (between W Polk and W Harrison Sts). 427.2610

Chicago movie critic Roger Ebert is the only film critic ever to have won a Pulitzer Prize for his work.

Restaurants/Clubs: Red   Hotels: Blue

Shops/ ♟ Outdoors: Green   **Sights/Culture: Black**

10 Moonraker ★$$ This neighborhood tavern is in the midst of a transformation. A new French chef has introduced a mix of bistro-style fare and eclectic dishes like wild mushroom pizza while retaining the out-of-this-world crabcakes. Tables move outdoors in the summer. ♦ International ♦ M-F, Su lunch and dinner; Sa breakfast, lunch, and dinner. 733 S Dearborn St (at W Polk St). 922.2019 &

11 Lakeside Press Building This eight-story brick building, on the National Register of Historic Places, was originally a printing factory owned by the R.R. Donnelley Company (note the company seal with Indian chief heads on the facade). It was designed in 1897 by **Howard Van Doren Shaw,** an architect better known for luxurious residential commissions. The solidity of the masonry walls, with their strong corners and thick piers that visually support a massive top story, contrasts with the delicate metal-and-glass window areas of the middle stories. In 1986, a major rehabilitation was done and in 1992 it became a dormitory for nearby **Columbia College.** ♦ 731 S Plymouth Ct (at W Polk St)

12 Dearborn Station The oldest surviving railroad passenger terminal in Chicago, this Romanesque Revival building of red sandstone and brick detailed in terra-cotta was designed by **Cyrus L.W. Eidlitz** in 1885 and restored by **Kaplan/McLaughlin/Diaz** in 1986. This landmark's facade is handsome, and the tower provides a wonderful terminus for Dearborn Street. Inside is a small sandwich bar and a large medical office. Several events are centered here during the Printer's Row Book Fair in mid-June. ♦ W Polk St (at S Dearborn St)

Within Dearborn Station:

Linda's Margaritas $$ An ordinary Mexican restaurant, but on a bright spring day the patio is a delightful spot for a margarita. Indoors, the florid paintings decorating the walls put you in the mood for anything hot and spicy. ♦ Mexican ♦ Daily lunch and dinner. 939.6600

13 River City These curvilinear poured-concrete buildings were designed in 1984 by **Bertrand Goldberg,** the architect who designed **Marina City** 25 years earlier. Apartments surround the courtyard atrium, which contains interior streets lined with shops. Complete with a 70-slip marina, restaurants, and other services, it's a "city within a city." ♦ 800 S Wells St (at W Polk St)

14 Chicago Fire Department Academy
Standing on the very spot where the Great Fire of 1871 is believed to have begun, this academy trains today's fire fighters. Visitors are welcome to drop by for an impromptu tour, but calling in advance can ensure that you're here when recruits are actually going through their paces—running through drills on three-story fire escapes, rappeling along ropes down brick walls, jumping into nets, or chopping up cars to extricate imaginary auto accident victims. ♦ M-F. 558 W DeKoven St (between S Clinton and S Jefferson Sts). 747.7239 ♿

15 Dearborn Park This community sprang up from abandoned railroad yards in the late 1970s. The diverse dwellings include town houses, garden apartments, and high-rises landscaped to suggest a suburb in the city. ♦ Bounded by W 18th and W Polk Sts, and S State and S Clark Sts

16 Powell's Bookstore One of Chicago's top used bookstores, Powell's carries 200,000 scholarly, academic, general interest, and out-of-print titles. ♦ Daily; M-F until 11PM. 828 S Wabash Ave (between E 9th and E 8th Sts). 341.0748. Also at: 2850 N Lincoln Ave (between Diversey Pkwy and George St). 248.1444 ♿; 1501 E 57th St (at Harper Ave). 955.7780 ♿

17 Buddy Guy's Legends Bluesman Buddy Guy, owner of the South Side blues bar the **New Checkerboard Lounge,** co-owns this spacious club with Marty Salzman. Buddy plays here regularly, as do other legendary blues musicians, while visitors such as Ron Wood and Bill Wyman often join in. ♦ Cover. Daily until 2AM; Sa until 3AM. 754 S Wabash Ave (at E 8th St). 427.1190

18 Merle Reskin Theatre Originally named the **Blackstone Theater,** this facility has been owned and operated by **DePaul University** since 1988. Designed in 1910 by **Marshall & Fox** in French Renaissance style with interior finishes of walnut and gold, the theater resembles a European opera house. It stages a series of student productions, including presentations for children. The renovated 1,340-seat facility also hosts opera and dance companies. ♦ 60 E Balbo Dr (between S Michigan and S Wabash Aves). 325.7900

19 Universal Bowling and Golf Corporation Bowling balls made to order, golf clubs, and pool tables and supplies fill this large sports shop. ♦ M-Sa. 619 S Wabash Ave (at E Harrison St). 922.5255 ♿

20 American Floral Art School Everything a budding florist could want to know about opening a flower shop and more is taught here. Visitors are welcome. ♦ M-F. 529 S Wabash Ave (between E Harrison St and E Congress Pkwy), Sixth floor. 922.9328

21 Museum of Contemporary Photography The first museum in the Midwest exclusively devoted to photography was founded in 1967 by **Columbia College,** a four-year alternative arts college at the same address. Works on exhibit are by both eminent and emerging artists from around the world. The diverse roles photography plays—as a medium of artistic expression, documenter of life and the environment, and technological and commercial tool—are presented. ♦ Free. M-Sa; closed August. 600 S Michigan Ave (at E Harrison St). 663.5554 ♿

22 Spertus Museum of Judaica The largest Jewish museum in the Midwest boasts an excellent permanent collection of religious and decorative art objects representative of Jewish life and culture through the centuries. Special exhibitions range from works by Jewish artists to broad topics relevant to Judaism; the **Zell Holocaust Memorial** is unforgettable. The **Rosenbaum Artifact Center** is a unique, hands-on exhibition that enables children (and grown-ups) to play at being archaeologists in the ancient Near East. ♦ Admission. M-F, Su. 618 S Michigan Ave (between E Balbo Dr and E Harrison St). 922.9012 ♿

23 Blackstone Hotel $$

Designed by **Marshall & Fox** and opened in 1910, this hotel has seen a lot of Chicago history. The phrase "smoke-filled room" was coined here during the 1920 Republican convention, when clouds of cigar smoke enveloped reporters waiting to learn the name of the party's presidential nominee (Warren G. Harding). More recently, the banquet scene in *The Untouchables* was filmed here. The ballroom, Victorian lobby, and many of the 305 rooms and suites have been refurbished in an ongoing restoration of this Registered National Landmark building. Rooms have period furnishings, and many overlook **Grant Park** through large windows that can be opened to let in a lake breeze. Amenities include discounts at nearby health facilities. In the hotel are the **Burnham Park Tap** bar and **Chequers,** a cheerful 1940s-style restaurant with an exhibition kitchen and a mesquite grill. The hotel's rates are a bargain

for this great location; weekend packages are also available. ◆ 636 S Michigan Ave (at E Balbo Dr). 427.4300, 800/622.6330; fax 427.4300 ext 4736

Within the Blackstone Hotel:

Mayfair Theatre Chicago's longest-running play, *Shear Madness,* is a comic whodunit on the boards here since 1981. The audience participates in questioning the suspects to discover the murderer's identity. ◆ 786.9120

24 **Chicago Hilton and Towers** $$$ When designed in 1927 by **Holabird & Roche,** the former **Stevens Hotel** was billed as the largest in the world and offered such recreational extravagances as an 18-hole rooftop golf course. Renamed for owner Conrad Hilton in the 1950s, the hotel reflects its $185-million renovations of 1985-86. Public spaces and the 1,620 guest rooms and suites are grand and luxurious. The hallways drip with chandeliers, and the rooms are rich in cherrywood furnishings and plush fabrics. Amenities include a state-of-the-art health club complete with a heated skylit pool, spa, and saunas, as well as private offices for business travelers. The exclusive Towers,

with a separate registration desk and concierge, has a European air and offers the comforts of a small hotel. The complex includes five restaurants: **Buckingham's** for steak and seafood (see below); the **Lakeside Green,** an atrium and lounge with piano bar, good for people watching; the **Pavilion,** a coffee shop open from 5AM to 1AM; the **Fast-Lane Deli,** featuring takeout and eat-in (open when the hotel is full enough to warrant it); and **Kitty O'Shea's,** a cozy pub with authentic Irish food and live Irish folk music nightly. The weekend packages are a good deal. ◆ 720 S Michigan Ave (at E Balbo Dr). 922.4400, 800/445.8667; fax 922.5240 ♿

Within the Chicago Hilton and Towers:

Buckingham's ★★$$$$ Grilled steaks are served in anything but a steak house setting. From the polished marble floors to the rich upholstery, this dining room exudes gentility. Entrées come with a fluffy baked potato or rice and fresh vegetables al dente. The dessert cart seems ready to sink beneath the weight of rich, chocolaty confections, along with the most satisfying servings of ice cream and cheesecake. ◆ American ◆ Daily dinner. Reservations required. 922.4400 ♿

Vibrant Views

Chicago can be a beautiful sight to behold, especially from these top 10 vantage points, many of which are explained in further detail throughout the book:

Lake Shore Drive is scenic during the day and dramatic at night, especially from the three following vantage points: between **Grand Avenue** and **Wacker Drive** immediately across from the **Loop;** heading south just past **Fullerton Avenue;** and heading north from **Hyde Park.**

A rare close-up of the nighttime skyline is seen from **Grant Park** during such events as the Chicago Jazz Festival (otherwise, the park is unsafe at night). Nearby **Buckingham Fountain** shows off with a multicolored light show.

Burnham Park and **Olive Park,** both mini-peninsulas jutting out into the lake, provide wide-angle views of the city across the water.

All of **Michigan Avenue's** stunning architecture can be surveyed during the day from the steps of the **Art Institute.**

The **Michigan Avenue Bridge** presents a dazzling nighttime vista of buildings along the river plus the floodlit **Tribune Tower** and **Wrigley Building.**

Continue north along the **Magnificent Mile,** which is particularly pretty when lit up for the Christmas holidays.

A drive along **Roosevelt Road** between Michigan Avenue and **Canal Street** presents a startling sneak-up-from-behind view of both the **South Loop** and the Loop.

The **Ravenswood** and **Evanston CTA** el routes encircle the Loop, providing surprises around every curve with almost-close-enough-to-touch passages beside buildings.

Picture-perfect views of **Lincoln Park's** grassy meadows, trees, and lagoons with the skyline in the background can be found at the **Fullerton Avenue Bridge** just west of Lake Shore Drive, the northern tip of **Diversey Harbor,** and from paddleboats in the **South Pond.**

A secret of many an early-bird runner and bicyclist are the stunning sunrises over **Lake Michigan** from any place along the shore.

The observation decks atop the 1,450-foot-tall **Sears Tower** and the 1,123-foot-tall **John Hancock Center** offer fantastic bird's-eye views for miles around.

25 Tommy Gun's Garage Roaring '20s-style flappers and dancing gangsters present a corny but entertaining dinner-theater revue. A decent three-course meal comes with the show. You may opt to see the show only, with a cover charge and two-drink minimum. The **Untouchables Tour** (see page 77) offers an optional stop here. ♦ Shows Tu-Su evenings. Reservations required. 1239 S State St (between E 13th St and E Roosevelt Rd), rear entrance. RAT.ATAT (728.2828) ⚭

26 N.A.M.E. Gallery Relocated from River West, this cooperative gallery exhibits emerging artists, mainly Chicagoans, plus frequent student work in a program called *Fresh*. ♦ Tu-Sa noon-5PM. 1255 S Wabash Ave (between E 13th St and E Roosevelt Rd). 554.0671

27 Landfall Press Gallery A well-established printmaker who teaches at the **University of Illinois** started this gallery 25 years ago on the North Side. In its present location for 10 years, the printing shop with a small gallery has an excellent inventory of contemporary lithographs, woodcuts, and etchings by such Chicago artists as Roger Brown and Ed Paschke, plus John Buck, Christo, and others. Despite its out-of-the-way location, this place is worth a visit. ♦ Tu-F; Sa by appointment; closed in August. 329 W 18th St (on the bridge, between S Clark and S Canal Sts), Suite 601. 666.6709 ⚭

28 American Police Center & Museum Established in 1974 by friends and family of police in response to tensions that escalated after the antiwar and inner-city riots of the 1960s, the museum pays homage to police here and around the world, with low-key displays of uniforms, equipment, and law enforcement procedures. Displays include sawed-off gangster shotguns from the Capone era, confiscated drug paraphernalia, and a touching memorial to Chicago police officers recently killed in the line of duty. ♦ Donation requested. M-F. 1717 S State St (at E 17th St). 431.0005 ⚭

29 Cotton Club Behind an ordinary commercial storefront lies a sophisticated jazz club. Modeled after the New York City original, the interior is done in gold tones, chrome, and Art Deco mirrors. The staff serves in tuxes, and the talent, such as Cassandra Wilson and the Art Porter Quartet, is always tops. On Friday and Saturday nights, jazz in the front room is supplemented by disco dancing in a dark room in back. ♦ Cover. Daily 6PM-2AM; F-Sa until 4AM. 1710 S Michigan Ave (between E 18th and E 16th Sts). 341.9787 ⚭

30 Prairie Avenue Historic District After the 1871 fire that ravaged the city's center, Chicago's leading entrepreneurs—including Potter Palmer, Philip Armour, Marshall Field, George Pullman, and John Glessner—built elegant mansions in every style in this area, which had escaped the blaze and was convenient to the business district. Around the turn of the century, when the neighborhood became more industrial, the elite left Prairie Avenue behind, relocating to the city's North Side. While only a few of the grand residences remain, this historic district—a veritable outdoor architectural museum—is well worth a visit. For tours, contact the **Glessner House** or **Clarke House** (see below). ♦ S Prairie Ave (between E 22nd and E 18th Sts, two blocks east of S Michigan Ave). 326.1480

30 John J. Glessner House Designed in 1886 for industrialist John Glessner, this unique and elegant home of rusticated granite is Chicago's only surviving building by premier American architect **Henry Hobson Richardson.** Much of the interior has been restored in the English Arts and Crafts style favored by the Glessners. The Chicago Architecture Foundation maintains the house as a museum. ♦ Admission. Tours: F 1PM, 2PM, 3PM; Sa-Su 1PM, 2PM, 3PM, 4PM. House open only for tours. Reservations required for groups of 10 or more. Discounted tickets for combined tour of Glessner House and Clarke House (see below). 1800 S Prairie Ave (at E 18th St). 326.1480

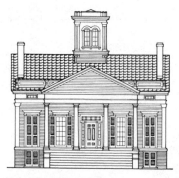

James Novak, Chicago Architecture Foundation

30 Henry B. Clarke House Also known as the **Widow Clarke House,** this 1836 Greek Revival–style home (pictured above) is Chicago's oldest surviving building, and one of the only wood-frame structures to have escaped the Great Fire of 1871. Now located within a few blocks of its original site, it has been moved twice. Meticulously restored and furnished, the house is a museum operated by the Chicago Architecture Foundation. Tours begin at the **Prairie Avenue Tour Center** in the **Glessner House** museum next door (see above). ♦ Admission. Tours F noon, 1PM, 2PM; Sa-Su noon, 1PM, 2PM, 3PM. House open only for tours. Reservations required for groups of 10 or more. Discounted tickets for combined tour of Clarke House and Glessner House (see above). Behind the Glessner House. 326.1480 ♿

31 Second Presbyterian Church In 1874 **James Renwick,** famous for the Smithsonian Institute building in Washington, DC, designed this Neo-Gothic structure using mottled limestone from nearby quarries. The building burned in 1900, and **Howard Van Doren Shaw,** a member of the church, rebuilt the interior with muralist-decorator Frederic Clay Bartlett. Wealthy parishioners lavished artwork on their church, including spectacular stained-glass windows by Sir Edward Burne-Jones, Louis C. Tiffany, and John La Farge. ♦ 1936 S Michigan Ave (at E Cullerton St). 225.4951 ♿

32 McCormick Place This massive convention center was built in 1971 to replace one that burned down in 1969. Architect **Gene Summers** was clearly influenced by **Mies van der Rohe.** His roof cantilevers 75 feet over walls of painted steel that frame seven-by-eight-foot plates of gray glass. The center, along with the newer north building designed by **Skidmore, Owings & Merrill,** hosts some of the largest conventions in the country. The ever-popular annual auto and boat shows, held in January and February, are open to the public; the National Restaurant Association show (for the trade only) draws huge crowds in June. ♦ 2301 S Lake Shore Dr (at E 23rd St). 791.7000; fax 791.6543 ♿

Within McCormick Place:

Arie Crown Theater This cavernous theater is notorious for its atrocious acoustics. *The Nutcracker* is an annual Christmas event here. The rest of the year, concerts and some traveling performances are interspersed with convention events. ♦ 791.6000 ♿

33 Burnham Harbor From early May through late October, anyone is permitted to launch a boat from here. If you don't have one, sailboats are available for rent (747.0737). During the summer, many Chicago yacht owners live here aboard their vessels. For a pleasant warm-weather stroll, walk along the harbor through **Burnham Park** from **McCormick Place** up to the **Adler Planetarium.** ♦ Off S Lake Shore Dr (between E 23rd St and E Roosevelt Dr).

Chicago natives who have won Academy Awards include actors Charleton Heston, Jason Robards, Mercedes McCambridge, Marlee Matlin, and Elizabeth McGovern.

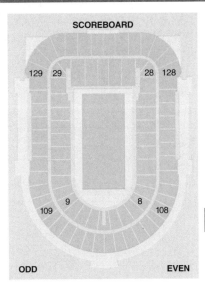

34 Soldier Field A colonnade of hundred-foot concrete Doric columns rises majestically behind **Chicago Bears** fans braving icy winds to support their football team. In warmer weather, the stadium hosts performers such as Bruce Springsteen and Madonna. Originally constructed in 1926 by **Holabird & Roche** as a war memorial, the stadium (seating plan above) has since been remodeled to accommodate the football team. Glassed-in boxes, added in 1981 to protect corporate clientele from the elements, cost about $7,500 per game (less if rented for the full season). ♦ Bounded by E Waldron and William McFetridge Drs, and S Lake Shore Dr and S Lake Shore Dr W. Ticket information 747.1285

35 Field Museum of Natural History It took more than 20 years for the natural history collection that originated at the 1893 World's Columbian Exposition to secure a permanent home in this vast Georgia marble and terra-cotta building (floor plan pictured on page 46). Endowed by Marshall Field Sr., it was designed by **D.H. Burnham & Co.** and **Graham, Anderson, Probst & White** to resemble a Greek temple—the ultimate architectural form at the time. **Harry Weese & Associates** planned the 1975 renovation and the 1986-87 restoration. Despite the acres of floor space, less than one percent of the museum's artifacts and specimens are on view. Exhibition vice president Michael Spock (son of the famous baby doctor) leads an ongoing campaign to enliven the museum with hands-on exhibits and more exciting displays. A $4-million *DNA to Dinosaurs* exhibit, which is dominated by a skeletal reconstruction of a 72-foot-long apatosaurus and includes a walk-through environment of a Coal Age forest, opened in June 1994. Other major new exhibits are *Messages from the Wilderness* and *Africa.* The

FIELD MUSEUM OF NATURAL HISTORY

Second Floor
1 Maori House
2 Earth Sciences
3 Pacific Spirits
4 Traveling the Pacific
5 Tibet
6 China
7 Gems
8 Moving Earth
9 Families at Work
10 Jades
11 DNA to Dinosaurs
12 Teeth, Tusks & Tarpits
13 Plants of the World
14 Dinosaur Hall
15 Plants

First Floor
1 World of Mammals
2 Rice Wildlife Research Station
3 Mammals of Africa
4 World of Birds
5 North American Birds
6 Messages from the Wilderness
7 Mammals of Asia
8 Nature Walk
9 Africa
10 Bird Habitats
11 Reptiles & Amphibians
12 Animal Biology
13 What Is an Animal?
14 Egypt Tomb
15 Stanley Field Hall
16 Insects
17 Gallery
18 Webber Resource Center
19 Place for Wonder
20 Plains Indians and Indians Before Columbus
21 Indians of the Woodlands and Prairies, Pawnee Earth Lodge
22 Eskimos and Northwest Coast Indians
23 Indians of the Southwest
24 Mexico and Central America
25 South America
26 Gallery
27 Sizes

Ground Floor
1 Education Department
2 James Simpson Theatre
3 Bushman
4 Sea Mammals
5 Picnic in the Field
6 Inside Ancient Egypt
7 Special Exhibits

held daily throughout the museum. A **McDonald's** is located on the ground floor, and there's a **Starbucks Coffee** in the basement.
♦ Admission; free Wednesdays. Daily. S Lake Shore Dr (at E Roosevelt Dr). 922.9410

36 John G. Shedd Aquarium The world's largest indoor aquarium (see the floor plan below) was the gift of John G. Shedd, president and chairman of the board of **Marshall Field & Company,** in 1930. Inhabited by more than 6,000 aquatic animals of every shape and hue, the aquarium is endlessly fascinating. Don't miss the sea anemones, river otters, or the feedings in the *Coral Reef* exhibit (daily 11AM, 2PM, 3PM; no 3PM feedings Monday through Friday September through April). Divers enter this 90,000-gallon re-creation of a Caribbean coral reef and talk to visitors through a microphone while they feed sharks, sea turtles, eels, and hundreds of tropical fish. Tear yourself away long enough to take a look at the architectural details of this **Graham, Anderson, Probst & White** building. Wave and shell patterns border the central room, and colorful mosaics of crabs and lobsters march across the tops of majestic doorways framed by Classical columns.

Harmoniously appended to the aquarium's lake side, the vast **Oceanarium** is the world's largest indoor marine mammal facility. Designed by **Lohan Associates** and opened in 1990, it is home to Pacific black whales, beluga whales, sea otters, dolphins, and seals. Visitors can wander through the main exhibit, which re-creates the rocky coastlines of southeast Alaska and the Pacific Northwest, complete with nature trails, streams, rocks, and forest vegetation. A 60,000-gallon penguin habitat is another great feature.
♦ Admission. Daily. Advance ticket purchase recommended for Oceanarium. 1200 S Lake Shore Dr (at Solidarity Dr). 939.2426, recorded message 939.2438 ♿

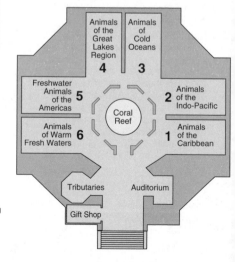

tomb of Pharaoh Unis-ankh, excavated and brought to Chicago in 1908, is at the core of the *Inside Ancient Egypt* exhibit. In the *Place for Wonder* children can handle meteorites, shells, skeletons, and countless other objects to their hearts' content. *Traveling the Pacific* transports visitors from Chicago's mercurial weather to a re-created coral island, complete with the sounds of birdcalls and crashing waves, and a life-size, glowing lava flow that was cast from an active volcanic flow in Hawaii. *Into the Wild* is an enormous diorama of nearly every species of bird in North America; with sound effects, it's like a walk in the woods. Check the "Field Notes" posted inside the main entrances for special events

Adler Planetarium

P. KAHLER

37 Adler Planetarium This pink granite dodecahedron (each of its 12 sides representing a sign of the zodiac), designed in 1930 by **Ernest A. Grunsfeld Jr.**, was the country's first planetarium. Like the **Field Museum** and the **Shedd Aquarium**, it was built with money made by merchandising: **Sears, Roebuck & Company** executive Max Adler financed the building and imported its Zeiss projector from Germany, where it had been designed in 1923. Antique astronomical instruments are displayed, and navigation, the history of exploration, and space travel are the subjects of exhibition dioramas. Narrated *Sky Shows* in the domed theater change throughout the year and are always engrossing and informative. After the Friday-night show visitors can tour the **Doane Observatory**, where a 20-inch telescope provides dramatic celestial views. Weekend *Sky Shows* for the six-and-under crowd are popular.

Spectacular views of the city skyline may be seen from the promontory leading to the planetarium, a perfect place for a warm-weather picnic or watching the sun set. The promontory is also home to three impressive pieces of sculpture. The *Thaddeus Kosciuszko Memorial* (1904, by Kasimir Chodzinski) is a bronze equestrian statue honoring the Polish hero who fought in the American Revolution and later for the freedom of his native country. *Nicolaus Copernicus* (1823, by Bertel Thorvaldsen) depicts the father of modern astronomy holding a compass and an armillary sphere, a model of the solar system. The bronze *Sundial* (1980, by Henry Moore) directly in front of the planetarium stands 13 feet high, marking the hour of the day. ♦ Admission; free on Tuesdays. Daily; F until 8PM. To find out what to look for in the sky, call the Nightwatch 24-hour hotline (322.0334). Solidarity Dr (at Lake Michigan). 322.0300 &

38 Meigs Field Built in 1947 and named for Merrill C. Meigs, publisher of the *Chicago Herald Examiner* and the *Chicago American*, this airport is used primarily by small commuter airlines and private planes. At press time, there is controversy about whether it should be expanded to allow instrument landings or closed and returned to park land. ♦ South of Adler Planetarium (off Solidarity Dr). 744.4787

Wally Phillips
WGN Radio

Great Day! Visit the **Museum of Science and Industry** (Chicago's most popular attraction). Then drive the lakefront to **Wilmette,** see the non-denominational **Baha'i House of Worship** . . . then north to the **Botanical Gardens.**

Navy Pier. One mile promontory on **Lake Michigan** . . . shops . . . flower gardens . . . restaurants . . . a 150-foot, 15-story-high Ferris wheel . . . a Grand Ballroom that seats 3,000.

Michigan Avenue. Visit the **Art Institute** then walk north across the **Chicago River** (dyed green every St. Pat's day) past the **Chicago Tribune,** the **Wrigley Building,** Michigan Avenue shopping, the **Gold Coast.**

Lake Michigan boat ride. Spectacular skyline view includes three of the five tallest buildings in the world **(Sears Tower, Standard Oil Building, Water Tower).**

Lincoln Park Zoo. Free daily all year, walking distance from Michigan Avenue and other hotels.

Shedd Aquarium. World's largest sea-life collection. **Adler Planetarium.** Celestial display, stars, planets, sky shows. The planetarium and the aquarium are next door to each other on the lakefront downtown.

Lyric Opera . . . **Chicago Symphony** (voted world's finest) . . . **Grant Park** free concerts . . . **Ravinia Festival** (June-Sept) . . . Home of the blues . . . Jazz clubs.

Restaurants: Steak, **Morton's** (the first of 25 now in US; 48-ounce porterhouse!), **Eli's;** Seafood, **Cape Cod Room, Drake Hotel;** Italian, **Rosebud;** French, **Charlie Trotter's, Le Francais, Carlos, Everest Room;** International, **Yoshi's Cafe, Un Grand Café;** Sports bars, **Michael Jordan's, Harry Caray's.**

Magnificent Mile/ Streeterville

Glitzy and ritzy, the Magnificent Mile is a shopper's dream come true. **Saks Fifth Avenue, Neiman Marcus, Bloomingdale's,** the 125-store **Water Tower Place,** and scores of specialty shops, fine restaurants, and luxury hotels stretch the just-under-a-mile length of **Michigan Avenue** from the **Chicago River** north to **Oak Street,** where consumerism gets even more serious in ultrachic designer boutiques. An architectural showplace, the avenue is anchored at its southern tip by the Gothic **Tribune Tower** and terra-cotta–clad **Wrigley Building,** and on the north by the palatial **Drake Hotel** and the polished pink granite office and shopping complex known as **One Magnificent Mile.** Some of the city's most exclusive residences—among them **Benjamin Marshall**'s mansard-roofed **999 Lake Shore Drive** and **Mies van der Rohe**'s twin apartment buildings— hug **Lake Michigan** as the roadway curves south into Streeterville, where trendy restaurants and around-the-clock action at **North Pier Chicago** are all the rage.

Difficult though it may be to envision today, much of this part of town was under water until a hundred years ago when a seedy character who called himself Captain Streeter ran a boat aground off **Chicago Avenue.** When he could not free his boat, he began his own landfill project. The area along the Chicago River thrived until the 1950s, packed with factories, railheads,

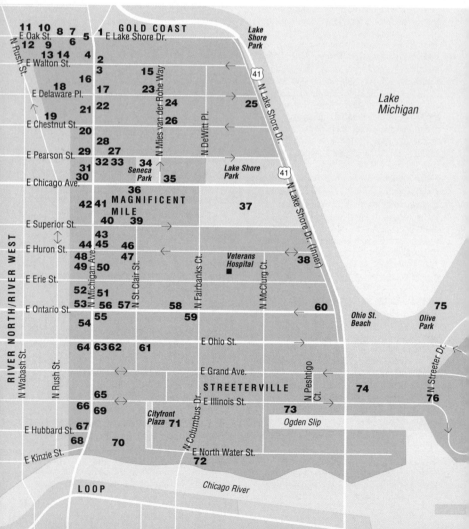

warehouses, and shipyards. Its growth has long been linked to that of the adjacent Near North Side, which was being settled in the late 19th century by wealthy citizens. Among the signs of prosperity was the **Fourth Presbyterian Church** at Grand Avenue and Wabash Street, which held its first service only hours before the 1871 Chicago Fire ravaged the community. Famous survivors of the fire were the **Water Tower** and its **Pumping Station**; completed just two years prior to the blaze and still standing today, they are landmarks on the avenue.

The 1920 opening of the **Michigan Avenue Bridge** connecting the city's North and South Sides was a major spur to growth. In 1921 the **Wrigley Building**, home office of the chewing gum company, rose beside the river at the avenue's southern end. **Raymond Hood** and **John Mead Howells's** winning entry in the international design competition for the **Tribune Tower** went up nearby in 1924. The grand **Drake Hotel**, by **Benjamin Marshall**, crowned the opposite end of the avenue in 1920. The nearby 14-story **Palmolive Building** (later to be called the **Playboy Building**, and today known as **919 North Michigan Avenue**), was a veritable skyscraper when it was built in 1929, topped by an airplane navigational beacon. That same year, Shriners flocked to their extravagant new **Medinah Athletic Club**; it went bankrupt just five years later during the Depression, when economic activity up and down the block screeched to a halt. The building has since been restored as the luxurious **Hotel Inter-Continental Chicago.**

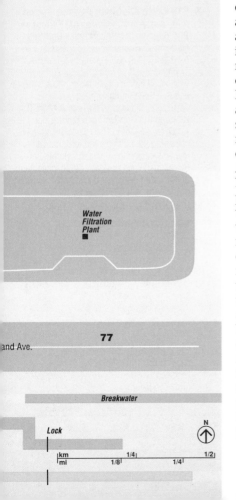

Water
Filtration
Plant
■

and Ave.

77

Breakwater

Lock

N
⊕

km   1/4| 1/2|
mi   1/8| 1/4|

The Michigan Avenue/Streeterville area remained an affluent community after the Depression, and it wasn't until the late 1960s and early 1970s that it developed its current identity as a high-end retail district. The 1970 arrival of the quarter-mile-high **John Hancock Center**, a combination of apartments, offices, and commercial space, played a part. But the real turning point was the 1976 construction of **Water Tower Place**. Anchored by a major branch of **Marshall Field's**, a downtown presence for more than a century, this seven-story vertical mall signaled the determined march of retail northward from the Loop. Retail development has continued virtually nonstop ever since, from the 1983 unveiling of **One Magnificent Mile**, to the 1989 revitalization of the abandoned North Pier Terminal into **North Pier Chicago**, a collection of upscale stores and restaurants. Another major project has been the rehabilitation of **Navy Pier** as a suitable site for Chicago's famed annual international art exposition (now called **Art Chicago**) and other public events.

Eager for business to support the high rents, most stores along Michigan Avenue and Oak Street are open seven days a week, though it's always wise to check before going. Crowds can get thick on weekends; to avoid the hordes, shop on weekdays. Make a day's excursion of it, with a break for lunch or dinner at one of the many restaurants in the area. Add a relaxing stroll along the posh residential streets on the northern end near the lake and you can say you've seen the sights.

1 Lakefront Underpass Cross beneath North Lake Shore Drive to the Gold Coast's Oak Street Beach and miles of paved paths perfect for a walk, run, or bike ride. Other underpasses in this area are at East Superior Street and East Grand Avenue. ♦ Between E Oak St and N Lake Shore Dr

2 Drake Hotel $$$ Modeled after Renaissance palaces by architect **Benjamin Marshall,** this hotel has played host to kings, queens, and presidents since 1920. The public areas are opulent, and most of the 535 rooms and suites follow suit with plush fabrics and period pieces. Some rooms, however, are surprisingly drab and cramped; check in advance that yours isn't. The Executive Business Women's Suites have foldaway beds, so the bedroom can be converted to a conference room with ease. For the business traveler, secretarial service, fax and telex, and a notary public are available. There are a number of adequate restaurants, plus the **Palm Court,** an exceptionally pretty, flowery refuge for afternoon tea or cocktails. Weekend packages are available. ♦ 140 E Walton St (at N Michigan Ave). 787.2200, 800/55.DRAKE; fax 951.5803 &

Within the Drake Hotel:

Oak Terrace $$ This large, attractive, all-purpose hotel dining room is popular for lunch and Sunday brunch, but the menu—from chicken breast *divan* to chef's salad—holds no surprises. Try to get a table at the north end overlooking the lake. ♦ American ♦ Daily breakfast, lunch, and dinner. 787.2200 &

Cape Cod Room ★$$$ Once the city's premier seafood house, this cozy New England-style spot with red-checkered tablecloths and nautical decorations remains popular, though the food has lost its luster. The Bookbinder soup (red snapper in a tomato-vegetable broth enhanced with sherry) is a signature item. ♦ Seafood ♦ Daily lunch and dinner. Reservations recommended. Jacket and tie required. 787.2200 &

Coq D'Or ★$$ Dimly lit regardless of the time of day, this clubby place pours countless cocktails and serves hearty food such as cheese omelettes, roast beef sandwiches,

and strip steaks. But the real draw is legendary pianist-singer Buddy Charles, who plays jazz, ragtime, show tunes, ballads, and requests with finesse. ♦ American ♦ Daily lunch and dinner. Music: Daily 9PM-1:30AM. 787.2200 &

Long Grove Confectionery Delectable chocolate-covered pecan-and-caramel candy and English toffees are among the goodies gobbled up at this gourmet candy shop. ♦ Daily. 642.1684

Georg Jensen Jewelry and lines of fine china, crystal, and silver from the famed Danish company are sold here. Prices are high, and service can be haughty. A bridal registry is available. ♦ M-Sa. 642.9160

3 919 North Michigan Avenue Known to Chicagoans for years as the **Palmolive Building** and later the **Playboy Building, Holabird & Root**'s elegant limestone tower built in 1930 is one of the city's finest Art Deco skyscrapers. It is both graceful and powerful, with finely balanced setbacks and a lighting scheme that emphasizes its dramatic verticality. **Skidmore, Owings & Merrill** restored the storefronts to their original Art Deco elegance. The 150-foot-tall mast crowning the building was originally an airplane navigational beacon visible for 60 miles. It went dark after high-rises were constructed nearby and residents complained of the light. ♦ At E Walton St

Within 919 North Michigan Avenue:

Mark Shale Catering primarily to a yuppie clientele, this appealing five-level store has a good selection of relatively conservative men's and women's attire and accessories. Semiannual sales at Christmas and in early summer offer great bargains. Alterations are gratis. ♦ Daily. 440.0720 &

Bally of Switzerland The sole Chicago branch of the leather-goods company famous for high-quality shoes and accessories is located here. ♦ Daily. 787.8110

Arturo Express $ Popular with the lunch crowd, this charming little place offers tempting baked goods and delectable salads. ♦ Cafe ♦ M-Sa breakfast and lunch. 751.2250

Restaurants/Clubs: Red	**Hotels:** Blue
Shops/ ♥ Outdoors: Green	**Sights/Culture:** Black

Magnificent Mile Shopping Map

OAK STREET

One Magnificent Mile
shops within include:
Chanel
Barry Bricken
Polo Ralph Lauren
Rosenthal Furs

Drake Hotel
shops within include:
Georg Jensen *jewelry, china, crystal, and silverware*

WALTON STREET

900 North Michigan Avenue
more than 60 shops on seven levels including:
Bloomingdale's
women's fashions **Henri Bendel**
fine silver **Pavillon Christofle**
men's and women's fashions **Gucci**

Mark Shale *men's and women's businesswear*
Bally of Switzerland *shoes and accessories*
Bulgari *fine jewelry*
Westin Hotel

MICHIGAN AVENUE

DELAWARE PLACE

Fourth Presbyterian Church

John Hancock Center *94th-floor observatory*

CHESTNUT STREET

Plaza Escada
toys **F.A.O. Schwarz**
Filene's Basement
Borders Books

Water Tower Place
seven stories of shops and restaurants including:
Marshall Field's
Lord & Taylor

PEARSON STREET

Old Water Tower

Chicago Visitors' Center

CHICAGO AVENUE

men's and women's fashions **Banana Republic**

Neiman Marcus

SUPERIOR STREET

Chicago Place
more than 80 shops on eight levels including:
Saks Fifth Avenue
Talbot's

Tiffany & Co. *fine jewelers*
Brooks Brothers *men's clothing*

HURON STREET

Compagnie International Express
men's and women's sportswear
Terra Museum of American Art
men's shoes **Hanig's**

Gap Kids *children's sportswear*
The Gap *sportswear*
Cole Hahn *shoes*
Niketown *sports clothing*
Sony *electronics*

ERIE STREET

cookware and home furnishings **Crate & Barrel**
crystal and china **Waterford/Wedgwood**
fine jewelers **Cartier**

NordicTrack *exercise equipment*
B. Dalton Bookseller
Burberrys *men's and women's classic apparel*

ONTARIO STREET

(currently under construction)

American Express Travel Service
Bigsby & Kruthers *men's clothing*

MICHIGAN AVENUE

OHIO STREET

Chicago Marriott Hotel
Circle Gallery
Rand McNally Map and Travel Store
Wrigley Building

Atlas Galleries
Shabahang Persian Carpets
The Forgotten Woman *larger women's fashions*
House of Hunan
Hammacher Schlemmer
Hotel Inter-Continental Chicago
Tribune Tower

4 One Magnificent Mile Three hexagonal cubes of polished pink granite—variously 21, 49, and 58 stories high—brace each other vertically and are oriented to avoid casting summer shadows on Oak Street Beach. This 1983 **Skidmore, Owings & Merrill** design was the most striking addition to the North Michigan Avenue skyline until the arrival of the **900 North Michigan** building on the next block. Offices and condos fill the towers of the skyscraper, while expensive shops and restaurants afford visitors browsing, buying— and dining options at the base. In addition to the listings below, **Barry Bricken, Chanel, Giacomo, Polo Ralph Lauren, N.H. Rosenthal Furs,** and **Matthew C. Hoffman Jewelers** are located here. ◆ 940-980 N Michigan Ave (between E Oak and E Walton Sts)

Within One Magnificent Mile:

Spiaggia ★★$$$$ The prices may empty your pocketbook, but this handsome bilevel restaurant, with its dramatic floor-to-ceiling windows overlooking the lake, is a winner, thanks partly to the knowledgeable staff. Thin-crust boutique pizzas are among the best starters. Main courses range from succulent roast chicken and other game birds to inventively garnished meats and fish. Everything is beautifully presented, but you won't be overwhelmed by the quantity. They have an extensive, expensive wine list. ◆ Northern Italian ◆ M-Sa lunch and dinner; Su dinner. Reservations and jacket required. 980 N Michigan Ave (at E Oak St), Second floor. 280.2750 &

Cafe Spiaggia ★★$$ **Spiaggia**'s casual little sister, done in the same decor on a reduced scale, proffers pizzas and pastas in two narrow rooms. Wines are available by the glass or bottle. The easygoing, friendly service and excellent coffee win praise. It's worth a stop, if only for an incomparable cup of espresso or cappuccino made from Italy's foremost brand of beans *(illycaffè)*. ◆ Northern Italian ◆ Daily lunch and dinner. 980 N Michigan Ave (at E Oak St), Second floor. 280.2764 &

Shaxted Exquisite bed linens and towels are sold here, many from Italy and Madeira and exclusive to this store. Custom-made linens also are available for a pretty penny, but might even be worth the price. ◆ M-Sa. 940 N Michigan Ave (between E Oak and E Walton Sts). 337.0855 &

5 Oak Street On a lovely day, when you don't feel the need to escape the elements by ducking into a nearby vertical mall, this one-block stretch is a shopper's paradise. Elegant boutiques for men's and women's

clothing, shoes, jewelry, linens, and stationery, plus wonderful salons to pamper you with a manicure or new hairstyle, will entertain browsers and buyers for hours. The stores' hours are as individualized as their selections: Some are open Sundays, others aren't; some close at 5PM, others at 6:30PM. Call first if there's a specific store you want to visit. ◆ Between N Michigan Ave and N Rush St

In Oak Street:

Giorgio Armani The renowned Italian designer's first couture boutique in the Midwest has three floors of men's and women's suits, eveningwear, leather goods, and accessories. ◆ M-Sa. 113 E Oak St (between N Michigan Ave and N Rush St). 427.6264

Ultimo This ultimate fashion boutique is frequented by both celebrities and the merely well-dressed looking for the latest from Valentino, Armani, and Sonia Rykiel, among others. Don't expect the salespeople to fall all over themselves to assist you. ◆ M-Sa. 114 E Oak St (between N Michigan Ave and N Rush St). 787.0906

Marilyn Miglin Makeup designers in this tiny boutique sit across from their customers at lighted booths, demonstrating proper technique by applying cosmetics to half of the client's face and letting her do the other half. Founded by a former model and dancer, the custom, nonanimal-tested products are made in a nearby lab. ◆ M-Sa. 112 E Oak St (between N Michigan Ave and N Rush St). 943.1120

6 Water Mark If none of a variety of package invitations suits your fancy, special-order from a vast selection of Crane's and the like. You can also choose stationery to be personalized. ◆ M-Sa. 109 E Oak St (between N Michigan Ave and N Rush St). 337.5353

7 Sonia Rykiel The designer's signature knits, dresses, velours, separates, and outerwear for women, as well as some items for kids, are featured in this smart little boutique. ◆ M-Sa. 106 E Oak St (between N Michigan Ave and N Rush St). 951.0800

7 Charles Ifergan Salon With offerings from a wash and style before a night on the town to a major makeover, this is one of the most popular salons around. On Saturday mornings, especially in June, the shop is filled with brides and attendants getting pampered for the big day. ◆ Tu-Sa. 106 E Oak St (between N Michigan Ave and N Rush St). 642.4484

8 Betsey Johnson The New York designer, who has a dozen boutiques around the country, produces body-conscious outfits that reveal every ripple and curve. As if that weren't enough of an attention-getter, items come in loud floral prints, paisleys, and plaids

Something's always on sale. ♦ Daily. 72 E Oak St (between N Michigan Ave and N Rush St). 664.5901

9 Pratesi Shop here for the world's most luxurious bed linens, manufactured in Florence for generations. ♦ M-Sa. 67 E Oak St (between N Michigan Ave and N Rush St). 943.8422

9 Nicole Miller One of several scattered around the country, this individually owned shop features Miller's famed "conversation" prints (because they always get talked about) in scarves, ties, tops, plus distinctive fragrances and bath products. ♦ Daily. 61 E Oak St (between N Michigan Ave and N Rush St). 664.3532

9 Luca Luca Very classy Italian fashions for women, many in strong pastels and distinctive fabrics, are on hand here. ♦ Daily. 59 E Oak St (between N Michigan Ave and N Rush St). 664.1512

9 Lester Lampert Specializing in expertly refashioned antique jewelry, this store has been in the same family for four generations; many pieces are produced on the premises. ♦ M-Sa. 57 E Oak St (between N Michigan Ave and N Rush St). 944.6888

9 Sulka Selling private-label menswear, this boutique specializes in fine silks and absolutely gorgeous ties. ♦ M-Sa. 55 E Oak St (between N Michigan Ave and N Rush St). 951.9500

10 Esquire Theatre Designed in 1938 by **Hal** and **William L. Pereira,** this snazzy, bilevel Art Moderne theater borrowed its name from *Esquire* magazine (founded a few years earlier in Chicago) to project an image of sophistication. Unfortunately, the large space has been chopped up into six theaters showing first-run films. ♦ 58 E Oak St (between N Michigan Ave and N Rush St). 280.0101

10 Bogner This is a branch of the German retailer specializing in high-end skiwear, cashmere, and leather goods. ♦ M-Sa. 56 E Oak St (between N Michigan Ave and N Rush St). 664.6466

11 Isis/My Sister's Circus Specializing in fashionable and distinctive one-size-fits-all casual clothing, it also has a jewelry department that includes the work of talented Chicago designers. ♦ Daily. No credit cards accepted. 38 E Oak St (between N Michigan Ave and N Rush St). 664.7074

Oak Street Shopping Map

MICHIGAN AVENUE

men's and women's fashions **Ultimo**	**Optica** *eyewear*
cosmetics **Marilyn Miglin**	**Stephanie Kelian** *shoes and accessories*
leathergoods **Hermès**	**Giorgio Armani** *men's and women's fashions*
women's apparel **Sonia Rykiel**	**Trabert & Hoeffer** *jewelry*
women's apparel **Janis**	**Billy Hork Gallery** *posters and original art*
bridal fashions **Ultimate Bride**	**The Water Mark** *writing accessories*
hair and makeup **Charles Ifergan Salon**	**Bottega Veneta** *Italian accessories*
silver jewelry **Great Lakes Jewelry**	**Ann Taylor** *women's apparel*
jewelry and handicrafts **Alaska Shop**	**Gianni Versace Boutique** *Italian fashions*
women's clothing **Betsey Johnson**	**Pratesi** *fine linens*
art and gifts **Unique Accents**	**In Chicago** *men's sportswear*
women's clothing **Jilsander**	**Nicole Miller** *women's fashions*
maternity clothes **Pea in a Pod**	**Luca Luca** *women's fashions*
hair salon **Cote d'Or**	**Lester Lampert** *jewelry*
clothing and jewelry **Isis/My Sister's Circus**	**Glasses, Ltd.** *eyewear*
women's and children's fashions **Sugar Magnolia**	**CP Shades** *women's fashions*
hair and nail salon **Robert-Lucas**	**Sulka** *menswear*
shoes **Precis**	**Ilona of Hungary** *hair and skin care salon*
	Atlas Galleries *contemporary and classic art*
	Private Lives *bedroom and bath accessories*
	Barneys *men's and women's fashions*

(OAK STREET runs between the two columns)

RUSH STREET

11 Sugar Magnolia Women's and children's attire and accessories that delight and surprise are available here. Flannel nightgowns, 1940s-style wool overcoats, and kids' leather jackets are equally smart. This is probably the most affordable clothing shop on Oak Street. ◆ Daily. 34 E Oak St (between N Michigan Ave and N Rush St). 944.0885

11 Robert-Lucas This bright white salon with light streaming through 21 windows specializes in peroxide-free enzyme hair coloring. ◆ Tu-Sa. Appointment recommended. 30 E Oak St (between N Michigan Ave and N Rush St). 642.6640

12 Private Lives Linens for bed and bath by top makers such as Laura Ashley, Ralph Lauren, and ESPRIT are attractively displayed and offered at discount prices. You can order certain items custom-made. ◆ Daily. 39 E Oak St (between N Michigan Ave and N Rush St). 337.5474. Also at: 662 W Diversey Pkwy (at Orchard St). 525.6464 &

12 Boogie's Diner $ This Aspen-based food and clothing store combines a fun 1950s-style soda shop atmosphere for dining with up-to-date fashions for the young at heart. Food is all-American basic—burgers, club sandwiches, and fries. Featured fashions include name-brand leathers and boots. ◆ American ◆ Daily lunch and dinner. 33 E Oak St (between N Michigan Ave and N Rush St). 915.0555 &

12 Barneys The Big Apple's legendary men's clothier has evolved into an upscale purveyor of fashions and accessories for both men and women. Its doors opened in the Windy City in September 1992. ◆ Daily. 25 E Oak St (at N Rush St). 587.1700 &

13 Malcolm Franklin Antiques Dan Sullivan upholds his grandfather's standard of carrying only the very best English antique furnishings, here and in the New York branch; both are considered to be among the best antiques stores in the country. ◆ M-Sa. 56 E Walton St (between N Michigan Ave and N Rush St). 337.0202

PANE CALDO
RISTORANTE ITALIANO
•

14 Pane Caldo ★$ Regional Italian antipasti and pasta are featured at this charming cafe and bakery. There's a large take-out menu. ◆ Italian ◆ Daily breakfast, lunch, and dinner. 72 E Walton St (between N Michigan Ave and N Rush St). 649.0055 &

14 T'ang Dynasty ★$$ Enjoy good Mandarin and Szechuan food in a rambling series of rooms adorned with Asian artworks. There are few surprises, but the dishes are nicely seasoned and presented in generous portions. Service is cheerful but erratic; servers also tend to praise whatever you order, so don't hope for much guidance. There's a full bar, plus wines and some Asian beers. ◆ Chinese ◆ Daily lunch and dinner. 100 E Walton St (between N Michigan Ave and N Rush St). 664.8688 &

15 Knickerbocker Chicago $$ Each room in this recently renovated, attractive hotel has a comfortable sitting area; some of the 256 rooms even have canopy beds. Rooms on the 14th floor offer a taste of 1920s Chicago: secret doors leading to a central staircase are carved into the walls, enabling guests who used the rooms as Prohibition-era speakeasies to make a quick getaway. Restaurants include the **Prince of Wales** and the more casual **Cafe**. Weekend packages are available. ◆ 163 E Walton St (between N Mies van der Rohe Way and N Michigan Ave). 751.8100, 800/621.8140; fax 751.0370 &

16 900 North Michigan Avenue In 1989 **Kohn Pedersen Fox** with **Perkins & Will** designed this king-size addition to the North Michigan Avenue skyline. The tower (pictured bottom right) contains restaurants and high-end retail stores on the first eight floors, anchored by **Bloomingdale's** and the **Four Seasons Hotel**, with offices and condominiums rising above. The department store is nicer than its New York counterpart; the linens, housewares, and fine china departments are among the best in the city. More than a hundred shops ring the marble-clad atrium, among them the **Coach Store, Cashmere Cashmere, Charles Jourdan,** and **Gucci.** ◆ Daily. Reduced-rate parking is available with tickets validated by the tenants. Between E Walton St and E Delaware Pl

Within 900 North Michigan Avenue:

Henri Bendel Designed by **François Cautreaux** to resemble a 1920s French mansion, this four-story "Lady's Paradise" is a mass of golden wallpaper, crystal chandeliers, plush carpeting, and stunning attire. Start at the top of the curving staircases and work your way down. Customer service is legendary. None of this, naturally, is for the faint of purse. ◆ Daily. Street level. 642.0140 &

Pavillon Christofle The first Chicago location of France's premier silversmith carries a lovely assortment of silverplate, sterling, stainless and gold-plated flatware, fine French crystal and china, and select pieces of 18-karat gold and sterling silver jewelry. ◆ Daily. Street level. 664.9700 &

Jessica McClintock Cinderella could have a ball in these dresses. Bolts of silk, satin, velvet, linen, and lace go into San Francisco–based McClintock's designs for old-fashioned, romantic dresses. Her exquisite bridal gowns are laden with beading and lace, and her pint-size party dresses are every little girl's fantasy. ◆ Daily. Third level. 944.2025 ♿

Glove Me Tender The only store in the country exclusively devoted to handwear carries more than 80 lines for men, women, and children, from evening gloves to designer dishwashing gloves. ◆ Daily. Fourth level. 664.4022 ♿

Tucci Benucch ★$$ This lighthearted, crowded, reasonably priced takeoff on an Italian villa serves fine pizzas, good roast chicken, seafood, and pastas. A nice touch: Crusty bread comes with a puddle of lushly herbed olive oil. ◆ Italian ◆ Daily lunch and dinner. Fifth level. 266.2500 ♿

Four Seasons Hotel $$$$ From the street-level lobby, guests take an elevator to the seventh-floor reception desk, lounges, and restaurants. This vast floor is elegantly furnished, with plush seating areas everywhere. An inviting, darkly paneled bar is a great place for drinks. In the beautiful, airy **Conservatory,** lacy cloths cover the low tables for afternoon tea and scones, and a pianist plays in the late afternoon; it's also a perfect spot for a cocktail in the evening, when a mellow jazz combo plays. One restaurant is for light meals, while **Seasons** (see below) provides a more formal dining experience. The 344 rooms are opulent with English furnishings, three two-line phones, a stocked bar, and bathrooms complete with robes and cotton balls. Maid service is twice daily. For the business traveler, soundproofed boardrooms with audiovisual equipment and adjoining windowed dining salons are available. Other features include a skylit swimming pool, rooftop running track, aerobics room, and exercise equipment. Weekend rates are available. ◆ 120 E Delaware Pl (at N Michigan Ave). 280.8800, 800/332.3442; fax 280.1748 ♿

Within the Four Seasons Hotel:

Seasons ★★$$$$ The menu, which changes with the seasons (naturally), features light preparations, among them delicious fish and fowl dishes and crisp fresh vegetables. Signature dishes include braised Maine lobster and Kobe beef. The wine list is extensive, and the surroundings are elegant, with dark woodwork and warm, red-patterned carpets. Request a table overlooking the lake. A children's menu is available. ◆ American ◆ Daily breakfast, lunch, and dinner. Reservations recommended. Jacket required. 649.2349 ♿

17 Westin Hotel $$$ Though popular with conventioneers, this gray concrete slab houses 740 rooms of average comfort and negligible character. The Executive Level offers additional perks: a welcome gift, complimentary hors d'oeuvres, and continental breakfast. All guests enjoy concierge services, plus free health club, sauna, and reasonably priced laundry service. Weekend packages are available. There are three restaurants, one of which often features live jazz in the evening. ◆ 909 N Michigan Ave (at E Delaware Pl). 943.7200, 800/228.3000; fax 649.7447 ♿

900 North Michigan Avenue

Terrific Tours

You can have a great time exploring Chicago on your own, but if you have special interests, limited time, or just like a little help getting acclimated, here are a few options:

The Chicago Architecture Foundation (224 S Michigan Ave, at E Jackson Dr, 922.3432, recorded information 922.TOUR) offers more than 50 tours, providing a chance to visit and learn about different sections of the city. Guided by well-informed docents, some of the more popular tours include *Loop Architecture Walking Tours* and *Frank Lloyd Wright in Oak Park.* Inquire about special tours geared toward children. Tours are offered daily.

Art Encounter (927 Noyes St, between Ridge and Sherman Aves, Evanston, 708/328.9222) offers two tours for art aficionados. One Saturday a month there's *Gallery Walk*—a walk through different art districts and art galleries conducted by local artists. On Wednesday afternoons the *Expanded Visions* tour provides an opportunity to visit artists' studios and collections in private homes. There are no tours offered during the summer months.

The Chicago Historical Society (N Clark St, at W North Ave, 642.4600) offers periodic tours of Chicago churches. With its immense immigration from Ireland, Poland, Bavaria, and other predominantly Catholic areas—and the wealth generated around the turn of the century—Chicago became home to an extraordinary number of magnificent church buildings. Though many have fallen on hard times due to population shifts, the windows and sculptures are still awe-inspiring. Call for tour schedules.

Chicago Horse and Carriage Ltd. (E Pearson St, at N Michigan Ave, 94.HORSE) provides old-fashioned and romantic horse-drawn carriage rides through the **Magnificent Mile** and **River North** areas. Tours are offered year-round; call for departure times.

Chicago Motor Coach and **London Motor Coach** (750 S Clinton St, at W Polk St, 922.8919) provide double-decker buses with wacky tour guides to visit the usual tourist spots, from the **Hancock Building** to the **Field Museum of Natural History.** Buses can be boarded at numerous places in the downtown area, and you can hop on and off as many times as you like for the price of one ticket. The buses run daily, year-round.

Chicago Supernatural Tours (708/499.0300) is a company for those who are interested in ghost stories and supernatural tales, offering day, night, and river tours of the Chicago area. Owner Richard Crowe even says that minor psychic occurrences have happened during the tours themselves. Call for information and departure points.

The Friends of the Chicago River (407 S Dearborn St, at W Van Buren St, 939.0490) is devoted to drawing interest to the often neglected river. The organization sponsors frequent walking tours and also provides maps for self-guided walks. Some of these river walks extend beyond the city into its environs. Call for tour schedules.

Graceland Cemetery (N Clark St, off W Irving Park Rd, 922.3432, recorded information 922.TOUR) is the final resting place for any number of Chicago scions of industry and architecture, and few expenses were spared for their monuments. This elegantly landscaped cemetery is also home to **Louis Sullivan**'s **Getty Tomb,** representing the change in **Sullivan**'s style which in turn influenced a movement in modern American architecture. The **Chicago Architecture Foundation** offers guided walking tours of the cemetery each Sunday at 2PM from August to October; it also sells a book for self-guided tours. Cars are welcome to drive through the cemetery (no parking), and it is accessible by **CTA** *Bus #22* **(Clark St Bus)** or *Bus #80* **(Irving St Bus).**

Chicago From the Lake (North Pier, 465 E Illinois St, 527.2002) and **Chicago's First Lady** (Michigan Avenue Bridge, 708/358.1330) offer guided tours of the city's history and architecture from the lake and the river (the latter in conjunction with the **Chicago Architecture Foundation**). The tours are 90 minutes long and operate daily from April through November.

The Spirit of Chicago (Navy Pier, 836.7899) lets you view Chicago from **Lake Michigan** while listening to Broadway show tunes performed by the waitstaff, dancing to live music, and indulging in a buffet. Cruises depart daily for brunch, lunch, and dinner. Sunset cocktail cruises and children's rates are available, too.

Untouchables Tours (Here's Chicago Visitor's Center, Water Tower Pumping Station, N Michigan Ave at E Pearson St, 881.1195) offers a two-hour bus tour of Prohibition-era gangster hangouts and hit spots, followed by an optional dinner-theater package. Tours are offered daily in summer, on weekends in winter.

18 Sidney Garber This well-established jeweler is known for his exceptional selection of fine gems in classic styles. ♦ M-Sa. 118 E Delaware Pl (between N Michigan Ave and N Rush St). 944.5225 ♿

18 Amico's Grand What sounds like a service station is actually a full-service salon and day spa featuring hair care, manicures and pedicures, facials, body wraps, and massages. Video imaging helps you visualize a new haircut or makeup style. ♦ M-Sa. Appointment recommended. 110 E Delaware Pl (between N Michigan Ave and N Rush St). 787.7876 ♿

19 Material Possessions Everything for your table in every medium, including handwoven mats, highly stylized contemporary place settings, earthy pottery, and sparkling glass, is carried here. Most pieces would not be found in a department store, and many are unique. ♦ Daily. 54 E Chestnut St (at N Rush St). 280.4885

19 Tremont Hotel $$$ This small, attractive hotel was renovated in 1985 in the style of an English manor. The brass-and-wood-detailed lobby has the aura of a comfortable men's club, and the 137 rooms and penthouse suites have period furnishings. There's a concierge, multilingual staff, and turndown service complete with cognac. The hotel's **Crickets** restaurant is closed and has been replaced by **Cafe Gordon** (under the management of Gordon Sinclair of River North's stellar **Gordon** restaurant). ♦ 100 E Chestnut St (between N Michigan Ave and N Rush St). 751.1900, 800/525.4800; fax 751.8691 ♿

20 Plaza Escada This German import's Eurochic decor, with bright lighting and lots of white marble, focuses attention on the designer's ready-to-wear fashions, all artfully displayed more by color than by style. Prices are high; be prepared to mortgage the farm. ♦ Daily. 840 N Michigan Ave (at E Chestnut St). 915.0500 ♿

Within Plaza Escada:

Escada Cafe ★★$$ For a **Spiaggia**-like lunch with a view, and at a lower cost, visit this restaurant on the store's fourth floor. A Brazilian chef does fascinating things with the freshest of vegetables and tiny pieces of meat; it's all very healthful, and tasty too. ♦ Cafe ♦ M-Sa 11:30AM-3PM. Group high tea available by reservation. 840 N Michigan Ave (at E Chestnut St). 915.0500 ♿

20 FAO Schwarz Is it a toy store or an amusement park? You decide. A life-size gorilla welcomes customers onto an escalator, which climbs up under a roller coaster for bowling balls, all to the tune of music and pealing bells. Keys turn, gears shift, and (stuffed) kangaroos box amid the extraordinary collection of toys arrayed over three floors. ♦ Daily. 840 N Michigan Ave (at E Chestnut St). 587.5000 ♿

21 Fourth Presbyterian Church The founding congregation worshiped in its new church at another location for the first time on 8 October 1871, just hours before the Chicago Fire began and burned it to the ground. All but five of the 321 members lost their homes in the flames. This impressive Gothic Revival church, the congregation's second, was built in 1914 by **Ralph Adams Cram. Howard Van Doren Shaw,** one of the church's many prominent members, designed the parish house and the fountain in the ivy-trimmed courtyard (the most romantic church courtyard in the city). The ceiling murals were designed by Frederic C. Bartlett. (This duo also collaborated on the **Second Presbyterian Church** near Prairie Avenue.) Excellent concerts are offered periodically at lunchtime and on Sunday afternoons. Holiday services are standing room only. ♦ N Michigan Ave (between E Delaware Pl and E Chestnut St)

Fourth Presbyterian Church

P. KAHLER

22 John Hancock Center The tapered profile of "Big John" has anchored North Michigan Avenue since it was built by **Skidmore, Owings & Merrill** in 1970. Layers of retail, parking, office, and residential spaces make up this multiuse giant. Its sunken plaza fronting the avenue underwent a badly needed overhaul in 1994. The dramatic cross-bracing is part of an ingenious framing system that creates a rigid, tubelike tower, structurally efficient and resistant to wind. Although the **Hancock** is 327 feet shorter than the **Sears Tower,** its observation deck offers views of the lake and the Loop that make it a favorite of Chicago natives. Ride a high-speed elevator to the **Skydeck Observatory** on the 94th floor or sit down to a meal in the **Signature Room** on the 95th floor (see below); both offer spectacular vistas in every direction, especially at night. A better bargain is a visit to the massive **Images Lounge** on the 96th floor, where you can sip a drink—kids can have a soda—and take in the view for about the same price you'd pay for entry to the **Observatory.** Everyone else has the same idea, though, so expect to wait in long lines for a seat, and be prepared to settle for one without much of a view. ◆ Fee for Observatory. Daily 9AM–12PM. 875 N Michigan Ave (between E Delaware Pl and E Chestnut St). 751.3681 ⅃

John Hancock Center

Within the John Hancock Center:

Signature Room ★★$$$ Incredible views of the city and lake provide a backdrop for meals at this lofty, dramatic perch. The ambitious, au courant food is good, but not great; dishes sometimes taste as experimental as they sound. Those with hearty appetites may opt for roast pork tenderloin with sausage and cornbread stuffing. The prix-fixe American epicure dinner is a delicious choice. For breathtaking vistas at a slightly gentler cost, try the luncheon buffet or Sunday brunch. ◆ American ◆ M-F lunch and dinner; Sa dinner; Su brunch and dinner. Reservations required for dinner. No tennis shoes or athletic wear allowed. 787.9596 ⅃

23 Guest Quarters Suite Hotel $$$ Each of the hotel's 345 spacious three-room suites is equipped with a mini-bar, two telephones, and two TVs with free cable. Amenities include a rooftop health club with pool, an exercise room, a sauna, a whirlpool, and panoramic views of the city and Lake Michigan. Meeting rooms and boardrooms can be reserved for business functions. Within the hotel are **Mrs. Parks Tavern** and the **Park Avenue Cafe,** a bistro/bar and a second-floor restaurant specializing in grilled foods. Packages for weekends and extended stays are available. ◆ 198 E Delaware Pl (at N Mies van der Rohe Way). 664.1100, 800/222.8733; fax 664.9881 ⅃

24 Raphael Hotel $$ This extremely reasonably priced 172-room hotel is perfect for those looking for intimacy and tastefully furnished rooms. The two-story lobby boasts cathedral windows, and the quaintly decorated rooms have sitting areas, stucco walls, and beamed ceilings. While it can't offer the features of a large, expensive hotel, it does have extremely attentive service. Weekend packages are available. ◆ 201 E Delaware Pl (at N Mies van der Rohe Way). 943.5000, 800/821.5343; fax 943.9483 ⅃

Within the Raphael Hotel:

Raphael Restaurant $$ Bountiful breakfasts, reasonably priced lunches, and more formal dinners that include free-range chicken and Long Island duckling are the fare at this clubby, 40-seat dining room. The intimate bar is a pleasant place for a drink ◆ American ◆ Daily breakfast, lunch, and dinner. Reservations recommended for lunch and dinner. 943.5000

25 860-880 North Lake Shore Drive Apartments The detailing in this pair of sleek steel-and-glass apartment towers, built in 1952, is masterful and subtle, the trademark of their architect, **Mies van der Rohe.** He later designed the apartments at **900-910 Lake Shore Drive,** and both pairs of buildings are home to many practicing Chicago architects. ◆ At E Delaware Pl

26 The Saloon ★★$$$ Vegetarians need not stop here. The meaty menu includes dishes like surf and turf and even huge surf and turf, a large lobster tail and Kansas City bone-in strip steak. Other succulent dishes are a slow-smoked one-pound pork chop, blackened prime rib, and whole roasted chicken. Brunch features a Santa Fe–style menu with southwest barbecue and Texas chili. ♦ American ♦ Daily lunch and dinner. 200 E Chestnut St (at N Mies van der Rohe Way), Street level. 280.5454

26 Chalfins' Deli ★$ This compact New York–style deli is colorful, lively, and full of great smells and tastes. Scrambled eggs with Nova Scotia salmon, thick-cut challah French toast, and other breakfasts can be ordered all day. Real winners are the pastrami and corned beef sandwiches served with spicy New York mustard. Takeout and delivery are available. ♦ Deli ♦ M breakfast and lunch; Tu-Su breakfast, lunch, and early dinner. 200 E Chestnut St (at N Mies van der Rohe Way), Lower level. 943.0034

27 Ritz-Carlton Hotel $$$ The 12th-floor lobby is grand, complete with a skylit fountain. All of the 431 spacious rooms have king-size beds, plush and polished furnishings, and two-line speaker phones. A health club with a swimming pool, exercise equipment, a whirlpool, steam rooms, a sauna, and massages are offered courtesy of the hotel. A concierge is very helpful, and attention to guests' personal needs is exceptional. You can have lunch or afternoon tea in the lobby **Greenhouse,** and the popular Art Deco bar presents live jazz or blues most nights. The **Cafe** offers good casual fare with a nice view of the lobby. The lobby is especially attractive at Christmas, when it is ablaze with poinsettias. Weekend rates are available. ♦ 160 E Pearson St (off N Michigan Ave). 266.1000, 800/332.3442; fax 266.1194 &

Within the Ritz-Carlton Hotel:

The Dining Room ★★★$$$$ This beautiful room, laden with exquisite flowers and romantically lit, is a perfect setting for a special occasion. The food is special, too, beginning with the complimentary appetizers. Among the excellent entrées are crepes filled with spinach and lobster tail, and fresh salmon served on a bed of smoked bacon, savoy cabbage, and tomatoes. Provocative desserts include rich Cointreau mousse sprinkled with berries and candied orange peels. Dainty little postdessert sweets perfectly cap the meal. A prix-fixe menu and good low-calorie spa selections are offered, and there's a very good wine list, too. Presentations, table appointments, and service meet the same high standard. A fine pianist plays during dinner. ♦ French ♦ M-Sa dinner; Su brunch and dinner. Reservations required. 266.1000 &

28 Water Tower Place Designed in 1976 by **Loebl Schlossman Dart and Hackl** with **C.F. Murphy Associates,** this marble-clad, reinforced-concrete building is one of the first and most successful vertical shopping malls in the country. **Lord & Taylor** and **Marshall Field's** are the anchors, and shops and restaurants fill seven stories. Movie theaters on two levels, each with several screens, provide another entertainment alternative should you run out of steam riding the escalators or glass-enclosed elevators between retail stops. Shops include **Banana Republic, FAO Schwarz, Laura Ashley,** and **Crabtree & Evelyn.** ♦ Most stores open daily. 835 N Michigan Ave (between E Chestnut and E Pearson Sts) &

Within Water Tower Place:

Rizzoli Bookstore Wood-framed windows filled with richly colored books lure you in. Classical music soothes as you browse through the extensive selection of architecture and art books. A wide selection of journals and periodicals includes European and Japanese art and fashion magazines. ♦ Daily; F-Sa until 9PM. Third level. 642.3500 &

Accent Chicago Get your Chicago souvenirs here: T-shirts, tote bags, **Cubs** baseball hats, the recipe and the pan for deep-dish pizza, and zillions of postcards. ♦ Daily 9AM-10PM. Seventh level. 944.1354. Also at: Sears Tower, 233 S Wacker Dr (between W Adams St and W Jackson Blvd). 993.0499 &

When the play, *The Wizard of Oz,* ran in Chicago in 1900 it took in $160,000 in 14 weeks and played to an audience of 180,000. The author, L. Frank Baum, lived in Chicago for almost twenty years.

Weather Facts:
Average wind speed in the Windy City: 10.2 miles per hour

Number of days a year the temperature is 32 degrees F or below: 121

Number of days a year the temperature is above 90 degrees F: 21

Percentage of clear days during a typical year: 23 percent

29 Bistro 110 ★★$$ Garlic lovers will find paradise in this bustling spot the instant they sample a buttery roasted bulb spread on good French bread. Wood-oven–roasted meats, fish, and fowl are pungent with garlic and herbs. The decor is bright, with polished light wood floors and murals by Judith Rifka. ◆ French ◆ Daily lunch and dinner, F-Sa until midnight. Reservations recommended. 110 E Pearson St (between N Michigan Ave and N Rush St). 266.3110 ♿

30 Park Hyatt Hotel $$$ Opulent, contemporary elegance characterizes this expensive hotel. Afternoon teas in the two-story travertine lobby allow you to fully appreciate an ambience dramatic with floor-to-ceiling windows, velvet couches, chandeliers cascading with crystals, and the tinkling of ivories on a grand piano. The 355 guest rooms are done in tones of deep green or peach and feature marble-topped rosewood furnishings. Among the treats are at least two telephones (one in the bathroom, which is also equipped with a TV), a morning newspaper, terry-cloth robes, and concierge service. ◆ 800 N Michigan Ave (at E Chicago Ave). 280.2222, 800/233.1234; fax 280.1963 ♿

Within the Park Hyatt Hotel:

Jaxx $$$ Originally located in the **Omni Chicago,** this eatery was transplanted here in 1994 when that hotel was sold by the Hyatt chain. Specials include penne with grilled chicken and sun-dried tomatoes. Unfortunately, in this location, the food hasn't drawn as much praise as the sleek and polished decor that harks back to a 1930s supper club. Dinner entrées include smoked chicken linguine, grilled lobster salad, and Dover sole *meunière* (lemon butter sauce). ◆ American ◆ Daily lunch and dinner. 280.2230 ♿

31 Water Tower
In 1869 **W.W. Boyington,** one of Chicago's first architects, designed the **Water Tower** (pictured at right) in a naive imitation of the Gothic style. This is one of the few buildings to survive the Great Fire of 1871. In 1882 Oscar Wilde visited Chicago and described this structure as a "castellated monstrosity with pepper boxes stuck all over it." It enjoys greater popularity today; its stone steps and the

Courtesy of the Department of Public Works, City of Chicago

surrounding grassy square are favorite places for an alfresco, people watching lunch. The **Chicago Visitors' Center** is located on the first floor. ◆ 800 N Michigan Ave (between E Pearson St and E Chicago Ave). 744.2400 ♿

32 Chicago Horse and Carriage Company
Top-hatted drivers with horse-drawn carriages are lined up and ready to take you for a romantic tour of the northern end of the Magnificent Mile, or elsewhere by request ◆ Southeast corner of E Pearson St and N Michigan Ave. 944.6773

33 Here's Chicago The **Old Water Tower**'s **Pumping Station** now houses a good tourist's introduction to the city: a wide-screen movie that takes you up the Chicago River as the bridges open, then flies you around the skyline. An animated Old Abe Lincoln offers comments about Chicago (he replaces an Al Capone doing the same thing—the latter may have amused tourists, but he aggravated city officials). A shop with all sorts of Chicago items, many gangster-related, should sate your taste for Al and his boys. ◆ Admission. Daily. 163 E Pearson St (off N Michigan Ave). 467.7114 ♿

34 Seneca Park/Eli M. Schulman Playground Local apartment dwellers and visitors alike do well to bring their kids to this compact public playground—the only one in this part of town—to let them burn off pent-up energy on the swings and slides. Funds for the facilities were raised by the Schulman family (of the popular **Eli's** across the street), who personally donated a good part of them. Note sculptor Deborah Butterfield's *Horse* on the park's eastern side; rising behind it is the new home of the **Museum of Contemporary Art.** ◆ E Chicago Ave (between N Mies van der Rohe Way and N Michigan Ave)

35 Museum of Contemporary Art Founded in 1967 to expand the Chicago art world beyond the bounds imposed by the conservative **Art Institute,** the **MCA** is dedicated to the avant-garde. The $46-million building, opened in the summer of 1996, covers 220,000 square feet, almost seven times the space of its former incarnation. The building and sculpture garden were designed by Berlin architect **Josef Paul Kleihues.** It includes a museum shop, a 15,000-square-foot studio-classroom facility, a 15,000-volume art library, and a 300-seat theater for film screenings and lectures. Although the museum is completely wheelchair accessible, many visitors will climb the 32-step grand staircase which **Kleihues** likens to the propyleia of the Acropolis. ◆ Admission; free Tuesdays. Tu, Th-Su 11AM-6PM; every Wednesday and the first Friday of each month until 9PM. 220 E Chicago Ave (between N DeWitt Pl and N Mies van der Rohe Way). 280.2660 ♿

36 Eli's ★$$$ Founded by the late Eli Schulman (whose likeness in faux stained glass dominates the dining room) and now run by his wife, Esther, this place enjoys a loyal clientele of steak lovers. The belt-busting prix-fixe dinner includes appetizers of sautéed calf's liver and broiled sole, followed by salad, steak and potatoes, and Chicago's best cheesecake. The last item is the founder's own famous creation—a rich, velvety concoction that comes in more than a dozen flavors and is distributed nationwide from the family's bakery at another location. Chicago booster Marc Schulman (Eli's son) even got Bill Clinton to sample it when he was campaigning here. You may skip a full meal and simply enjoy a slice in the piano lounge. ♦ American ♦ M-F lunch and dinner; Sa-Su dinner. Reservations and jacket required in the dining room. 215 E Chicago Ave (between N Mies van der Rohe Way and N Michigan Ave). 642.1393 ♿

37 Northwestern University School of Law/American Bar Association At the eastern edge of the campus, along Lake Shore Drive, is the university's law school and the high-rise headquarters of the ABA. Completed in 1984, **Holabird & Root**'s complex is an exceptionally subtle and well-detailed modern addition to the neighboring Collegiate Gothic buildings of **James Gamble Rogers,** built from 1926 to 1927. Note the four-story atrium that joins old and new buildings on Chicago Avenue, and the granite buttresses that echo the earlier limestone forms. ♦ Northwestern University School of Law: 357 E Chicago Ave (at N Lake Shore Dr). ABA: 750 N Lake Shore Dr (at E Superior St)

38 680 North Lake Shore Place In 1926 **Nimmons & Dunning** added a blue and brown Gothic Revival tower to their brick and terra-cotta building, which had been erected two years earlier as the American Furniture Mart. Renovated in 1984 by **Lohan Associates,** it now houses condominiums, a retail arcade, and offices, including those of the Playboy empire. Before Playboy moved in, the building's address had been 666 North Lake Shore Drive. It was changed because the original numerals led some to call it the "Sign-of-Satan Building." ♦ Between E Erie and E Huron Sts

Within 680 North Lake Shore Place:

Gold Star Sardine Bar★★$ It was once a well-kept secret, but now the word is out, so on weekends expect a long wait; after all, this tiny bar barely seats 50 people, even fewer on the evenings when the likes of the **Count Basie Orchestra** or Pia Zadora with full orchestral backup take the floor. Well, that's part of the charm, and it's usually worth standing in line. A no-smoking, no-talking policy is sometimes enforced during performances. The kitchen serves up meat loaf and burgers at lunchtime. ♦ American ♦ Cover charge Friday and Saturday nights. M-Sa lunch. Shows begin at 8PM. No reservations accepted. 664.4215 ♿

Treasure Island This gourmet grocery store has a fantastic take-out deli catering to every possible taste, from roasted chicken to bulging hand-carved sandwiches to a bounteous salad bar. It makes for a perfect summertime picnic at the lakefront right across the street. ♦ Daily. 664.0400 ♿

Tulip's Cafe $$ Although it doesn't compare with Chicago's top Italian restaurants, this trattoria is an agreeable place for a leisurely, reasonably priced lunch. ♦ Italian ♦ M-Sa lunch and dinner. 787.2782 ♿

39 Summerfield Suites $$ This totally remodeled hotel has a traditional style with loads of amenities: Each of the 121 suites is equipped with a microwave, coffee maker, VCR, and ironing board; a common laundry room is available as well. There's no restaurant, but a 24-hour shop on the premises sells snacks, frozen food, and ice cream for those with an attack of midnight munchies. Guests can enjoy the outdoor pool in the summer months and a gleaming new fitness center all year round. The reasonable rates include a full breakfast buffet. ♦ 166 E Superior St (at N St. Clair St). 787.6000, 800/833.4353; fax 787.6133 ♿

40 Gino's East Pizzeria ★$$ Some of the best deep-dish pizza in the city is served in seedy surroundings of vinyl-covered tables and rough wooden walls dense with graffiti. Beaming down from above the bar are black-and-white photos of celebrity diners including Bruce Springsteen and Ronald Reagan. As many as 10,000 pies, crunchy-crusted and oozing with tasty, cheesy fillings, are dished out every week, including individual-size pizzas at lunchtime. To avoid the crowds, pick up a take-out order or frozen pizza at their store next door. ♦ Pizza ♦ Daily lunch and dinner; F-Sa until midnight. 160 E Superior St (off N Michigan Ave). 943.1124

41 Neiman Marcus Just the place to pick up that perfect little $1,000 christening gown—it simply wouldn't be **Neiman Marcus** at a lesser price. Designer salons on the second floor include Chanel and Ungaro. The fourth floor boasts the outstanding Epicure Department, a gourmet shop that carries caviars, exotic cheeses, chocolates from around the world, and freshly prepared items from local restaurants. The store also has a full-service salon to pamper customers with hair care, makeup, and massages. The four-story building is actually part of the **Olympia Center** (built in 1984 by **Skidmore, Owings &**

Merrill), a 63-story, pink granite office and condominium tower that fronts Chicago Avenue. Note the glass "keystone" in the Michigan Avenue arch. ♦ Daily. 737 N Michigan Ave (between E Superior St and E Chicago Ave). 642.5900 ♿

42 Banana Republic Of this contribution to Chicago architecture by New York's famed **Robert A.M. Stern**, one local critic commented, "Well, at least it's not any larger." Distinctly out of place in its surroundings, this branch of the national clothing chain looks like the Nairobi Airport hangar transported to North Michigan Avenue. Inside, hide stretches over the hanging lamps, leather and slate cover the floor, and a glass staircase somehow manages to look like a rope bridge. Architecture purists may scoff at this tribute to a land of pith helmets that never was, but shoppers who like the chain's merchandise are likely to enjoy this store. ♦ Daily. 744 N Michigan Ave (between E Superior St and E Chicago Ave). 642.0020 ♿

43 Brooks Brothers
Traditional styles for men, women, and boys fill the two floors of this classic haberdashery. ♦ Daily. 713 N Michigan Ave (between E Huron and E Superior Sts). 915.0060 ♿

43 Tiffany & Co. Whether dressing for a game of tennis or an inaugural ball, those with dollars to spend come here for their dazzling jewels. The boutique carries special collections by Paloma Picasso and Elsa Peretti. ♦ M-Sa. 715 N Michigan Ave (between E Huron and E Superior Sts). 944.7500 ♿

43 Elizabeth Arden Splurge on a Maine Chance Day (which includes a one-hour body massage; facial; manicure and pedicure; lunch; a haircut, shampoo, and styling; and makeup application) or just take A Red Door Beauty Break (which includes a half-hour neck, shoulder, back massage; manicure; and makeup application). ♦ M-Sa. 717 N Michigan Ave (between E Huron and E Superior Sts). 988.9191 ♿

"Hog butcher for the world,
Tool maker, stacker of wheat,
Player with the railroads and
  the nation's freight handler,
Stormy, husky, brawling,
City of the big shoulders."

Chicago, Carl Sandburg

Restaurants/Clubs: Red   **Hotels:** Blue
Shops/ ⚲ Outdoors: Green   **Sights/Culture:** Black

44 Chicago Place Built in 1990, this 43-story multiuse complex consists of an eight-floor retail mall designed by **Skidmore, Owings & Merrill** and a 272-room apartment tower designed by **Solomon Cordwell Buenz & Associates.** The three-part clear, stained-glass, and colored windows on the exterior of the eight-story base are classic Chicago School references, and the curving corners evoke **Louis Sullivan**'s **Carson Pirie Scott & Company** building. The first two stories are clad in various shades of pink and green granite, while the upper levels of the base and tower are painted concrete. Inside, the mall is decorated with Prairie School colors and motifs, with space for 80 specialty shops and restaurants. Note Mrs. O'Leary's cow and other local icons in the lobby mural. Anchors are the seven-story Midwest flagship store of **Saks Fifth Avenue, Ann Taylor,** and **Bockwinkel's Grocery,** Michigan Avenue's only full-service grocery store. The top floor of the mall has a palm garden/food court with a flowing stream; covered by a barrel-vaulted glass roof, it evokes European winter gardens of the late 19th century. Other stores include **Talbots** (women's clothing), **The Real Nancy Drew** (painted furniture, silk-screened T-shirts, and original artwork), and **Chiasso** (knickknacks). ♦ Daily. Free parking (with a validated ticket) is available in a small lot at the lower level. 700 N Michigan Ave (bounded by E Huron, E Superior, and N Rush Sts).

Within Chicago Place:

Body Shop Based in Brighton, England, this boutique for lotions and potions now has branches in a number of US cities. Whether you prefer Grapefruit Shampoo or Peppermint Foot Lotion, you'll be happy to know that all the products are animal- and environment-friendly. ♦ First level. 482.8301 ♿

Chiaroscuro An art gallery that's also a gift shop, this is a browser's heaven full of wall art, statuary, whimsical folk sculpture, hand-painted furniture, handwoven apparel, an outstanding selection of jewelry, and handmade art cards. ♦ Fourth level. 988.9253 ♿

Sassparella Ltd. This charming store features a complete selection of bed, bath, and table linens, including the largest assortment of shower curtains and bath accessories in the city. Among the many European imports are Le Jacquard Français table linens to set off your Limoges, and Palais Royale sheets to let you sleep like a king. ♦ Seventh level. 642.7340 ♿

45 Allerton Hotel $ What was once an elegant Art Deco hotel is now faded and past its prime. Formerly plush furnishings in the 450 rooms are a bit worn, too, but the rooms are comfortable and the prices very reasonable for the location. Weekend rates are available.

♦ 701 N Michigan Ave (at E Huron St).
440.1500, 800/621.8311; fax 440.1819 &

Within the Allerton Hotel:

The Avenue $$ Once home to one
of Chicago's first fine French restaurants
(**L'Escargot**), this place has been turned into
a bower of flowers, all pale green and pink.
The menu runs to lots of fresh fish and pasta
at reasonable prices. An outdoor cafe serving
salad niçoise and similar dishes is a welcome
addition to the avenue. ♦ Cafe ♦ Daily
breakfast, lunch, and early dinner. 944.8200 &

46 Radisson Hotel & Suites $$$ Formerly
the **Sheraton Plaza,** this new $9-million
renovation has 341 rooms with 90 suites
appointed with comfortable contemporary
furnishings. Definitely geared to the business
traveler, the hotel has computer ports in
every room; there's also a health club and an
outdoor pool. ♦ 160 E Huron St (at N St. Clair
St). 787.2900, 800/333.3333; fax 787.5158 &

Within the Radisson Hotel:

Cassis ★★$$$ Informal chic and hearty
portions are de rigueur at this Southern
French bistro. Standard bistro fare—*steak
frites*, bouillabaisse, and grilled seafood over
couscous—head the list; those with lighter
appetites may choose a gourmet pizza or
an unusual salad, perhaps roasted beets
and goat cheese with a bacon vinaigrette.
Not surprisingly, there's an extensive wine
list. ♦ French ♦ Daily breakfast, lunch, and
dinner. 255.1600 &

47 Avanzare ★★$$$ This glossy, chic, noisy
spot is Lettuce Entertain You Enterprises'
toniest Italian restaurant. Though the quality
varies, the restaurant is deservedly popular
for inventive pastas, seafood, and seasonal
game specials. Meals start with good crusty
bread and herbed virgin olive oil. For a savory
appetizer, try the marinated seafood. Tortellini
stuffed with smoked chicken is a winning
entrée, and you can choose from rich ricotta
cheesecake, tiramisù, and homemade gelati
to finish. This is a top spot for power brokers

and other VIPs, especially at lunch.
The sidewalk cafe is fun in good weather.
♦ Northern Italian ♦ M-F lunch and dinner;
Sa-Su dinner. Reservations required. 161
E Huron St (at N St. Clair St). 337.8056 &

48 City Place
Boisterously decorated
with red granite and
blue reflective and tinted
glass and accented
with medallions and
chevrons, this 40-story
mixed-use complex
(pictured at right)
was built by **Loebl
Schlossman & Hackl** in
1990. The **Omni Chicago
Hotel** occupies floors 5
through 25, and there are
13 floors of offices above
that. ♦ 678 N Michigan
Ave (at E Huron St)

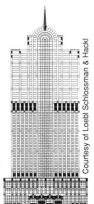

Courtesy of Loebl Schlossman & Hackl

Within City Place:

Omni Chicago Hotel $$$ All of the
347 suites here are luxuriously furnished
in fine upholsteries and polished woods and
equipped with a wet bar and two telephones;
all offer incredible views. Guests are
pampered with nightly turndown service,
complimentary newspaper, overnight laundry,
and 24-hour room service. A fully equipped
health club with an indoor pool sits beneath
a skylight on the top floor. For $1,000 a night,
guests can select from a few suites designed
in the signature styles of **Frank Lloyd Wright,
Charles Rennie Mackintosh,** and **Mies
van der Rohe,** among other darlings of
Modernism. Business services and two deluxe
boardrooms are available. Two lounges are
also on the premises. Weekend packages
are available. ♦ 944.6664, 800/843.6664;
fax 266.3015 &

Within the Omni Chicago:

Cielo ★$$$
The sky seems
to be the limit
here, with
floor-to-ceiling
windows
overlooking
Michigan
Avenue and a
trompe l'oeil
mural of the sky
on the domed
ceiling (hence
the name). A
wood-burning

oven and grill add an Italian accent to the
menu, but the focus is on foods from the
Adriatic, Mediterranean, and Atlantic coasts.
Dinner entrées include roast duckling basted
with lavender honey and rabbit with muscat

wine and figs. Pianist Michael Laird sings popular songs and show tunes. ♦ Mediterranean ♦ Daily breakfast, lunch, and dinner. Music Tuesday through Saturday nights. 944.7676 ♿

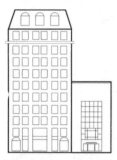

49 Terra Museum of American Art
The museum's permanent collection of 19th- and 20th-century American paintings, particularly strong in the Impressionists, was and still is being amassed by businessman Daniel J. Terra, formerly President Reagan's ambassador-at-large for cultural affairs. Originally located in Evanston, the museum (pictured above) moved to this prime location, designed by **Booth/Hansen & Associates,** in 1987. Changing exhibitions of American art, usually organized by other museums, are shown in the galleries, along with part of the permanent collection. ♦ Admission. Tu noon–8PM; W-Su noon-5PM. 666 N Michigan Ave (between E Erie and E Huron Sts). 664.3939 ♿

50 Cole-Haan Fine footwear and leather fashion accessories, many of hand-sewn construction, plus Italian-made handbags, briefcases, and luggage are sold here. ♦ Daily. 673 N Michigan Ave (between E Erie and E Huron Sts). 642.8995 ♿

N I K E T O W N

50 Niketown This glossy, high-tech, three-level store features every kind of athletic gear imaginable for adults and children. Packed with sports memorabilia, innovative displays (the wall behind the swimming equipment is alive with tropical fish), and a basketball court for trying out your new high-tops, it's worth a visit just to take a look. ♦ Daily. 669 N Michigan Ave (between E Erie and E Huron Sts). 642.6363 ♿

50 Sony Gallery of Consumer Electronics Experience three floors packed with the latest in electronic marvels for business and entertainment. Unlike at discount stores, where you're more likely to buy these things, the knowledgeable staff here has time to demonstrate. ♦ M-F until 8PM. 663 N Michigan Ave (between E Erie and E Huron Sts). 943.3334 ♿

51 Burberrys Expect quality and high prices at this two-floor emporium of fine British clothing for men and women. The specialty is outerwear and raincoats. ♦ Daily. 633 N Michigan Ave (between E Ontario and E Erie Sts). 787.2500 ♿

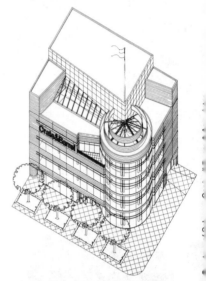

52 Crate & Barrel Designed in 1990 as an elegant "machine for selling" by **Solomon Cordwell Buenz & Associates,** this five-story glass-and-white-aluminum building (pictured above) is the flagship store of the housewares and home furnishings chain. Chicagoan Gordon Segal started the business in 1962 in a small store in the Old Town neighborhood, using overturned crates and barrels as merchandise displays. (That location later became an outlet store and has been replaced by an even bigger outlet on West North Avenue where bargain hunters can find last season's merchandise at rock-bottom prices.) This store, which has the sleek look of an ocean liner, stands out among the traditional masonry buildings of Michigan Avenue. A glassy corner rotunda is full of escalators that carry you past tempting displays of everything from culinary equipment to contemporary furniture. ♦ Daily. 646 N Michigan Ave (at E Erie St). 787.5900 ♿ Also at: 101 N Wabash Ave (and E Washington St). 372.0100 ♿; Outlet at: 800 W North Ave (at N Halsted St). 787.4775 ♿

52 Waterford/Wedgwood A beautiful selection of Irish crystal and British china is presided over by the very nicest group of salespeople. You will be much better attended to here than in one of the large department stores. ♦ M-Sa. 636 N Michigan Ave (between E Ontario and E Erie Sts). 944.1994 ♿

53 Cartier Now that native jeweler **C.D. Peacock** (founded the same year as the city) has closed, this is Chicago's preeminent jewelry store, carrying impeccably crafted gold rings, necklaces, and bracelets, extraordinary gemstones, and handsome wristwatches, as well as china and stationery. ♦ M-Sa. 630 N Michigan Ave (at E Ontario St). 266.7440 ♿

54 Richard Gray Gallery Modern and contemporary paintings, drawings, sculpture, and prints from the masters of the 20th century as well as current avant-garde artists are sold here. Works by Picasso, Matisse, Moore, and Susan Rothenberg, among others, are displayed. ♦ Tu-Sa. 620 N Michigan Ave (between E Ohio and E Ontario Sts). 642.8877 ♿

55 Hunan Cafe ★★$$ Opened by a popular Chinese restaurateur, this spot features dim sum and noodle dishes served alongside specials ranging from moo-shu pork to sautéed swordfish. Expect good regional cuisine. ♦ Chinese ♦ Daily lunch and dinner. 625 N Michigan Ave (at E Ontario St). 482.9898

56 Howard's Bar & Grill If Chicago's (self-declared) best burger is more your style, try this cozy tavern, which has been around since the days when this was still a neighborhood. A back terrace is open in summer. ♦ American ♦ Daily lunch and dinner. 150 E Ontario St (between N St. Clair St and N Michigan Ave). 787.5269

Child's Play

After taking the children on the requisite trip to the top of the **Sears Tower** and a ride on the Ferris wheel at **Navy Pier,** what's a parent to do? Not to worry—Chicago offers plenty of activities to please the most curious and fidgety kids, and here are 10 of the best:

Museum of Holography. This small museum is filled with astonishing holographic images of such varied personalities as Tyrannosaurus rex, Dracula, and Michael Jordan. For the really curious kid, there are tours that explain the physics of light and the laser process.

Old Town School of Folk Music. Offering music classes for six-month-old children and concerts for kids between the ages of two and 10, this school is a music-loving parent's dream come true. On Sundays in autumn the school hosts the *Music Maze,* where children can build cardboard instruments and participate in sing-alongs and rhythm and drawing classes. There's always something swinging here.

Museum of Broadcast Communications. The public archives here contain 6,000 TV programs, 10,000 commercials, and 49,000 hours of radio programs—pick your kid's favorite and plug in. For a unique souvenir of your visit head over to the *Kraft Television Center:* Up to four family members can don gold blazers and read from news teleprompters while museum staffers videotape a 3-minute segment that you can take home for a cost of $20.

Chicago Children's Museum. Now in a 57,000-square-foot space in **Navy Pier,** the museum offers something for every personality; there's a three-story *Climbing Schooner,* the *Inventing Laboratory, Waterways* exhibit where children can experiment with the wet stuff without getting in trouble, and even a replica of a landfill, among other attractions.

John G. Shedd Aquarium. Children and their adult companions love the *Coral Reef* exhibit, a 90,000-gallon re-creation of a Caribbean coral reef complete with divers who talk to visitors through a microphone while they feed sharks, sea turtles, eels, and hundreds of tropical fish.

Museum of Science and Industry. *Curiosity Place* is an interactive exhibit where kids (it's most suited for those under six) and their parents can move freely between areas filled with water, sound, blocks, sand, machines, and light to experiment with action and reaction in a fun and educational way.

Farm-in-the-Zoo. Cows, horses, sheep, pigs, and other creatures some city dwellers have never before seen in the flesh reside in a five-acre replica of a Midwestern farm. Goat milking, butter churning, and meet-the-animals pet-fests are scheduled throughout the day.

Lincoln Park Zoo. More than 2,000 swans, a **Great Ape House,** and the **Rookery,** a serene habitat filled with winged creatures cavorting amid ponds and waterfalls, are just some of the delights at this zoo within the city.

Planet Hollywood. Filled with enough Hollywood memorabilia to interest anyone, knowing that this place is owned by Bruce Willis, Arnold Schwarzenegger, and Sylvester Stallone should be sufficient to fascinate your kids. There are also hamburgers, pizzas, and a store vending movie-themed merchandise.

Rock 'n' Roll McDonald's. This neon-flickering "Micky D's" is packed with 1950s memorabilia, from a flaming-red 1963 Corvette to Archie and Veronica dolls and arcade games. While your kids devour their Big Macs, you'll enjoy listening to the sounds of Buddy Holly, Connie Francis, and Elvis.

56 Bice ★★$$$ Trendsetters and beautiful people pack this trattoria, a branch of a growing international chain, where the decor (sort of a Postmodern Deco) is as sleek as the patrons. The menu is extensive, with a good selection of pasta, risotto, veal, and chicken prepared in a variety of ways, sometimes with exotic or unexpected ingredients. However, the quality of the food is uneven, and, though legions of waiters mill around, often none appears to be assigned to your table—unless, of course, you are known to them. Ah well, sit back and enjoy the show. The best people watching is in the bar and, in good weather, the sidewalk cafe. ♦ Italian ♦ M-Sa lunch and dinner; Su dinner. Reservations recommended. 158 E Ontario St (between N St. Clair St and N Michigan Ave). 664.1474

57 Motel 6 Chicago $ An unbeatable price and a prime location make this 191-room link in the motel chain one of the best deals in town. Standard, clean, and comfortable, the rooms are equipped with voice mail, cable TV (including HBO), and a service of free local phone calls. The **Il Toscanaccio** restaurant is one of the best outdoor cafes in the neighborhood for people watching and serves a terrific grilled portobello mushroom sandwich. ♦ 162 E Ontario St (at N St. Clair St). 787.3580, 800/466.8356; fax 787.1299 ㅂ

58 Joy Horwich Gallery Once this street was the center of Chicago's gallery district, but most galleries have moved several blocks west. This holdout has contemporary drawings, paintings, and sculpture, many by Chicago artists. ♦ Tu-Sa. 226 E Ontario St (between N Fairbanks Ct and N St. Clair St). 787.0171

58 Ron of Japan $$$ This branch of an Osaka-based chain of steak houses has a flair for the dramatic. Seating is at huge seashell-shaped red-vinyl booths, and many meals are prepared tableside at *teppanyaki* tables. Waitresses scurry about in kimonos, and the prime rib is presented on a samurai sword. Some seafood is available. ♦ Steak house ♦ Daily dinner. 230 E Ontario St (between N Fairbanks Ct and N St. Clair St). 644.6500

59 Schatz Building This place has a history: Once home to Chicago's famed **Chez Paree** nightclub and, briefly, the school that began as the **American Bauhaus** and became the **Institute of Design**, it's now owned by a sculptor named Lincoln Schatz; a few other artists have studios here too. Inside is a lively little restaurant, **Cucina Italiana,** offering quick and inexpensive meals, and a jazz and blues place called **Milt Trenier's.** Along the North Fairbanks Court side of the building is a massive mural inspired by Michelangelo's *Moses.* ♦ 247 E Ontario St (at N Fairbanks Ct)

Within the Schatz Building:

West Egg Cafe $ Order breakfast all day at this noisy, friendly spot. Also available at table or counter are salads, sandwiches, and pasta. ♦ American ♦ M-Sa breakfast, lunch, and dinner; Su breakfast and lunch. 620 N Fairbanks Ct (at E Ontario St). 280.8366

60 Days Inn Lake Shore Drive $ Enjoy lakefront views at budget rates. The trade-off for the price is luxury—you'll find none here. The 580 rooms are standard, although well-kept. Traffic noise might get to you, since the hotel sits right on busy Lake Shore Drive. However, the outdoor pool is nice in summer and guests have privileges at a nearby health club. The revolving **Pinnacle Restaurant** on top of the hotel is only open for private affair. ♦ 644 N Lake Shore Dr (at E Ontario St). 943.9200, 800/325.2525; fax 649.5580 ㅂ

61 Gypsy ★$$ The theme is American eclectic with numerous fresh fish and aged steak specials, but the trimmings are a hodgepodge of international tastes and sounds. A flamenco guitarist plays on Wednesday and Thursday nights, a selection of tapas are served during Happy Hour, and the kitchen regularly offers tastings of various dishes made with ostrich and kangaroo meat. A good wine list makes this a fine stop for any hungry gypsy. ♦ International ♦ Daily lunch and dinner. 215 E Ohio St (at N St. Clair St). 644.9779 ㅂ

62 Sayat Nova ★$$ The walls of this romantic room are adorned with Oriental tapestries and curve into semiprivate alcoves. A compact menu features mostly familiar Middle Eastern cuisine, from hummus to shish kebab. ♦ Middle Eastern ♦ Daily lunch and dinner. 157 E Ohio St (between N St. Clair St and N Michigan Ave). 644.9159

63 Timberland This shop is part of a chain specializing in rugged outdoor clothing, boots and shoes, and accessories. ♦ Daily. 545 N Michigan Ave (at E Ohio St). 494.0171 ㅂ

63 Forgotten Woman High-style business and dress clothes for the larger woman (sizes 14 to 24) are supplemented by a line of stockings, shoes, and boots. ♦ Daily. 535 N Michigan Ave (between E Grand Ave and E Ohio St). 329.0885 ㅂ

The baggage for O'Hare International Airport is marked ORD because the original name for the field was Orchard.

63 House of Hunan ★$$$ Regional specialties reign supreme at this cavernous and rather formal restaurant. Start with a cold appetizer, such as vegetarian duck or drunken chicken, which are much better than the greasy hot appetizers. As a main course, whole pike steamed with ginger and ham and topped with mushrooms and scallions is both tasty and handsomely presented. If you long for something spicy-hot, opt for the Szechuan-style pike braised in chili sauce, or the Szechuan eggplant with mushrooms and peppers. ♦ Chinese ♦ Daily lunch and dinner. 535 N Michigan Ave (between E Grand Ave and E Ohio St). 329.9494 ♿

64 Circle Gallery This highly commercial gallery premiered the paintings and lithographs of disco queen Donna Summer. The gallery's "Art To Wear" collection of limited-edition art jewelry includes wristwatches with faces by LeRoy Neiman. ♦ Daily. 540 N Michigan Ave (at E Ohio St). 670.4304 ♿

64 Chicago Marriott $$ Huge yet comfortable, this bustling hotel is one of the city's most popular convention venues. Long registration lines snake through the marble-floored lobby, which is just a step away from an extravagant atrium bar and lounge. Both lobby and lounge are encircled by retail shops. The more than 1,100 rooms are fairly standard, with modern furnishings and anonymous artwork on the walls. The top-level (and more expensive) Marquis floor boasts more spacious quarters, a private lounge, and a concierge—all at a premium price. A health club, an indoor swimming pool, and outdoor tennis courts are available to all guests. Restaurants within the hotel are **J.W.'s Steakhouse** and **Allie's Bakery.** ♦ 540 N Michigan Ave (at E Ohio St). 836.0100, 800/228.0265; fax 836.6139 ♿

65 Hotel Inter-Continental Chicago $$$ Designed By **Walter W. Ahlschlager,** the hotel opened in 1929 as the **Medinah Athletic Club,** an opulent leisure site for members of the Shriners and their families. When the Depression hit, the place went bankrupt. In ensuing years, the property operated as a succession of hotels, collecting more layers of paint and plaster with each new identity. Multimillion-dollar renovations undertaken by **Harry Weese & Associates** in the late 1980s uncovered long-forgotten terra-cotta frescoes, murals, marble walls and floors, and bronze and brass trim, all of which have been painstakingly restored under the direction of Lido Lippi, who was involved in preliminary research for the restoration of Rome's Sistine Chapel. The 41-story Indiana limestone facade was cleaned and the original gold leaf and gold-plate highlighting renewed. The building is crowned with a mosquelike dome that was gilded and illuminated to shimmer at night.

Ask to tour the hotel's meeting-room and ballroom areas, which are a mélange of fantastic styles from many cultures, including Egyptian, Roman, Greek, Spanish, and Asian—from the Assyrian hall of lions to the massive French Renaissance ballroom.

The 341 guest rooms have tasteful Biedermeier-style European furnishings, mini-bars, and telephones in the bathrooms as well as bedrooms. Electronic hookups to the front desk allow you to review your bills, and receive and relay messages via your TV screen. The discriminating business traveler may opt for quarters in the more expensive Executive Club, which includes personal butler service and access to the private Executive Lounge. All hotel guests may use the health club, which boasts a mosaic-tiled indoor swimming pool that was once the training site for Olympic gold medalist and future Tarzan Johnny Weissmuller. The hotel's first-floor bar and salon serve cocktails; the latter also serves afternoon tea. During summer, a sidewalk cafe off the salon serves lunch and light supper. The luxurious **Boulevard Restaurant** (see below) overlooks the lobby.

The former **Forum Hotel** next door has been incorporated into the **Inter-Continental** as the **North Towers,** adding 517 more rooms that have been renovated in comfortable, contemporary fashion. ♦ 505 N Michigan Ave (at E Illinois St). 944.4100, 800/327.0200; fax 944.3050 ♿

Within the Hotel Inter-Continental Chicago:

Boulevard Restaurant ★$$$ The horseshoe-shaped second-floor dining room looks over the hotel's lobby and sports a hand-stenciled ceiling. If the lighting were brighter, one might imagine Fred Astaire and Ginger Rogers dancing down the staircase. China created by Tiffany & Co., floral carpeting, and striped upholstery make for a rich environment. However, there is room for improvement in the food—basically haute American cuisine with European touches. Best are the simple offerings such as panfried trout fillets lightly cooked and complemented with fresh herbs and walnut butter. A daily prix-fixe lunch includes three courses plus dessert. ♦ Continental ♦ Daily breakfast, lunch, and dinner. Reservations recommended. 944.4100 ♿

Chicago-based Sears, Roebuck and Co. introduced the benefit of profit sharing to its employees in 1916.

Native Chicagoan Quincy Jones has won more awards than any other musician. His work includes producing Michael Jackson's "Thriller" album, writing the movie score for *The Color Purple,* and producing the 1996 Academy Awards show.

66 Rand McNally Map and Travel Store
You'll find maps of every state, more than 30 types of globes, travel guides, and all manner of travel-related items that will get you there and back in one satisfied piece. This store is a smaller version of the one at 150 South Wacker Drive (at West Adams Street). ♦ Daily. 444 N Michigan Ave (at E Illinois St). 321.1751 ♿

Tribune Tower

67 Billy Goat Tavern $ This journalists' hangout was the inspiration for the late John Belushi's "cheebugga, cheebugga" short-order routines on "Saturday Night Live." Otherwise, it's an underground greasy spoon serving merely adequate hamburgers It's located on Lower Michigan Avenue; access is down the stairs from North Michigan Avenue. ♦ Burgers ♦ Daily 7AM-2AM. 430 N Michigan Ave (at E Hubbard St). Lower level. 222.1525

68 Wrigley Building Graham, Anderson, Probst & White built this white terra-cotta–clad building in 1922. The clock tower has been a distinctive landmark at the gateway to North Michigan Avenue since the Michigan Avenue Bridge crossed the Chicago River. It has always been dazzlingly floodlit from the opposite bank. The chewing gum company's corporate offices are situated here (its factory is on the city's South Side). ♦ 400 N Michigan Ave (near the Chicago River)

69 Tribune Tower An international design competition held by the newspaper in 1922 yielded numerous famous designs in addition to **Hood & Howells**'s prizewinning Gothic tower, which many considered retro in an era of emerging modern style. Today it is the grand old gentleman of North Michigan Avenue, and Chicagoans wouldn't trade its buttressed tower for anything. At street level, the walls have embedded stones—each of them labeled—which were pirated from famous and ancient monuments worldwide by the newspaper's foreign correspondents. These include pieces of the Parthenon, Notre Dame, and the Pyramids. Set into the north wall of the lobby is a stone from the Cave of the Nativity in Bethlehem, where Christ is said to have been born.

Also at street level is a fully equipped **WGN Radio Studio.** (**WGN** is owned by the *Chicago Tribune,* and its call letters derive from the newspaper's old boast of being the "World's Greatest Newspaper.") Here you can watch through a glass window as traffic, sports, and business reports are given by local radio personalities with whom you can converse through a microphone when they are off the air. The newspaper is printed at the **Freedom Center;** free 45-minute tours are given during business hours Monday through Friday. ♦ Daily. Tours offered every hour, by reservation. Tribune Tower: 435 N Michigan Ave (between the Chicago River and E Illinois St); Freedom Center: 777 W Chicago Ave (at N Halsted St). Tour reservations 222.2116

70 Pioneer Court This well-kept plaza is a handsome addition to the cityscape. Tall prairie grasses and fir trees predominate in a graceful series of plantings interspersed with fountains. Walk through here to reach **NBC Tower.** ♦ Between the Chicago River and Tribune Tower

71 NBC Tower Harking back to the streamlined Deco skyscrapers of the 1920s and 1930s, this building's strong vertical lines rise to a spire emblazoned with the corporate peacock emblem. Built by **Skidmore, Owings & Merrill** in 1989, this is an elegant addition to the Chicago skyline. In the lobby, note Chicago artist Roger Brown's *City of the Big Shoulders:* barns and trucks and skyscrapers in Day-Glo browns and greens. On the North Columbus Drive side of the building, visit the **NBC Store,** which sells hats and bags and jogging clothes with insignias from shows like "Seinfeld" and "Saturday Night Live." ♦ Daily. NBC Tower: Cityfront Center, 200 E Illinois St (at N Columbus Dr). NBC Store: 454 N Columbus Dr (between E North Water and E Illinois Sts). 836.5760 &

NBC Tower

Within the NBC Tower:

Pazzo's NBC $$ With wine bottles lining the bar and walls painted to resemble Roman ruins (peeling plaster, exposed brick) and a vegetable market, this place sells ambience as well as food. The latter runs to wood-fired pizzas, generous antipasti, and California-style Italian fare, and the service is pleasant. ♦ Italian ♦ M-F lunch and dinner; Sa dinner. 455 Cityfront Plaza. 329.0775 &

72 Sheraton Hotel and Towers $$ Bordering the Chicago River, the city's largest convention and business hotel boasts the Midwest's largest ballroom (nearly 40,000 square feet) as well as 1,200 guest rooms. The **Towers** section offers upgraded accommodations and services on four private floors. Guests can use the private health club or take advantage of easy access to bike and jogging trails. The **Streeterville Grill and Bar** serves Italian-style lunch and dinner daily; the **Riverside Cafe** is convenient for breakfast or lunch; and a lobby bar, **Waves,** offers nightly entertainment and a view of the river. In the summer, the riverside **Esplanade** is a lovely place for a drink or light meal. ♦ 301 E North Water St (at Cityfront Center). 464.1000, 800/325.3535; fax 329.7045 &

72 Clock Sculpture If you've ever wanted to see a time machine, visit the plaza in front of the hotel. There, sculptor Vito Acconci's *Floor Clock* goes round in a circle twice daily; the minute hand is about 20 feet long. ♦ 301 E North Water St (at Cityfront Center)

William Wrigley Jr. became a successful soap and cleaning products salesman by giving away chewing gum as a premium. The gum was so popular that in 1893 he started manufacturing his own Wrigley's Spearmint and Juicy Fruit gum.

McClurg Court was named after a mild mannered bookseller, Alexander C. McClurg, who led one of the bloodiest charges of the Union forces in Atlanta. Although he was offered a career in the military he returned to Chicago to resume selling books.

Restaurants/Clubs: Red   **Hotels:** Blue
Shops/ Outdoors: Green   **Sights/Culture:** Black

73 North Pier Chicago This former commercial shipping pier is now one of the most popular spots in town with the younger set, especially suburbanites and out-of-towners. But even jaded sophisticates can't help but be enthralled by the waterside view of the skyline. There are more than 40 restaurants and shops to divert you, plus tour boats departing hourly from the dock. ♦ 435 E Illinois St (between N Lake Shore Dr and N McClurg Ct). 836.4300

Within North Pier Chicago:

Baja Beach Club A monument to the short attention span, this place is always jammed with packs of people, especially on weekends. While a live band and crowded dance floor are the central attractions, other rooms are ringed with every type of video game; if you get bored with that, have a game of pool or ski-ball. Expect long waits in a "staging area" (with another live band to keep you entertained) on weekends. If you're hungry, head upstairs for some Texas-style barbecue at the **Original A-1** restaurant, operated by Lettuce Entertain You Enterprises, Inc. ♦ Daily. 222.1992

Dick's Last Resort ★$$ Large groups can have a good time at this boisterous restaurant with long rows of tables, a warm-weather patio on the pier, and a good Dixieland band contributing to the atmosphere. The burgers are big and juicy, and tin buckets keep your french fries hot or your beer cold. The huge beer list includes a 25-ounce Africa Mamba, something of a house specialty. ♦ American ♦ Daily lunch and dinner; M-Th, Su to 2AM; F to 4AM; Sa to 5AM. 836.7870

Old Carolina Crab House ★$$ This casual spot has the feel of an oversize Southeast coast seafood shack, and tables by the window of the glass-enclosed patio offer a pretty view of the water. Fresh seafood is the specialty: Options include crabs in season, seafood cocktails, crab salad, Florida-style shrimp in lime butter, and grilled fish. Steer clear of the seafood linguine, which is soupy and heavy on the garlic. ♦ Seafood ♦ Daily lunch and dinner. 321.8400

Virtual World Battletech Center No two adventures are ever the same at this virtual reality playground. Computer games put you in the driver's seat of a humanoid war machine called Mech. ♦ Admission. Daily to 11PM; F-Sa to 1AM. 836.5977

CityGolf Chicago This indoor miniature golf course is complete with reproductions of Chicago landmarks, including the **John Hancock Center.** ♦ M-Th 10AM-10PM; F-Sa 10AM-midnight; Su noon-6PM. 836.5936

Bicycle Museum of America As the home of Schwinn (now defunct) and Sears, which respectively made and sold more bicycles than anyone else in the land, it's appropriate that Chicago should be home to the country's only bicycle museum. Displays and lectures on the history and preservation of bicycles give you new respect for these extraordinary two-wheeled vehicles, and special exhibits tackle a variety of topics from the bicycle's impact on women's liberation to international bike races. ♦ Admission. Daily. 222.0500

Chicago From The Lake, Ltd. A variety of boat tours depart from this spot, including a 90-minute architectural lecture in which members of the **Chicago Architecture Foundation** expound on sites along the Chicago River (10AM, noon, 2PM, and 4PM), and a historical cruise along the lake and river that traces the history and development of Chicago (11AM, 1PM, and 3PM). ♦ Admission. Daily May through November. Reservations recommended. 527.1977

74 Lake Point Tower In 1968 **Schipporeit-Heinrich** and **Graham, Anderson, Probst & White,** whose architects had been students of **Mies van der Rohe** at the **Illinois Institute of Technology,** based the design of this curving three-lobed tower on a visionary skyscraper **Mies** had proposed for Berlin almost 50 years earlier. This condominium building is located near the foot of Navy Pier and rises to a height of 645 feet, affording its residents extraordinary views. Its two-story base features a private landscaped park with a lagoon and a swimming pool. ♦ 505 N Lake Shore Dr (between E Illinois St and E Grand Ave)

75 Olive Park This public park, built to camouflage a water filtration plant on the lake shore, boasts a wonderful view of the skyline. The grass and park benches are perfect for a picnic. During the summer, this is the site of several festivals. A small public beach sits immediately to the west. Access is by an underpass at East Grand Avenue or from Navy Pier parking lots. ♦ N Lake Shore Dr (at E Grand Ave)

76 Streeter Drive This short curve of a street at the head of **Navy Pier** is named for Captain George Wellington Streeter, who, with his wife, Maria, was beached near here in the late 19th century when their excursion boat accidentally ran aground on a sandbar. When they couldn't free their boat, they decided to fill up the lake around it with dirt from nearby construction sites. Streeter was aided by other squatters, who built shanties on the new land. The Chicago police tried many times to remove the Streeters and other residents of what had grown to a 180-acre shantytown (Streeter was briefly imprisoned after someone was killed during an attempted ouster). He officially lost his battle in 1918, when a court ordered his removal and the burning of the shanties. All but one square mile of the original 180-acre area is now landfill. ♦ Between Navy Pier and Lake Shore Dr

77 Navy Pier Built in 1916 as the **Municipal Pier,** this 3,000-footlong structure was intended to serve both commercial and excursion boats, but commercial shipping moved to South Side Lake Calumet and the automobile came into general use, knocking the wind out of the sails of the excursion-boat business. That left Chicago with a magnificent promenade that extends nearly a mile out into the lake. For decades the city tried to figure out what to do with it. The US Navy occupied it during World War II (hence its name), and it was later the first Chicago campus for the **University of Illinois.** The spacious domed auditorium at the eastern end was modestly renovated by the city in 1976; the annual International Art Expo started using it at about the same time. After that, the pier drew various ethnic festivals, food fairs, and other art shows. In 1991, the city finally embarked on a multimillion-dollar renovation, which included shoring its pilings and tearing down all but the two main buildings at the western end of the pier and the auditorium.

Today, the pier is one of Chicago's major attractions with over 40,000 square feet of restaurants and retail shops. A six-story glass atrium houses the **Crystal Gardens,** a year-round, one-acre, indoor botanical park featuring lush gardens, and palm trees and evergreens surrounding fountains and public seating. The **Ferris Wheel** rises to 150 feet and is modeled after the very first Ferris wheel (built for Chicago's **1893 World Columbian Exposition**). This one can accommodate 240 passengers for each seven-and-a-half minute ride; at night, it's illuminated by thousands of lights. The **Musical Carousel** documents the history of the pier with hand-painted scenes on the rounding boards and the 38 hand-painted animals were designed to represent the different styles used throughout the history of the carousel. ♦ Daily; Ferris wheel and carousel operate seasonally. E Grand Ave (off N Lake Shore Dr)

Within Navy Pier:

Chicago Children's Museum
Known for its interactive and creative exhibits, the 57,000-square-foot facility offers exhibits like the *Inventing Lab,* where children are given the raw materials to create their own computer software programs, musical instruments, and flying machines. Other exhibits include *Waterways,* where children don raincoats to experiment with water, and the *Climbing Schooner,* which allows youngsters to climb the riggings 35 feet to the crow's nest and then slide down a ladder to the lower deck. ♦ Admission. Tu-Su. 527.1000 &

Navy Pier IMAX Theater This 440-seat theater has a five-story-high, 80-foot-wide screen with a film format 10 times than that shown in conventional theaters. The one-ton movie projector magifies the image 300 times. Recent shows included "Africa: The Serengeti." ♦ Admission. M-Sa 10AM-9PM; Su 1-7PM. 595.7437 &

In 1914 Chicago Police Chief Schuettler approved bloomer-style swimsuits for thin women but said they were "immoral, dangerous, and ridiculous on fat women." In 1916 a law was passed freeing women from the requirement to wear stockings under their bloomer bathing suits on Chicago beaches.

Charles A. Dana, a newspaper editor from New York, gave Chicago its nickname of the "Windy City." That was in reference to the bragging by city residents during the Columbian Exposition of 1883, but the nickname soon became associated with the winds blowing from Lake Michigan. In fact, Chicago ranks only 16th in windiest US cities. (Great Falls, Montana is first).

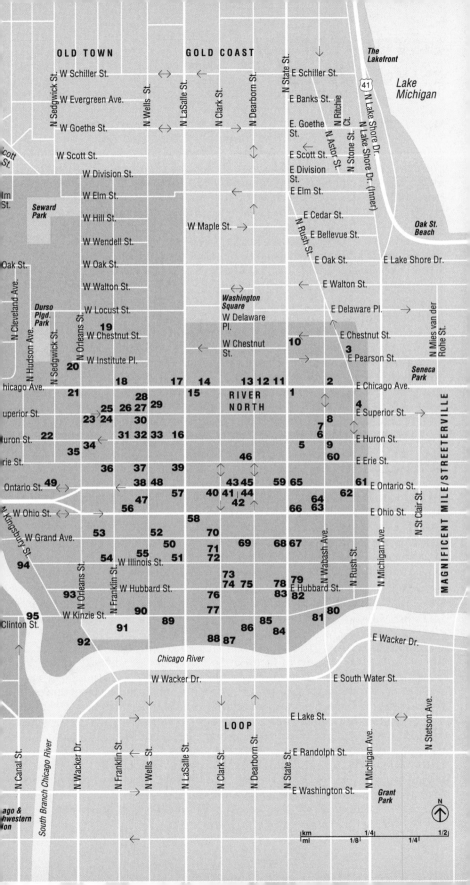

OLD TOWN

GOLD COAST

The Lakefront

Lake Michigan

W Schiller St.
E Schiller St.

W Evergreen Ave.
E Banks St.

N Sedgwick St.
N Wells St.
N LaSalle St.
N Clark St.
N Dearborn St.
N State St.

W Goethe St.
E. Goethe St.

N Ritchie Ct.
N Astor St.
N Stone St.
N Lake Shore Dr.
N Lake Shore Dr. (Inner)

W Scott St.
E Scott St.

E Division St.

W Division St.

W Elm St.
E Elm St.

Seward Park

W Hill St.
E Cedar St.

W Maple St.
E Bellevue St.

Oak St. Beach

N Rush St.

W Wendell St.
E Oak St.

E Lake Shore Dr.

Oak St.
W Oak St.

W Walton St.
E Walton St.

W Locust St.
E Delaware Pl.

Durso Plgd. Park

N Cleveland Ave.
N Hudson Ave.
N Sedgwick St.
N Orleans St.

19

W Chestnut St.
Washington Square

W Delaware Pl.
10
E Chestnut St.

N Mies van der Rohe St.

W Institute Pl.
W Chestnut St.
3
E Pearson St.

20

Seneca Park

18
17
14
13 **12** **11**
2
E Chicago Ave.

chicago Ave.
21
15
1

RIVER NORTH

uperior St.
25
26 **27**
29
28

8
E Superior St.
4

7

23 **24**
30
6

Huron St.
22
31 **32** **33**
16
5
9
E Huron St.

35
34

60

36
37
39
46
E Erie St.

MAGNIFICENT MILE/STREETERVILLE

rie St.

Ontario St.
49
38 **48**
43 **45**
59 **65**
61
E Ontario St.

47
57
40 **41** **44**
62

56
42
64

W Ohio St.
58
66
63
E Ohio St.

N St Clair St.

N Kingsbury St.

W Grand Ave.
53
52
70
69
68 **67**

50
71

54
55
51
72

W Illinois St.

N Orleans St.
N Franklin St.
N Wabash Ave.
N Rush St.
N Michigan Ave.

94

W Hubbard St.
73
79

93
90
74 **75**
78
E Hubbard St.
82

83

W Kinzie St.
76

95
91
89
77
81 **80**

Clinton St.
92
88 **87**
86
85
84

E Wacker Dr.

Chicago River

W Wacker Dr.
E South Water St.

E Lake St.

LOOP

N Canal St.
N Wacker Dr.
N Franklin St.
N Wells St.
N LaSalle St.
N Clark St.
N Dearborn St.
N State St.
E Randolph St.
N Michigan Ave.
N Stetson Ave.

Grant Park

E Washington St.

ago & hwestern ion

South Branch Chicago River

km
mi
1/8
1/4
1/4
1/2

N

River North/ River West

If the Magnificent Mile is all splash and flash, River North is substance and stability. Perched confidently behind Michigan Avenue are turn-of-the-century brownstones, the Roman Catholic **Holy Name Cathedral**, and the **Episcopal Cathedral of St. James**, as well as the national headquarters of the American Medical and American Library Associations. A generous smattering of shops and restaurants makes the community as inviting as it is imposing. A few blocks to the west, **Wells Street** rivals New York City's SoHo in the number and variety of art galleries and offers plenty of fine dining and lively entertainment—from **Michael Jordan's** restaurant to the late-night **Ontario Street** restaurant-row scene that includes the **Hard Rock Cafe** and **Ed Debevic's**. And farther west again, just beyond the **Chicago River**, is the lower-rent district of River West, home to experimental art galleries and a phalanx of chic dance clubs along **Fulton Street**. Combined, the two neighborhoods are bounded more or less by **Division Street, Rush Street**, the Chicago River, and the **Kennedy Expressway (I-90/94)**.

The Irish were the first European immigrants to arrive in the area, settling near the river and north to **Erie Street**. In the 1840s they provided labor for the iron foundries, mills, and shipyards along the east bank. In 1849 they built their own simple church, **Holy Name Chapel**. Today, the massive **Holy Name Cathedral** stands on the same site, on **State Street** at **Chicago Avenue**. In 1856 industrial growth was hastened by the construction of a bridge (which no longer exists) at Rush Street that linked the city's **North** and **South Sides**, and German and Swedish settlers joined the area's Irish. After the Great Fire of 1871, wealthy Anglo-Saxons were able to rebuild rapidly and remained in the area, but the first wave of immigrants moved on (they were eventually replaced by Italians).

In 1920 the **Michigan Avenue Bridge** went up, and **LaSalle Street** was widened for automobiles, giving River North residents improved access to the Loop. Manufacturing continued to thrive along the river, but in the decade following World War I, industry faltered and many factories were converted into warehouses for downtown businesses. In 1930, **Marshall Field & Company** opened a gigantic warehouse beside the river; now known as the **Merchandise Mart**, this wholesale showroom is still the largest commercial building in the world.

During the 1950s, portions of River North began to slip in status, and its huge mansions became seedy rooming houses or ticky-tacky apartments. Subsequent renovation helped remedy this situation, and except for the infamous Cabrini-Green housing project along the river between Chicago Avenue and Division Street, it's all rather high rent today. The area has seen dramatic change since the 1970s: First, economic downturns led to the widespread shuttering of factories and warehouses; then these deserted buildings were snatched up by artists, photographers, and other creative souls in need of large, cheap spaces. Next came a handful of art galleries, their owners fed up with cramped quarters and sky-high rents on the other side of Michigan Avenue. Even a disastrous fire in 1989, which destroyed millions of dollars in artwork when nine galleries burned to the ground, did not deter growth. Today, at least 50 galleries are situated within a six-block-square area along **Superior** and **Huron Streets**. Additional galleries began appearing in the River West area in the mid-1980s. The conversion of abandoned warehouses into late-night dance clubs along Fulton Street, where other warehouses still serve as a major meat-and-produce wholesale market during the day, is a 1990s phenomenon.

iver North is especially fun to visit during festive Friday-night openings, /hen any number of galleries introduce new shows and the crowds can be as ffbeat as the artwork. The biggest blasts take place on the Friday after Labor)ay and the first or second Friday in January, when all the galleries have penings at once. Many stay open Sundays during the month of May, when n international art exposition is in town. Also nearby are attractions of a ifferent sort: **Planet Hollywood, Capone's Chicago,** and **Rock 'n' Roll** 1cDonald's.

---

1 Holy Name Cathedral Designed by **Patrick C. Keely,** this has been the cathedral of the Catholic Archdiocese of Chicago since 1874, when its dedication drew a crowd of more than 5,000 and featured a parade of 18 bands and a 25-priest choir. The 1979 visit of Pope John Paul II attracted a huge audience, as have performances by Luciano Pavarotti and the **Chicago Symphony Orchestra.** The interior of the Victorian Gothic church is warm and welcoming, with an ornate wooden ceiling and elaborate stone carving. Of particular note are the impressive organ loft at the back of the church and the three wide-brimmed hats hanging above the main altar. Tradition decrees that a departed cardinal's official hat, or *galeros,* be suspended from the ceiling of his cathedral. (These belonged to the late cardinals Mundelein, Stritch, and Meyer.) The cathedral has been renovated twice: in 1914, by **Henry J. Schlacks,** and in 1968, by **C.F. Murphy & Associates.** ♦ 735 N State St (at E Chicago Ave). 787.8040

2 Hotel St. Benedict Flats This lively 1883 Victorian Gothic composition of brick and stone designed by **James J. Egan** is a charming part of the 19th-century streetscape, with apartments above small shops. Note the variety of bay treatments and the incised lintels and art glass transoms above the windows. The owner repeatedly threatened to tear the building down to make way for something more lucrative, but it was saved by acquiring landmark status in 1990 after much community agitation. ♦ 50 E Chicago Ave and 801 N Wabash Ave

Within the Hotel St. Benedict Flats:

Streeter's Tavern Named after the raucous boatman who built up Streeterville, the community east of Michigan Avenue, this is your basic popcorn and beer spot, popular with college students. ♦ Daily. 944.5206

3 St. James Chapel/Quigley Seminary Step through an arched entryway on busy Rush Street and enter another world. A complex of Gothic buildings designed in 1917 and 1925 by **Gustav Steinbeck** surrounds a paved courtyard. The fact that it's filled with parked cars only heightens the illusion that you have been magically transported to Paris. Gargoyles, statue-filled niches, and spiky copper-covered dormers and towers complete the effect. The exteriors are a jewel-box setting for the real treasure—the seminary's chapel.

Modeled after Sainte-Chapelle in Paris, the chapel features a brilliant display of stained glass. The 14 windows, designed and executed by Robert Giles, contain more than a half-million pieces of handmade English glass. The seminary was named for Chicago's Archbishop James Quigley, who in 1905 established **Cathedral College** to prepare boys for the priesthood. He died 10 years later, and his plans for a larger seminary were fulfilled by his successor, Archbishop George Mundelein. ♦ M-F 8AM-4PM. Pick up a visitor's pass around the corner at 103 E Chestnut St. 831 N Rush St (at E Pearson St). 787.9343

4 Giordano's ★$$ This is a great stop for tasty stuffed pizza, but insist on a table on the first floor, preferably near a window overlooking Rush Street, or they'll seat you in the dark cavern upstairs. ♦ Pizza ♦ Daily lunch and dinner. 747 N Rush St (at E Superior St). 951.0747. Also at: 236 S Wabash Ave (at Jackson Blvd), Basement level. 939.4646; 1840 N Clark St (at W Lincoln Ave). 944.6100 &

5 Suntory ★★$$$ Designed as an authentic Japanese villa, this place offers a choice of three dining rooms, each with its own menu. There's a sushi bar, one of the city's best, with an amazing array of selections; a *shabu shabu* room, where diners cook their own meals in boiling broth at the table; and a *teppanyaki* grill, where steak, seafood, and vegetables are dramatically prepared before your eyes. Free hors d'oeuvres are served Mondays through Fridays starting at 4:30PM. ♦ Japanese ♦ M-F lunch; Sa-Su lunch and dinner. 11 E Huron St (between N Wabash Ave and N State St). 664.3344

6 City Source/City Stitcher Part of this store's charm is its setting in an old mansion. It specializes in gifts, home accessories, and needlework. The real treasures are up a staircase on the second floor, where the mansion's original woodwork and fireplaces remain; hundreds of needlepoint and cross-stitch canvases cover the walls, and the stock of all-natural threads is like a rainbow and fills an entire room. ♦ M-Sa. 28 E Huron St (at N Wabash Ave). 664.5499

7 Biba Rich colors and fabrics enliven this tiny boutique of women's clothing. Most items are European imports. Note the rack of fab faux furs. ♦ M-Sa. 712 N Wabash Ave (between E Huron and E Superior Sts). 642.7728

8 Blackhawk Lodge ★$$ The rustic decor is reminiscent of a comfortable North Woods hunting retreat. Signature starters include crab cakes and cheese grits with a fresh mushroom sauce. Choose from a wide variety of such comfort foods as roast turkey, ribs, steak, and fish. With lunch served until 5PM, this is a great spot for an early supper while talking about the one that got away. ◆ American ◆ Daily lunch and dinner. 41 E Superior St (at N Wabash Ave). 280.4080

9 Episcopal Cathedral of St. James Designed by **Edward Burling** in 1857 and then reconstructed by **Burling & Adler** in 1875, the cathedral's English Gothic exterior (pictured above) conceals the city's most unusual and beautiful ecclesiastical interior. The walls are covered with Arts and Crafts stencil patterns in 25 colors, designed in 1888 by New York architect **E.J. Neville Stemt** and carefully restored in 1985. Most US church interiors are copies of Old World designs, but the decoration here is pure 19th-century Americana, done at the height of the stenciling craze, and the effect is highly original. The **Chapel of St. Andrew** was built by **Ralph Adams Cram** and **Bertram G. Goodhue** in 1913. In 1985 **Holabird & Root** completed a restoration. ◆ 65 E Huron St (at N Wabash Ave). 787.7360

10 Tempo ★$ Good food is served in large portions, especially at breakfast (omelettes come in frying pans). In warm weather, opt for a table on the sidewalk. This is also a terrific spot for people watching. ◆ Coffee shop ◆ Daily 24 hours. 1 E Chestnut St (at N State St). 943.4373

11 Yanase ★$$ This family-style Japanese restaurant serves reasonably priced sushi and excellent tempura. Sit at the downstairs sushi bar. ◆ Japanese ◆ M-F lunch and dinner; Sa dinner. 818 N State St (at W Chicago Ave). 664.1371

12 Michael Reese Thrift Shop Bargain hunters will find antique furniture, good books, and great hand-me-downs that doctors and other affluent types have donated to benefit **Michael Reese Hospital.** ◆ M-Sa. 54 W Chicago Ave (at N Dearborn St). 337.8266

13 Santa Fe ★$ Tasty Southwestern barbecue and a casual atmosphere make this bar a fine spot to down a cold beer and catch a quick meal. In summer months there's an outdoor cafe. ◆ Southwestern ◆ Daily lunch and dinner. 800 N Dearborn St (at W Chicago Ave). 944.5722

14 Pattaya ★$ Not just another Thai place, this clean and quiet storefront restaurant serves a variety of very good, reasonably priced, regional dishes. Some of the notable noodle dishes here include *pad thai* (thin noodles with almonds, egg, peanut sauce, and bean sprouts), *lad na gai* (wide noodles with broccoli, curry, and garlic), and *pad cee-ew gai* (chicken on top of wide noodles with egg, bean sprouts, and garlic). ◆ Thai ◆ M-Sa lunch and dinner. 114 W Chicago Ave (between N Clark and N LaSalle Sts). 944.3753

15 la locanda ★★★$$$ There are many Chicago restaurants that claim to serve authentic Italian cuisine, but this one is the real McCoy. You'll pay for the privilege, which may include a wait even if you have reservations. Complimentary bread, fresh tomatoes spiced with basil, and bel paese cheese are served while you peruse the sumptuous appetizer list. Pastas are terrific, and the risottos are perfection. Main courses include a mixed seafood grill, osso buco with polenta, and herbed chops. A superior wine list highlights small Italian wineries. *Buon appetito!* ◆ Italian ◆ M, W-F lunch and dinner; Sa-Su dinner. Reservations required. 745 N LaSalle St (at W Chicago Ave). 335.9550 &

16 Caspian Oriental Rugs This is the Midwest's largest dealer of exotic carpets—a 6,000-square-foot bazaar with 10,000 new and antique rugs imported from Iran, China, and India. ◆ Daily. 700 N LaSalle St (at W Huron St). 664.7576

17 Moody Bookstore The inventory at Chicago's largest Christian bookstore is in doctrinal accord with the **Moody Bible Institute,** the seminary with which the store is affiliated. A huge selection of Bibles includes the *Businessman's Bible: Spiritual Directives for Excellence in Business* and computer software Bibles. There's also a wide range of titles on marriage, family, and finances; items for kids such as glow-in-the-dark bedtime prayer reminders; and a large selection of Christian music tapes and CDs. ◆ M-Sa. 150 W Chicago Ave (at N LaSalle St). 329.4352 &

18 Paper Source A paper fetishist's nirvana, this shop carries a fascinating variety of handmade, machine-made, and mold-made papers. The stationery and artists' supplies are imported from around the world. There's also an array of designs, from the novel to the normal, for rubber-stamp-art fans. ◆ Daily. 232 W Chicago Ave (at N Franklin St). 337.0798 &

Bad Boys in Gangland

Though the Mayors Daley and many civic boosters don't like to admit it, the mere name of Chicago conjures up scenes of Al Capone and his fellow gangsters shooting up the city, Godfather style. And little wonder: From 1920 to 1933 battles by the Mob (or Mafia) over control of bootlegging operations, gambling, prostitution, and other lucrative, illegal activities resulted in some 700 gangland murders. More than half a century has passed since then, but Chicago can't seem to shake its notorious reputation. Blame it on guys like these:

Big Jim Colosimo started out as a precinct captain and whorehouse owner at the turn of the century. Ultimately he controlled the South Side's liquor and gambling operations, pulling in a personal income of about $50,000 a month. The flamboyant gang leader also owned a restaurant where he regularly dished out spaghetti to Enrico Caruso and other opera stars he adored. In 1920 rivals shot him in the head outside the restaurant. His funeral was attended by 5,000 people, many of them judges and politicians. Al Capone, Colosimo's bodyguard, boasted that he pulled the trigger, but no one seems to know for sure.

Johnny Torio, Colosimo's successor, oversaw an army of about 800 gunmen and grossed about $70 million a year. He paid generous bribes to keep the law off his back: One police chief drew $1,000 a day. After barely surviving an assassination attempt in 1924, Torio relocated to New York and his operation was taken over by Al Capone.

Dion O'Banion, a florist and safecracker, had delivered newspapers as a kid and carried a press card throughout his life; once, when caught robbing a safe, he used the card to convince police that he was actually doing a news story. He controlled the North Side's bootleg supply and liked to hijack trucks carrying other gangs' liquor. One day in 1924, while making bouquets in the floral shop he operated across the street from **Holy Name Cathedral,** he was shot dead by three of Capone's boys.

Hymie Weiss, whose real last name was Polish and six syllables long, was an accomplished liquor hijacker, safecracker, jewel thief, and murderer. He is said to have coined the phrase "take him for a ride," in which a rival was driven to a secluded part of town and bumped off. He and rival Al Capone tried to kill each other several times. In 1926 Weiss was machine-gunned to death on the steps of **Holy Name Cathedral** (the cornerstone of the church was damaged by bullets and later replaced).

Alphonse "Al" Capone was one of the most violent gangsters Chicago has ever known. Nicknamed "Scarface" due to the scar on his left cheek from a dance-hall fight, he oversaw hundreds of gang killings and personally mangled many a foe with a baseball bat. In 1925 Bugs Moran's gang riddled his car with bullets, but Capone turned out not to be in it. The following year, a cavalcade of 10 cars sent by Hymie Weiss drove past a restaurant where Capone was eating and let loose with a reported 10,000 machine-gun rounds in less than 10 seconds; Capone survived by diving to the floor. In 1929 his boys lined up six of Bugs Moran's gang in a **Lincoln Park** garage (no longer there) and machine-gunned them to death in the infamous St. Valentine's Day Massacre. Capone finally found his match in the Internal Revenue Service. Indicted for tax evasion in 1931, he was found guilty and sentenced to 10 years in prison. Shortly after his release, he died of syphilis.

Though in Chicago and elsewhere the Mob is hardly a thing of the past, teenage drug dealers have been stealing the headlines in recent times, particularly in the city. Moblike activities have shifted to suburban areas and are said to maintain a hold on some workers at exposition centers and airports.

For a taste of gangster-era Chicago, take the **Untouchables Tour** (Here's Chicago/Chicago Visitor's Center, 163 E Pearson St, at N Michigan Ave, 881.1195) or visit **Capone's Chicago** (605 N Clark St, at W Ohio St, 654.1919), a museum featuring exhibits and shows starring lifelike figures who retell the high points of Prohibition.

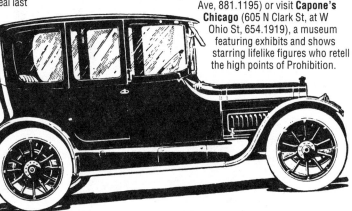

19 Kiki's Bistro ★★$$$ A dining room resembling a rustic country cottage provides a charming setting in which to enjoy typical French bistro fare. Start with puree of salted cod with white truffle oil or sausage wrapped in pastry. For your main course, consider grilled sea bass in-onion vinaigrette or sautéed calf's liver with pearl onions and wine vinegar sauce. Be sure to order the rich chocolate-laced crème brûlée for dessert. ♦ French ♦ M-F lunch and dinner; Sa dinner. Reservations recommended. 900 N Franklin St (at W Chestnut St). 335.5454 ♿

20 Gold's Gym Briefcase toters arrive in BMWs to trade dress shirts for muscle Ts and pump iron in a serious way. For visitors, a daily membership rate provides access to cardiovascular equipment, free weights, computerized resistance-training systems, and barking personal coaches. ♦ Daily. 820 N Orleans St (at W Institute Pl). 664.6537

21 750 North Orleans Street The lobby of this converted warehouse, now filled with art galleries, boasts six murals that attract crowds who try to identify the local personalities portrayed. Chicagoan Robbie Boijeson painted the primitive-style series while she attended medical school. The mural facing the entryway depicts Chicago's late mayor Harold Washington and syndicated newspaper columnists Ann Landers and Mike Royko, among others. The last mural features the **Bears** football coach Mike Ditka and fellow sports celebs. ♦ At W Chicago Ave

Within 750 North Orleans Street:

Ehlers Caudill Gallery The work of contemporary photographers such as Steven Foster, Irving Penn, and Sandy Skoglund is featured in this gallery, along with vintage photographs. ♦ Tu-Sa; closed weekends in July and August. 642.8611 ♿

Abraham Lincoln Bookshop Civil War and Lincoln history buffs from around the country are attracted to this warm and inviting store, which is more like a museum. Floor-to-ceiling glass-doored bookcases display art, books, and documents from the era. Proprietor Daniel Weinberg is frequently called upon to authenticate Lincoln memorabilia. He's glad to share his knowledge, even with browsers. ♦ M-Sa. 357 W Chicago Ave (between N Orleans and N Sedgwick Sts). 944.3085

22 Scoozi! ★★$$ At the front of yet another restaurant from Lettuce Entertain You Enterprises, a big red tomato beckons. Inside, the noisy crowd at the bar is packed three deep; the bustling 320-seat dining room has a decadent European feel with distressed walls, dark woods, and old-fashioned embellishments; and Italian talk radio blares in the bathrooms. Despite the scene, the chef turns out some serious Italian fare, including a wonderful *pizza boscaiola* (with roasted portobello mushrooms, fontina cheese, prosciutto, walnuts, and truffle oil). Desserts include a super ricotta cheesecake. Expect a wait for dinner. ♦ Italian ♦ M-F lunch and dinner; Sa-Su dinner. 410 W Huron St (at N Sedgwick St). 943.5900 ♿

23 Club Lago ★$ A neighborhood restaurant and bar, this has been a River North fixture since the 1950s, before the area got chic. The large lunch crowd jams the bar and packs the tables. Old-fashioned Italian standards include decent chicken Vesuvio (roasted chicken, potatoes, and peppers) and fried calamari. ♦ Italian ♦ M-Sa lunch and dinner until 8PM; Sa lunch. 331 W Superior St (at N Orleans St). 337.9444

24 Phyllis Kind Gallery The big-name American contemporary artists exhibited here include Ed Paschke, Roger Brown, and Robin Woodsome. The gallery also features artists from the former Soviet Union, such as Eric Bulatov, Yuri Dyshlenko, and Oleg Vassilyev. ♦ Tu-Sa; closed Saturday in July and August. 313 W Superior St (between N Franklin and N Orleans Sts). 642.6302

24 Printworks Gallery Works on paper, including limited-edition prints, drawings, and photographs, are on display here. Artists' books are a specialty; artists such as as Audrey Niffenegger, who wrote the text hand-set the type, wood-cut the images, and bound the books herself, create these one-of-a-kind volumes. The gallery represents emerging and major artists whose prints do not generally appear elsewhere, among them Leon Golub, Richard Hunt, Ellen Lanyon, Seymour Rosofsky, and Hollis Sigler. Amicable gallery directors Sidney Block and Bob Hiebert enthusiastically pore through their collection for visitors and explain aspects of the printmaking process. ♦ Tu-Sa, and by appointment. 311 W Superior St (between N Franklin and N Orleans Sts). 664.9407

24 Michael Fitzsimmons Decorative Arts Concentrating on 20th-century US architectural and decorative art, this gallery is also the world's largest dealer of original **Frank Lloyd Wright** furniture, leaded glass, and drawings. ♦ Tu-Sa. 311 W Superior St (between N Franklin and N Orleans Sts). 787.0496

24 Schwebel Gallery This gallery deals in exceptional 19th- and 20th-century American antique furnishings and accessories. ♦ M-Sa. 311 W Superior St (between N Franklin and N Orleans Sts). 280.1998

24 Gwenda Jay Gallery Emerging regional contemporary artists are featured, along with innovative works by architects, including drawings, furniture, and installations. Shows have included steel-and-pine furniture by Los Angeles architect **Thom Mayne.** ♦ Tu-Sa. 301 W Superior St (at N Franklin St). 664.3406

24 Signet Fine Art Guang Xin Qian's gallery concentrates on contemporary works by Chinese artists, among them Mao Jie, who blends traditionalist Chinese art with Western abstractions, and the collaborative paintings of the Zhao brothers. Qian also publishes the fine-arts quarterly *New Era in Chinese Painting.* ♦ Tu-Sa. 301 W Superior St (at N Franklin St). 621.1119

25 Catherine Edelman Gallery Exhibits change frequently at this premier photography gallery. Among the contemporary works have been pieces by Barbara Crane, David Plowden, and Richard Misrach. ♦ M-Sa. 300 W Superior St (at N Franklin St). 266.2350

25 Carole Jones Gallery Jones carries a variety of contemporary art and sculpture by established international artists. The emphasis is on work steeped in myth and symbol. ♦ Tu-Su. 300 W Superior St (at N Franklin St). 587.8820

25 Van Straaten Gallery Wayne Thebaud's still lifes, and master prints by Jasper Johns are among the contemporary drawings, prints, and paintings featured here. ♦ Tu-Sa. 300 W Superior (at N Franklin St). 642.2900

26 Marx Gallery This small gallery features contemporary glass art, including Michael Rogers's delicate cast crystal, John Wolfe's cast laminated glass, and blown glass sculpture by Vernon Brejcha. ♦ Tu-Sa. 230 W Superior St (between N Wells and N Franklin Sts). 753.1400

26 Schneider Gallery Handmade jewelry and ceramics by a variety of international artists are the focus here. ♦ Tu-Sa. 230 W Superior St (between N Wells and N Franklin Sts). 988.4033

26 Gruen Galleries A strange but wonderful juxtaposition of African artifacts and Old World–style forged iron objects is found here. Among the African works are towering carved wood funerary figures from Zaire and intricately beaded chairs from Cameroon. Ironwork table bases, chairs, bedframes, chandeliers, candelabra, and more are produced by Erwin Gruen, a Berlin-born blacksmith. Ask to see his gigantic shop of whirring machinery in the basement. ♦ M-Sa. 226 W Superior St (between N Wells and N Franklin Sts). 337.6262

26 Ann Nathan Gallery The emphasis is on three-dimensional objects, whether functional or fantastic. Notable pieces have included Brian Sauve's four-foot–diameter globe of 1950s floral TV trays riveted together patchwork style; Lynn Zetzman's *Portrait of a Contemporary,* a male figure fashioned almost entirely from men's ties; and hand-painted cabinets and mosaic tile figures by Leslie Hawk. ♦ Tu-Sa. 218 W Superior (between N Wells and N Franklin Sts). 664.6622

26 Betsy Rosenfeld Contemporary paintings, drawings, photography, and sculpture are featured here, one of only a handful of galleries that show glass, both blown and hot-form. ♦ Tu-Sa. 212 W Superior St (between N Wells and N Franklin Sts). 787.8020

27 Manifesto The ultimate source for architect-designed furniture, lighting, and accessories, this gallery focuses on licensed reproductions of European and American pieces designed between 1890 and 1940, with some contemporary designs. The high-end wares include dining tables by Italian architect **Carlo Scarpa** and carpets, furniture, and tableware by Josef Hoffman. ♦ Tu-Sa. 200 W Superior St (at N Wells St). 664.0733

27 Carl Hammer Gallery Primarily nontraditional, self-taught, and outsider artists are represented, most notably Chicago's own Mr. Imagination, who produces carved works in sandstone. ♦ Tu-Sa. 200 W Superior St (at N Wells St). 266.8512

27 June Blaker This high-end men's and women's clothing and accessories store specializes in imported fashions, with an emphasis on the latest European designs. ♦ M-Sa. 200 W Superior St (at N Wells St). 751.9220

27 Isobel Neal Works by African-American artists are on display here, including powerful bronzes and Prisma color drawings by Preston Jackson, wall hangings by Carol Ann Carter, and life-size dolls by Barbara Ward. ♦ W-Sa, or by appointment. 200 W Superior St (at N Wells St). 944.1570

28 Nicole Gallery Along with Haitian art and Shona sculpture from Zimbabwe (including works by Henry Munyaradzi), Nicole features Chicago collagist Allen Stringfellow. ♦ Tu-Sa. 734 N Wells St (between W Superior St and W Chicago Ave). 787.7716

Chicago's South Side was the training ground for many great jazzmen who then moved on to Hollywood and New York, among them Benny and Harry Goodman, Louis Armstrong, Louis Panico, Eddie Condon, Hoagy Carmichael, and Jess Stacy.

Restaurants/Clubs: Red   **Hotels:** Blue
Shops/♥ Outdoors: Green   **Sights/Culture:** Black

29 Roy Boyd Gallery Roy and Ann Boyd represent contemporary abstractionists, most of them from Chicago. The gallery also has a collection of photography from Russia, Lithuania, and Estonia. Ask to see the lovely sculpture garden in back. ♦ Tu-Sa. 739 N Wells St (between W Superior St and W Chicago Ave). 642.1606

29 Farrago ★$$ At lunchtime, it's an attractive, bustling cafe, serving a menu of salads, sandwiches, and fresh-baked goods that changes daily. In the evening, it becomes a bistro brimming with such imaginative entrées as sautéed escarole with plantain-hominy cakes and barbecued pork chops with stuffed black-bean chilies. ♦ American ♦ M-F breakfast, lunch, and dinner; Sa brunch and dinner. 733 N Wells St (between W Superior St and W Chicago Ave). 951.7350 &

30 Northern Illinois University Gallery Students, alumni, and guest artists display their work at this nonprofit gallery. Exhibits have included Mary Jo Bang's *An Ever Rolling Stream,* a series of timeless, surrealistic black-and-white photos of France. ♦ Tu-Sa; closed in August. 215 W Superior St (between N Wells and N Franklin Sts). 642.6010

30 Maya Polska Gallery A tribute to the fall of the Iron Curtain, this place is an eye-opener. The Russian art world has been observing pre- and post-Perestroika society and turning what it sees into searing images, usually very realistic and not very complimentary. There's also art from Poland and elsewhere in Eastern Europe. A Russian herself, Ms. Polska generously describes the work and the artists. ♦ Tu-Sa. 215 W Superior St (between N Wells and N Franklin Sts). 440.0055

30 Kass/Meridian Gallery Prints by contemporary and modern masters include Alexander Calder lithographs from the 1960s and works by Roy Lichtenstein, Joan Miró, Robert Motherwell, Andy Warhol, and Pablo Picasso. ♦ Tu-Sa. 215 W Superior St (between N Wells and N Franklin Sts). 266.5999

30 Jean Albano Gallery Contemporary American painting, sculpture, and constructions by both established and emerging artists are the trade at this gallery, which emphasizes West Coast artists. ♦ Tu-Sa. 215 W Superior St (between N Wells and N Franklin Sts). 440.0055

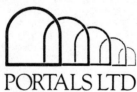

31 Portals Ltd. A fantastic arrangement of naive paintings by international artists is juxtaposed with fine 18th- and 19th-century furniture and decorative objects; for example, Karen Halt's *When a Man Loves a Woman* is displayed beside a handsome Gillows & Company writing desk. The inspiration of interior designer Nancy McIlvaine and her art-collector husband, William, the spacious seventh-floor gallery is beautiful, with wide arched windows providing great views of the neighborhood. ♦ M-Sa. 230 W Huron St (at N Franklin St). 642.1066

31 Parenteau Studios Entering this gallery is like going to a garage sale at Versailles. French and continental antique furniture and decorative arts have included a Louis XVI writing table and huge carved armoire circa mid-19th century. ♦ M-F. 230 W Huron St (at N Franklin St). 337.8015

32 Fly By Nite Gallery Despite the name, this gallery claims to offer the largest collection of European pottery circa 1890-1930 in the world. Some 850 pieces are in stock, including Art Nouveau, Art Deco, and *l'art pratique.* ♦ M-Sa. 714 N Wells St (between W Huron and W Superior Sts). 664.8136

32 Centro Ristorante Bar $$ The River North branch of Little Italy's **Rosebud,** this one serves such country dishes as *cavatelli* in a vodka-marinara sauce, chicken francese, and shrimp and broccoli (ordinary, some say) as well as a large assortment of antipasti. A sidewalk cafe makes it a popular stop in warm weather. ♦ Italian ♦ M-F lunch and dinner; Sa dinner. 710 N Wells St (between W Huron and W Superior Sts). 988.7775 &

32 Mongerson-Wunderlich Gallery Best known for Native American and Southwestern folk art, paintings, sculpture, and textiles, this gallery has everything from traditional Pendleton blankets to wild ladies' sling-back pumps with toes made of crocodile heads and mounted on roller skates. ♦ Tu-Sa; closed Saturdays in July and August. 704 N Wells St (at W Huron St). 943.2354

33 O'Hara's Gallery This huge gallery is filled to the rafters with European and Asian furniture, paintings, rugs, and decorative arts dating from the 17th to the 19th centuries. ♦ M-Sa. 707 N Wells St (between W Huron and W Superior Sts). 751.1286

34 Zolla/Lieberman Gallery Inc. In 1976, dealer Roberta Lieberman pioneered in the development of this area by moving into a nearly abandoned warehouse one block east of her current location, spurring an exodus of other galleries from Michigan Avenue and stimulating the rapid growth of Chicago's art community here. Her artists tend to be *avant,* although she represents Deborah Butterfield, whose graceful iron *Horse* adorns **Seneca Park** east of the **Water Tower.** This street-level gallery has windows all around, so you can look before going in. ♦ Tu-Sa. 325 W Huron St (at N Orleans St). 944.1990 &

HAT DANCE

34 Hat Dance ★★$$ Lettuce Entertain You
Enterprises strikes again, this time with a
busy, noisy, fun Mexican restaurant that looks
like a set from a bizarre black-and-white south-
of-the-border movie. The color scheme is
white—110 subtly different shades of white, in
fact—accented only by a few sombreros over
the bar. Inventive dishes include *chiles
rellenos* stuffed with chicken, olives, raisins,
and onions; wood-roasted chicken; and *tuna
asada,* seared on the outside and rare on the
inside. Dishes are served in both *pequeño* and
regular sizes to encourage experimentation.
Wash it all down with one of a dozen Mexican
beers. ♦ Mexican ♦ M-Sa lunch and dinner;
Su dinner. Reservations recommended. 325
W Huron St (at N Orleans St). 649.0066 &

Under Fire: Chicago's 1871 Inferno

No one knows for certain how Chicago's Great Fire
of 1871 started, though legend has it that the first
flames crackled in a haystack when Mrs. O'Leary's
cow knocked over a lantern in the barn behind her
cottage west of the **Loop.**

It was 8 October 1871, a Sunday evening, and the
weather was unusually dry. The fire department,
exhausted from battling a big blaze in another
neighborhood, didn't arrive quickly enough,
and the fire was soon out of control. Strong
winds swept it through the **West Side,** where
the fire destroyed ramshackle wooden houses
along with lumberyards and factories. The
voracious flames spread to the downtown area,
consuming financial buildings on **LaSalle Street**
and stores along **State Street,** including all the
supposedly fireproof structures.

Most of the city's 300,000 residents fled for safety
to the edge of the **Chicago River,** where they were
treated to a horrific panoramic view of the fire's
four-mile course. The Great Chicago Fire burned
steadily for three solid days.

Losses topped $200 million, and 1,688 acres
were leveled between the lake, the river, **Fullerton
Avenue** on the **North Side,** and **12th Street** on the
South Side. Downtown Chicago had practically
disappeared. Gone, too, were the homes of nearly
one-third of the city's population. The roaring
inferno bent streetcar rails, burned down telephone
poles, melted 15,000 water-service pipes, and
scorched 28.5 miles of wooden sidewalks. In the
aftermath, the bodies of 250 people were found,
and many more may have been killed.

Yet Chicago was quick to bounce back. Within
a week after the last flame flickered, more than
5,000 temporary structures had been built and
the construction of 200 permanent buildings
had begun. The City Council wisely passed an
ordinance that required new buildings in the
downtown area to be constructed of brick and
iron. Architects had a field day designing buildings
that were taller and more elaborate than their
predecessors. The homeless moved into wooden
cottages built a short distance from the center of
town, and soon were creating new neighborhoods
in the city's outskirts. Chicago was almost entirely
rebuilt within three years.

Ironically, one survivor of the fire was the
O'Leary cottage (although no one's quite sure
what happened to the cow). Today, the **Chicago Fire**

**Area destroyed
by the fire**

Addison St.

N Clark St.

W Fullerton Ave.

N Clybourn Ave.

N Lincoln Ave.

41

N Lake Shore Dr.

W North Ave.

Lake
Michigan

N Ashland Ave.

N Orleans St.

W Division St.

W Chicago Ave.

Chicago River

W Randolph St.

90

94

290

S LaSalle St.

S State St.

S Michigan Ave.

S Lake Shore Dr.

W Roosevelt Rd.

**Suspected
starting point
of the Great
Chicago Fire**

W Cermak Rd.

N

km   1   2
mi   1

Department Academy stands on the site.
Fascinating remnants of the blaze are on view
at the **Chicago Historical Society.**

34 Rhona Hoffman Gallery Focusing on American and European contemporary art, this gallery's exhibits change every four to six weeks. ◆ Tu-Sa. 325 W Huron St (at N Orleans St). 951.8828

35 Green Door Tavern ★$$ This cozy spot has been a bar since 1921. Set in one of the first buildings to go up after the Chicago Fire, it boasts many of its original fixtures, and has antiques hanging from the walls and ceiling. Crowds show up for the basic home cooking: hamburgers with baked beans and coleslaw, good meat loaf, mashed potatoes and gravy. There's a wide assortment of imported and domestic beers. ◆ American ◆ Daily lunch and dinner; closed Sunday in July and August. 678 N Orleans St (between W Erie and W Huron Sts). 664.5496

35 Mr. Beef ★$ You shouldn't leave Chicago without sampling one of the city's sloppiest and most delectable indigenous gastronomical delights: an Italian beef sandwich smothered in hot and sweet peppers. This River North restaurant does one of the best. ◆ Italian ◆ M-F breakfast, lunch, and early dinner; Sa lunch. 660 N Orleans St (between W Erie and W Huron Sts). 337.8500 ⴕ

36 Tuttaposto ★$$$ Seafood and meats cooked in an open wood-burning oven are the order of the day at this Mediterranean taverna. Popular appetizers include Sardinian focaccia with three spreads, Greek hillbilly salad, and Tunisian chicken wings. The extensive wine list features Greek, Spanish, and Italian vintages. ◆ Mediterranean ◆ M-F lunch and dinner; Sa-Su dinner. 646 N Franklin St (at W Erie St). 943.6262 ⴕ

36 303 West Erie Street Talk about climbing your way to the top! Scaling the brick wall of this renovated factory is artist Jim Stone's *Climbing Yuppies,* a life-size pair of male and female executives making their way up on ropes, briefcases at their sides. The artist dressed department-store mannequins in suits, pumps, and wingtips, then sprayed them with fiberglass to make them rock hard and weather resistant. Building co-owner Burt Lewis, who commissioned the project, originally envisioned burglars scaling the walls, but his partners suggested a sculpture that would reflect the target market which they are trying to interest in their renovated loft rentals. ◆ At N Franklin St

37 Jan Cicero Gallery Contemporary American paintings and drawings with a regional emphasis, from Milwaukee street scenes to the Chicago el, can be found at this gallery. ◆ Tu-Sa. 221 W Erie St (between N Wells and N Franklin Sts). 440.1904 ⴕ

37 America's Bar Retired **Bears** running back Walter Payton's multilevel nightclub is designed as a pseudo gymnasium, complete with waitresses attired as cheerleaders. There's dancing to music from the 1960s, 1970s, and 1980s, and plenty of spontaneous sing-alongs. A small cover charge and one-drink minimum entitle you to mounds of cocktail-hour food Tuesday through Friday from 5 to 7:30PM. ◆ Cover charge. Tu-Th to 2AM; F-Sa to 4AM. Must be 23 or older. No denim, shorts, or T-shirts permitted. 219 W Erie St (at N Wells St). 915.5986

38 Ed Debevic's ★$ Quite possibly the only diner in the world that has valet parking, this 1950s-style spot was opened by Lettuce Entertain You Enterprises in the mid-1980s. The atmosphere is frenetic and noisy. Food runs along the lines of burgers, mashed potatoes, and meat loaf, all washed down with Green River soda pop. The ever-friendly waitresses will urge coconut cream pie on you for dessert—go for it. It's a fun place to bring kids, but expect a wait. ◆ Diner ◆ Daily lunch and dinner. 640 N Wells St (at W Ontario St). 664.1707

39 Big Bowl Cafe ★$ This sidewalk cafe serves complete meals in bowls, featuring soups and salads. A popular item is three chix on stix (three skewers of chicken and a variety of vegetables served with chicken broth and a crispy noodle cake). ◆ American ◆ M-Sa lunch and dinner. 159½ W Erie St (at N LaSalle St). 787.8297

40 Rock 'n' Roll McDonald's $ The busiest and most visually stimulating "Micky D's" in the city, this neon-flickering place is packed with 1950s memorabilia, from a flame-red 1963 Corvette to Archie and Veronica dolls and working arcade games. Customers in line tap their feet to the sounds of Buddy Holly, Connie Francis, and Elvis. Too bad the food's no better than at any other **McDonald's.** There's free parking in a big lot, but don't leave your car here while you visit another Ontario Street spot or you'll help make a towing company rich. ◆ Fast food ◆ Daily 24 hours. 600 N Clark St (at W Ontario St). 664.7940 ⴕ

41 Capone's Chicago It had to happen, though city leaders and local image makers struggled to prevent it. For years, Libertyville native Michael Graham collected gangster-era memorabilia for the day he could put it all on display; now Chicago's rat-a-tat-tat gangland past is enshrined here. A lifelike Big Al (Snorkey to his friends, the sign says) greets visitors at the door; inside are shows in which other lifelike characters tell historically accurate tales, roughly chronologically; they run every half hour. There's also a shop called the **Four Deuces.** ◆ Admission. Daily 10AM-

10PM. 605 N Clark St (between W Ohio and W Ontario Sts). 654.1919 &

42 Hard Rock Cafe ★$$ From the outside this building, designed by **Tigerman, McCurry** in 1985, resembles a mammoth 18th-century orangerie. Inside, the collection of rock 'n' roll memorabilia dazzles, the ear-splitting music pounds, and the tourists—from teenagers to grandparents—keep coming. The burgers are good. ♦ American ♦ Daily lunch and dinner. 63 W Ontario St (between N Dearborn and N Clark Sts). 943.2252 &

43 Chicago Chop House ★★$$$ Served in a cozy two-story town house, the meat-and-potatoes meals here start with a whole loaf of fresh bread and a house salad, then get down to business with expertly cooked steak that can weigh up to 64 ounces. Chicken and seafood are also available. There's piano music every evening. ♦ Steak house ♦ M-F lunch and dinner; Sa-Su dinner. 60 W Ontario St (between N Dearborn and N Clark Sts). 787.7100

44 Commonwealth Edison Substation This 1989 building shares a lineage with the neighboring **Hard Rock Cafe,** and is an unusual case of an architect being contextual with his own recent work. Both were designed by **Stanley Tigerman,** whose handling of the restaurant's scale and window treatments was inspired by the 1929 Georgian Revival power station that was on this site. The substation was slated for demolition, but **Tigerman**'s replacement repeats its basic motifs and even reuses some fragments. The building looks like an English country pavilion—except for the large mechanical louvers that fill the limestone window surrounds. ♦ 600 N Dearborn St (at W Ontario St)

45 Excalibur Now a nightclub, this 1892 building by **Henry Ives Cobb** was known as "The Castle" in the 19th century, when it was built as headquarters for the Chicago Historical Society. The granite-faced fortress has dramatic arched windows and sharply pitched roofs and gables. Each of its four floors—three stories plus basement—spans 11,000 square feet.

Following the society's move to larger quarters in the 1930s, the building saw a succession of tenants. It served as everything from a Moose lodge to offices for the Federal Music Projects of the Works Progress Administration to the **Institute of Design,** founded by Bauhaus guru **László Moholy-Nagy.** In the late 1960s, a group of investors bought it to create a nightclub, a plan that finally materialized when attorney F. Lee Bailey purchased it from them and opened **The Gallery.** It went through two more incarnations before becoming **Excalibur** in the late 1980s. A gigantic entertainment complex popular among a mainstream crowd, the club offers billiards and video games in the basement, a main-floor cabaret with dance music from the 1950s to 1970s, and a gigantic multilevel dance club with current tunes. ♦ Cover charge. Daily to 4AM; Sa to 5AM. 632 N Dearborn St (at W Ontario St). 266.1944

46 Studio V Eye-catching items fill this Art Deco studio: graphics, telephones, perfume bottles, funny flamingos, fine clothing, funky earrings, and neon wall clocks reminiscent of old diners. ♦ M-Sa noon-6PM. 672 N Dearborn St (at W Erie St). 440.1937 &

46 Manikas Designs Here Tom Manikas designs and produces big, dangling earrings of every sort. Bring in an outfit and he will design the perfect earrings to complement it. He also makes bridal headdresses with complex beading and lace. ♦ M-Sa. Appointments recommended for custom work. 676 N Dearborn St (between W Erie and W Huron Sts). 337.7755

47 Carson's—the Place for Ribs ★$$ Big, meaty, moist, tangy-sweet ribs are presented on huge platters. Ditto for the steaks and barbecued chicken. All entrées are served with a choice of potato—choose au gratin—plus salad or coleslaw and fresh rolls. Desserts include giant chocolate sundaes. Heavy advertising makes this a major tourist trap, albeit one you might actually *want* to be trapped in. ♦ Ribs ♦ Daily lunch and dinner. 612 N Wells St (between W Ohio and W Ontario Sts). 280.9200 &

48 Planet Hollywood $$ A testament to our fascination with celebrities, this otherwise average restaurant packs customers in with movie mystique. One of a dozen such places around the country owned by Willis, Schwarzenegger, and Stallone, this place attracts the starstruck. It's filled with Hollywood memorabilia, with pawprints of Newman, Eastwood, Hawn,

Basinger, O'Toole, and the like adorning the entrance. You can't miss it; giant fluorescent palm trees announce its presence from the roof. There are hamburgers, pizzas, and a store vending movie-themed merchandise. ♦ American ♦ Daily lunch and dinner. 633 N Wells St (at W Ontario St). 266.7827 ♿

49 Reza's ★★$ This sprawling space has seen several restaurants come and go; even **Berghoff's,** the tourists' favorite in the Loop, didn't make it here. Now a branch of a popular budget-priced uptown restaurant, it seems to have the magic touch. Start with the hummus and eggplant dips, but save room for an ample portion of kabob, stew, lamb shanks, or game hen. The price of an entrée includes lentil soup, lots of raw veggies, fluffy rice, plus pita. The wine list is small, but adequate. This is a great spot for a crowd after gallery hopping. And you can usually find a parking place on the street, particularly in the evenings. ♦ Middle Eastern ♦ Daily lunch and dinner. 436 W Ontario St (between N Orleans and N Kingsbury Sts). 664.4500 ♿

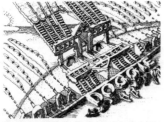

Courtesy of Stanley Tigerman & Associates

50 Anti-Cruelty Society Addition Constructed in 1978 by **Stanley Tigerman & Associates,** this is another of their billboard buildings (like the **Self-Park Garage** in the Loop). In this case, the whimsical design resembles a dog-food can, with a framed upright on the roof forming a pull tab. The two-story windows are curved to resemble the cheeks of a basset hound. ♦ 157 W Grand Ave (between N LaSalle and N Wells Sts)

51 Michael Jordan's ★$$; The world's most popular basketball player snared the title of most famous Chicagoan from Al Capone, and crowds of his fans are drawn here in hopes of running into the **Bulls'** No. 23. You aren't likely to spot him, but there's plenty of **Bulls** memorabilia here, from ties to collector mugs and plaques. The food runs to steaks and chops, as well as burgers and pizzas. A giant basketball atop this place will guide you, even from blocks away. ♦ American ♦ Daily lunch and dinner. 500 N LaSalle St (at W Illinois St). 644.3865 ♿

52 Grand & Wells Tap ★$$$ This quaint tavern with an ersatz 1930s atmosphere serves huge steaks in various ways, including plain, baked with grated parmesan broiled on top, or Tuscan-style with marinara sauce.

Pasta dishes and seafood are good, too. Political and big-business heavies tend to hang out here. ♦ Steak house/Italian ♦ M-F lunch and dinner; Sa-Su. Reservation required. 531 N Wells St (at W Grand Ave). 645.1255 ♿

52 Parrinello ★$$ Regional Italian food made with only the freshest ingredients is the fare this casual, airy Mediterranean cafe. Start wi a selection of cold antipasti. Entrées on the seasonally changing menu may include grille veal chops in wine or grilled beef with sweet gorgonzola. Celebrities and politicians are often spotted here. ♦ Italian ♦ M-F lunch; M-Sa dinner. 535 N Wells St (between W Grand Ave and W Ohio St). 527.2782

53 Orca Aart This gallery features art— including photographs, paintings, sculpture, tapestries, and baskets—from the Arctic, Africa, and the Pacific Northwest. Owner Jay Fahn is one of the country's foremost experts on Inuit art. ♦ Tu-Sa. 300 W Grand Ave (between N Franklin and N Orleans Sts). 245.5245 ♿

54 Club Gene & Georgetti, Ltd. ★$$$ Opened in 1941, this dark, clubbish Italian steak house evokes another age. Diners, many of whom have been regular customers for years, are served in one of the four small dining rooms within an old three-story flat. Fare runs to prime aged steaks and especiall good chicken Vesuvio. ♦ Steak house/Italian ♦ M-Sa lunch and dinner. 500 N Franklin St (at W Illinois St). 527.3718 ♿

55 Mario Villa Nicaraguan-born New Orleania Mario Villa creates "furniture that appears to have been dug up and dusted off, but is definitely New World," says London-based *World of Interiors* magazine. Chairs, beds, benches, chaises, tables, and lamps are created in materials such as bronze, steel, and copper, sometimes treated with muratic acid to add shades of turquoise or rusty red. Actress Joanne Woodward bought Villa's Arc de Triomphe lamp for husband Paul Newma and a table supported by the Three Graces decorates a model apartment in New York's Trump Tower. ♦ M-Sa. 500 N Wells St (at W Illinois St). 923.0993

55 Pimlico Antiques Ltd. Here's a wonderland of 18th- and 19th-century furniture and accessories to discover, including china, porcelain, and exquisite mirrors. ♦ M-Sa. 500 N Wells St (at W Illinois St). 245.9199

56 Tiffany Stained Glass Stained-glass pieces in the Tiffany style, from windows to wisteria lamps, are this store's specialty, and they are made on site. Former mayor Jane Byrne came here for the city's official gift to Pope John Paul II during his 1979 visi and left with a small made-to-order window depicting the pontiff on one side and the

Chicago skyline on the other. ♦ M-F noon-5PM; Sa 10AM-3PM. 216 W Ohio St (between N Franklin and N Wells Sts). 642.0680

57 SportMart For decades, this was **Morrie Mages,** the world's largest sporting goods store. Its eight floors were stocked with everything for golf, tennis, hunting, skiing, camping, aerobics, scuba diving, safari hunts—you name it—most at a good discount. Purchased by **SportMart,** the selection remains extensive. On the outside of the building, a wall of fame displays concrete handprints of Chicago sports celebrities past and present, among them **Bears** running back Walter Payton, **Blackhawks** hockey star Bobby Hull, and **DePaul University Demons** basketball coach Ray Meyer. ♦ Daily 10AM-9PM; Su to 6PM. 620 N LaSalle St (at W Ontario St). 337.6151

58 River North Hotel $$ Part of the Best Western chain and one of the best bargains in the area, this hotel offers 358 modern rooms and suites, a rooftop sundeck, an enclosed swimming pool, and exercise equipment. There's a restaurant on site, free valet parking, and special weekend packages are available. ♦ 125 W Ohio St (at N LaSalle St). 467.0800, 800/727.0800; fax 467.1665 ♿

59 Red Head In its previous incarnations (first **Outtakes,** then **The Fish Head**) this club aimed to be supercool, with bouncers admitting only the hip. Changing times and an aging clientele have turned it into another kind of chic bar, this one with live reggae music Sundays. The owners have kept the amazing 900-gallon, 50-foot-long aquarium that was the former club's trademark. ♦ W-Su 5PM-2AM. 14 W Ontario St (at N State St). 640.1000

59 Embassy Suites Hotel $$ Part of a rapidly expanding national chain, this attractive hotel located three blocks off Michigan Avenue offers a lot for your money, including complimentary breakfast and cocktails. Each of the 358 suites has a kitchen with a wet bar and a well-lit dining/work table. ♦ 600 N State St (at W Ontario St). 943.3800, 800/EMBASSY; fax 943.7629 ♿

Within the Embassy Suites Hotel:

Pa'pagus ★$$ Another theme restaurant from Lettuce Entertain You Enterprises, this

time a Greek-style taverna serving Mediterranean food. A cozy sidewalk cafe is open during warm weather. ♦ Greek ♦ Daily lunch and dinner. 642.8450 ♿

60 R.H. Love Gallery Once an art history professor, R.H. Love now runs a gallery that offers a veritable education in American painting and drawing. Housed in the historic **Samuel M. Nickerson House,** the collection begins with 17th-century colonial portraits, segues into classics by such artists as Mary Cassatt and Grant Wood, and concludes with contemporary works by Kenneth Noland, Robert Goodnough, and many others.

The building itself is as notable as the artwork. One of the few surviving mansions from Chicago's Gilded Age, it was designed in 1883 by **Burling & Whitehouse** for Samuel Nickerson, a transplanted New Englander who made a fortune in distilleries before founding the First National Bank of Chicago. The sober facade belies an interior so lavish it is known as the "marble palace." When the house went up for sale after World War I and prospective single-family buyers for a 30-room mansion were scarce, Charles Osborne spearheaded a campaign to buy the house and donate it to the **American College of Surgeons,** from which Love acquired it for his gallery. ♦ M-Sa. 40 E Erie St (at N Wabash Ave). 640.1300 ♿

61 Lawry's—The Prime Rib ★$$$ A former McCormick mansion (so many relatives of reaper manufacturer Cyrus McCormick lived in this neighborhood at one time that it was known as McCormickville) provides a suitably ornate setting for prime rib, the only entrée on the dinner menu. It's served in the English tradition from a silver-domed platter, accompanied by salad, mashed potatoes, and Yorkshire pudding. The lunch menu has more variety. ♦ American ♦ M-F lunch and dinner; Sa-Su dinner. Reservations recommended. 100 E Ontario St (at N Rush St). 787.5000

62 Lenox House $$ This all-suites hotel in an older, renovated building is just one block from the expensive digs on Michigan Avenue. Though the decor is plain, each of the 330 suites is furnished with a fully equipped kitchen and wet bar. Amenities include a daily newspaper, in-room movies, and access to a local health club. Special rates for weekends and extended stays are available. ♦ 616 N Rush St (at E Ontario St). 337.1000, 800/44.LENOX; fax 337.7217 ♿

Within Lenox House:

Houston's ★$$ The diverse menu at this dark, clubby restaurant—big with the business lunch and after-work crowd—includes delicious spinach artichoke dip for chips, cobb salads, homemade soups, fresh fish filleted in-house daily, and hickory-grilled steaks. ♦ American ♦ M-Sa lunch and dinner. 649.1121 ♿

63 Medinah Temple This ersatz Middle
Eastern temple, designed in 1911 by **Huehl
& Schmid,** is ornately decorated with terra-
cotta, Moorish arched windows filled with
stained glass, detailed metal grillwork, and
rooftop domes. It was built for the Shriners,
who named it after one of the most sacred
ancient Muslim shrines in Saudi Arabia.
The interior is a large auditorium used for
Shriner conventions and for ice shows,
circuses, and high school graduations; for
decades, Democratic presidential nominees
held their election-eve rallies here. ♦ 600 N
Wabash Ave (at E Ohio St). 266.5000

64 Pizzeria Due ★$ The younger (but bigger)
sister restaurant of **Pizzeria Uno** down the
block is situated in a handsome brick, stone,
and wood-trimmed mansion, built in 1872.
The stucco-walled interior retains little of the
original splendor. ♦ Pizza ♦ Daily lunch and
dinner. 610 N Wabash Ave (between E Ohio
and E Ontario Sts). 943.2400. Pizzeria Uno:
29 E Ohio St (at N Wabash Ave). 321.1000

65 Bukara ★$$ This branch of a New Delhi
restaurant is elaborately outfitted: The waiters
wear native *pathani* uniforms, tapestries
hang on the walls, and sitar music plays in the
background. Some of the seating is in private
dining alcoves. Kabobs and seafood stand
out on the North Indian frontier menu, but the
extraordinary prix-fixe lunch buffet Mondays
through Fridays is the best bet. You can watch
meals being prepared through the kitchen's
glass wall. ♦ Indian ♦ Daily lunch and dinner.
2 E Ontario St (at N State St). 943.0188

66 Tree Studios Building Lawyer and
philanthropist Lambert Tree had this three-
story building constructed by the **Parfitt
Brothers** in 1894 to offer Chicago artists
a place to work instead of the garrets and
basements they could typically afford.
Arranged around a courtyard behind Tree's
home, the studios provided charming if
spartan workspace for 17 artists. Natural light
streamed through the large windows on State
Street, and huge doors between the studios
could be opened for parties and exhibitions.
The ground floor was divided into small
shops housing galleries and art-supply
stores. In 1912 and 1913, additions on
Ontario and Ohio Streets were designed
by **Hill & Woltersdorf.**

Among the first to work here were popular
painters Wellington Reynolds, Pauline Palmer,
and Frederick Freer. At one time or another
in the mid-1900s, most of Chicago's better-
known artists have lived here, including
painters Macena Barton, Rowena Fry, and
Natalie Henry, muralist Louis Grell, sculptor
John Breyn, and James Alan St. John, who
first drew Edgar Rice Burroughs's *Tarzan.* In
the 1940s, actor/artist Burgess Meredith and
other movie stars were tenants, but they threw
such wild parties that they were kicked out.

Artists still work and live in the studios,
including sculptor Claire Prussian and city-
sketcher Bill Olendorf.

Lambert Tree is long gone, and the Medinah
Temple Association, whose main building
stands on the site of his home, now owns
the Tree Studios Building. But Tree continue
to look on—in a way. Carved in stone on
either side of the Ohio Street entrance are th
faces of Tree and his wife, Ann, daughter of
Marshall Field (the first). Be sure to notice th
original details of the storefronts within the
Tree Studios Building. ♦ Private residences.
4 E Ohio St (at N State St)

Within the Tree Studios Building:

Accents Studio Proprietor Simone
Flynn presents limited edition jewelry and
accessories crafted by over 200 artists, 25
of whom are Chicagoans. Some of the more
notable pieces include whimsical hand-cut
sterling silver pieces by Anni & Co. and an
amazing range of vintage-looking pieces
by Roxanne Assoulin. There are even some
funky limited-edition backpacks. ♦ M-Sa.
611 N State St (at E Ohio St). 664.1311 ♿

Tree Studio The first art and antiques
store in the neighborhood opened in the
1950s and still specializes in 1920s to 1940s
Works Project Administration and regional
paintings, pottery, and furniture, largely from
the Midwest. Jim Romano, a Tree Studios
resident, painter, and author of the *Original
Mafia Cookbook,* runs the business with
partner Julie Watt. Vincent Price and Edward
G. Robinson used to shop here; Catherine
Deneuve still does. ♦ M-Sa. 613 N State St
(between E Ohio and E Ontario Sts). 337.75

67 515 North State Street The American
Medical Association is headquartered in
this 30-story building, designed in 1990 by
famed Japanese architect **Kenzo Tange** with
Chicago's **Shaw & Associates. Tange**'s first
major commission in the US, it is promoted
as a "crisp, pure statement of assertive form
precise finish, and refined materials." It is
also one of the few strong new statements
of Modernism in a city whose architects
have turned largely to historical allusion. The
elegant two-story lobby contains a sculpture
metal-and-glass stairway that provides an
intriguing spatial experience. A **Chicago
Atheneum** gallery in the lobby mounts
interesting exhibitions of architecture
and design. ♦ At W Grand Ave

68 Rock Bottom Brewery ★★$ This huge
new bar and restaurant offers sampler-sized
portions of their house-brewed beers and a

ales. Along with the brewmaster's suggestions is a hearty American grill menu featuring good burgers, ribs, chicken, fish, salads, and more. Other attractions include seven billiard tables, and a children's and late-night menu. But perhaps the biggest draw of all is the Mug Club, in which members can bring their own mugs and order brews at reduced prices; not surprisingly, there is a waiting list. ◆ American ◆ Daily lunch and dinner. 1 W Grand (at N State St). 755.9339 ♿

69 Zinfandel ★$$ This stylized and comfortable American restaurant has a great portobello mushroom sandwich (with barbecue sauce) and other inventive variations on American cuisine such as a smoked flank steak sandwich and coleslaw with spicy peanut and sesame dressing. A small grocery sells such goodies as garlic mustard and lemon pear butter. ◆ American ◆ M-F breakfast, lunch, and dinner; Sa brunch and dinner. 59 W Grand Ave (between N Dearborn and N Clark Sts). 527.1818

70 Blue Chicago on Clark During the 1950s, this part of Chicago was quite "blue"—full of pornographic bookstores and bars that ripped off unsuspecting tourists. Now it's a chic restaurant row, with some delightful shops nestled between eateries. Fitting, then, that this successful spin-off of the original **Blue Chicago** (a little farther north on State Street) should have settled here, too. Both clubs feature performances by top local and national blues acts, such as Johnny B. Moore and Willy Cat and the Japs. A single, inexpensive cover charge is good for both venues. ◆ Cover charge. M-Sa 8PM-2AM; shows start 9PM. 536 N Clark St (at W Grand Ave). 661.0100

71 Maggiano's ★$$ Another successful Lettuce Entertain You Enterprises venture, this airy *ristorante* serves good pastas, veal, and other regional Italian dishes. Spectacular sandwiches and fresh breads can be ordered from the attached bakery. ◆ Italian ◆ Daily lunch and dinner. 516 N Clark St (between W Illinois St and W Grand Ave). 644.7700 ♿

72 Gordon ★★★$$$ The slightly bizarre interior—murals of sensuous women sweep across the walls—adds a sense of the surreal to one of Chicago's best restaurants, a perfect spot for a high-powered business lunch or dinner or a romantic interlude for two. Insiders quip that owner Gordon Sinclair has a revolving door for chefs, and the quality of the food has gone up and down with the changes in the kitchen. But whoever is at the helm can be counted on for up-to-the-minute creations,

be they seared fish with pickled ginger and peppered cucumber, or such classics as a paillard of veal. And whatever happens, there'll always be the artichoke fritter béarnaise, a signature dish. Most entrées are available in half orders for half price plus $1. Express lunches are available at the bar. A prix-fixe pretheater dinner is available from 5:30PM to 6:30PM every night but Saturday, and there's a delightful brunch Sundays. A jazz piano and trio plays every evening; there's also a small dance floor. ◆ American ◆ M-F lunch and dinner; Sa-Su dinner. Reservations and jacket required. 500 N Clark St (at W Illinois St). 467.9780 ♿

73 Frontera Grill ★★★$$ Named by *Chicago* magazine

as one of the city's best, this colorful restaurant serves regional Mexican cuisine. Owners Deanna and Rick Bayless wrote a book, *Authentic Mexican Regional Cooking from the Heart of Mexico*, on the very topic. The ever-changing menu often includes the house specialty, *tacos al carbon*, chicken, duck, or skirt steak folded into a homemade tortilla. Mahimahi with two sauces and Yucatecan-style marinated venison in a spicy sauce of fresh tomatoes, *habañero* chilies, and sour orange juice are out of this world. Anything with a mole sauce is excellent. The adjoining **Topolobampo**, also owned by the Baylesses, shares a bar and waiting area. ◆ Mexican ◆ Tu-F lunch and dinner; Sa dinner. Reservations recommended. 445 N Clark St (between W Hubbard and W Illinois Sts). 661.1434

73 Topolobampo ★★★ $$$ Regional Mexican cooking gets even more refined—and more expensive—than at the wonderful **Frontera Grill** next door, both under the stewardship of the acclaimed Baylesses.

Appetizers include extraordinary tamales stuffed with smoked mussels, shredded game, or other ingredients. Among the entrées is Oaxacan-style chili-marinated capon breast steamed in banana and avocado leaves. The meals served here and next door come with freshly made tortillas, cactus, chayote, and regional renditions of beans and rice. ◆ Mexican ◆ Tu-F lunch and dinner; Sa dinner. Reservations recommended. 445 N Clark St (between W Hubbard and W Illinois Sts). 661.1434

74 Golden Triangle This shop stocks a wonderful selection of native crafts and art objects from the Golden Triangle—Burma,

Laos, and Northern Thailand's Chaing Mai region. Carved objects of teak and rainwood include charming spirit houses. Thai legend has it that if you set one on the corner of your property, making sure that no shadow is cast upon it by your house, the spirits will peacefully live outside instead of dropping in on you. ◆ M-Sa. 72 W Hubbard St (at N Clark St). 755.1266

75 Court House Place The first Cook County courthouse was demolished soon after being built, having been poorly designed and too small. This is the second courthouse, built in 1892 by **Otto Matz** and renovated into offices by **Solomon Cordwell Buenz & Associates** in 1986. The handsome Bedford limestone facade is enhanced by the cast-iron and copper-coated metalwork of the arched entrance. Beautiful metalwork carries through to the lobby staircases.

As a courthouse, the building has a colorful history. In 1897 sausage maker Adolph Leutgert was tried, convicted, and sentenced to life imprisonment for the murder of his wife after her wedding ring and a small fragment of bone were found in a vat at his sausage factory. In 1924 Nathan Leopold and Richard Loeb were tried and convicted here for killing a 13-year-old boy for fun, as depicted in Meyer Levin's novel *Compulsion*. Their defense attorney was Clarence Darrow, whose impassioned arguments against capital punishment won them life sentences rather than the death penalty. In the 1920s Carl Sandburg served a reporter apprenticeship here. Ben Hecht, co-author with Charles MacArthur of *The Front Page*, honed his court-reporting skills here during the same era. ◆ 54 W Hubbard St (at N Dearborn St)

76 Baton Show Lounge And now, for something completely different, outrageous female impersonators, so good that you'll forget they're men. The Las Vegas–style revue is emceed by Leslie, a.k.a. Diana Ross. Chili Pepper, the best known of the performers, creates a whole host of characters. Club owner Jim Flint sometimes dresses up too, and always thinks he's the best. About a third of the audience is gay. The rest are straight couples, tourists, and the occasional celebrity. ◆ Cover charge, two-drink minimum. W-Su. Reservations recommended. 436 N Clark St (at W Hubbard St). 644.5269

77 Mambo Grill ★★$$ North Shore native Roger Greenfield hasn't quite got the Lettuce Entertain You touch, but he is adventure-some. This place is an experience, from the attention-getting decor—spiky brass ornament, mauve marbleized walls, a ceiling emblazoned with names of foods in bold browns and maroons—to the pan-Latin menu. Try the Anaheim pepper stuffed with portobello mushrooms, served over black

bean salsa and topped with three types of cheese and a roasted tomatillo sauce. ◆ Latin American ◆ M-Sa lunch and dinner; Su dinner. 412 N Clark St (between W Kinzie and W Hubbard Sts). 467.9797

77 Sawbridge Studios Selling "furniture with a story," this place will entice even the most casual visitor to learn more. The hand-crafted pieces range from birdhouses and CD racks to dining room sets and sleigh beds, with magnificently smooth wooden cutting boards, quilts, pillows, and Arts and Crafts–style pottery. Among the craftspeople featured are Chicagoan Jeff Miller (contemporary) and Vermonters Charles Shackleton (Scottish and Irish styles) and the McGuire family (Shaker). Many of the larger pieces are pictured and described on sepia-toned cards that shoppers can take home. ◆ M-Sa. 406 N Clark St (between W Kinzie and W Hubbard Sts). 828.0055 &

77 Mare ★★$$$ Several restaurants have come and gone at this corner spot as the neighboring blocks switch from adult bookstores to upscale retailers and restaurants, but **Mare** seems destined to last while. The murals—a romantic view of Venice on one wall, and Poseidon and a mermaid on the ceiling—reinforce the theme: seafood, all regional Italian in origin. Grilled calamari and ravioli stuffed with mushroom and ricotta cheese are among the appealing offerings. Vegetarian dishes are also a specialty. Diners rave about this place. ◆ Italian ◆ M-F lunch and dinner; Sa dinner. 400 N Clark St (at W Kinzie St). 245.9933

77 Roman Marble Import Company Antique marble art pieces from around the world include a hundred Victorian and French fireplaces, among them a mantel from a Potter Palmer residence. ◆ M-F; Sa 10AM-2PM. 120 W Kinzie St (at N Clark St). 337.2217

TUCC✦✦ILAN™

78 Tucci Milan ★$$ The sleek, loftlike dining room looks to be of Milanese design, with abstract artwork, striking lighting fixtures, Italian newspapers hanging on a rack, and an eight-seat cappuccino/espresso bar near the entrance. Actually, though, it's another restaurant set by Lettuce Entertain You Enterprises. The menu is a sophisticated variation on the one at sister eatery **Tucci Benucch** on the Magnificient Mile. Thin-crust pizzas are blanketed with a variety of innovative toppings; pastas range from the traditional to the au courant; and risottos include shrimp, fennel, cucumber, chives, and basil. Herb-roasted chicken and grilled swordfish in sun-dried tomato sauce are among the numerous satisfying entrées. The moderate prices are the same at lunch and dinner. ♦ Italian ♦ M-Sa lunch and dinner; Su dinner. Reservations recommended. 6 W Hubbard St (at N State St). 222.0044 ♿

79 Courtyard By Marriott $$ A suburban hotel in the city is the best way to describe this establishment. King-size beds and large desks are offered in the 336 guest rooms. The **Courtyard Cafe** serves predictable breakfast, lunch, and dinner. You'd do better to eat at one of the many alternatives nearby. ♦ 30 E Hubbard St (at N State St). 329.2500, 800/321.2211; fax 329.0293 ♿

80 Chicago Sun-Times Building One of Chicago's major daily newspapers is written, edited, and printed right here beside the Chicago River in a 1957 building by **Naess & Murphy.** (It's supposed to resemble an ocean liner.) A free tour of the editorial department, composing room, and pressroom is conducted Tuesdays through Thursdays at 10:30AM. You may also walk unescorted through the first-floor hallway and watch the presses in action through a long glass partition Mondays through Fridays from 7AM to 6PM. Tour reservations required. ♦ 435 N Wabash Ave (at the Chicago River). 321.3251

81 IBM Building IBM's regional headquarters are housed in an elegantly proportioned 52-story slab designed by the office of **Mies van der Rohe** and **C.F. Murphy Associates** in 1971. It was **Mies**'s last office building. The curtain wall of aluminum and bronze-colored glass is the ultimate refinement of this architectural form, which first appeared in **Mies**'s apartment buildings at 860-880 Lake Shore Drive. Modernists can pay homage to the master in the high-ceilinged lobby, which contains a small bust of the architect by sculptor Marino Marini. The granite plaza turns a cold shoulder to the river and is so windy that ropes are often set up to keep pedestrians from being blown away. ♦ 330 N Wabash Ave (at W Kinzie St)

82 Andy's ★$$ One of the best and certainly the busiest of Chicago's jazz bars, for many years this was a grungy hangout where printers from the nearby daily newspapers convened at all hours. It retains an essence of crumminess with beat-up floors, dirty bathrooms, and the scent of stale beer and cigarette smoke. When Dick Goodman and Scott Chisholm bought it in the late 1970s, they started offering jazz—which is now played here about 80 hours a week. There are lunchtime sets Mondays through Fridays from noon to 2:30PM, music for the after-work crowd at 5PM, and a final set at 8:30PM. The huge roster of musicians is composed mostly of nationally known locals, among them the John Bany Trio with supreme sax

player Brad Goode, the Mike Smith Quintet, and Dr. Bop and the Headliners. A menu of pretty good pizza, steaks, burgers, and ribs is offered from lunch until midnight. ♦ American ♦ No cover for lunch sets; cover during evening. M-Sa 11AM-2AM; Su 6PM-midnight. 11 E Hubbard St (at N State St). 642.6805 ♿

Shaw's

82 Shaw's Crab House and Blue Crab Lounge ★★$$$ The atmosphere is lively, sometimes almost frenetic, at this New England–style seafood house and lounge, yet another successful offering from Lettuce Entertain You Enterprises. The **Crab House** serves more than 40 fish entrées, plus chicken and pasta. Everything is absolutely fresh; in fact, a staff biologist inspects the seafood for purity. This place is so popular, however, that even with a reservation, you may get fed faster by opting for the adjacent **Blue Crab Lounge.** Here, seated on high stools, you'll find a limited but nevertheless good list of raw-bar items and hot dishes, not to mention a fantastic thick chowder. The lounge also offers ethnic cuisine at seasonal events like the Scandinavian crawfish feast. ♦ Seafood ♦ M-Sa lunch and dinner; Su dinner. Reservations recommended. 21 E Hubbard St (between N Wabash Ave and N State St). 527.2722 ♿

83 Gold Coast Dogs ★$ Charbroiled hot dogs and cheese fries, among other items, are delivered by friendly servers who seem thrilled to meet you after all these years. Arguably the best fast-food joint in the city, it also serves eggs and such for breakfast. A long line forms at lunchtime. ♦ Fast food ♦ M-F breakfast, lunch, and dinner; Sa-Su lunch and dinner. 418 N State St (at W Hubbard St). 527.1222. Also at: 330 S Wells (at Van Buren St). 427.8161

Every day more vehicles pass over the Dan Ryan Expressway on Chicago's South Side than any other road in the world.

In 1983 Chicago gangster/ex-con Ken "Tokyo Joe" Eto survived an assassination attempt when three bullets bounced off his skull. When asked how he felt shortly afterward, he responded, "I have a headache."

Restaurants/Clubs: Red   **Hotels:** Blue
Shops/♥ Outdoors: Green   **Sights/Culture:** Black

84 Marina City Chicago's first "city-within-a-city" was designed in 1959 by **Bertrand Goldberg Associates** for 24-hour use, with residential, commercial, and recreational components. A base building housing a restaurant and marina provides a platform for a 10-story office building and twin towers with 40 stories of apartments above 20 levels of parking. The trapezoid-shaped apartments have walls that range from eight feet long at the core to 21 feet at the balcony. They have maintained their popularity, even though the retail and entertainment businesses have failed miserably and the entire complex is badly in need of maintenance. Nevertheless, the buildings are a marvel of reinforced concrete construction and the finest example of **Goldberg**'s organic architecture. ◆ 300 N State St (at the Chicago River)

85 Harry Caray's ★★$$$ The Flemish Gothic building designed by **Henry Ives Cobb** in 1895 was originally owned by the Chicago Varnish Company, which made glosses for railroad equipment, coaches, carriages, pianos, and furniture. Now it's a restaurant co-owned by legendary **Cubs** radio sportscaster Harry Caray, and it's filled with sports photos and memorabilia. The bar is 60.5 feet long—the distance between the pitcher's mound and home plate. Italian-American fare includes the big hit, chicken Vesuvio. Harry comes in several times a week during baseball season. When the **Cubs** are playing at **Wrigley Field,** the place stays open until midnight. ◆ Italian/American ◆ Daily lunch and dinner. 33 W Kinzie St (at N Dearborn St). 465.9269 ৬

86 Hotel Nikko $$$$ One of a global group of Japanese-owned luxury hotels, this sleek building is elegantly decorated in a combination of international styles, from Japanese gardens to contemporary American art. Most of its 425 guest rooms, which include 26 suites, have spectacular views of the city and the Chicago River. Amenities include mini-bars, complimentary coffee with your morning wake-up call, 24-hour room service, a cardiovascular fitness center, and business support services. A huge lobby bar caters to jet-lagged travelers by offering piano music and drinks 24 hours a day. Special rates, as well as luxury packages, are available Friday and Saturday nights. ◆ 320 N Dearborn St (at the Chicago River). 744.1900, 800/645.5687; fax 527.2650 ৬

Within the Hotel Nikko:

ΓELEBRITY
(A F E

Celebrity Cafe ★★$$$ Overlooking the Chicago River, this glamorous dining spot is big for weekday power breakfasts and lunches. Dinner is romantic, with candles flickering on the tables and city lights twinkling outside the windows. Chef Jean-Pierre Henry prepares dinner entrées that include grilled veal medallions with corn cakes and herbed artichoke bottoms, and chicken breast sautéed with lemon and oregano, served with gnocchi and tomato coulis. Lunch includes similar dishes, as well as salads and soups. The attractive curved bar is a good spot for cocktails. ◆ International ◆ Daily breakfast, lunch, and dinner. Reservations recommended. 836.5499 ৬

Marina City

Benkay ★★$$$$ Chicago's food critics have singled out meals in the tatami rooms here, served by waitresses in traditional costume, as a gastronomical high point. Treat yourself to a traditional *kaiseki* prix-fixe dinner here, a seemingly never-ending stream of exquisite sushi, tempura, salads, soups, and stews. Cold country sakes accompany the meal and rich-flavored green tea concludes it. For adventurous early birds, a traditional Japanese breakfast, including a porridge of stewed sardine and salmon roe, is available. Be sure to ask for a room with a river view. ♦ Japanese ♦ Tu-F breakfast, lunch, and dinner; Sa-Su dinner. Reservations recommended. 836.5490 ᕕ

87 Sorriso $ Big with the after-work crowd, this friendly restaurant and bar is located a flight down from street level in the Quaker Building, yet offers a spectacular river view. The menu features Italian-style antipasti, soups, salads, and pizza. Complimentary appetizers come with cocktails. ♦ Italian ♦ M-F lunch and dinner; Sa dinner. 321 N Clark St (at the Chicago River). 644.0283 ᕕ

88 City of Chicago Central Office Building Designed in 1914 by **George C. Nimmons** as a food-processing factory for Reid, Murdoch & Company, this is now a paper-processing warren of city offices. The 320-foot-long facade rises eight stories above the river (12 stories at the clock tower), combining the horizontal emphasis of the Prairie School with the large windows and expressed structure of the Chicago School. The brick and terra-cotta detailing merits a close look. ♦ 320 N Clark St (at the Chicago River)

89 Asian House The city's largest selection of Asian housewares, among them rosewood furniture, coromandel screens, hand-painted furniture, hand-crafted brass lamps, and porcelain vases from the People's Republic of China, is offered here. ♦ M-Sa. 159 W Kinzie St (between N LaSalle and N Wells Sts). 527.4848

89 Jay Robert's Antique Warehouse Three floors and 54,000 square feet are filled with antique furniture, including rows of armoires, sideboards, buffets, desks, and even marble and wooden fireplaces. Items come from every period—from Chippendale to French Empire, country pine to Art Nouveau. And everything is in beautiful condition and reasonably priced. ♦ M-Sa. 149 W Kinzie St (between N LaSalle and N Wells Sts). 222.0167 ᕕ

90 Kinzie Street Chophouse ★★$$ An unusual selection of Mediterranean-style entrées, including herb-crusted salmon, steaks, and smoked mozzarella and chicken ravioli, are on the menu at this bright, friendly bistro. ♦ Continental ♦ M-Sa lunch and dinner; Su dinner. 400 N Wells St (at W Kinzie St). 822.0191

91 Merchandise Mart Built by Marshall Field in 1931 to house wholesale offices and showrooms, this behemoth's total floor area of four million square feet makes up the second-largest building in the US (only the Pentagon is bigger). The **Mart**'s thousands of showrooms display home and office furnishings, business products, and giftware, employing about 9,000 people and drawing 10,000 visitors every day (the showrooms are open only to the trade; i.e., architects and designers). It even has its own elevated train station on the **Ravenswood** line. Like many grandiose projects conceived in the Roaring Twenties, the building hit hard times soon after it opened, and Field sold it to Joseph P. Kennedy for a fraction of its worth; the Kennedys still own it today. The building underwent a 1986-91 renovation by **Graham, Anderson, Probst & White**, and a 1991 project by **Beyer Blinder Belle** converted the first two floors into a retail mall with 85 shops and restaurants. These include mostly chain stores such as **Coconuts Records, The Limited, Crabtree & Evelyn, Coach,** and other specialty shops. ♦ M-Sa. Between N Wells and N Orleans Sts (at the Chicago River. 527.4141 ᕕ

92 Chicago Apparel Center The **Mart**'s sister building, designed by **Skidmore, Owings & Merrill** in 1977, is connected to it by a bridge by **Helmut Jahn** that reflects the **Mart**'s design. More than 8,000 lines of women's, children's, and men's clothing and accessories from around the world are represented here. Showrooms are closed to the public. If you act as if you know where you're going, however, you might be able to saunter upstairs. Once there, you may *discreetly* ask if they sell any samples. Some shops will, some won't. ♦ M-F. 350 N Orleans St (off W Kinzie St). 527.7600 ᕕ

Within the Chicago Apparel Center:

Holiday Inn Mart Plaza $$$ Taking up the top floors (16 through 23) of the **Apparel Center**, this hotel offers fantastic city views. The 525 rooms are modernly decorated, and amenities include an indoor swimming pool and exercise facilities. A couple of restaurants and bars are on the premises, but you'll do better to go out. ♦ 836.5000, 800/HOLIDAY; fax 222.9508 ♿

93 California Pizza Kitchen ★$ The super-thin crust and imaginative toppings on the pizzas served at this popular cafe offer a welcome contrast to heavy, deep-dish, Chicago-style pizza. This is a pleasant spot for a leisurely lunch or a light late-night snack. ♦ Pizza ♦ Daily lunch and dinner. 414 N Orleans St (at W Hubbard St). 222.9030. Also at: Water Tower Place (835 N Michigan Ave, between E Pearson and E Chestnut Sts). 787.7300 ♿

93 Klay Oven ★★$$$ If Indian cuisine is your idea of ambrosia, you can find eternal happiness here. You'll also pay a stiff price. For starters, the *samosas* (fried pastries stuffed with potatoes and peas) are heavenly. Main courses include tandoori tiger prawns, perfectly seasoned lamb dishes, and quail. You'll be "sari" if you don't sample some of the chutneys. ♦ Indian ♦ Daily lunch and dinner. 414 N Orleans St (at W Hubbard St). 527.3999 ♿

94 East Bank Club Chicago's beautiful people come here to sweat. You need to know a member to gain admittance, but your hotel concierge might be of assistance. It's worth a try just to see the 450,000-square-foot, four-floor health club, with an indoor and outdoor swimming pool (the one outside has a two-acre poolside deck with a cafe and bar), giant aerobics and exercise equipment areas, 21 racket-sports courts, two indoor running tracks, an indoor driving range, and a white-linens restaurant. ♦ Daily. 500 N Kingsbury St (at W Illinois St). 527.5800

95 Kinzie Street Bridge Until April 1992, this was just another bridge across the north branch of the Chicago River—then it took on a historical significance equal to Mrs. O'Leary's cow. It was at this site that newly installed but faulty pilings caused a freight tunnel to collapse, causing the flood that ranks alongside the Great Fire in the history of city disasters. ♦ W Kinzie St (between N Kingsbury and N Canal Sts)

96 Shelter A few years ago, this was *the* place to be; now the rest of us can get in without waiting interminably. A steady stream of hipsters in black leather, spandex, and lace work out their dance fever in the industrial-strength, two-story, 30,000-square-foot club. The main dance floor upstairs has a booming 20,000-watt sound system and giant speaker platforms atop which club dancers strut their stuff. The conversation parlors are plump with overstuffed couches. A wall behind the bar glows with a superb collection of lava lamps. Progressive music jumps from rock to funk to rap, and the crowd is young, beautiful, and sprinkled with Chicago celebrities. Forgo jeans and sneakers if you want to pass the

intermittently enforced dress code at the doo ♦ Cover charge. Th-Sa 9:30PM-4AM. 564 W Fulton St (at N Jefferson St). 648.5500

97 Como Inn $$ Established in 1924, this restaurant is a generation-after-generation tradition for many Chicagoans, even though the fare is only fair. It's a sight to behold—a city block of room after room, all whimsically decorated in different styles, from an ornate 19th-century Florentine library to the Napoli Room, embellished with silk flowers and vines. As for the menu, pasta is the best choice. ♦ Italian ♦ Daily lunch and dinner. Reservations recommended. 546 N Milwaukee Ave (at W Grand Ave). 421.5222

98 Randolph Street Gallery Formed in 1979, in 1982 this cooperative gallery became the first to move to River West. They commission and present works by local and national artists, often in collaboration with other arts groups. Frequent musical performances are held weekends. ♦ Tu-Sa noon-6PM. 756 N Milwaukee Ave (at W Huron St). 666.7737

99 Ka-Boom! Opened in July 1991, this once cool hangout is aging by the usual dance club lifespan standard—but not gracefully. Glitzy and costly, it has five drinking and dancing areas, from the Billiard Room to the Kabaret to the VIP Room, where would-be-hip types cruise the bar hoping to attract scarce model types. ♦ Cover charge. M-Sa 9PM-4AM. 747 N Green St (at W Chicago Ave). 243.8600

100 Artemisia The often controversial women's cooperative gallery (named for Artemisia Gentileschi, an influential 16th-century Italian Renaissance painter) shows its members' works, as well as those of emerging and alternative artists. ♦ Tu-Sa. 700 N Carpenter St (off N Milwaukee Ave). 226.7323 ♿

101 Cortland-Leyten Gallery The focus is ethnographic and folk art of the Americas and Asia, including such exhibits as *Philippine Folk Art: Tribal and Colonial Expressions*, featuring items crafted in wood, textile, fiber, and metal. Contemporary art from North and South America is also on view. ♦ Sa noon-5PM, or by appointment. 815 N Milwaukee Ave (at W Chicago Ave). 733.2781

Bests

Roberta Lieberman
Art dealer, Zolla/Lieberman Gallery

If you don't mind the wind that sweeps in from Lake Michigan, my Chicago neighborhood—Streeterville—is a great place for walking.

If you are a jogger or cyclist you can run or ride for uninterrupted miles along the lake from the Museum of Science and Industry on the South Side to Hollywood Avenue on the north. If you're not, walk along Lake Shore Drive from Oak Street to North Avenue and admire the magnificent late–19th-century and early–20th-century apartment buildings.

If you're a shopper head south on Michigan Avenue (aka the Magnificent Mile), taking a detour down Oak Street for the boutiques, and don't stop till you reach Ohio Street. In the meantime you will have passed three formidable vertical malls—900 Michigan Avenue, Water Tower Place, and Chicago Place—not to mention almost every major department store of the Western world.

But should your fancy be culture, you can also walk to the Museum of Contemporary Art, the Art Institute, the Chicago Symphony Orchestra, the Lyric Opera, and (best of all) the multitude of galleries located in the River North district.

Michael Kutza
Director, Chicago International Film Festival

The Margarita: The perfect drink for a good time. It can only be found at ONE place! Frontera Grill on Clark Street. Problem is you can't get in the place. Two-hour waits and all that stuff, but find a way. The food is OK, too spicy for me.

Classiest Joint: If you want to impress, with quality food and service it's still Gordon . . . worth the money and your time. Besides, he's a friend of mine, so I can always get a table.

Blues & Jazz: All over town, but I hate the stuff, so can't help! Sorry. Ask your hotel or a taxi driver.

Architecture: We have the best design in the world, by all the great guys, see it from a boat! Yes, the best way to cover all of our new and classic architecture is while seated in a guided Chicago River boat tour. Check tour boat schedules, they go every few hours, weather permitting.

Fun & Food: Oo-La-La . . . The wildest restaurant you'll find in town. A little gay, a little too many models (all sexes), always beautiful people and food. Hard to get in but ask for Philip, he will find a way.

Drive along the Lake Shore: You may think you're in Rio, but it is Chicago. Miles of perfect beaches edge the city; wade in, walk along, watch the sun come up. . . or go down (you'll have to look the other direction for that!). Start at 22nd Street and drive north to Foster Avenue . . . all along Lake Shore Drive.

Sushi: I hang out at Kamehachi Sushi on Wells Street. Cute, fresh, friendly, and cheap, open very late, too.

Sports: All over the place! The Bulls, Da Bears, The Cubs. . . we got 'em. Try and find a ticket!

Theater: Lots of offbeat, off Broadway (if you will), it's all very good, very original, very Chicago. See it here before it goes on to fame and fortune . . . and Broadway! Steppenwolf Theatre is NUMBER ONE; Goodman Theatre and Second City should also be considered.

Shopping: The specialty shops are worth a look—Ultimo on Oak Street is an original; ask for Joan, she owns the place. 900 North Michigan Avenue is a mall with style. I don't know if you need any of the stuff, but you want to see this place.

Hotels: We've got 'em. I love the Swiss Grand Hotel! Fabulous rooms, all glass walls, and wrap-around views. Super health club on the roof too. The rich expense-account crowd (do they still exist?) love the Four Seasons . . . posh, costly, all the best of the best . . . but if you've done one, you've done them all. Still, if this is it for you, this is it. How about a small European hotel? Try the Claridge on North Dearborn; ask for Mike, he'll get you in.

The Chicago Theater: This is something special, very Chicago. The movie palace restored. A MUST SEE. Of course there has to be a play on stage for you to get in, same goes for the Auditorium Theatre—here's an architecture masterpiece of another kind. Perfect acoustics, grand style, turn of the century. Nowhere else but in Chicago will you see such grandness. . . and there are backstage tours for both.

Pizza: For some reason Chicago and pizza go hand in hand! I don't get it, but I do like a few pizzas in town. Forget that deep-dish thing that made us famous, you can get that back home FROZEN. Go to Scoozi and order the thin-crust Margherita with basil/cheese; it's fabulous. Or try Leona's and order thin–wheat-crust anything; even more fabulous!!

Ribs: How do you feel about barbecue baby back ribs? It's like pizza, we seem to be famous for them. Best is Carson's—The Place For Ribs. They have locations all over town and their coleslaw is also terrific.

Asian Treats: Yoshi, from Tokyo, runs a "hands-on" favorite dining spot in Chicago. It is a rare combination of service, style, flavors, and comfort. French cooking with all the simplicity of a fine Japanese sushi spot.

Buddy Guy
Musician

My club, Buddy Guy's Legends, where I can hear great blues seven nights a week, meet and greet my friends and fans from around the world when I am not on tour.

Love the city skyline from the Observatory, and the new Navy Pier; trying to catch a White Sox or Bulls game; picking up a Maxwell Street–style Polish sausage; driving through one of the many forest preserves; and, like almost everyone else, marveling at the politics of this great city.

Gold Coast

Century-old stone mansions rub shoulders with contemporary high-rises in the class-conscious Gold Coast community, bordered by **Chicago Avenue**, **North Avenue**, **Lake Michigan**, and **Rush** and **LaSalle Streets**. Chicago's power brokers live here: captains of commerce, the high-society set, even the city's Roman Catholic archbishop, not to mention ambitious up-and-comers who can toss off the steep rents. Highlights include the architecturally and historically significant **Astor Street District** and the striking swath of luxury

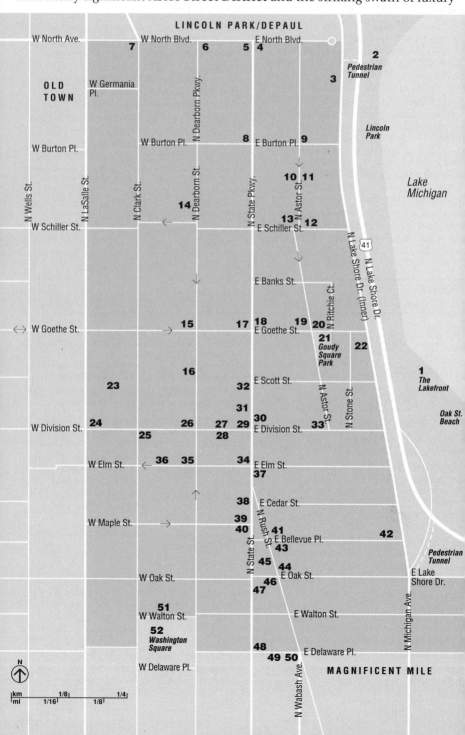

LINCOLN PARK/DEPAUL

W North Ave.

W North Blvd.

E North Blvd.

OLD TOWN

W Germania Pl.

Pedestrian Tunnel

Lincoln Park

W Burton Pl.

W Burton Pl.

E Burton Pl.

N Dearborn Pkwy.

Lake Michigan

N Wells St.

N LaSalle St.

N Clark St.

N Dearborn St.

N State Pkwy.

N Astor St.

W Schiller St.

E Schiller St.

N Lake Shore Dr. (Inner)

N Lake Shore Dr.

E Banks St.

N Ritchie Ct.

W Goethe St.

E Goethe St.

Goudy Square Park

The Lakefront

E Scott St.

N Astor St.

N Stone St.

Oak St. Beach

W Division St.

E Division St.

W Elm St.

E Elm St.

E Cedar St.

W Maple St.

N Rush St.

N State St.

E Bellevue Pl.

Pedestrian Tunnel

E Lake Shore Dr.

W Oak St.

E Oak St.

N Michigan Ave.

W Walton St.

E Walton St.

Washington Square

W Delaware Pl.

N Wabash Ave.

E Delaware Pl.

MAGNIFICENT MILE

N

km 1/8 1/4
mi 1/16 1/8

partments along **Lake Shore Drive.** A bit inland, first-class dining and famous Old World hotels, such as the **Omni Ambassador East,** cater to epicurean tastes, while the infamous Rush Street bar scene draws late-night throngs.

The Gold Coast was born in 1882, when entrepreneur Potter Palmer filled in a frog pond on Lake Shore Drive and put up a quarter-million-dollar "mansion to end all mansions," constructed under the direction of architects **Henry Ives Cobb** and **Charles Sumner Frost.** (In 1950 "Palmer's Castle," as it was called, was demolished and replaced by a high-rise apartment building at 1350 North Lake Shore Drive.) Other opulent homes followed. "On the shore the mansions of the millionaires form an uninterrupted line of sumptuous dwellings," wrote a visitor to the community in 1905. "They are of different sizes and styles. . . all are attempts to create something impressive." Among them was the Roman Catholic archbishop's residence, built in 1885 on a spacious plot of land on North Avenue. Soon after, the archdiocese sold some of its nearby landholdings and neighboring houses were built, but the original residence continues to serve as home to Chicago's leading Catholic. Aristocratic dwellings, including town houses in Queen Anne, Romanesque Revival, and Georgian Revival styles, appeared along the side streets, most prominently on **Astor Street** and **Dearborn Parkway.**

Between 1895 and 1930, deluxe apartment buildings sprang up in the area, many of them elegant and ornate designs by architect **Benjamin Marshall.** During the Depression and World War II, construction slowed and the original housing began to deteriorate; many opulent homes were converted to apartments. Construction began anew in the 1960s and 1970s, but most of the more recent structures do not begin to approach the magnificence of their predecessors. Thankfully, many of the wonderful older buildings remain. The Astor Street District alone has about 300 buildings listed on the National Register of Historic Places. A walk along this or another of the quaint, tree-lined streets in the community is truly a pleasure.

Rush Street, in the neighborhood's midsection, is a different world altogether. In a tradition dating back to the 1920s, Rush Street is endowed with more restaurants and nightclubs per square foot than any other part of the city. For some time, it was an enclave of B-movie houses and adult bookstores. In the 1960s Chicago's raucous singles bar scene was born at **Butch McGuire's on Division Street,** just north of Rush Street. Hence, the term "Rush Street" today actually designates Rush and Division Streets combined, a nightly cacophony of merrymaking as local and out-of-town visitors descend to eat, drink, and dance the night away. It's such a mob scene on Friday and Saturday nights that the Chicago Police Department closes Division Street to automobile traffic to accommodate the hordes.

---

1 Lakefront Unlike other North Side neighborhoods, the Gold Coast possesses little in the way of a park along the lake, except for one tiny patch of green with a gazebo across from the Magnificent Mile's **Drake Hotel.** Otherwise, the lake here is fronted by concrete pathways and rocks—not all bad, since it makes for a great place to walk, run, or ride a bicycle. And what the area lacks in grass, it makes up for in sand, with the glorious **Oak Street Beach,** *the* beach for Chicago's young and beautiful to see and be seen. Bronze-skinned volleyball players, perfect-10 models, all-American Frisbee-tossing frat brothers and sorority sisters, jet-setting flight attendants, plus ordinary folks from the neighborhood and voyeurs from all over—they all blanket the sands weekend after steamy summer weekend. ♦ Pedestrian access via underpass across from the Drake Hotel (N Michigan Ave and E Lake Shore Dr/E Oak St). Another passageway is near E North Blvd and N Lake Shore Dr. By car, take the LaSalle Dr exit off Lake Shore Dr, park in the lot near E North Blvd, then walk south

2 Chess Pavilion On the lake at the northern end of the Gold Coast, this concrete structure with built-in chessboards attracts a mixed crowd of serious and not-so-serious chess players. If you're interested in playing, bring your own chess pieces, and introduce yourself to an opponent. The view of the city from this vantage point is spectacular. ♦ Lakefront (just south of E North Blvd)

3 **International Museum of Surgical Science** This 1918 building designed by **Howard Van Doren Shaw** and its neighbors at 1516 and 1530 North Lake Shore Drive are all Chicago landmarks. A sculpture on the front lawn by French artist Edouard Chaissing entitled *Hope and Help* portrays a heroic physician propping up his sickly patient. Inside, 32 rooms of displays depict the history of surgery in a degree of detail both gruesome and fascinating, including such early methods as trephining (drilling through the skull to release evil spirits), bloodletting by leech, wound-licking by serpent, cauterization with hot irons and boiling oil, bone-crushing orthopedic procedures, early caesarean sections, plus amputations, gallstone operations, and plastic surgery. You name it, they've got it, in exhibitions that incorporate vivid paintings, early medical textbooks, and actual pieces of surgical equipment. Thankfully for the queasy, exhibits also feature anesthesia, pharmaceuticals, X-rays, laser surgery, and other modern techniques. ♦ Donation requested. Tu-Su. Tours available by advance reservation. 1524 N Lake Shore Dr (between E Burton Pl and E North Blvd). 642.6502

4 **1555 North State Parkway** The private residence of the Roman Catholic Archbishop of Chicago is the oldest structure still standing in the Astor Street District. It was constructed in 1880 according to the design of **Alfred F. Pashley** on spacious grounds, before the surrounding area began to be developed. The 2.5-story Queen Anne–style building is constructed of redbrick with limestone trim and elaborate brick- and ironwork. Its steeply pitched roofs, numerous gables, and dormers are topped by 19 elaborate chimneys. The building, surrounded by beautifully landscaped grounds, is probably the largest and best preserved in the area. ♦ At E North Blvd

5 **1550 North State Parkway** When it was completed in 1912, this **Marshall & Fox** structure was the city's most luxurious apartment building. It's still one of the most gracious. On the north side, overlooking the park, used to be a hundred-footlong suite of public rooms: a grand salon with a gracefully curving bay, petit salon, a dining room, and an orangery. The apartments each had 15 rooms occupying an entire floor. Bedrooms were arranged along the east side, with views of the lake, and the kitchen and service areas were tucked into the southwest corner. The building has since been subdivided into smaller apartments. ♦ At W North Blvd

6 **Latin School of Chicago** Housing one of the city's finest and most expensive progressive schools, with a high-school student body of about 400, this five-story brick building has an Olympic-size swimming pool, a full-service cafeteria with an outdoor terrace, and art studios and a botanical garden soaking up sunlight on the top floor. Lower grades are taught at a separate building down the block at 1531 North Dearborn Parkway. There, nannies line the sidewalks every afternoon to pick up their young charges. ♦ 59 W North Blvd (at N Dearborn Pkwy).

6 **1547 North Dearborn Parkway** Built in 1892, this Richardsonian town house (still a private residence) was originally the **Jacob Rehm House.** Rehm was a successful brewer who became Chicago's chief of police in the mid-1880s. He was instrumental in the creation of **Lincoln Park** and was one of the Chicago Park District's early commissioners. ♦ At W North Blvd

7 **Village Theater** This is one of the last movie theaters in town whose wide screen has not been subdivided into two or three microscopic-size ones. Unfortunately, it's also one of the noisiest. Movies are close to first-run, and ticket prices are low, low, low. ♦ 1548 N Clark St (at W North Ave). 642.2403

8 **Madlener House** Designed by **Richard E. Schmidt** and **Hugh M.G. Garden** in 1902 and renovated by **Brenner, Danforth & Rockwell** in 1963, this architectural landmark (pictured above) is a simple, almost severe, cubical building that shows influences of the Arts and Crafts and Prairie School movements. **Garden** designed the Sullivanesque ornament around the doorway. The Graham Foundation for

Restaurants/Clubs: Red   Hotels: Blue
Shops/ ♥ Outdoors: Green   Sights/Culture: Black

Advanced Studies in the Fine Arts restored the house and uses it for offices, lectures, and a small display area. In the courtyard is a sculpture garden of architectural fragments. ♦ M-Th by appointment. 4 W Burton Pl (at N State Pkwy). 787.4071

9 Patterson-McCormick Mansion This 1892 Georgian Revival palazzo by **McKim, Mead & White** was commissioned by Joseph Medill, former Chicago mayor and editor and part owner of the *Chicago Tribune,* as a gift to his daughter, Mrs. Robert Patterson. The house was the setting for many lavish society gatherings, and hosted kings and queens. It set new standards architecturally as well as socially: New York architect **Stanford White**'s meticulous Georgian design sounded the death knell for the picturesque Queen Anne and Romanesque Revival styles in favor of symmetrical, Classical facades. When the industrialist Cyrus McCormick II bought the house in 1927, he commissioned an addition by **David Adler** that doubled its size. A rehabilitation and conversion was completed in 1979 by **Nagle Hartray & Associates** with restoration architect **Wilbert R. Hasbrouck.** It's now been divided into condominiums. ♦ 20 E Burton Pl (at N Astor St)

10 1444 North Astor Street A superb example of an Art Deco town house, this 1929 building was designed for Edward P. Russell by the firm **Holabird & Root,** architects of the **Board of Trade** and **919 North Michigan Avenue.** The sleek facade is of smooth limestone trimmed in highly polished black granite. A slightly projecting three-story curve of black iron creates a stylized bay for the upper floors. The house remains a private residence. ♦ Between E Schiller St and E Burton Pl

10 1406 North Astor Street Built in 1922 for Joseph T. Ryerson Jr. of the Ryerson Steel family and for many years chairman of the board of Inland Steel, this home was designed by the prominent society architect **David Adler** in the formal style of Parisian boulevard houses of the Second Empire. The elegant facade is symmetrical (including chimneys at *both* ends of the house) and features rustication at the base and corners; tall, narrow windows on the second and third floors; a mansard roof with dormers; and delicate iron balconies. An interesting later addition to this private residence is visible only from a distance—a two-story rooftop pavilion capped by a steep slate roof. ♦ Between E Schiller St and E Burton Pl

11 1451 North Astor Street Built for Peter Fortune, who with his brothers ran the Fortune Brothers Brewing Company, this 1912 building is another by **Howard Van Doren Shaw.** Shaw designed several of the houses on Astor Street, including the Georgian Revival **Goodman House** at **No. 1355.** This is one of his most fanciful designs, an eclectic

English Tudor brick-and-limestone house with elaborate carving above the front door. It was renovated in 1989 by **Marvin Herman & Associates** and remains a private residence. ♦ Between E Schiller St and E Burton Pl

11 1447 North Astor Street Built for jeweler C.D. Peacock circa 1903, this is now the headquarters of the Junior League of Chicago. The severe facade is enlivened by geometric brickwork at the top story. ♦ Between E Schiller St and E Burton Pl

11 1443 North Astor Street The **H.N. May House** is a good example of the Richardsonian Romanesque style that became popular in the late 1880s. The rock-faced granite facade has deep-set windows, a prominent gable, and an arched entrance. The rough wall contrasts wonderfully with the smooth carving of the third-floor window lintels and columns and the first-floor entry arch with carved panels. Completed in 1891, the design is by **Joseph Lyman Silsbee,** an early employer of **Frank Lloyd Wright.** The house is still a private residence. ♦ Between E Schiller St and E Burton Pl

Courtesy of Marvin Herman & Associates

11 1425 North Astor Street Originally this was the home of William D. Kerfoot, a prominent realtor best remembered in Chicago as the man who, just two days after the Great Fire of 1871, erected the first business structure in the burned district. The Georgian Revival residence (pictured above) was built in 1895 and is plain except for the pair of small arched windows under an elaborate pediment on the second floor. In 1990 it was renovated by **Marvin Herman & Associates;** it's a private residence. ♦ Between E Schiller St and E Burton Pl

11 1421 North Astor Street A Romanesque Revival house of rusticated sandstone, this was built for lumber dealer George Farnsworth in 1889 (it's still privately owned). Notice how the glass in the windows curves to fit the bay. The entrance is on the south through an elegant iron-and-glass porch. ♦ Between E Schiller St and E Burton Pl

Cycling in Chicago

When the weather is fine there's no better way to enjoy the day than biking along the scenic lakefront path, with glittering highrises and green parks on one side of you and windswept **Lake Michigan** on the other. This 20-milelong blacktop trail runs parallel to **Lake Shore Drive,** stretching all the way from **Foster Avenue** in the north to **71st Street** in the south. Created and maintained by the parks department, the trail is a favorite place for Chicagoans to take in the great outdoors; in addition to cyclists, you'll find rollerbladers, dog walkers, joggers, and people out for an old-fashioned stroll.

The trail's most interesting and widely used section is from **Belmont** to **16th Street.** (South of 16th Street, it's wise to ride with a companion for safety purposes). This stretch of trail skirts the edges of the **Lincoln Park, Gold Coast,** and **Magnificent Mile** neigborhoods, offering the visitor a great way to see the sights. Many of Chicago's top attractions—including the **Adler Planetarium, Field Museum, Shedd Aquarium, Grant Park, Burnham Harbor, Buckingham Fountain, Lincoln Park Zoo,** and **Navy Pier**— are accessible from this section of the bike path. If that sounds too ambitious, pack a picnic and head for **Oak Street** or **Fullerton** beach.

12 Charnley House This three-story, seven-room house built for James Charnley was designed in 1892 by **Adler & Sullivan,** who apparently gave this commission to their 25-year-old chief draftsman, **Frank Lloyd Wright.** Although the house's blocky mass is unlike that of later Prairie School homes, it makes the most of the confining site. The client requested grand spaces, so more than half of the interior space is devoted to a central skylit stairwell. The intricate copper cornice and the balcony with its Sullivanesque design are the only significant ornamentation. Unlike the other houses on the street, this private home was not a re-creation of architecture from days past; it looked ahead to the 20th century. A restoration was completed in 1988 by **Skidmore, Owings & Merrill.** ♦ 1365 N Astor St (at E Schiller St)

12 1355 North Astor Street This large-scale Georgian mansion (still privately owned) was designed in 1914 by **Howard Van Doren Shaw** for lumberman William C. Goodman, who lived in it only briefly. **Shaw** also designed the Loop's **Goodman Theatre**—donated by Goodman in honor of his deceased playwright son—and the family mausoleum at Graceland Cemetery. ♦ At E Schiller St

12 1349 North Astor Street The facade of this circa-1880 building, which was remodeled by **Howard Van Doren Shaw** in 1920, makes an interesting contrast with his earlier work next door at **No. 1355.** This is a much less literal interpretation of the Georgian style, with elegant proportions but without applied ornament—an almost Modernist treatment. This private residence is often called the Court of the Golden Hands, after the detailing over the entrance. A 1990 renovation was drafted by **Michael Lustig & Associates.** ♦ At E Schiller St

13 38-50 East Schiller Street A series of seven row houses (all still privately owned) built in 1885 mixes Queen Anne, Romanesque Revival, and other influences. **No. 38** is faced with pale green stone and trimmed in red sandstone for an unusual polychrome effect. ♦ At N Astor St

13 36 East Schiller Street This 1894 house was built for Carter Henry Harrison Jr. who served five terms as Chicago's mayor (1897-1905, 1911-15). His father had also served five terms as mayor, four of them consecutive, but was murdered by a crazed rival during the **1893 World's Columbian Exposition.** William Wrigley Jr. was the second owner of this house; it remains a private residence. ♦ At N Astor St

14 St. Chrysostom's Church An English Gothic church built in 1894 by **Clinton J. Warren** for the neighborhood's elite Episcopal congregation, this structure underwent a major face-lift in 1923 and 1924, courtesy of consulting architects **Walcott, Bennett, Parsons & Frost.** An adjoining building was removed, and others were incorporated into the complex. In 1926 the American Institute of Architects awarded the church a gold medal for design. The altar and sanctuary were designed by **David Adler.** The resounding 43-bell carillon, manufactured in Croydon, England, was donated by steel manufacturer Charles R. Crane. ♦ 1424 N Dearborn St (between W Schiller St and W Burton Pl). 944.1083

15 Three Arts Club Designed in 1914 by **Holabird & Roche,** this club was founded by Gwetholyn Jones and friends—among them Jane Addams and Mrs. Ogden Armour (wife of the meatpacking giant)—to provide shelter in the "wicked city" to young women who were studying any of the three arts (painting, drama, or music) at such places as the **School of the Art Institute.** In today's more liberated climate, men are allowed in the summer, when tour groups often find shelter here, and the arts umbrella has been expanded to include fashion, interior design, and architecture. Similar clubs existed in London, Paris, and New York City, but only this one remains.

The four-story building, which has been designated a Chicago landmark, resembles a formal Tuscan villa built around an open-air courtyard. On the first floor is a recital room with a marble fireplace and two grand pianos, a library, sitting room, drawing room, tearoom, and dining room, all with tall ceilings, decorative terra-cotta, and stenciling. Several of these rooms look out onto the central courtyard through tall, arched windows. Visitors are welcome to tour the first floor. Simply ring the doorbell, enter, and sign in at the front desk. ♦ Daily. 1300 N Dearborn St (at W Goethe St). 944.6250

16 3rd Coast $ While away the hours at this artsy coffeehouse and wine bar, sipping delicious San Francisco spiced iced tea, cappuccino, or California wines, savoring salads and scones, reading trashy magazines, and gossiping with friends. ♦ American ♦ Daily 24 hours. 1260 N Dearborn St (between W Division and W Goethe Sts). 649.0730

16 Claridge Hotel $$ This small European-style hotel—quiet and quaint, with a cozy lobby (and lobby bar) and a personable staff—gets a thumbs-up for offering high quality at reasonable rates. Six of the 172 rooms are suites, three of them with wood-burning fireplaces. Perks include mini-bars, complimentary daily newspapers and continental breakfast, health club access, limousine service, and a multilingual concierge staff. Though owned by a Japanese firm, this hotel has a definite Chicago accent, with library shelves filled with books by homegrown writers, music composed by Chicago musicians in the lobby, and art by local artists on the walls. ♦ 1244 N Dearborn St (between W Division and W Goethe Sts). 787.4980, 800/245.1258; fax 266.0978 ♿

Within the Claridge Hotel:

Passports ★$$ Lined with watercolors by Chicago artist Bill Olendorf, this pleasant little restaurant offers a combination of Asian and continental cuisine. Start with salmon cakes or Japanese-style brochettes of deep-fried chicken or beef over salad. For an entrée, try grilled salmon, Thai glazed chicken, or country-style pork ribs. ♦ International ♦ Daily breakfast, lunch, and dinner. 787.4980 ext 676

17 Ambassador West, A Grand Heritage Hotel $$$ In 1919 **Schmidt, Garden & Martin** designed this hotel, which has long been a luxurious home away from home for visiting celebrities. Over the years it became a bit down-at-the-heels, but it reclaimed its glory in 1989 following extensive restorations of the original English decor. The posh lobby has a marble floor, oak paneling, and custom-made crystal chandeliers. English artifacts in the **Guildhall** ballroom include a restored 17th-century portrait of Lady Faversham from the original Guildhall in Bath, England. There are 219 rooms and suites with wet bars, and complimentary continental breakfast, newspapers, and shoe shine. The **Beau Nash** serves breakfast daily and dinner Fridays and Saturdays. A bit of interesting history: Ernie Byfield inherited the hotel from his father in 1926 and had an exact duplicate, the **Ambassador East** (now the **Omni Ambassador East;** see below) constructed nearby. The two hotels used to be connected by a large underground passageway called Milsom Street. The passageway is no longer, and the hotels are now under separate management. ♦ 1300 N State Pkwy (at W Goethe St). 787.3700, 800/300.WEST; fax 640.2967 ♿

17 1340 North State Parkway Built in 1899 by **James Gamble Rogers** for prominent surgeon George Isham at a cost of $50,000, the residence gained notoriety in the 1960s as the **Playboy Mansion,** home to magazine publisher Hugh Hefner and his bunnies. Among other amenities, Hef installed a bowling alley, a firepole for getting from floor to floor, an indoor swimming pool, and a bar with an underwater view of the swimmers. After he moved to California, the house served as a dormitory for students of the **School of the Art Institute;** more recently, it's been divided into privately owned condominiums. ♦ Between W Goethe and W Schiller Sts

18 Omni Ambassador East $$$ In 1926 **Robert S. De Golyer** designed this hotel as a mirror image of the **Ambassador West** across the street. The only Chicago member of the Historic Hotels of America, it boasts a gleaming green-and-white Italian marble lobby with German crystal chandeliers. Celebrity guests throughout the years have included Margaret O'Brien, Tallulah Bankhead, Frank Sinatra, Judy Garland, Cary Grant, Shirley MacLaine, David Bowie, Richard Pryor, and Alfred Hitchcock, who in 1958 shot scenes for *North by Northwest* here. The British band Led Zeppelin had a memorable stay in 1977, when they destroyed their suite to the tune of $23,000, breaking lamps, tearing molding off the wall, and throwing a couch out their 11th-floor window. Those who stay in one of the 275 rooms and suites enjoy complimentary newspapers, temporary membership at nearby health clubs, limousine rides to downtown, and 24-hour room service from the **Pump Room.** ♦ 1301 N State Pkwy (at E Goethe St). 787.7200, 800/THE.OMNI; fax 787.4760 &

Within the Omni Ambassador East:

Pump Room ★$$$$ Stop in, if only to say you've been here. The restaurant, named for an 18th-century spa in Bath, England, opened in 1938 and became popular almost immediately: Ronald Reagan and Jane Wyman held hands here; Humphrey Bogart and Lauren Bacall celebrated their marriage over breakfast in the highly coveted Booth One; and such notables as Marilyn Monroe, Paul Newman, Salvador Dalí, and Milton Berle all ate here. In those days the waiters were garbed in red swallow-tailed coats, the coffee-pourer sported a gold turban, and anything that could be impaled—from olives to flaming steaks—was served on swords. Celebrity dogs were treated royally in the nearby **Pup Room,** which served beef bones au naturel.

When the place went belly-up in 1976, Lettuce Entertain You Enterprises took it over, adding clubby leather upholstery and black tuxedos for the waiters. An over-40 Chicago socialite crowd still congregates here, coveting seats along the voyeuristic wall of windows overlooking State Parkway. The menu has simple food, and the house specialties are prime rib and crispy roasted duck. A free Happy Hour buffet Mondays through Fridays from 5PM to 7PM is one of the best such spreads in the city. Live entertainment is presented nightly, and there's dance music on weekends. ♦ American ♦ Daily breakfast, lunch, and dinner, F-Sa until midnight. Reservations recommended. Jacket required after 4:30PM. 266.0360

19 Astor Tower At 28 stories, one of the first skyscrapers to invade the Gold Coast is more than twice as tall as the earlier generation of apartment buildings. The units begin on the fourth floor, raised on thin concrete columns above the neighboring row houses. The columns run the full height of the building, and are filled in with glass concealed by metal louvers that provide privacy and protection from the sun and wind. The louvers are adjustable from within, with difficulty; residents tend to leave them in a fixed position. **Bertrand Goldberg,** the architect of **Marina City,** designed this building in 1963, and although it lacks the characteristic curving shapes of his later work, it does show his fondness for exposed concrete and his willingness to experiment. ♦ 1300 N Astor St (at E Goethe St)

19 1308-12 North Astor Street The famous architect **John Wellborn Root** lived and died in the center town house of this series of three that he designed in sandstone and red brick in 1887. After his death in 1891, his widow and his sister-in-law Harriet Monroe, founder of *Poetry* magazine, made their home here. The townhouses are still private residences. ♦ Between E Goethe and E Banks Sts

19 1316-22 North Astor Street These Romanesque Revival town houses were built in 1889 by **Charles W. Palmer** for the entrepreneur Potter Palmer. It was a speculative venture—he didn't have any specific tenants in mind, he just believed the need was there—that turned out well for him. Note the unusual treatment of the rusticated stone on **Nos. 1316** and **1318.** They are private residences. ♦ Between E Goethe and E Banks Sts

20 1301 North Astor Street This high-rise apartment building with its understated Art Deco style was designed in 1928 by **Philip B. Maher.** Windows and recessed spandrels create a vertical rhythm. The second-generation Potter Palmer family originally occupied a three-story apartment at the top of the building. Just as the senior Palmers had made this neighborhood fashionable by building a mansion on uncharted territory, their offspring made it socially acceptable to live in cooperative apartments rather than houses. A similar building, designed three years later by the same architect, is located diagonally across the intersection at 1260 North Astor Street. ♦ At E Goethe St

21 Goudy Square Park This tree-shaded park is named after William C. Goudy, who was a prominent Chicago attorney. In 1990, neighborhood residents raised $350,000 to create a delightful children's play area. ♦ N Astor and E Goethe Sts

22 1260 North Lake Shore Drive This 1906 **Holabird & Roche** Georgian Revival residenc on the corner was designed a decade after th same architects had created its neighbor to the south, **No. 1258** (see below), but the difference in the two buildings' styles spans four centuries. The house is privately owned. ◆ At E Goethe St

22 1258 North Lake Shore Drive You can easily imagine Romeo courting Juliet from beneath the stone balcony of this three-story Venetian Gothic town house, designed in 1895 by **Holabird & Roche.** It's a private residence. ◆ Between E Scott and E Goethe Sts

22 1254 and 1250 North Lake Shore Drive These two buildings, together with their neighbors, convey a sense of what bustling Lake Shore Drive must have been like in its heyday—an elegant promenade lined with mansions in a variety of historical styles, mostly Queen Anne, Romanesque, and Georgian. These two are wonderful examples of Richardsonian Romanesque, with rough-hewn blocks of stone, recessed entrances, arches, squat columns, and carved details (note especially the grinning face depicted on one of the column capitals of **No. 1254**). Both were designed by **Gustav Hallberg** and **Frank Abbott.** The house to the north was built for lawyer and businessman Mason Brayman Starring, the other for the prominent realtor and developer Carl Constantine Heisen. After the original owners sold them, the houses fell into disrepair and subsequently were divided into churchmouse-size apartments that never quite took off. Later renovations by **Marvin Herman & Associates** joined the structures and turned them into four multimillion-dollar private residences. They are topped by a shared roof deck and have a live-in concierge. ◆ Between E Scott and E Goethe Sts

23 Carl Sandburg Village This massive complex of high-rises, town houses, gardens, and shops was the product of urban renewal, constructed on land cleared of similarly grand houses fallen on hard times. Named after the Chicago poet and built from 1960 to 1972 by **Solomon Cordwell & Associates,** the village attracted thousands of young professionals to the neighborhood, stimulated the development of new retail businesses, and helped reinvigorate the whole area. ◆ Bounded by N Clark and N LaSalle Sts, and W Division St and W North Ave

24 LaSalle Towers When viewed from the east, this 1920 building appears to have three-dimensional bay windows. The northern facade features **Adolph Loos**'s design for the **Tribune Tower** competition, while the south side copies the archway from the Transportation Building designed by **Louis Sullivan** for the **1893 World's Columbian Exposition.** All of this is a masterpiece of trompe l'oeil by artist Richard Haas, who honors **Sullivan, Daniel Burnham, John Wellborn Root,** and **Frank Lloyd Wright** in portraits beneath the arch. Originally a hotel, this is now an apartment building, which was

renovated in 1980-81 by **Weese Seegers Hickey Weese.** ◆ 1211 N LaSalle St (at W Division St)

25 Chicago Athenaeum Amid the honky-tonk of Division Street is an aesthetic delight, the **Daniel H. Burnham Center.** Part of the **Chicago Athenaeum,** the nation's only independent museum of architecture and design, the center was named after Chicago's famed turn-of-the-century architect and urban planner ("Make no small plans; they have no magic to stir men's souls."). This showplace of the three-branch museum, on the second floor above an **Osco's** drugstore, is worth a visit. The frequently changing exhibitions include such varied subjects as computer chips, Philco radios, **Mies** furniture, and Tyrolean architecture. ◆ Donation suggested. Tu-Sa. 1165 N Clark St (at W Division St). Also at: 515 N State St (at E Grand Ave); 333 W Wacker Dr (at S Franklin St). Same telephone for all three sites: 280.0131

26 Edwardo's ★$$ There are several **Edwardo's** in the city offering tasty pizza with all-natural ingredients, including a whole-wheat crust. The spinach pizza is incredible. ◆ Pizza ◆ Daily lunch and dinner. 1212 N Dearborn St (at W Division St). 337.4490. Also at: Numerous locations throughout the city

27 Mother's Best known for its giant basement dance floor jammed with people gyrating like maniacs, this club draws a crowd that tends to be younger and more suburban—not to mention more energetic—than those at other bars. Light shows, karaoke record-a-hit, lip-sync contests, and roaring rock music are overseen by hyperactive DJs. ◆ M-F, Su 8PM-4AM; Sa until 5AM. 26 W Division St (between N State Pkwy and N Dearborn St). 642.7251

27 Butch McGuire's Chicago's original singles bar opened its doors in 1961. Proprietor McGuire estimates that his establishment has been instrumental in the meetings and marriages of more than 3,000 couples. The small menu  features burgers and such in big portions. Your best bet for food here is the whopping weekend brunch, starting with one of the best Bloody Marys in town. ◆ M-Th, Su 10AM-2AM; F until 4AM; Sa until 5AM. 20 W Division St (between N State Pkwy and N Dearborn St). 337.9080

27 Five Faces $ The famous five are James Dean, Marilyn Monroe, Elvis, Lucy, and Bogie, whose countenances are painted on the facade. Inside, the fare ranges from gyros and cheese fries to taffy apples. Frankly, the place is a dive, but in the middle of the night when you're done bar hopping and are absolutely starving, you can order something here—just eat it someplace else. ♦ Fast food ♦ Daily 10:30AM-5AM. 10 W Division St (between N State Pkwy and N Dearborn St). 642.7837

28 The Lodge Small and somewhat lodgelike with a dark wood decor, this neighborhood hangout is lively even when other bars on the street are dead. There's a great jukebox and complimentary chili bar. ♦ Daily to 4AM; Sa to 5AM. 21 W Division St (between N State Pkwy and N Dearborn St). 642.4406

28 Alumni Club $ Decorated to excess with college memorabilia and sports trophies, this bar and grill draws a predictable crowd for burgers, chili, omelettes, sandwiches, and the inevitable brewskies. ♦ American ♦ Daily 4PM-2AM; Sa until 5AM. 15 W Division St (between N State Pkwy and N Dearborn St). 337.4349

28 Bootleggers Loud rock 'n' roll and a big dance floor draw a young suburban crowd. ♦ Daily 4PM-4AM. 13 W Division St (between N State Pkwy and N Dearborn St). 266.0944

28 P.O.E.T.S. The sign out front proclaims this is not "just another meat market." While that may be true, there's got to be a better way to say it, perhaps by mentioning that it attracts more of a neighborhood crowd and sometimes shows concerts and movies on its large-screen TV. But there's nothing particularly poetic about the place. ♦ Daily 4PM-4AM; Sa to 5AM. 5 W Division St (at N State Pkwy). 943.7638

29 P.J. Clarke's $ It has been called the "divorce bar"—it often seems as though most customers are either getting a divorce or getting over one. But what's important is that they're all enjoying themselves at this casual, ersatz old-fashioned tavern. The Caesar salad is great, and the beef barley soup is famous. The menu otherwise consists of burgers and Italian items. ♦ American ♦ Daily lunch and dinner. 1204 N State Pkwy (at W Division St). 664.1650

29 Yvette ★$$$ Little tables, glass doors that open onto the sidewalk. and a jazzy piano bar make for an atmosphere that's part romantic French cabaret and part fine dining. A dance trio plays on weekends. The tiered dining room in back, one of the city's first bistros, can get noisy when music is playing out front. *Poisson fumé,* or Norwegian smoked salmon,

is a house specialty. Pâtés and breads are freshly made. Come as you are. ♦ French ♦ M-F lunch and dinner; Sa-Su brunch and dinner. 1206 N State Pkwy (between W Division and E Scott Sts). 280.1700 ᕀ

29 St. Germain Bakery & Cafe ★$$ Dine in a Parisian sidewalk cafe, savoring such traditional treats as crepes, pâtés, onion soup, quiche, and arguably the best chocolate mousse in Chicago. Lively and bustling, with an extensive wine list, this is a great late-night spot for wonderful pastries and espresso. It's also become the place for Sunday brunch. Though its patisserie only gets so-so marks, the atmosphere compensates. ♦ French ♦ Daily breakfast, lunch, and dinner; F-Sa until midnight. 1210 N State Pkwy (between W Division and E Scott Sts). 266.9900 ᕀ

30 1209 North State Parkway A narrow wall of curving brick and glass conceals the **Frank Fisher Apartments,** an attractive example of Art Moderne forms executed in brick in 1938 by **Andrew N. Rebori.** Artist Edgar Miller designed the terra-cotta plaques on the facade, some of which, unfortunately, are missing. ♦ At E Division St

31 Zebra Lounge This tiny piano bar describes itself as a "civilized watering hole at the jungle's edge," and you half expect to see Tarzan or Jane swing by for a drink. Zebra stripes rule—on the wallpaper, the light fixtures, in paintings, and on zebra artifacts. When the 20 or 30 people who cram into the room get loosened up, it's one big sing-along with the piano player. Casts from touring musicals sometimes drop in unexpectedly and do a number or two just for fun. ♦ M-F, Su until 2AM; Sa until 3AM. 1220 N State Pkwy (between W Division and E Scott Sts). 642.5140

32 1236-52 North State Parkway These circa-1872 Italianate limestone row houses were the first residences built on the Gold Coast after the Great Fire of 1871. **Nos. 1240-44** were remodeled in 1916 by society architect **David Adler. No. 1240** later became the home of **Nathaniel Owings,** founding partner of the firm **Skidmore, Owings & Merrill,** and their renovation of **Nos. 1242-44** was one of the fledgling firm's first commissions. The houses are still privately owned. ♦ At E Scott St

33 McConnell Apartment Building When built in 1897 by **Holabird & Roche,** this elegant apartment building, with seven stories plus English basement, was considered a skyscraper. It's the oldest fireproof apartment building on the North Side and is closely related to the architects' Chicago School office buildings downtown. The simple, unornamented design expresses the structure within, and gracefully curving corner bays are similar to those of the firm's **Old Colony Building.** ♦ 1210 N Astor St (at E Division St)

34 Estaloca $$ A sleek Italian trendsetter, all white on white, occupied this site until the early 1990s. But as tastes shifted toward coziness and comfort, that too-cool scene was replaced by this Southwestern spot. The decor has been warmed up Santa Fe style, in yellow and aqua with lots of Mexican pottery and cactus. Offerings include barbecue pork sandwiches, pizza, and inventions like guacanachos and Monterrey potato skins. With owner Phil Stefani in charge, this place is likely to become as hearty and boisterous as his long-popular eponymous Lincoln Park restaurant. There's an outdoor cafe in summer. ♦ Tex-Mex ♦ Daily dinner. Closed Mondays in winter. 1148 N State St (at W Elm St). 337.5622

35 Ranalli's $$ Lots of nine-to-fivers congregate at lunchtime and after work for pizza and beer and wide-screen TV sports. When the weather is right, the best place to sit is on the second-floor balcony that wraps around the corner, the perfect people-watching perch. ♦ Pizza ♦ Daily lunch and dinner. 24 W Elm St (at N Dearborn St). 440.7000. Also at: 1925 N Lincoln Ave (south of Armitage Ave). 642.4700; 337 S Dearborn St (between Jackson and Van Buren Sts). 922.8888

36 Albert's Cafe ★$ Their white-chocolate mousse cake will send you to heaven. This cozy European-style pastry and espresso shop also serves light meals such as Belgian waffles and salad niçoise. ♦ Cafe/Patisserie ♦ Tu-Su lunch and dinner. 52 W Elm St (between N Dearborn and N Clark Sts). 751.0666

37 West Egg Cafe $ Party all night on Rush Street, then breakfast here all day. Meals start with big homemade muffins that stand to ruin your appetite for eggs prepared some 30 different ways. Salads, sandwiches, and pasta are also served. ♦ American ♦ M-Th, Su 6:30AM-10PM; F-Sa 24 hours. 1137 N State St (at E Elm St). 951.7900. Also at: 620 N Fairbanks Ct (at Ontario St). 280.8366; 525 W Monroe St (at Canal St). 454.9939

37 Latham Limited If you're serious about women's designer threads, check out these racks packed with business and casualwear by designers like Kenar and Chicagoans Caroline Rose and Richard Dayhoff. ♦ M-Sa. 1133 N State St (at E Elm St). 787.9349

38 Melvin B.'s ★$ This is the place to fraternize alfresco with Chicago's youth culture. On hot afternoons there's hardly a table to be had. The food runs to burgers, ribs, and chicken salad; drinks to margaritas and beer. ♦ American ♦ Daily to 2AM. 1114 N State St (between W Maple and W Elm Sts). 751.9897 &

39 The Waterfront ★$$ If looking at the exteriors of all those houses on Astor Street leaves you craving an interior view, visit this cozy bar. The best time to stop by is between 4 and 7PM or after 10PM, when it offers specially priced hors d'oeuvres. Upstairs, a seafood restaurant exudes a nautical air from copper tabletops to walls mounted with old lanterns and rusty anchors. The hearty clam chowder and the authentic San Francisco cioppino are practically meals in themselves. The menu includes a delicious *sole en sacque*—fillet of sole baked in a brown paper bag that you tear open on your plate, releasing flaky fish in simmering juices. ♦ Seafood ♦ Daily lunch and dinner until midnight. 16 W Maple St (between N State and N Dearborn Sts). 943.7494

40 Blue Agave ★$$ A dozen Mexican beers and six kinds of margaritas (all with fresh-squeezed lemon juice) are served here, which tells you something about the crowd. A stuffed burro and wooden wagon dominate the entrance, and sombreros and serapes hang from the balconies. If you want to eat, head upstairs; all the standard Mexican fare is offered in abundance, plus a surf-and-turf dish called *monte-mar.* ♦ Mexican ♦ Daily lunch and late dinner. 1050 N State St (at W Maple St). 335.8900

40 Morton's ★★$$$ The renowned steak house chain began right here, and it's still the best steak in the whole city. The double filet mignons, 24-ounce porterhouses, 20-ounce strip steaks, and other generous cuts are perfectly prepared to order. Choose between steaming baked potatoes, crisp hash browns, or toasted potato skins, all extra on the à la carte menu. Gigantic lobster, whole chicken, and a good assortment of vegetables served in big portions round out the menu. Only entrée prices are listed on the menu so you'll have to ask for the cost of appetizers, salads, and side dishes. ♦ Steak house ♦ Daily dinner. Reservations recommended. Newberry Plaza, 1030 N State St (at E Bellevue Pl), Lower level. 266.4820 ♿

41 Kronie's/Elliot's Nest This roll-up-your-sleeves bar with a sports/faux antiques motif is situated in adjacent town houses. Large picture windows overlook Bellevue Place. The only food served is at the taco bar, but the friendly young crowd isn't here to eat. When things get hopping, everybody sings along with Frank Sinatra or Van Morrison on the jukebox. A recent addition provides some more competitive entertainment at the bar. It's NTN, the national trivia-game network, via cable TV. ♦ Daily noon-4AM. 18 E Bellevue Pl (at N Rush St). 649.6500

41 Original Pancake House $ It's an odd sight—a little whitewashed house right across the street from the gleaming glass and granite of the **Sutton Place Hotel.** Locals come throughout the day for breakfast in a dining room that looks much like a sunny kitchen. ♦ American ♦ Daily breakfast and lunch. 22 E Bellevue Pl (between N Lake Shore Dr and N Rush St). 642.7917

42 Fortnightly of Chicago Originally the **Bryan Lathrop House,** this 1892 building was designed by his friend, the noted New York architect **Charles McKim** of **McKim, Mead & White.** A guidebook published in 1933 called this "the most perfect piece of Georgian architecture in Chicago"—a judgment few would dispute. The symmetry of the graceful facade is gently broken by the off-center placement of the entrance. The only jarring note is struck by the longer central window of the third floor, which lacks its original balcony. In 1922 the building was remodeled by one of **McKim**'s former pupils for **The Fortnightly,** the city's oldest women's club, which was described in the same guidebook as "the most truly highbrow of many women's organizations of this amazing city." In 1972 the building was again remodeled, this time by **Perkins & Will.** The ladies' literary society still inhabits the building and does not allow nonmembers to tour the building. ♦ 120 E Bellevue Pl (at N Lake Shore Dr). 944.1330

43 Sutton Place Hotel $$$ In the late 1980s the sumptuous **Hotel 21** was built on this site, but it was sold after two years. Then it was the **Le Meridien,** which retained its luxury from the striking glass and gray granite exterior to the Art Deco–inspired interior, the three-story atrium bar, and the state-of-the-art remote-controlled boardroom. Now **Sutton Place,** it will soon undergo some refurbishment, but it is still basically the same establishment. All 247 guest rooms and 41 suites have VCRs, CD players, and three phones with voice mail and a speakerphone. Six of the suites are duplex penthouses with spiral staircases. Weekend discounts and packages are available. ♦ 21 E Bellevue Pl (at N Rush St). 266.2100, 800/810.6888; fax 266.2103 ♿

Within Sutton Place Hotel:

Brasserie Bellevue ★$$ Art Deco decor, soft lighting, and an inventive French menu with lots of fresh fish and meats raise this dining room a notch above your average hotel restaurant. It's an especially good spot for weekend brunches. ♦ French ♦ Daily breakfast, lunch, and dinner. 266.9212 ♿

44 Backroom This small, subterranean jazz club is housed in a former horse stable. The dozen or so tables are packed like sardines in front of the stage. Larger weekend crowds fill a balcony, too. The audience ranges from music students to jazz fans, who come to hear the greats, including regulars Gahlib Ghallab, Bobby Lewis, and the Ken Chaney Xperience. ♦ Cover, two-drink minimum. Daily from 8PM. Nightly shows start at 9PM. 1007 N Rush St (at E Oak St). 751.2433

45 Hamburger Hamlet $ This Beverly Hills–based chain of fancy hamburger joints serves consistently good giant burgers with guacamole and other toppings, as well as chili and omelettes. ♦ American ♦ Daily lunch and dinner until midnight. 1024 N Rush St (between E Oak St and E Bellevue Pl). 649.6601 ♿

46 Tender Buttons Button lovers Diana Epstein and Millicent Safro have enjoyed years of tremendous success with their flagship buttons-as-works-of-art emporium in Manhattan. Their Chicago shop carries a comparable inventory of thousands of buttons in every possible style and material from around the world, all displayed in a serene environment of antique furniture and display cases. You will find Art Deco celluloid buttons; playful children's buttons; buttons depicting Egyptian figures, animals, fruits, and vegetables; and 500 styles of men's blazer buttons. Many are antiques, such as those of English hand-carved horn or vintage Chinese enamel. ♦ M-Sa. 946 N Rush St (at E Oak St). 337.7033

47 Papa Milano $$

Densely packed tables covered with old-fashioned red-and-white checkered cloths set the tone for generous portions of homemade spaghetti or lasagna with the now-departed Papa's famous tomato sauce. Local pols hang out here; it's been around forever. ♦ Italian ♦ Daily lunch and dinner. 951 N State St (at E Oak St). 787.3710

48 Talbott Hotel $$ On cold days the fireplace in the lobby of this all-suites hotel crackles invitingly. There are 147 suites, each composed of living room, bedroom, and fully equipped kitchen. Their decor is decidedly modern, in contrast to the charming Old World lobby. Guests enjoy concierge service, nightly turndown, and complimentary continental breakfast and morning newspaper. Weekend packages and special rates for stays of a month or more are available. ♦ 20 E Delaware Pl (at N State St). 943.0161, 800/825.2688; fax 944.7241 ♿

49 Entre-Nous Duska Kuhlmann's resale shop sells dresses, sweaters, eveningwear, shoes, hats, coats, and more by the likes of Valentino, Yves St. Laurent, Christian Dior, and Charles Jourdan—all for nondesigner prices. Some items have never been worn. While digging through the jam-packed racks is enough to throw your shoulder out, it could be worth it. The most expensive goods— $2,000 evening gowns for $200—go first. ♦ M-Sa. 21 E Delaware Pl (between N Wabash Ave and N State St). 337.2919

49 Bottega Contessa Born and bred in Greece but laying claim to royal status via her father, a Roman count, designer Contessa Helena Kontos attracts a celebrated clientele with her glamorous collection of slinky, sensual eveningwear and showstopping daywear. Customers include Oprah Winfrey, Nancy Wilson, and Whitney Houston, who normally purchase made-to-order. The staff is friendly. ♦ M-Sa. 1 E Delaware Pl (between N Wabash Ave and N State St). 944.0981

50 3rd Coast on Delaware ★$ Linger here for hours sipping cappuccino or fresh juice, nibbling on a muffin or a scone made daily on the premises in such tempting flavors as orange pecan and lemon raisin. Sit outdoors when the weather is fine. In or out, the people watching is great entertainment. ♦ Coffee shop ♦ Daily 7AM-2AM. 888 N Wabash Ave (at E Delaware Pl). 664.7225

51 Newberry Library Designed in 1892 by **Henry Ives Cobb** in the Romanesque Revival style, this is more formal and less fortresslike than his Chicago Historical Society building (now the **Excalibur** nightclub). The carving around the first-floor arches is particularly beautiful. A 20-year renovation ended in 1982 with the opening of **Harry Weese**'s 10-story addition to the north, which provided climate-controlled storage facilities for some of the library's 1.4 million books, five million manuscript pages, and 75,000 maps.

Subjects span Western Europe and the Americas from the Middle Ages to the 20th century. Among some 20 areas of special strength are the Italian Renaissance and the history of cartography. Anyone age 17 or older may make use of the library's noncirculating material. The Chicago Genealogical Society, founded here in 1967, houses one of the finest collections of genealogical data in the country and offers free monthly meetings on conducting family-tree searches. The library also sponsors classes, lectures, concerts, and art exhibits. ♦ M-Sa. Genealogical meetings first Saturday of the month, except July and August. 60 W Walton St (between N Dearborn and N Clark Sts). 943.9090

52 Washington Square Directly in front of the **Newberry** is Chicago's first public park, the site of many a rousing public event in its early years. In 1855 Germans who owned and patronized Chicago's many beer gardens held a protest here over increases in liquor-license fees by the City Council, as well as over the *Chicago Tribune*'s diatribes against the "Lager-beer-swilling and Sabbath-breaking Germans" who carried on a tradition of Sunday drinking. The Germans eventually prevailed. The site became known as **Bughouse Square** in the 1920s, when crowds gathered every Sunday evening to hear radical soapbox speakers. Today the park is a warm-weather gathering place for lunchtime strollers and assorted vagrants. ♦ Bounded by W Delaware Pl and W Walton St, and N Dearborn and N Clark Sts

Chicago businessman Walter L. Newberry, founder of the Newberry Library, died at sea on his way to Paris in 1868. He was entombed in a rum barrel, which served as his coffin when he returned to Chicago.

Restaurants/Clubs: Red **Hotels:** Blue

Shops/♥ Outdoors: Green **Sights/Culture:** Black

Old Town

This section of Chicago is home to an eclectic mix of people: longtime residents, offbeat artists, and briefcase-toting professionals. Anchored for a century by **St. Michael's Church**, the community is bounded by **Division** and **Wisconsin Streets**, **Lincoln Park**, and **Larrabee** and **Halsted Streets.** Quaint shops, celebrated restaurants, and evening entertainment—from the audience-participatory **Tony n' Tina's Wedding** to the **Second City** comedy troupe—form a diverse commercial core on **Wells Street.** Also prominent is the **Old Town Triangle District,** with its fastidiously renovated 19th-century workers' cottages.

In the mid-1800s Old Town was known as the "Cabbage Patch," a patchwork of truck gardens and cow pastures near the city cemetery. The cemetery's 1868 conversion to **Lincoln Park** helped spawn Old Town's growth. Three years later, the Chicago Fire prompted a massive influx of working-class Germans from the burned-out areas—the first in a series of immigrant groups who have lived here. The new arrivals earned their living in factories such as the Western Wheel Works bicycle company (now apartments on Wells Street) and the Oscar Mayer Sausage Company (now closed). Many of the small, solid homes they built stand today, most within the Old Town Triangle District.

By the end of the century, the German population had become a dominant force in Old Town, and **North Avenue,** known as "German Broadway," developed into one long strip of shops, restaurants, and saloons catering to their tastes. **St. Michael's Church,** organized in 1852 by German Catholics, had become Chicago's largest German parish by 1892. As the 20th century dawned, however, the Germans began to depart for newer housing in northern neighborhoods, making way for new groups of immigrants. By 1920, North Avenue stores were owned by Russian Jews and frequented by Hungarians.

The end of World War II brought additional waves of ethnic groups to Old Town. The massive Cabrini-Green housing project, built in the neighborhood's southwest corner in the late 1950s, became home to lower-income residents. Relatively cheap housing in the area also attracted artists and urban pioneers who began renovating and revitalizing older buildings. Thanks largely to their efforts, the Old Town Triangle District was declared a Chicago Landmark in 1977 and listed on the National Register of Historic Places in 1984—and housing was no longer inexpensive.

Old Town is perhaps best known for the Haight-Ashbury character taken on by Wells Street in the 1960s, when hippies and tourists descended to buy incense and psychedelic tie-dyes, listen to Pete Seeger and fellow folkies at the **Earl of Old Town,** a now-defunct club, and see the likes of Elaine May and Mike Nichols perform their special brand of social satire at **Second City.** While the flower children and most of the businesses that served them are long gone, some (such as **Second City**) have survived. The neighborhood still has an offbeat, creative atmosphere that supports such traditions as the immensely popular **Old Town and Wells Street Art Fairs,** which annually (on the second weekend of June) showcase work by local and other artists.

---

1 Moody Church This independent church devoted to evangelism and Bible education was designed in 1925 by **John R. Fugard.** The church was founded by Dwight L. Moody, a shoe salesman who came from Boston to Chicago to pursue a personal ministry serving poor street children. It now occupies one of the largest Protestant church buildings in the country, and sends radio and television broadcasts of many of its services around the world. The immense Romanesque structure, redbrick trimmed in terra-cotta, is a 140-by-225-foot rectangle with a semicircle facing Clark Street. It seats 4,000 people on the main floor and the cantilevered balcony. Everyone has an unobstructed view of the

pulpit and choir because there are no interior columns. The vaulted ceiling and supporting piers were suggested by the design of the ancient Church of St. Sophia in Istanbul. Interior stained-glass windows were bestowed in memory of various pastors and lay members of the church. ♦ 1630 N Clark St (between W North Ave and W Eugenie St). 943.0466

2 Chicago Historical Society Designed in 1932 by **Graham, Anderson, Probst & White,** this is the Society's fourth location since its founding in 1857. One of its earlier homes went up in flames, and another now serves as the **Excalibur** nightclub in River North. Its current home, with **Lincoln Park** as its backyard, was erected with much pride and fanfare. The original building is a Georgian Revival structure of redbrick with limestone. It's oriented to the east, with a columned portico and broad stairway stretching down to sloping lawns and a statue of *Abraham Lincoln* by Augustus Saint-

Gaudens. The 1972 annex, designed by **Alfred Shaw,** shifted the entrance to Clark Street and allowed the museum to expand, but to many it resembled a mausoleum. In 1988 a second addition, designed by **Holabird & Root,** concealed the first in a modern wrapping of brick and limestone accented with white painted steel. The inviting entrance incorporates large areas of gridded glass that visually open the museum to the street.

Among the museum's numerous holdings are one of the nation's largest 19th-century women's costume collections, extensive artifacts from the Civil War and the Chicago Fire, and Chicago architectural records and drawings. A historical library is available to the public and is frequently used by students and scholars. The museum hosts special programs throughout the year, including tours of many city neighborhoods. ♦ Admission; free on Mondays. Daily. 1601 N Clark St (between W North Ave and W Eugenie St). 642.4600

Chicago Historical Society

Courtesy of the Chicago Historical Society

Within the Chicago Historical Society:

Big Shoulders Cafe $ A sunny, pleasant, two-story cafe is dominated by **Daniel Burnham**'s impressive terra-cotta arch, which originally served as the main entrance to the Union Stock Yard National Bank. The cafe serves refreshing salads and sandwiches, luscious soups, vegetarian dishes, and irresistible desserts such as warm brownies topped with ice cream then drizzled with caramel sauce and sprinkled with toasted coconut. ♦ American ♦ M-Sa lunch; Su breakfast and brunch. 587.7766

Gift Shop Yes, they sell Chicago souvenirs, but better still are the beautifully illustrated books on local history, architecture, and culture. There's a large section on Chicago's ethnic groups, and another on Abraham Lincoln and the Civil War. ♦ Daily. 642.4600

2 **Couch Mausoleum** Opened in 1868, **Lincoln Park** sits on land that was once a cemetery. Mass exhumations relocated almost all the remains to private cemeteries. The Couch family, however, won a lawsuit against the city to keep the tomb of Ira Couch exactly where it was—which is now in a clump of trees behind the **Chicago Historical Society**. Couch was a tailor who later owned the **Tremont House Hotel** at its original location downtown. (It's now in the Michigan Avenue area.) One other grave remains in the park, near the **Farm-in-the-Zoo**. Dating from 1852, it marks the remains of David Kennison, a participant in the Boston Tea Party who lived to be 115. ♦ Behind the Chicago Historical Society

Damen Avenue (2000 W from 7546 N to 10058 S) was named after Rev. Arnold Damen (1815-1890), the Jesuit priest who founded Loyola University, Holy Family Church, and St. Ignatius High School. During the Chicago Fire of 1871 Damen vowed that if his church was spared, a candle would burn forever at Holy Family Church. Even though the fire started just blocks from the church, winds blew it in the other direction. A light has burned perpetually at the church for over a hundred years.

Restaurants/Clubs: Red **Hotels:** Blue

Shops/ ♥ **Outdoors:** Green **Sights/Culture:** Black

3 **164-72 West Eugenie Street** Built in the 1880s, these row houses are elaborate examples of the Queen Anne style so popular in the late 19th century. These private residences feature a variety of window types and building materials—brick, stone, slate, terra-cotta—and a lively roofline punctuated by dormers, gables, and turrets. ♦ Between N LaSalle and N Wells Sts

4 **Nookies** $ Somewhere between greasy spoon and restaurant, this place has been a neighborhood institution for years. On weekends people line up for omelettes, pancakes, burgers, and coffee. ♦ American ♦ Daily breakfast, lunch, and dinner. 1746 N Wells St (at N Lincoln Ave). 337.2454. Also at: 2114 N Halsted St (between W Dickens and W Webster Aves). 327.1400; 3343 N Halsted St (between Belmont Ave and Addison St). 248.9888

5 **Topo Gigio at the Park** ★$$ This open, airy *ristorante* with a view of **Lincoln Park** was spawned from its sister a few blocks south. Both are named after the Italian equivalent to Mickey Mouse, but the ambience is distinctly grown-up in appeal. Homemade pasta is a crowd pleaser, as are herb-roasted chicken and veal. ♦ Italian ♦ M-Sa lunch and dinner; Su dinner. 1800 N Lincoln Ave (at N Wells St). 751.8070. Also at: 1516 N Wells St (at W Schiller St). 266.9355 ♿

6 Fire Relief Cottage Within a few days of the Chicago Fire in 1871, small cottages known as relief shanties sprang up. Built by the city at about $75 each for people who had been left homeless, some also served as distribution centers for food and clothing. This diminutive house is believed to have been one; today it's a private residence.
♦ 216 W Menomonee St (at N Wells St)

7 1802 North Lincoln Park West This 1872 structure (still a private residence) is one of the few wooden farmhouses remaining in Old Town. Note the contrast between the relatively plain long facade on Menomonee Street and the elaborate Italianate treatment of windows and cornice on the narrow end facing North Lincoln Park West. ♦ At W Menomonee St

Historic American Buildings Survey.
Courtesy of the Art Institute of Chicago

8 1826-34 North Lincoln Park West
These five brick row houses (pictured above), designed by **Adler & Sullivan** from 1884 to 1885, are rare examples of **Louis Sullivan**'s early residential work. Their Queen Anne design is enlivened considerably by his distinctive geometric ornamentation. Vertical bands decorated with terra-cotta distinguish the second and fourth houses. Those two have plain window openings to set off the ornament, while the other three have decorated arched window tops whose motif is repeated in the cornice. All are private homes. ♦ Between W Menomonee and W Wisconsin Sts

8 Charles Wacker House Charles was the son of Frederick Wacker, and this circa-1870 home was originally the carriage house at the back of his father's property next door. One of the directors of the **1893 World's Columbian Exposition** and chairman of the Chicago Plan Commission for 17 years, Charles was instrumental in implementing the 1909 Burnham Plan for the development of Chicago. Part of that legacy is the double-level Wacker Drive. The long front entrance stairway here—a trademark of Chicago houses of that era—was built high to accommodate a "modern" sewage system. The house remains a private residence.
♦ 1836 N Lincoln Park W (between W Menomonee and W Wisconsin Sts)

8 Frederick Wacker House A successful brewer and a leader in the city's German community, Wacker hired a Swiss architect to create this elaborate chalet in 1874. The basic form of the 2.5-story Chicago cottage— a gabled clapboard structure above a simple brick ground floor—proved well suited to this fanciful Alpine style. A wide overhanging veranda is supported by large carved brackets, and smaller brackets are paired below the cornice. Elaborate wood carving decorates the window tops and the balustrades. Housepainter James F. Jereb gave the house a "Painted Lady" color scheme in 1987 and then signed and dated the lower left of the facade. This is a private residence.
♦ 1838 N Lincoln Park W (between W Menomonee and W Wisconsin Sts)

9 Midwest Buddhist Temple One of the largest immigrant groups to settle in Old Town in the 1940s and 1950s were the Japanese. In 1972 **Hideaki Areo** built this temple, which, despite its small size, dominates the area because it's raised on a one-story base and stands clear of surrounding buildings. The striated concrete base contains a large meeting room as well as classrooms and offices; its roof forms a terrace for ceremonial processions. The temple itself is of stucco and heavy timber with translucent clerestory windows and a traditional Japanese roof. The interior is simple: A small, gold Buddha and an altar with candles and flowers are the primary embellishments in an airy room of white walls and ceilings. Visitors are welcome for meditational services. One weekend each summer, the temple sponsors the popular Ginza Festival, providing an introduction to Japanese food, dancing, and culture. ♦ 435 W Menomonee St (at N Hudson Ave). 943.7801

10 St. Michael's Church This landmark defines Old Town, since tradition decrees you are within the neighborhood's boundaries if you can hear the church's bells. The chiming carries farther than you might think, with each of the five bells weighing between 2,500 and 6,000 pounds. The growing German community built a small church here in 1852 and replaced it with a larger one 17 years later, only to see it gutted by the 1871 Chicago Fire. (The *Daily Tribune* referred to the remains of the tower and walls as "the most impressive ruins on the North Side.") The determined parishioners rebuilt their church in just a year, and a decade later hired New York artist Karl Labrecht to design the lavish interior. In 1888 an exterior renovation by **Herman T. Gaul** was completed and a steeple was added to crown the tower. Circus acrobats thrilled crowds at the dedication ceremony when they hung by their heels from the cross at its summit. The four-sided steeple clock was added the following year. Parishioners have included prizefighter Nick Castiglione and actor Johnny Weissmuller, who was an altar boy here before learning to swing from the trees as Tarzan. ♦ 1633 N Cleveland Ave (at W Eugenie St). 642.2498

11 A 1000 Nites Cafe ★$$ Steps away from a busy street and tucked into a frame house, this restaurant aims for romance with candles, bud vases, and a slightly exotic air. Kabobs—chicken, beef, or lamb grilled after being marinated in secret sauces—are the house specialty. The lamb stew sopped up with bits of pita bread is a most satisfying meal. ◆ Middle Eastern ◆ Daily lunch and dinner. 1612 N Sedgwick St (at W North Ave). 944.4811

12 Twin Anchors ★$$ Opened in 1932, this may be the city's oldest rib joint. People from around the world show up at the lodgelike wood-paneled bar and restaurant after having heard about it over beers in Germany or during a snowstorm in Switzerland—or so say members of the Tuzi family, owners since 1978. Though the place is known for its baby-back pork ribs, the filet mignon and New York strip steak are also specialties. Arrive before 6PM to beat the crowd, or have a drink and spin a few discs on the Jolson-to-Springsteen jukebox. ◆ American ◆ M-F late dinner; Sa-Su lunch and dinner. Reservations accepted for large groups only. 1655 N Sedgwick St (at W Eugenie St). 266.1616

13 Crilly Court This charming street is just a block away from busy Wells Street, but seems a century apart. It was developed between 1885 and 1893 by Daniel F. Crilly, a South Side contractor who bought the block bounded by North Park and St. Paul Avenues, and Wells and Eugenie Streets, cut a north-south street through the middle of it, and named it **Crilly Court.** On the west side he built two-story Queen Anne–style row houses and on the east side a four-story apartment building. Above the apartment doors are carved the names of his four children: Isabelle, Oliver, Erminie, and Edgar. Doors on the north and south sides are marked with the street names Eugenie and Florimond (the original name of St. Paul Avenue). Crilly then built another apartment building to the east; its Wells Street facade offers a wonderful example of late–19th-century storefronts with apartments above. In the 1940s Crilly's son Edgar renovated these buildings extensively, replacing the rear wooden porches with steel balconies and closing off the alleys to create private courtyards. His success led the way for others interested in reviving Old Town while preserving its architectural heritage.

Over the years, the Crilly estate has leased units to many well-known Chicagoans, among them poet and journalist Eugene Field and Cyrus DeVry, director for many years of the **Lincoln Park Zoo.** Another resident was George K. Spoor, an early movie producer known for his films with Charlie Chaplin and the Keystone Cops; he sometimes preserved his films in his Crilly Court icebox. Commercial artist Haddon Sundbloom, creator of the Quaker on the Quaker Oats cereal box and Aunt Jemima, lived here, often using people in the neighborhood as his models. ◆ Bounde by W Eugenie St and W St. Paul Ave, and N Wells St and N North Park Ave

14 Green, Inc. For nearly two decades, this shop has been luring plant lovers to its conservatorylike space. One room overflows with unusual house plants; in another, exotic flowers grow in wild profusion. Its proprietor is full of good advice. ◆ Daily. 1718 N Wells S (between W Eugenie St and W St. Paul Ave). 266.2806

14 Design Source, Inc. Owned by an interior designer, this shop offers an eclectic array of decorative home accessories, from 18th-century Chippendale chests to hammered-tin lamps from Mexico. **S'Agaro,** the adjoining shoe store, was opened by the proprietor's daughter. It features imported, but not overpriced, women's shoes. ◆ Tu-Sa. 1710 N Wells St (between W Eugenie St and W St. Paul Ave). 751.2113

Handle With Care

14 Handle With Care One-of-a-kind creations by hot designers from Chicago or Paris hold center stage here. In addition to women's clothing, this boutique carries stunning jewelry. ◆ Daily. 1706 N Wells St (between W Eugenie St and W St. Paul Ave). 751.2929

14 Heartworks It's the place to go for a year's supply of birthday cards, plus memorable gift items such as a wooden comb and brush set, birdhouses made of twigs, rubber duckies for the bath, handmade vegetable-oil soaps, and gorgeous wrapping paper. They'll have the perfect little picture frame to take home to the neighbor who's been watering your plants ◆ Daily until 9PM. 1704 N Wells St (between W Eugenie St and W St. Paul Ave). 943.1972

14 Savories $ A simple neighborhood place for coffee, tea, sandwiches, pastries, and gift items. Locals come in to read their paper, buy coffee beans or a new mug, or pick up desser to take home for dinner. ◆ Cafe ◆ Daily. 1700 N Wells St (at W Eugenie St). 951.7638

15 The Real You Merchandise in this small shop is the usual assortment of costume jewelry. The malachite, cultured pearls, and rose quartz are noteworthy, but what draws most customers here is the hope of giving old, broken favorites a new life. They'll repair even the trashiest costume jewelry with nary a you've-got-to-be-kidding stare. ◆ M-Sa, Su 11AM-2PM. 1657 N Wells St (between W North Ave and W Eugenie St). 787.3239

15 A New Leaf There are many florists in Chicago, but this shop has an exceptional selection of fresh-cut flowers. Considering its high-rent location, the prices are especially reasonable. ◆ Daily. 1645 N Wells St (between W North Ave and W Eugenie St). 642.1576

16 Second City A list of just a few of the people who have cut their comedic teeth here makes an all-star roll call: Alan Arkin, Ed Asner, Elaine May, Jerry Stiller, Anne Meara, John Belushi, Bill Murray, and Shelley Long. The club was founded at this location in 1959 by a small group of theater lovers that included Mike Nichols and Sheldon Patinkin. (They proudly snatched the name "Second City" from essayist A.J. Liebling's derisive profile of Chicago published in *The New Yorker* in the early 1950s.) Their unique brand of satirical comedy was an instant hit, not only locally but in the global theater community. An official Touring Company was formed in 1967 and continues to make appearances worldwide. In the early 1970s, another **Second City** opened in Toronto, where John Candy, Gene Levy, Dan Aykroyd, and Gilda Radner all honed their skills.

The revue has stuck to its original format: On an empty stage, using few props, six or seven actors lampoon contemporary life in a series of skits. Then the actors ask the audience for ideas, from which they improvise new sketches. (With fine-tuning, these improvisations eventually become parts of new shows, of which there are two or three every year.) This theater has blossomed into two cabaret-style settings next door to each other and one suburban outpost in Rolling Meadows—three different troupes presenting three different revues at the same time. Cocktails and hot beverages can be purchased during the shows.

Incidentally, the original building's ornamental facade is from the once-glorious **Garrick Theatre** downtown, designed by **Adler & Sullivan** and demolished in 1961. ◆ Shows Tu-Su. Reservations recommended; required for Friday and Saturday. Credit cards accepted for drinks only. 1616 N Wells St (between W North Ave and W Eugenie St), 1608 N Wells St (at W North Ave). 337.3992.

16 That Steak Joynt ★ $$$ Ribs, steaks, chicken, and fish are served in trencherman portions. Reserve a dinner-theater package here to guarantee a seat at **Second City** or **Zanies**, or stop by after either show to hear Bruce Meils on the piano. ◆ American

◆ Daily dinner. 1610 N Wells St (between W North Ave and W Eugenie St). 943.5091

16 Piper's Alley What began as the Piper family bakery in the 1880s became the enclosed **Piper's Alley** in the 1960s, a lively collection of shops hawking love beads and Grateful Dead albums to hippies and tourists. Many of the shops are gone today, but the ones that remain are enjoying a resurgence of interest in their peacenik goods. Another renovation in 1992 added the **Piper's Alley Theater,** four small screens showing first-run movies. ◆ Daily. 1608 N Wells St (at W North Ave). 642.7500

16 Tony n' Tina's Wedding An interactive spoof of an Italian-American wedding may seem like an unlikely theatrical hit, but that's exactly what this has become. The audience of "guests" mingles with the "bridal party" of actors, dances to a band, eats an Italian wedding supper, observes family spats, and drinks champagne. The only difference between this and a real wedding is that you pay your way in rather than buying a gift. ◆ Shows Tu-Su. Reservations required. 230 W North Ave (at N Wells St). 664.1456

17 Old Town Ale House Dark, damp, dingy, and like home to its faithful, this bar serves construction workers elbow-to-elbow with **Second City** actors. A mural on the wall pays tribute to regulars over the years. The jukebox plays everything from Billie Holiday to Maria Callas. ◆ Daily to 5AM. 219 W North Ave (at N Wieland St). 944.7020

18 Vintage Posters With far more than posters, this is the Midwest's largest collection of European decorative items from the Belle Epoque: mirrors, frames, bowls, throws, plus distinctive posters of the era. ◆ Daily. 1551 N Wells St (at W North Ave). 951.6681

18 Stella d'Italia ★ ★ $$ The owners imported Italy's leading risotto maker to prepare that delectable rice dish in such splendiferous varieties as *nettuno* (with seafood), *all'aragosta* (with lobster), and *ai porcini* (with porcini mushrooms). Other specialties include tortellini *bolognese,* grilled tuna, and tableside dessert flambés. ◆ Italian ◆ M, W-Sa lunch and dinner; Su dinner. 1547 N Wells St (between W Burton Pl and W North Ave). 654.1416

19 Up-Down Tobacco Shop This shop has been on Wells Street since the 1960s, when many customers no doubt bought rolling papers here for uses other than tobacco. Owned by Diana Gits, the store takes you back to an even earlier era, when smoking was a sign of refinement: The air is rich with the scent of tobacco, and beautiful hand-carved pipes, gold cigarette cases, and a large selection of imported cigars and cigarettes are on display. ◆ M-Th, Su 11AM to 11PM; F-Sa 11AM-12PM. 1550 N Wells St (between W Burton Pl and W North Ave). 337.8505

Musical Chairs

Always famous for its blues and jazz, and a superb symphony orchestra, Chicago's musical repertoire continues to grow. Today the city is becoming increasingly known as home to hot new rock artists like Liz Phair and Smashing Pumpkins; whether you're into opera or reggae, Greek ballads or gospel, you can probably hear it in Chicago. Below is a sampling of some of the city's best listening posts. For information on specific acts or schedules, call the individual location or consult weekly entertainment listings in the *Reader, Tribune,* or *Sun-Times* newspapers.

Blues

Blue Chicago 937 N State St (at E Walton St), 642.6261

B.L.U.E.S. 2519 N Halsted St (at W Lill Ave), 528.1012

B.L.U.E.S. Etc. 1124 W Belmont Ave (at N Clifton Ave), 525.8989

Buddy Guy's Legends 754 S Wabash Ave (at E 8th St), 427.1190

Kingston Mines 2548 N Halsted St (at W Wrightwood Ave), 477.4646

Rosa's 3420 W Armitage Ave (at N Kimball Ave), 342.0452

Smoke Daddy 1804 W Division (at N Wood St), 772.6656

Classical and Opera

Civic Opera House 20 N Wacker Dr (between W Washington and W Madison Sts), 332.2244

Orchestra Hall 220 S Michigan Ave (between E Adams St and E Jackson Blvd), 435.6666

Country and Folk

Carol's Pub 4659 N Clark (at Leland Ave), 334.2402

Club Bub at Bub City 901 W Weed St (at N Sheffield Ave), 266.1200

Old Town School of Folk Music 909 W Armitage Ave (at N Fremont St), 525.7793

Whiskey River 1997 N Clybourn Ave (at N Racine Ave), 528.3400

Eclectic Offerings

Cubby Bear Lounge 1059 W Addison St (at N Clark St), 327.1662

Elbo Room 2871 N Lincoln Ave (at W George St), 549.7700

FitzGeralds 6615 Roosevelt Rd (between East and Clarence Aves), Berwin, 708/788.2118

Gospel

Christ Tabernacle Missionary Baptist Church (home of the Thompson Community Singers) 854 N Central Ave (at Division St), 921.2554

Greek

Deni's Den 2941 N Clark St (at W Oakdale Ave), 348.8888

Irish

Abbey Pub 3420 W Grace St (at Elston St), 478.440?

Augenblick 3907 N Damen Ave (at W Irving Park Rd), 929.0994

Kerrigan's 2310 W Lawrence (at Western Avenue), 334.0620

Kitty O'Shea's 720 S Michigan Ave (at E Balboa Dr), 922.4400

Jazz

Andy's 11 E Hubbard St (at N State St), 642.6805

Bop Shop 1807 W Division St (at N Wood St), 235.3232

Bossa Nova 1960 N Clybourn (at W Racine St), 248.4800

The Bulls 1916 N Lincoln Park W (at W Wisconsin St), 377.3000

Gold Star Sardine Bar 680 N Lake Shore Pl (between E Erie and E Huron Sts), 664.4215

Green Dolphin Street 2200 N Ashland Ave (at W Webster Ave), 395.0066

The Green Mill 4802 N Broadway (at W Lawrence Ave), 878.5552

Jazz Showcase 59 W Grand (at State St), 670.2473

Pops for Champagne 2934 N Sheffield Ave (at W Oakdale Ave), 472.1000

Latin

Tania's 2659 N Milwaukee Ave (at N Kedzie Ave), 235.7120

Polka

Baby Doll Polka Club 6102 S Central (at 61st St), 582.9706

Reggae

Equator Club 4715 N Broadway (between Lawrence and Leland Aves), 728.2411

Wild Hare & Singing Armadillo Frog Sanctuary 3530 N Clark St (at W Cornelia Ave), 327.4273

Rock, Pop, and Dance Clubs

Beat Kitchen 2100 W Belmont (at Paulina St), 281.4444

Crobar 1543 N Kinsbury (at W Weed St), 413.7000

Empty Bottle 1035 N Western Ave (at Cortez St), 276.3600

Ka-boom! 747 N Green St (at W Chicago Ave), 243.8600

Lounge Ax 2438 N Lincoln Ave (at W Fullerton Ave), 525.6620

Metro 3730 N Clark St (at W Waveland Ave), 549.0203

Phyllis' Musical Inn 1800 W Division (at N Wood St), 486.9862

Red Dog 1954 W North Ave (at Damen St), 278.1009

Shelter 564 W Fulton St (at N Jefferson St), 648.5500

19 Zanies Chicago's premier stand-up comedy club is small, cramped, and very conducive to laughter. Featured performers range from national names like Jay Leno to local talent. Comedian Emo Phillips got his start here. ♦ Cover and two-drink minimum. Shows Tu-Su. Reservations recommended. 1548 N Wells St (between W Burton Pl and W North Ave). 337.4027

20 Trattoria Roma ★$$ When it opened down the block in 1987 in a space the size of a postage stamp, this was arguably Chicago's first authentic trattoria. It has since spawned all sorts of imitators. This larger location is done in a vaguely surreal style, with plaster copies of Roman architectural fragments on the walls that give you the sense of dining amid the ruins. Good starters include crisp-crusted mini-pizzas or mussels marinara. Regular features include spaghetti scampi and rigatoni mozzarella. It's always busy, and reservations are not accepted, so line up early. ♦ Italian ♦ M-F lunch and dinner; Sa-Su dinner. 1535 N Wells St (between W Burton Pl and W North Ave). 664.7907. Also at: 1119 W Taylor St (at May St). 226.6800

21 Old Town Aquarium In addition to servicing home aquariums, this store carries the largest selection of saltwater fish in the city. A look in the spectacular aquarium in the front window reveals beautiful breeds of every color and stripe. The store specializes in locating rare species, and will ship anywhere in the world. ♦ Daily, Th to 9PM. 1538 N Wells St (between W Burton Pl and W North Ave). 642.8763

21 Fresh Choice $ This cheery yellow-and-white restaurant offers a choice of healthy meals, from the salad bar to the weekend omelette bar that gives you the option of an egg-white omelette. The true health fanatic can get a shot of wheat grass (a single two-ounce shot equals two pounds of vegetables) or fresh squeezed carrot juice. Sandwiches are available, as are smoothies, yogurt, and Italian ice. ♦ Cafe ♦ Daily breakfast, lunch, and dinner; open until midnight June through August. 1534 N Wells St (between W Burton Pl and W North Ave). 664.7065

21 Fudge Pot Indulge yourself. The Dattalo family has perfected the art of homemade candy making over two generations. The chocolate-covered English butter toffee melts in your mouth, and fudge comes in 10 flavors. It's hard to walk by too many times without having one of their taffy apples, made with fat Granny Smith or Delicious apples, depending on the season, and hand-dipped in homemade caramel. They're the best in the city! ♦ Daily. 1532 N Wells St (between W Burton Pl and W North Ave). 943.1777

21 O'Brien's Restaurant $$ With a posh men's-club atmosphere—dark wood, deep green hues, and two-ton chandeliers—this is truly a traditional steak house. The menu is heavy on substantial steaks and steaming baked potatoes. Try their famous thick cabbage soup. A piano bar deep within entertains until midnight. ♦ Steak house ♦ M-Sa lunch and dinner; Su dinner. 1528 N Wells St (between W Burton Pl and W North Ave). 787.3131

22 West Burton Place There's a tiny park where Burton Place stops short of Wells Street, and it's worth a brief detour to walk along this quiet block to get to it (the street ends at LaSalle Street and starts again on the other side of Sandburg Village, in the Gold Coast). **No. 155** is a brick apartment building that was whimsically remodeled in 1927 by **Sol Kogen** and artist Edgar Miller. It's a sort of folk version of Art Deco, with a patchwork of glass block, mosaic, marble, terra-cotta, and old brick salvaged from demolished neighborhood buildings. Note, too, the interesting tile work on the sidewalk. ♦ Between N LaSalle and N Wells Sts

23 Burton Place $ On a winter's night, go ahead and jockey with the regulars for a prime seat next to the crackling fireplace in this neighborhood bar. While you're here, try one of their great burgers. ♦ American ♦ Daily until 4AM. 1447 N Wells St (at W Burton Pl). 664.4699

24 Byron Roche Gallery Harry Waller is a songwriter and producer whose passion is painting Chicago's fire stations in their myriad styles; several of these are here, along with contemporary paintings, Raku pottery, sculptures of wood and glass, plus antiques. Roche himself is full of intriguing stories about the art and artists. ♦ Tu-Su. 1446 N Wells St (at W Burton Pl). 654.0144

25 Old Jerusalem ★$ The atmosphere is reminiscent of lunchroom, but the Middle Eastern cuisine is delicious, from the freshest parsley-packed tabbouleh to the crisp, perfectly seasoned falafel. Share three or four different appetizers with companions for a very satisfying—and cheap—meal. ♦ Middle Eastern ♦ Daily lunch and dinner. 1411 N Wells St (between W Schiller St and W Burton Pl). 944.0459

Cabrini Street (828 S, from 500 W to 1334 W) was named after St. Frances Xavier Cabrini (1850-1917), the first American to be canonized by the Catholic Church. She founded Columbus Hospital in 1905, and the public housing projects on the Near North Side were also named after her.

25 Orso's ★$$ Most restaurants come and go as the neighborhood changes, but this one has staying power. Quaint, relaxed, and romantic, with a piano player, flickering candles on the tables, and a lovely patio and garden out back, it serves predictable pastas, eggplant parmigiana, roasted chicken, and such. ♦ Italian ♦ M-F lunch and dinner; Sa-Su dinner. 1401 N Wells St (at W Schiller St). 787.6604 &

26 Kamehachi ★★$$ For years, a Nisei woman ran a popular sushi bar a few blocks up the street; her granddaughter has taken over and expanded into this new space, but maintains the long commitment to freshness and consistent quality of the food. For those unfamiliar with Japanese delicacies, the restaurant offers a "beginner's" meal that consists of all cooked items, as well as a wide variety of raw fish dishes for aficionados. An outdoor patio is available for summer dining. ♦ Japanese ♦ Daily lunch and dinner. 1400 N Wells St (at W Schiller St). 664.3663

27 Noble Horse Equestrian Center Horses are indeed nobly stabled in this renovated 1917 building. In addition to supplying the steeds used for carriage rides along Michigan Avenue, in movies, and on TV, the stable offers complete boarding and training services to horse owners. It also provides riding lessons for all levels in English, hunt seat, and dressage. The public is welcome to drop in to admire the horses. ♦ Daily. 1410 N Orleans St (at W Schiller St). 266.7878

28 Cobbler Square Built in 1889, this former factory complex originally housed Western Wheel Works, the world's largest bicycle manufacturer. In 1911 the bikers moved out and a doctor with arthritic feet moved in, intending to make therapeutic foot products—and the rest, they say, is history. Dr. Scholl's footwear firm was one of Old Town's largest employers until 1981, when it left this location to seek cheaper labor. In 1985 the redbrick buildings, which encompass an entire square block, were renovated by **Kenneth Schroeder** into 295 loft apartments surrounding landscaped courtyards. What was probably the Evergreen Avenue entryway, flanked by pillars and topped with a little balcony, is now permanently closed by a cast-iron gate; the main level on the Wells Street side has retail stores. ♦ 1350 N Wells St (between W Evergreen Ave and W Schiller St)

The first female surgeon in the country was Dr. Mary Harris Thompson. After graduating from New England Female Medical College in 1865 she came to Chicago and founded the Chicago Hospital for Women and Children, where she served as chief physician and surgeon.

Within Cobbler Square:

Barbara's Bookstore From the time it opened in 1963 at a different location just up the block, this store has served as the neighborhood hippie/intellectual bookshop. The literary and socially conscious spirit survives even in this most modern new site. A wide array of Chicago's alternative newspapers is available, most of them free, and popular authors make frequent appearances. ♦ M-Sa until 10PM; Su until 9PM. 1350 N Wells (between W Evergreen Ave and W Schiller St). 642.5044. Also at: 3130 N Broadway St (at Belmont Ave). 477.0411; Navy Pier, 700 W Grand. 222.089; 1100 Lake St (at Merrion Ave), Oak Park. 708/848.9140

29 Broadway Home Furnishings You can find nearly any piece of furniture here—bed, table, lamp, wastebasket, CD rack. All of it is sturdily made, and the prices are reasonable. ♦ Daily. 1361 N Wells St (between W Evergreen Ave and W Schiller St). 587.8788. Also at: 3843 N Broadway St (at Grace St). 327.4320

29 Kenyon Oppenheimer, Inc. Open since 1969, this gallery is devoted to original prints by 19th-century naturalist John James Audubon. Prices range from two to five figures. The building that houses it is listed on the National Register of Historic Places. Built in 1875 and restored in 1985, its original architect is unknown. By all means visit the fairy-tale courtyard garden in back. Hidden away in a coach house behind the garden is a laboratory where experts conserve and restore artwork on paper. ♦ Tu-Sa. 1357 N Wells St (between W Evergreen Ave and W Schiller St). 642.5300

29 Village Cycle Center Here is one of the city's largest emporiums selling specialized and custom bikes. ♦ Daily. 1337 N Wells St (at W Evergreen Ave). 751.2488

30 Fire Engine Company No. 27 The city had just purchased a fire engine from a manufacturer in Seneca Falls, New York, and needed a new building in the neighborhood to house it. In 1874 the Chicago Board of Public Works filled the order. The resulting two-story structure featured an Italianate design that was without precedent for a building of this type. It's now part of the North Wells Street Historic District, which includes the buildings from 1240 to 1260 North Wells Street, and is on the National Register of Historic Landmarks. The tower that was used for drying the hoses and watching for fires has been shortened, and office workers now toil where firefighters used to sleep. ♦ 1244 N Wells St (at W Scott St)

31 House of Glunz Limousines double-park out front while the drivers run in to pick up a case of this rare vintage or that special Champagne for their well-to-do employers. The store and the building—one of the first constructed after the Great Fire, in 1872—don't look much different than they did when Louis Glunz started his wine and spirits business here in 1888. The exterior has a handsome dark green, gold-trimmed facade and an ornate cast-iron sign. Inside are stained-glass windows imported from Germany, all of the original wooden wine racks, rich-hued murals of wine-related scenes, and numerous antique wine bottles from the days when the company ordered wine by the barrel and decanted it into its own bottles. The shop specializes in rare vintage California cabernets from smaller wineries, such as **Heitz, Grgich Hills,** and **Jordan,** and rare French wines, cognacs, and armagnacs. They will prepare custom gift packages and ship anywhere.

For a trip back in time, ask to visit the old wine-tasting room and the museum. The former, a dark, moody place, has bottles of significant wines arranged in racks and a wonderful collection of antique crystal wine glasses. The museum, which was the popular **Glunz Tavern** before Prohibition (when the shop switched to the legal sale of home-brewing ingredients), still has the original sandwich menu tacked to the wall, plus a number of well-worn cooperage tools. There's also a Schlitz memorabilia corner, the **House of Glunz** having been the first Chicago distributors of "the beer that made Milwaukee famous." Tours are available. ♦ M-Sa. 1206 N Wells St (at W Division St). 642.3000

Bests

Miriam Santos
Chicago City Treasurer

Nuevo Leon: My favorite place for authentic and inexpensive Mexican food in the center of **Pilsen,** Chicago's Mexican community. Take time to walk around and check out the bakeries and everything else this wonderful neighborhood has to offer.

Daniel J's: A very cozy and romantic restaurant, Daniel J's is still an unexpected, but welcome addition to **North Ashland Avenue.** Wonderful fish entrées, but make sure that you leave room for dessert. It's always crowded so make reservations.

Shopping on Michigan Avenue: Stroll down the **Magnificent Mile** and window or *really* shop in some of the best stores in Chicago.

Exploring Neighborhoods: Chicago is truly a city of neighborhoods. Get out of the hotels and walk! Whether it's in **Hyde Park, Andersonville, Humbolt Park,** or **Uptown,** Chicago is a walking city with many communities to take in and enjoy.

Lincoln Park Zoo: Take a walk through the only zoo in the United States that is still free to the public. While you are there, don't miss the Great Ape House where you will find the largest variety of great apes of any zoo in the country.

Harold Washington Library: One of Chicago's most beautiful structures, both inside and outside. Don't miss the Harold Washington Room to learn about the city's first African American mayor.

Hubbard Street Dance: Chicago is fortunate to host one of the best dance troupes in the country. Make sure to get reservations in advance.

Afternoon Tea: When you really need to wind down and let someone else take care of you, enjoy an afternoon tea at either the **Drake Hotel** or the **Four Seasons.** It's a perfect way to make a relaxing transition into the evening's activities.

Art Institute: One of the best ways to spend an afternoon in Chicago. When you get tired of walking and want something to eat, take a break in the Art Institute's beautiful outdoor cafe.

Pops for Champagne: Drop by for live jazz and great Champagne any night. But for a great Sunday brunch with live jazz and an incredible selection of Champagnes and wines, Pops is a great place to wrap up a weekend that you don't want to end.

Public Art Tours: Chicago has some of the best public art one can see. Take a tour and learn about all of the famous (and less famous) artists who have made sightseeing in Chicago so intriguing.

Summer Parades: If you are visiting Chicago during the summer, there's a good chance that a parade is going on somewhere. Every community takes pride in its parades and while some are held in the neighborhoods, many take place downtown.

City Council Meetings: In Chicago, where politics is a spectator sport, attend a City Council meeting in **City Hall** and see many of the notorious aldermen you have heard so much about.

Buddy Guy's Legends: No one visiting Chicago should leave without having heard Chicago blues. There are many blues clubs throughout the city, but if you have to pick one, go to Buddy Guy's.

Red Lion Pub: Enjoy an ale and some fish-and-chips at this haunted, but popular, English pub. Talk to the proprietor or some of the regulars about their experiences with the visitor who frequents the second floor (there really is a ghost). When you're done, browse through the wonderful used book stores across the street and along **Lincoln Avenue.**

Music Box Theatre: No matter what movie is shown, it's going to be a good one at the Music Box. But the real attractions include the pipe organ that is still played before every feature and the stars that twinkle from the sky (ceiling) above.

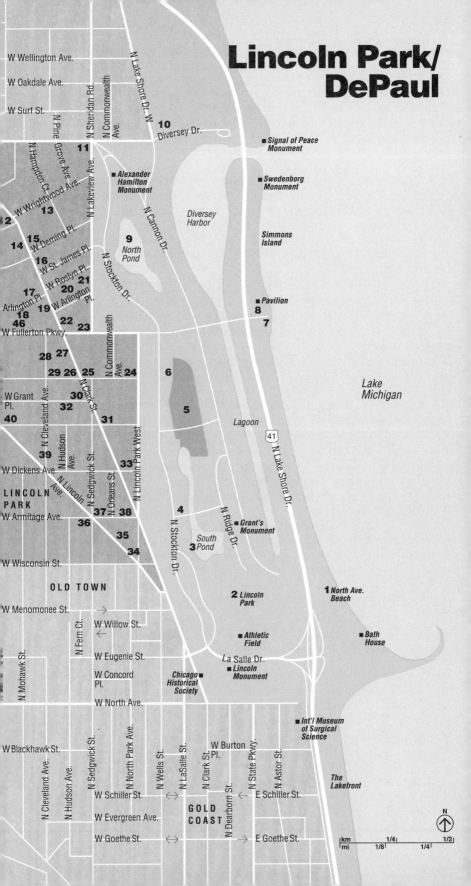

Lincoln Park/DePaul

W Wellington Ave.

W Oakdale Ave.

W Surf St.

N Sheridan Rd.

N Commonwealth Ave.

N Lake Shore Dr. W

10 Diversey Dr.

■ Signal of Peace Monument

11

N Pine Grove Ave.

N Lakeview Ave.

■ Alexander Hamilton Monument

■ Swedenborg Monument

N Hampden Ct.

W Wrightwood Ave.

13

Diversey Harbor

Simmons Island

2

15 W Deming Pl.

14

9 North Pond

N Cannon Dr.

16 W St. James Pl.

W Roslyn Pl. **21**

17 **20**

Arlington Pl. **19** W Arlington Pl.

18

46

22 **23**

W Fullerton Pkwy.

N Stockton Dr.

N Commonwealth Ave.

■ Pavilion

8

7

28 **27**

29 26 25

24

6

Lake Michigan

N Clark St.

30

W Grant Pl.

32

5

40

31

Lagoon

[41]

N Lake Shore Dr.

39

N Hudson Ave.

N Cleveland Ave.

W Dickens Ave.

N Lincoln Ave.

N Sedgwick St.

33

N Orleans St.

N Lincoln Park West

LINCOLN PARK

W Armitage Ave.

37 **38**

4

N Ridge Dr.

■ Grant's Monument

36

35

N Stockton Dr.

3 South Pond

34

W Wisconsin St.

1 North Ave. Beach

OLD TOWN

2 Lincoln Park

W Menomonee St. →

■ Athletic Field

■ Bath House

N Fern Ct.

W Willow St.

←

W Eugenie St.

La Salle Dr.

W Concord Pl.

Chicago ■ Historical Society

■ Lincoln Monument

N Mohawk St.

W North Ave.

■ Int'l Museum of Surgical Science

W Blackhawk St.

N Sedgwick St.

N North Park Ave.

N Wells St.

N LaSalle St.

N Clark St.

W Burton Pl.

N Dearborn St.

N State Pkwy.

N Astor St.

N Cleveland Ave.

N Hudson Ave.

W Schiller St. ↔

E Schiller St.

The Lakefront

W Evergreen Ave.

GOLD COAST

W Goethe St. ↔

→ E Goethe St.

N

km
mi   1/8   1/4   1/4   1/2

Lincoln Park/ DePaul

A lakefront park, beaches with sky-blue waters, and the **Lincoln Park Zoo** draw affluent residents and envious visitors to the bustling Lincoln Park neighborhood, ringed by **Diversey Parkway, North** and **Clybourn Avenues,** and **Lake Michigan.** Local architecture provides more attractions, from **Mies van der Rohe** towers overlooking the park to 19th-century town houses on tree-lined streets in the landmark **Mid-North** and **Sheffield Historic Districts.** At the community's heart, the **DePaul University** campus spans many acres and lends its name to a gentrified neighborhood that combines the collegiate with the urbane. Award-winning restaurants, original boutiques, first-class bookstores, and much more vie for your attention along **Lincoln Park West, Clark Street,** and **Fullerton, Armitage,** and **Lincoln Avenues.** And then there's the famous nightlife, including productions by the **Steppenwolf** and **Victory Gardens Theaters,** get-down Chicago sounds at **B.L.U.E.S.,** and billiards and bar hopping along **Halsted Street** and Armitage and Lincoln Avenues.

Lincoln Park's evolution into something more than pastoral scenery began with the arrival in the mid-1850s of the **McCormick Theological Seminary** (which has since moved to Hyde Park), named after industrialist benefactor Cyrus Hall McCormick. In the middle of farmlands, the seminary constructed chapels, academic buildings, and the **McCormick Row Houses,** an enclave of handsome town houses that still stand today. Another boost was the 1868 opening of the park from which the community draws its name. **Lincoln Park,** built upon what had been a depressing city cemetery, quickly became one of the city's most popular places to visit. It remains so today; it boasts a fascinating zoo, a plant and flower conservatory, pretty lagoons, and grassy lawns. The Great Fire of 1871 also led to the area's construction boom, as burned-out Chicagoans moved in.

Quite the high-class residential district throughout the 1920s and 1930s, Lincoln Park suffered setbacks during World War II, when many homes were converted into poorly maintained rooming houses. By the 1950s suburban flight had left the community in such a sorry state that city administrators officially declared it a blighted area. The designation proved fortuitous, however, as city funds became available for urban renewal. Dangerously dilapidated buildings were demolished, numerous vintage structures were beautifully rehabilitated, and new homes, apartment buildings, and retail stores were built. In the 1960s **DePaul University** embarked upon a long-range expansion program that continues to this day.

Now Lincoln Park rates as one of the city's most desirable—not to mention expensive—places to live, especially among young professionals. Whereas urban pioneers once picked up property for peanuts, the price of a town house these days can hover near a half-million dollars—and apartment rentals don't come cheaply, either. As a result, many middle-class residents have moved on to more affordable pastures. Some have relocated to the neighborhood's western edge, where the long-neglected **Clybourn Corridor** is undergoing a dramatic conversion to upscale housing and retail stores.

This part of the city is active around the clock; restaurants, theaters, and clubs are packed at night, especially on weekends. In warm weather, a steady stream of people wends its way to the park, zoo, and beach. So take along a good measure of patience wherever you're headed; you'll encounter crowds.

1 North Avenue Beach Unlike the Gold Coast's trendy Oak Street Beach, the sands of North Avenue are everyone's. Fit or fat, hip or hopelessly outdated, well-to-do or waiting to win the lottery—all are welcome. The beach curls out into Lake Michigan just above North Avenue and stretches a long, lazy mile north. From May to September, volleyball nets sprout like mushrooms—bring your own gear or reserve a court at the beach house (it's actually a ship onshore), which contains changing rooms, rest rooms, and a small concession stand. By car, exit Lake Shore Drive at LaSalle Drive. Look for parking in the lot just south of the beach, or head west and check for spaces along the streets through **Lincoln Park.** You can also bus or cab it to North Avenue, then take the pedestrian bridge over Lake Shore Drive. ◆ Along the shore of Lake Michigan (north of W North Ave)

2 Lincoln Park The park's thousand acres of lakefront land sweep north of West North Avenue with broad, grassy meadows, mature shade trees, two lagoons, and paths that wind around and through it all. Chicago's parks are meant to be used, and this one certainly is: running, bicycling, strolling, barbecuing, badminton playing—if it's fun, it's done. (See the "Lake View/Wrigleyville" chapter for information about **Lincoln Park**'s southern sector.) ◆ Bounded by Ardmore Ave, W North Ave, N Lincoln Park W, N Lakeview Ave, N Lake Shore Dr W, Marine Dr, and Lake Michigan

3 South Pond Don't just stand on the shoreline looking at the water—get onto it! Paddleboats are for rent from the boathouse near **Cafe Brauer** (see below) by the hour May through October. In winter, however, heed the signs: Stay off the ice. ◆ Lincoln Park (off W Wisconsin St)

3 Farm-in-the-Zoo The sign over the cattle barn used to read "Beef Animals" until somebody realized that it wasn't a respectful way to refer to Bossy. Cows, horses, sheep, pigs, and other creatures some city dwellers have never before seen in the flesh reside in a five-acre replica of a Midwestern farm. Goat milking, butter churning, and meet-the-animals pet fests are scheduled throughout the day. ◆ Free. Daily. Lincoln Park (at W Wisconsin St). 935.6700

4 Cafe Brauer A superb example of Prairie School architecture, this two-story building overlooking the South Pond was built in 1908 by **Dwight H. Perkins** of **Burnham & Root** as the **Lincoln Park Refectory.** Chicago businesspeople frequented the cafe for lunch in the early part of the century, when a complete meal cost 65 cents. Over the years, however, business declined, largely as a result of a state law prohibiting the sale of liquor in public parks. In 1941 the cafe closed and sat neglected for 50 years until the Chicago Park District, the Lincoln Park Zoological Society,

the Levy Organization, and a group of architects and historians teamed up to restore it to its original state. The building is now on the National Register of Historic Places. Partners in the restoration were **Harry J. Hunderman** of **Wiss, Janney, Elstner Associates; Meisel & Associates;** and **Lawrence B. Berkeley & Associates.** Fastidious attention was paid to detail: The company that manufactured the original French pan roof tiles was contracted to produce replacements, which required the reinvention of a glaze to match the originals. The walls were peeled down to the original salt-glazed bricks. Designs for new light fixtures were based on old lighting found during renovations.

The second-floor Great Hall, which is rented out for gala events, boasts polished hardwood floors, decorative stained glass, Rookwood-style tile murals, a dramatic skylight, and stained-glass and bronze chandeliers. On the first floor is a cafeteria decorated with handsome tile, oak paneling, and brass rails. Unfortunately, the food—hot dogs, hamburgers, little pizzas—isn't up to the setting. The fare at the old-fashioned **Ice Cream Shoppe,** also on the main level, is better. ◆ Daily; until 3PM November through March. 2021 N Stockton Dr (at W Armitage Ave). 281.2565

5 Lincoln Park Zoo A gift of two swans from New York's Central Park to Chicago in 1868 gave rise to a booming population of more than 2,000 of these graceful birds a century later. As for other zoo highlights, head for the **Great Ape House**, where primate families cavort just a thick pane of glass away from your face. Then escape the world in the **Rookery**, a serene habitat filled with winged creatures cavorting amid ponds and waterfalls. And on a hot day, there's nothing as refreshing—or mesmerizing—as watching the sea lions make waves in their little blue pond. The zoo adds a touch of the wild to the city: On warm summer nights, high-rise neighbors can hear the wolves howling. ◆ Free. Daily. 2200 N Cannon Dr (at W Webster Ave). 742.2000 &

Chicago Prohibition officer Eliot Ness, mythologized in film and TV, admitted in his autobiography that he never actually met Al Capone.

6 Lincoln Park Conservatory Three acres of greenhouses built here in 1891 provide a lush home to plant life from all corners of the earth. In the dead of winter, you can walk into a warm tropical garden of banana palms and spider plants. Four seasonal flower shows, including Christmas poinsettias and Easter lilies, draw oglers by the busload. A stately garden of some 20,000 flowers, most of them started from seed in the greenhouses, is planted each spring in the promenade out front. The fountain sculpture *Storks at Play,* by Augustus Saint-Gaudens and Frederick MacMonnies, serves as the outdoor backdrop to a million wish-you-were-here snapshots. ◆ Free. Daily. N Stockton Dr (near W Fullerton Ave). 742.7736 &

7 Rocks at Fullerton Avenue These immense stone steps which lead to the lake are a veritable outdoor theater on summer weekends. The beautiful people walk their beautiful dogs; cool dudes swerve on Rollerblades, balancing blaring boom boxes on their shoulders; and teenagers in love stroll arm-in-arm dressed in matching skin-tight studded black-leather swimsuits. ◆ W Fullerton Ave at Lake Michigan

8 Theatre on the Lake At this community theater owned and managed by the Chicago Park District, amateur actors strut their stuff in a summer series that has them belting out tunes from *The Music Man, Evita,* and other Broadway hits. A show at the screened-in theater can be fun when the weather is right; otherwise the absence of air-conditioning makes it stifling. The low ticket prices help compensate. ◆ Box office Tu-F 3-9PM; Sa 4- 9PM. Shows Tu-Sa 8PM. Reservations recommended. Lakefront (just north of W Fullerton Ave). 742.7771

9 North Pond Tool around in a paddleboat (the boat house is on the northeast side of the pond). Practice angling (bring your own pole, there are no rentals here) at the south end in the casting pond, or just rest on a grassy hill and enjoy the great view of the city to the south. ◆ Lincoln Park (between W Fullerton Pkwy and W Deming Pl)

10 Diversey Driving Range Golfers of all ages and skill levels line up to practice their swing at 35 tees at this Chicago Park District facility bounded by Diversey Harbor, Lake Shore Drive, and several high-rises. For those who prefer to putter around, there's also a miniature golf course. ◆ Fee. Daily April through November. W Diversey Pkwy (at N Lake Shore Dr W). 245.0909

11 Elks National Memorial Building Built in 1926 by **Egerton Swartwout** in recognition of members of the Benevolent and Protective Order of Elks who died in World War I, and rededicated after subsequent wars, this is the city's most lavish memorial. The building is a massive circular structure with a flattened dome above an enormous colonnade. Beneath the colonnade is a frieze, five feet high and 16 feet long, with allegorical carvings of war and peace. Elks medals, photos, and memorabilia are available for viewing in the archives room. The adjacent **Elks Magazine Building** was designed in 1967 by **Holabird & Root.** ◆ Donation requested. M-F. 2750 N Lakeview Ave (at W Diversey Pkwy). 477.275◑

12 2nd Hand Tunes This friendly, crowded shop sells used records—vinyl, that is. Its sister store a block south stocks CDs and cassettes, and its other sibling sells all three. They all carry everything from to punk to show tunes. ◆ Daily. 2604 N Clark St (at W Wrightwood Ave). 929.6325. Also at: 2550 N Clark St. 281.8813; 1375 E 53rd St (between Dorchester and Kenwood Aves). 684.3375

12 Wiener Circle $ Energetic staffers work elbow-to-elbow at a frantic pace to keep the condiment-laden "char dogs" and greasy fries coming. They accommodate nighthawks by staying open until the wee hours. ◆ Fast food ◆ Daily lunch and dinner until 4AM; F-Sa until 5AM. 2622 N Clark St (between W Wrightwood and W Schubert Aves). 477.744◑

12 Aphidistra The gruff intellectual types who run this place seem put off if you ask for help finding something amid the dusty jumble of used books (with rather high price tags). For a quick in/out, check the recent-arrivals table at the door, then cross the room and pick through the cheap paperbacks. ◆ M-F 12:30-9PM; Su noon-8PM. 2630 N Clark St (between W Wrightwood and W Schubert Aves). 549.3129

13 Francis J. Dewes House Designated a Chicago landmark in 1974, this house was built in 1896 for a wealthy German brewer in the Baroque Revival style by two European architects, **Adolph Cudell** and **Arthur Hercz.** The elaborate ornamentation of this privately owned home includes finely carved stonework and detailed cast-iron railings. Caryatids support a second-floor balcony at the Wrightwood Street entrance, and the western facade boasts a large staircase window of stained and leaded glass. The house at the west side of the lot, a typical Chicago town house dressed in the Baroque finery of its neighbor, was built by Dewes for his brother. ◆ 503 W Wrightwood Ave (at N Hampden Ct)

14 Frances' $ This restaurant has been serving home-style meals to Lincoln Park folk since the 1930s. Some people swear by the mashed potatoes, while others go for the potato pancakes. No one seems to

remember who Frances was, but her melt-in-your-mouth cheese blintzes are still a mainstay. Other offerings are largely cafeteria-quality. ♦ Deli ♦ Tu-Su breakfast, lunch, and dinner. 2552 N Clark St (between W Deming Pl and W Wrightwood Ave). 248.4580

15 Raymond Hudd For more than 46 years, this milliner has been designing hats for such celebrities as Phyllis Diller, and for a long list of Chicago bridesmaids. Hudd's hats for every occasion range from the classic to the fanciful—from pillboxes to straw bonnets adorned with plastic spiders. Whatever the style, the workmanship is always impeccable and the prices usually reasonable. ♦ Tu-Sa 2545 N Clark St (between W Deming Pl and W Wrightwood Ave). 477.1159

16 Dr. Wax Used and new records, tapes, and CDs, from Janis Joplin to Die Warsau, pack this dusty shop. You probably won't be able to browse for long unless your eyes don't mind cave-level lighting. ♦ Daily. 2529 N Clark St (at W Deming Pl). 549.3377

ALTERNATIVES

16 Alternatives These are some of the trendiest shoes for male and female twentysomethings you'll ever see. Given the quality and the neighborhood, the prices are surprisingly low. How does owner Sandro Ciurcina do it? He has friends and relatives in the shoe business back home in Florence. ♦ Daily. 2523 N Clark St (between W St. James Pl and W Deming Pl). 281.4801. Also at: 942 N Rush St (at E Oak St). 266.1545

16 Presence Ultracomfortable women's clothes, in styles that don't require wearers to work out at a gym five times a week. Most are made of natural fibers and are reasonably priced. Notice the fine selection of scarves, from Parisian silk to Indian cotton. ♦ Daily. 2501 N Clark St (at W St. James Pl). 248.1761

17 Steve Quick Jeweler If the *Starship Enterprise* crew were into fine jewelry, they could find something here to accent their outfits. Futuristic earrings, bracelets, necklaces, and wedding bands combine diamonds and other precious and semiprecious stones (such as tourmaline and quartz), many cut at odd angles and mounted untraditionally. You can watch the staff designer at work inside the shop. ♦ Daily. 2464 N Clark St (at W Roslyn Pl). 404.0034

RISTORANTE

18 Salvatore's ★$$ Down a quiet side street, away from the hubbub on Clark, Northern Italian classics are served by candlelight. Choose from a dozen pasta dishes, scampi, scungilli, clams, beef, chicken, and veal. For dessert try chocolate cheesecake smothered in raspberry sauce or ice cream truffles in assorted flavors. ♦ Italian ♦ Daily dinner. 525 W Arlington Pl (off N Clark St). 528.1200

19 Jerome's ★$$ The good, fresh, reasonably priced food runs the gamut, from juicy burgers with melted cheddar to vegetable stir-fries. Pastries and hearty millet bread are baked on the premises. Meals start with a basket of bread; if that whets your appetite for more, request a free loaf on your way out. The elevated patio, shaded by trees, overlooks the action on Clark Street. They also offer take-out service—and feed the homeless with the same fine food at a local church. ♦ American ♦ M-F lunch and dinner; Sa-Su brunch and dinner. 2450 N Clark St (at W Arlington Pl). 327.2207

19 Ouzeri ★$$ The Greek word *ouzeri* means a small local restaurant where friends gather to relax and enjoy themselves. This one specializes in *mezethes*—hot and cold appetizer-size portions of Greek specialties. The menu also includes extensive seafood and shish kebab entrées, chargrilled meats, and a traditional dish of smelt fried in olive oil and spiced with oregano. ♦ Greek ♦ Daily lunch and dinner. 2442 N Clark St (at W Arlington Pl). 477.6644

20 Arlington and Roslyn Place District If you'd like a respite from the 20th-century commercialism on this stretch of Clark Street, relief is literally just around the corner. Turn east at Roslyn or Arlington Place, tree-lined streets of century-old houses that together form a Chicago Landmark District. The wildly overgrown lot on Arlington just east of Clark Street is a small refuge for birds. St. James and Deming Places between Lakeview and Clark Streets are lined with charming town houses. When you return to Clark Street and look south from the west side of the street at Deming Place, you're back in the 20th century, with a view of the **John Hancock Center** and **900 North Michigan Avenue.** ♦ Between N Lakeview Ave and N Clark St

21 Theurer/Wrigley House Built in 1896 by **Richard E. Schmidt** and **Hugh M. G. Garden,** this is the only remaining mansion on Lakeview Avenue. Schmidt had apprenticed with **Adolph Cudell,** architect of the nearby **Francis J. Dewes House** (see above), and was well versed in German Neo-Classicism.

The richness of materials used here is striking, with green copper and black iron trim set off against the orange facade. Terra-cotta is used for the long narrow quoins, window frames, and the frieze and pediment above the entry porch. The conservatory at the southwest corner is original, but the sunroom above the entrance was added later. **Schmidt** and **Garden** went on to design several Prairie School landmarks, including the **Madlener House** and the **Montgomery Ward Warehouse.** William Wrigley of chewing gum fame bought the house in 1911; it remains a private residence. ♦ 2446 N Lakeview Ave (at W Arlington Pl)

22 My π $$ Although it appears small from the outside, this place is actually cavernous, with brick walls, stained-glass windows, and a fireplace. Ordering pizza entitles you to all you can eat at the giant salad bar. ♦ Pizza ♦ Daily lunch and dinner. 2417 N Clark St (at W Fullerton Ave). 929.3380 ♿

23 2400 North Lakeview Avenue This 1963 high-rise was the last apartment building in Chicago designed by **Mies van der Rohe,** master of the elegant glass-and-aluminum curtain wall. Floor-to-ceiling windows provide residents with fabulous views of **Lincoln Park** and the lake. ♦ At W Fullerton Ave

Ambria

24 Ambria ★★★$$$$ Set in an elegant Art Nouveau dining room in the Belden-Stratford Building (formerly a luxury hotel), this restaurant's excellent French nouvelle cuisine places it among the city's top dining spots and makes it popular for business entertaining. Chef Gabino Sotelino's imaginative menu subtly blends East and West in such dishes as Japanese *mizuna* greens salad with warm, creamy, goat-cheese dressing. The dinner menu has wonderful seafood dishes, such as charcoal-grilled sea bass served on tomato *coulis* with sautéed thinly sliced potatoes. Desserts range from sorbets and unusual ice creams to the signature white chocolate mousse served with dark chocolate fudge. A five-course prix-fixe degustation dinner is available. ♦ French ♦ M-Sa dinner. Reservations and jacket required. 2300 N Lincoln Park W (at W Belden Ave). 472.5959

24 Un Grand Café ★★$$$ This handsome and lively French bistro is the more casual, less expensive sister of **Ambria** (see above) across the Belden-Stratford Building lobby. Service is friendly and excellent. The satisfying entrées include *steak frites* (steak with french fries), roasted country-style chicken, and tender braised lamb shank in a basil-aioli sauce. Finish with a fresh-fruit tart or cobbler. ♦ French ♦ Daily dinner. Reservations recommended. 2300 N Lincoln Park W (at W Belden Ave). 348.8886

25 Tower Records/Video/Books The famous West Hollywood record store opened its Chicago outlet in 1991. Boasting a huge inventory of CDs, tapes, and laser discs in every musical category, it also hosts signings by bands in town on tour. An attached video store with an impressive selection of rental tapes has challenged the local **Blockbuster** for neighborhood supremacy. The book section carries the latest in contemporary fiction, as well as music magazines from around the globe. ♦ Daily until midnight. 2301 N Clark St (at W Belden Ave). 477.5994 ♿

26 Nonpareil Look no further for that special gift: a full-size carved wood alligator head from Guatemala, ceramic coffee mugs decorated with Mexican Day of the Dead skulls, and purse-size plastic fez-capped Shriners, to name just a few of the choices at this eclectic shop. ♦ Daily. 2300 N Clark St (at W Belden Ave). 477.2933

26 Distinctive Interior Designs Every piece is a beauty; glass serving bowls from Poland, Royal Doulton dinner plates, Italian glazed tile coasters, hand-painted majolica dishes from France, and sturdy American pewter pitchers. Items are shipped anywhere in the US. ♦ Daily. 2322 N Clark St (between W Belden Ave and W Fullerton Pkwy). 248.0738 ♿

27 Neo Despite its name, this club opened in 1980 and is now an elder statesman of the city's dance club scene. Enter via an alleyway painted with bright geometric designs. Young urban professionals and die-hard clubsters dance to industrial and house music into the wee hours. The place doesn't get moving until midnight, at the earliest. ♦ Cover charge. Daily 9PM-4AM. 2350 N Clark St (between W Belden Ave and W Fullerton Pkwy). 528.2622

28 2300 Block of North Cleveland Avenue Tour guides describe the house at **No. 2314** (circa 1880) as "riotously eclectic." The facade is a mixture of brick and stone, false slate mansard, Gothic detailing, and a large gable with a finial and hooded dormer. The Georgian Revival porch was probably added later. The brick and sandstone residence at **No. 2325** (circa 1885) has an unusual corner rectangular bay in turret form. At **Nos. 2339** and **2343** stand two of the area's three wooden structures that predate the Great Fire of 1871 (**Policeman Bellinger's Cottage** is the other; see below). They probably escaped damage because the fire had almost died out by the time it got this far north. These are all private residences. ♦ Between W Belden Ave and W Fullerton Pkwy

Tales from the Windy City

Chicago is often depicted as a tough, hustler's town; the penetrating edge of city life makes it a perfect backdrop for mystery and crime novels. It is also one of the best examples of the immigrant experience, not to mention political chicanery. Here are a few of the books that evoke both the historical and present-day atmosphere of this constantly changing metropolis.

And Now, Your Chicago Bulls! A Thirty-Year Celebration by Ronald Lazenby (Taylor Publishing, 1995). This lavishly illustrated book is actually a fawning tribute to one of the greatest team franchises in sports history and to the illustrious Michael Jordan.

Another Dead Teenager by Thomas E. Krupowicz (TERK Publishing, 1995). Written by a retired Chicago police officer and fingerprint expert, this collection of 10 short stories intrigues and horrifies.

Black Metropolis: A Study of Negro Life in a Northern City (University of Chicago Press, revised edition 1993). This sociological study chronicles the rise of Chicago's African-American community through the first half of the 20th century.

Boss: The Life and Times of Richard J. Daley by Mike Royko (NAL-Dutton, 1988). The prizewinning newspaper columnist offers a scathing portrayal of the reign of the first Mayor Daley.

Chicago, City on the Make by Nelson Algren (McGraw-Hill, 1951). In hard-boiled prose, Algren tells the story of the city through stories of its people—from the native Potawatomi, to the 1919 Black Sox, to gangster Al Capone, and finally, social worker and former Jane Addams.

Hard Case by Barbara D'Amata (Scribners, 1994). Fictional freelance reporter Cat Marsala solves another mystery in the trauma unit of a major Chicago hospital.

Homeland by John Jakes (Doubleday, 1993). Jakes weaves an evocative portrait of the turn-of-the-century immigrant experience through the rise of one German family.

Horseshoes and Nuclear Weapons by Mike Hatch (New Publishing, 1994). The subject of this thriller is a radical terrorist cult that is trying to overthrow the government and destroy the city.

Jaded by Eugene Izzi (Simon and Schuster, 1996). Fictional detective Jake Philips investigates dirty Chicago cops.

The Jungle by Upton Sinclair (NAL-Dutton, reissued 1989). Written as an indictment of the harsh treatment of immigrants who worked in the Chicago stockyards, this book resulted in the first regulation of the food industry and the passage of the Pure Food and Drug Act.

Killer on Argyle Street by Michael Raleigh (St. Martin's Press, 1995). This murder mystery set in Uptown Chicago abounds with vivid descriptions of the neigborhood's diversity and its Vietnamese and Cambodian residents.

Windy City by Hugh Holton (Forge, 1995). Holton, a real-life Chicago police lieutenant, wrote this mystery about a fictional local mystery writer who solves a real-life murder. Now *that's* twisted!

Windy City Blues: V.I. Warshawski Stories by Sara Paretsky (Delacorte Press, 1995). The queen of Chicago detective fiction writes of the neigborhoods that nonlocals rarely see in this collection of stort stories featuring private eye V.I. (Vic) Warshawski. Check out some full-length V.I. Warshawski mysteries, too, like *Guardian Angel* or *Tunnel Vision*.

Writing Chicago: Modernism, Ethnography, and the Novel by Carla Cappetti (Columbia University Press, 1993). A comparison and parallel study of the fiction of Chicago writers Nelson Algren, Richard Wright, and James Farrell.

29 Ann Halsted House Built in 1883, the oldest known residential commission of **Adler & Sullivan** was begun when the firm was still known as **D. Adler & Company.** The 27-year-old **Louis Sullivan** was integrating the Beaux Arts training he'd received in Paris (hence the facade's strict symmetry), the unusual Egyptoid ornamentation he'd seen in the Philadelphia office of architect **Frank Furness** (as in the rigid lotus flower in the gable pediment), and the picturesque use of materials that made the Queen Anne style so popular (as found on the elaborate chimneys). The house remains privately owned. ◆ 440 W Belden Ave (at N Cleveland Ave)

30 Panache Welcome to accessories heaven, laden with one-of-a-kind belts, earrings, necklaces, bracelets, scarves, and hair clips. The friendly sales staff is quick to assist. ◆ Daily. 2252 N Clark St (between W Grant Pl and W Belden Ave). 477.4537

30 Christina's An old house turned boutique, this shop features women's suits, casual separates, and eveningwear hanging on racks and over a fireplace mantel. ◆ Daily. 2248 N Clark St (between W Grant Pl and W Belden Ave). 549.2442

30 Degagé Women's conservative suits, trendy sportswear, and designer jewelry are on the second floor of a Victorian town house. The French 1930s-style handmade jewelry and the silk kimono vests are especially nice. ◆ Daily. 2246 N Clark St (at W Grant Pl). 935.7737

31 Francis W. Parker School Named for the 19th-century educator who successfully promoted the idea of schools for teacher training, **Parker** has long been known as Chicago's "progressive" private school, while the **Latin School of Chicago** is considered more traditional. Alumnus Abbott Pattison sculpted the figures of children at the main Clark Street entrance, which was designed by **Holabird & Root** in 1962. The school's parents include numerous Chicago celebs like Gene Siskel, who often volunteer for the school's extensive adult education classes. ◆ 330 W Webster Ave (at N Clark St). 549.0172

32 Mid-North District The sign at West Grant Place says that this area is significant for its concentration of 19th-century brick row houses. And it is. For a brief walking tour, head south and west to Hudson and Webster Avenues, walk south on Hudson to Dickens Avenue, then go west a block to Cleveland Avenue and walk north to Fullerton Avenue. You will see a wide range of building types, from early cottages that survived the 1871 fire to a stark modernist dwelling, along with many beautiful renovations of late 19th-century architecture. ◆ Enter at W Grant Pl (at N Clark St)

Within the Mid-North District:

2200 Block of North Cleveland Avenue Some houses on this block were built in the last decade while others have been here since the 1860s. None is more than four stories high, and the mix makes for a spectacular sight. The modernist fortress at **No. 2215** was the home of **Bruce Graham,** the retired **Skidmore, Owings & Merrill** partner who designed the **John Hancock Center** and **Sears Tower,** as well as this 1969 house. Working here on a considerably smaller scale, he created a very private residence of reinforced concrete with a black steel-bar gate. Italianate duplex town houses at **Nos. 2234-36** share an ornate cornice and columned porch. They were constructed around 1874, just before the fire zone (where wood construction was prohibited) was extended to this area. The blockiness and large scale of the freestanding residence at **456 Belden Avenue** (circa 1890) set it apart from its neighbors. Although most architects advised the owner to tear it down and start over, he opted for renovation. The 1972 remodel by **Harry Weese & Associates** divided the basement into two apartments and left the top floors for the owner's home. ◆ Between W Webster and W Belden Aves

Policeman Bellinger's Cottage This 1869 house is one of the few wood structures to survive the Great Fire of 1871. Bellinger and his brother-in-law apparently kept the fire at bay by dousing individual sparks as they landed on the roof, rather than wasting precious water trying to keep the whole building wet. Coincidentally, it was designed by **W.W. Boyington,** the architect of the **Chicago Water Tower,** another famous survivor of the fire. The building, a private residence, is a typical Chicago cottage with a raised basement and high first floor. Charming details include decorative shingles, brackets, and a false front over the gable reminiscent of Wild West storefronts. ◆ 2121 N Hudson Ave (at W Dickens Ave)

Chicago has 131 forest preserves, 572 parks, and 31 beaches. Its public lakefront is 27 miles long.

Actor John Malkovich was the co-founder of Chicago's renowned Steppenwolf Theater Company. Other famous Steppenwolf alumni are "Frasier"'s John Mahoney, *Forest Gump's* Gary Sinise, and "Roseanne"'s Laurie Metcalf.

Restaurants/Clubs: Red	**Hotels:** Blue
Shops/ 🍴 Outdoors: Green	**Sights/Culture:** Blac

Mr. Grunt

33 R.J. Grunts ★$$ The first of Chicago restaurateur Rich Melman's many hot spots is credited with introducing the salad bar to America. **Grunts** is an animated spot with checkered tablecloths and a menu covered with cartoon characters. Grub includes half-pound burgers. ◆ American ◆ Daily lunch and dinner. 2056 N Lincoln Park W (at W Dickens Ave). 929.5363

34 The Bulls There's no connection to the basketball team, but this bistro claims fame in its own right: It's been a neighborhood fixture for as long as most current residents can remember. Smoky, crowded, and open every night of the year, it's also heaven for jazz club junkies who can't live without their daily fix. ◆ Daily 8PM-4AM; Sa to 5AM. 1916 N Lincoln Park W (between W Armitage and N Lincoln Aves). 337.3000

35 Ranalli's on Lincoln $$ Although the pizza is just average in quality and above average in price, on summer evenings patrons fill the 75 or so outdoor tables while crowds gather on the sidewalk to wait for their names to be bellowed through a megaphone. If your wallet is full, this is a good place to relax and sample some unusual brews—the menu features more than a hundred brands of beer. ◆ Pizza ◆ Daily lunch and dinner. 1925 N Lincoln Ave (off W Armitage Ave). 642.4700

36 Chalet Wine and Cheese Shop Adventurous sorts can find more interesting and reasonably priced fare in the ethnic neighborhoods, but this shop—one of four in the city—is still a good place to stock up on cheeses, pâtés, beverages, and such for a picnic in the park. ◆ Daily. 405 W Armitage Ave (between N Sedgwick St and N Hudson Ave). 266.7155 &

37 Geja's Cafe ★★$$$ Fondue lives on at this romantic hideaway, with subdued lighting, intimate booths, and live flamenco and classical guitar music. Dinners include abundant portions of meat

Geja's cafe

or seafood and fresh vegetables, ready to cook at your table. Save room for dessert, perhaps fruit and cake dipped in chocolate. One warning: The air here grows thick with the smells of sterno and cigarette smoke (there is a nonsmoking section, which is a little better). ◆ Fondue ◆ Daily dinner. 340 W Armitage Ave (between N Lincoln Ave and N Orleans St). 281.9101

37 Ben & Jerry's The Vermont-based ice-cream company with a social conscience scoops up rich, natural ice cream in tempting flavors such as rainforest crunch and chocolate-chip cookie dough. Take along a few friends for a Vermonster: 20 scoops of ice cream topped with gobs of ice goo. ◆ Daily 11AM-1OPM. 338 W Armitage Ave (between N Orleans St and N Lincoln Ave). 281.5152 &

38 Park West First it was a concert hall, then a dance hall, then a concert hall again. Now it's both. Concerts have included performers like Yoko Ono and range from reggae to rock to classical. Sometimes dancing follows; other times dancing is the main event, with a band or recorded music. Flexible seating accommodates hundreds. ◆ Tickets or cover charge. Hours vary. 322 W Armitage Ave (at N Clark St and N Lincoln Park W). Box office and events schedule 929.5959

39 2100 Block of North Cleveland Avenue An unfortunate example of what the *Old House Journal* calls "remuddling" is seen at **2125 North Cleveland Avenue.** The owners' desire to modernize their building (which probably seemed hope-lessly outdated in the 1960s) resulted in a suburbanized facade that has no relationship to the original scale, forms, or materials. The two-story house at **No. 2147** (circa 1883) is sometimes attributed to a youthful **Louis Sullivan** because of the Egyptoid ornamentation and the unusual triangular bay. Alterations to the facade have made the composition awkward. A wonderful Art Deco facade gave **No. 2150** a face-lift early in the Depression. The spectacular two-story leaded-glass window is the highlight of a jazzy geometric composition. Irene Castle, of the dance team Vernon and Irene Castle, once lived here. These are all private residences. ◆ Between W Dickens and W Webster Aves

40 Bacino's $$ They claim to serve "America's first heart-healthy pizza," a stuffed spinach pizza that meets American Heart Association nutritional guidelines. But that's if you eat only one piece. Still, the pizzas are made with only natural ingredients. A no-reservations policy explains the long lines that form outside on weekends. ◆ Pizza ◆ Daily lunch and dinner. 2204 N Lincoln Ave (at W Webster Ave). 472.7400

40 Sterch's In the midst of the Lincoln Avenue rat race, this cozy neighborhood bar stands out for its simplicity. It's just a quiet place to meet a friend for a beer. ♦ Daily to 2AM. 2238 N Lincoln Ave (between W Webster and W Belden Aves). 281.2653

40 Big Nasty One whiff will bring memories of fraternity parties rolling in. The lager-soaked furniture, the warm beer served in plastic cups, the stained pool table and bargain prices attract people who yearn to relive their college days, as well as those who are still living them. Predictably, the crowd gets rowdy. Beware: Regulars enjoy dowsing other patrons with beer and spraying each other with Silly String (sold behind the bar for $3 a can). ♦ Tu-F 7PM-2AM; Sa to 3AM; usually closed Tuesday and Wednesday from September through March. 2242 N Lincoln Ave (between W Webster and W Belden Aves). 404.1535

41 Natural Selection Gifts of every variety are displayed in a tiny space redolent of scented candles and potpourri. Decorative ceramic items and jewelry, with standouts such as Czechoslovakian glass earrings delicate in design and color, are the specialty. ♦ M-Sa. 2260 N Lincoln Ave (between W Webster and W Belden Aves). 327.8886

42 Cafe Equinox ★$ This light and breezy coffeehouse is on the site of one of the oldest drugstores in Chicago and contains the original woodwork and cabinets. The inventive menu features light fare, including soups and salads. In warm weather, sidewalk tables provide a nice vantage for watching the street action while sipping designer coffee. ♦ Coffeehouse ♦ Daily until midnight. 2300 N Lincoln Ave (at W Belden Ave). 477.5126

43 John Barleycorn Memorial Pub $$ In 1890 this sprawling neighborhood pub was built as a saloon. During Prohibition, it fronted as a Chinese laundry. Customers were served by deliverymen who rolled in laundry carts loaded with bottles of bootleg liquor. The pub got its new name sometime in the 1960s. It serves 11 beers on tap and pretty good hamburgers, accompanied by classical music and a nonstop slide show of museum paintings and sculpture. Retire to the beer garden, weather permitting, or throw darts at the real bristle boards in the lounge. Weekday all-you-can-eat specials attract starving artists. ♦ American ♦ Daily lunch and dinner to 1AM. 658 W Belden Ave (at N Lincoln Ave). 348.8899 &

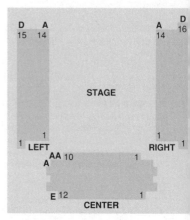

44 Victory Gardens Theater The company has presented nearly 175 plays since its founding in 1974, with an emphasis on the work of Chicago playwrights and world premieres. A number of productions, among them *Beau Jeste* by James Sherman, have gone on to popular acclaim in New York City. A Readers' Theater series features staged readings of new and not-yet-completed works. The 195-seat main stage and a 60-seat studio, which is used for smaller productions, classes, auditions, and rehearsals, are on the first floor of a building **Victory Gardens** shares with the **Body Politic Theatre**. ♦ Tu-Su. 2257 N Lincoln Ave (between W Webster and W Belden Aves). 871.3000 &

44 Body Politic Theatre One of the city's first Off-Loop theaters, the **Body Politic** (seating plan above) was founded in 1969 with a mission to revitalize the city through the arts. The company has provided extensive theatrical training, supported the formation of small theaters, and nurtured the talents of such playwrights as David Mamet and Alan Gross. In June the theater hosts one of the city's most enjoyable street fairs to raise funds for new productions. ♦ Tu-Su. 2261 N Lincoln Ave (between W Webster and W Belden Aves), Second floor. Box office 871.3000

45 600-700 West Fullerton Parkway In the late 1800s, Fullerton Parkway was one of the most fashionable residential streets on the North Side. This tree-lined block is still one of the prettiest in the city, with rows of three-story bay-fronted buildings of brick and stone. The block is anchored by **Lincoln Park Presbyterian Church**, a sturdy Romanesque structure designed by **Clinton J. Warren** in 1888. ♦ Between N Geneva Terr and N Orchard St

46 Church of Our Savior When the Presbyterians left this site for their new church a block away in 1889, the Episcopalians bought it, razed the old building, and replaced it with a fashionable Romanesque church. Architect **Clinton J. Warren,** who designed the new churches for both denominations, later designed the **Congress Hotel** downtown. The church's main entrance is at the base of the turreted bell tower. Inside are five stained-glass windows by Louis Tiffany and walls of unusual unglazed terra-cotta. ♦ 530 W Fullerton Pkwy (between N Clark St and N Geneva Terr). 549.3832

Courtesy of Holabird & Root

47 St. Clement's Catholic Church George D. Barnett built this church (pictured above) in 1917-18. The interior was restored in 1989 by **Holabird & Root** and it's now one of the most beautiful spaces in the city. Every surface is embellished, from the painted dome to the marbleized columns, and the overall effect is sublime. Architect **Walker Johnson** of **Holabird & Root** designed the hanging light fixtures that provide computer-controlled illumination yet look as though they've been here forever. ♦ 642 W Deming Pl (at N Orchard St). 281.0371 &

48 Children's Memorial Hospital Established in 1892, this well-known hospital has a rooftop helipad for flying in patients from all over the country. The building was designed in 1961 by **Schmidt, Garden & Erickson.** ♦ 707 W Fullerton Ave (at N Burling St). 880.4000

49 Peter's $ This neighborhood diner once was popular with the late-night postconcert crews that dribbled over from the blues bars on Halsted and the **Deja Vu Bar Room** on Lincoln. When it expanded into an adjacent storefront and cut its 24-hour service, the place lost a bit of local flavor (and most current patrons are likely to be home asleep before last call). The solid diner fare is still a nice way to start a Saturday, though. ♦ Diner ♦ Daily breakfast, lunch, and dinner. 742 W Fullerton Ave (at N Halsted St). 880.5730

50 B.L.U.E.S. A dark, narrow nightclub with a little stage showcases the big talents of blues stars Sunnyland Slim, Little Ed and the Imperials, Albert King, and many others. ♦ Cover charge. Daily; shows start at 9PM. 2519 N Halsted St (at W Lill Ave). 528.1012. Also at: 1124 W Belmont Ave (at N Racine Ave). 525.8989

51 Terrain Natural-product devotees David Winters and Robert Lang feature hard-to-find products for the hair and skin, including the lines of Kiehl's from New York, Ahava from Israel, Decleor and Phytotherathrie from France, and their own Terrain line. The in-house salon specializes in such treatments as moortherapy, in which the hair and scalp are massaged with mud from Belgium. ♦ Daily. Treatments by appointment. 2542 N Halsted St (between W Lill and W Wrightwood Aves). 549.0888

51 Kingston Mines When in town, movie stars and musicians inevitably show up in the audience at this blues club, which is creeping up on its third decade. Two stages feature live blues seven days a week. Regular talent includes Lonnie Brooks, Valerie Wellington, and Junior Wells. The place gets packed quickly, so arrive early or be prepared to stand all night. ♦ Cover. Daily; shows start at 9:30PM. 2548 N Halsted St (at W Wrightwood Ave). 477.4646

52 Corner Pocket The real hotshots shoot pool elsewhere, so customers here can enjoy a nice, quiet game at one of six tables. There's also a backyard beer garden. ♦ M-F 4PM-2AM; Sa-Su from noon. 2610 N Halsted St (at W Wrightwood Ave). 281.0050

52 Itto Sushi ★$$ Sushi and sashimi seem to be highly revered here, since *itto* refers to a spiritual gathering. You can watch the sushi chef prepare your selections and ceremoniously set them before you on the blond-wood counter at the sushi bar. Broiled fish and meat, teriyaki, and tempura are also served. The restaurant has its own parking lot, a rarity in this area. ♦ Japanese ♦ M-Sa lunch and dinner. 2616 N Halsted St (between W Wrightwood and W Schubert Aves). 871.1800

The four stars in the flag of Chicago represent the Fort Dearborn Massacre (1812), the Great Fire (1871), the World's Columbian Exposition (1893), and the Century of Progress Fair (1933).

Can We Talk?

Chicago is home to three of the top talk shows in the country— "Oprah," the "Jenny Jones Show," and the "Jerry Springer Show." If your life isn't colorful enough to be a panelist, you can at least be a member of the studio audience. Admission to all three shows is free, but you must reserve well in advance. The more flexible your dates, the better your chances, or try your luck on a standby line; call for taping schedules.

Jenny Jones

(NBC Tower, 454 N Columbus Dr, at E Illinois St, 836.9485). Call to request tickets or to suggest topics for the show.

Jerry Springer

(NBC Tower, 454 N Columbus Dr, at E Illinois St, 321.5365). Tickets by phone reservation; you must be at least 18 years old to be a member of the studio audience.

Oprah

(Harpo Studios, 1050 W Washington St, at N Aberdeen St, 591.9222). Make telephone reservations at least one month in advance; staffers will take your name and later confirm your seat reservation.

52 Uncle Tannous ★$$ The arabesque inner sanctum and sunny indoor patio at this restaurant provide the perfect setting for a Lebanese feast. Start with *maza,* a mass of appetizers that fills the table with dishes ranging from pickled vegetables to stuffed grape leaves. Juicy lamb chops or *shawarma,* a seasoned mixture of beef and lamb, are recommended entrées. ♦ Middle Eastern ♦ M dinner; Tu-Su lunch and dinner. 2626 N Halsted St (between W Wrightwood and W Schubert Aves). 929.1333

53 Steve Starr Studio Midnight-blue "Evening in Paris" perfume bottles, Art Deco lamps, chrome toasters, and eerie lighting make you feel like you're in a time warp. All of the aforementioned are for sale. What's not for sale, but is on view here, is owner Steve Starr's personal collection of gorgeous Art Deco picture frames containing smiling photos of such famous customers as Diana Ross and Bette Midler. (You can, however, take some of them home in *Picture Perfect,* the Rizzoli-published art book Starr wrote.) ♦ M-F noon-6PM; Sa-Su noon-5PM. 2779 N Lincoln Ave (at W Diversey Pkwy). 525.6530

53 Delilah's The sign hanging outside this alternative music pub bears a portrait of Snow White on one side and the Evil Queen on the other—an apt reflection of the contrast between the staff and clientele's pleasant demeanor and their occasionally menacing appearance. The goateed boys and black-clad punkettes that run the place are surprisingly friendly, even to guys in ties. DJs play tunes by unknown local bands when the well-stocked jukebox is idle. Upstairs is a small room with comfy chairs and a pool table. Sample one of the 26 kinds of whiskey available. ♦ Daily to 2AM; Sa to 3AM. 2771 N Lincoln Ave (between W Schubert Ave and W Diversey Pkwy). 472.2771

54 Star Top Cafe ★★$$$ Named for the star-shaped iron burners on its stovetop, this cafe has an offbeat look. Regulars love the windows and signs outside, which are redecorated every six months or so: There have been psychedelic paisleys, zebra stripes, and little primitive cave man designs. There is also bizarre modern art hanging on the walls inside; it gets changed every few months or so, too. Owner Bill Ammons describes the menu as fusion cuisine, an eclectic variety of spicy foods from around the planet. Rock music is played at high volume. ♦ International ♦ M-Sa dinner. Reservations recommended. 2748 N Lincoln Ave (between W Schubert Ave and W Diversey Pkwy). 281.0997

55 Act I This shop has the city's largest collection of theater books, plus trade magazines such as *Variety* and *Backstage.* ♦ M-F until 8PM; Su noon-6PM. 2632 N Lincoln Ave (at W Wrightwood Ave). 348.6757

55 950—Lucky Number The dance floor is big and black with a disco ball overhead, and the taped music is progressive at this no-frills club. ♦ Cover charge Friday and Saturday. W-F 8PM-2AM; Sa to 3AM. 950 W Wrightwood Ave (at N Lincoln Ave). 929.8955

56 Healing Earth Resources With incense-drenched air and New Age music in the background, it's a cinch you'll find crystals here. You will, along with Indian weavings, silver jewelry, self-help books, air cleaners, and ionizers. The adjacent **Earth Cafe** sells organic juices, fresh wheat grass, and light vegetarian meals (such as avocado sandwiches) to eat in or take out. ♦ Daily. 2570 N Lincoln Ave (at W Wrightwood and N Sheffield Aves). 327.8459 ♿

In 1918 Illinois, Wisconsin, and Michigan became the first states to give women the right to vote in national elections.

57 Apollo Theater Center This striking 350-seat space is one of the oldest commercial theaters outside the Loop. Producers often book the space for big-budget productions of Off-Broadway hits such as *Lend Me a Tenor,* which attract suburbanites by the busload. Seating is in five sections around a thrust stage. Try to avoid row F; it has less leg room. ♦ 2540 N Lincoln Ave (between W Altgeld St and W Wrightwood Ave). Box office 935.6100

57 Spacetime Tanks Located in an unsightly 1970s condo/retail complex, this unique day spa specializes in isolation float tanks. These sealed pods (not for the claustrophobic) are filled with warm water laced with float-inducing minerals. Strip down, hop in a tank, and let your mind go free. Massages and sound-and-light experiences with earphones and goggles are also available. ♦ Daily until 9PM. Appointment necessary. 2526 N Lincoln Ave (between W Altgeld St and W Wrightwood Ave). 472.2700

58 Lilly's Stuccoed caverns connected by archways, a long window overlooking Lincoln Avenue, a creaky wooden floor, and a little stage with a piano make for a neat, quirky place to come for live blues. Local talent predominates. ♦ Cover charge. Daily 4PM-2AM. 2513 N Lincoln Ave (between W Altgeld St and W Lill Ave). 525.2422

59 Kongoni Co-owners Kim Clark and Dan Vulinovic fell in love with each other and with African handicrafts at about the same time. Their inventory includes musical instruments, Zulu baskets, and dolls. Best of all are the necklaces made of antique trade beads, and a line of clothing designed by Clark and constructed from African fabrics. ♦ Daily. 2480½ N Lincoln Ave (between W Montana and W Altgeld Sts). 929.9749 ♿

60 Fiber Works Weaver Kathy Jahnke sells yarn and other supplies for knitting and weaving, along with finished pieces (including sweaters, bags, and scarves) by herself and others. Classes are taught at looms lined up in the back of the store. ♦ Daily. 2457 N Lincoln Ave (between W Fullerton Ave and W Altgeld St). 327.0444 ♿

60 Booksellers Row This store has rolling wooden ladders reaching up to shelves full of books, but none of the musty, mildewy odors of other used bookstores—which is just as proprietors Howard and Alison Cohen like it. They carry used books, fine and rare volumes, and many review copies, all reasonably priced. ♦ M-Sa 11AM-10:30PM; Su noon-8:30PM. 2445 N Lincoln Ave (between W Fullerton Ave and W Altgeld St). 348.1170 ♿. Also at: 408 S Michigan Ave (between E Congress Pkwy and E Van Buren St). 427.4242

60 Biograph Theater Gangster John Dillinger was lured here to see the movie *Manhattan Melodrama* one evening in 1934, little realizing that FBI agents were gathering outside to gun him down (thanks to a hot tip from his friend Anna Sage, the notorious "Lady in Red"). The theater has since been divided into four screens. It shows first-run features. ♦ 2433 N Lincoln Ave (between W Fullerton Ave and W Altgeld St). 348.4123

61 Blake Fashion-forward European designs are featured in this uncluttered women's clothing store. Owners Marilyn and Donnie have pared the selection down to only the best of everything the upscale trendsetter *must* have. Labels include Ghost and Helmut Lang. ♦ Daily. 2448 N Lincoln Ave (between W Fullerton Ave and W Montana St). 477.3364 ♿

61 Red Lion Anglophiles congregate at this authentic English pub that serves Sam Smith Nut Brown Ale and other imports. Posters of London line the walls. The triple-deck patio in back is great in warm weather. ♦ Daily to 2AM. 2446 N Lincoln Ave (between W Fullerton Ave and W Montana St). 348.2695

61 Uncle Dan's Army-Navy Camping and Travel This surplus-plus store stocks its shelves with everything from sub-zero–rated sleeping bags to French Foreign Legion kepis. The establishment caters to both serious campers and college students looking for funky winter hats. The staff is knowledgeable and friendly. Seasonal clothing is often on sale, so keep an eye peeled for bargains. ♦ Daily. 2440 N Lincoln Ave (between W Fullerton Ave and W Montana St). 477.1918

61 Lounge Ax A few years ago, owners Julia Adams and Susan Miller turned a neighborhood tavern into the hottest club in the city for alternative music. In the process, they became the doyennes of the local rock scene and friends of many bands around the country. They have welcomed top local and national acts, including The Sea & Cake, Golden Smog, Red Red Meat, and The Mekons. If you're looking for an intimate rock club, this one is a must. ♦ Cover charge. M-F 8PM-2AM; Sa to 3AM; music starts at 9PM. 2438 N Lincoln Ave (between W Fullerton Ave and W Montana St). 525.6620

61 Three Penny Theater Although it's a little run-down, this cinema is a great place to catch double features of art and foreign films before they leave town. ♦ Daily. 2424 N Lincoln Ave (at W Fullerton Ave). 935.5744

62 DePaul University This Catholic university was established in 1898 as **St. Vincent's College.** It was chartered as **DePaul University** in 1907, and for the next 50 years remained relatively small. In the 1960s it embarked on a major expansion program, and in 1973 acquired the nearby campus of Presbyterian **McCormick Theological Seminary.**The purchase added considerable real estate to the university's holdings. **McCormick,** originally known as the **Indiana Theological Seminary,** had moved here in 1859 from New Albany, Indiana, thanks to a $100,000 gift from industrialist Cyrus McCormick. In subsequent decades, a Gothic chapel, many classroom halls, and a group of homes now known as the **McCormick Row House District** (see below) were built on the property. By 1892 the seminary was one of the largest landowners in the Lincoln Park area, with holdings valued at $1.3 million. In 1973 it moved to Hyde Park to affiliate with theology schools at the **University of Chicago,** providing **DePaul** with its own growth opportunity. **DePaul** now covers some 25 acres in the area, and also maintains a separate campus downtown. Its student enrollment is nearly 15,000. ♦ Bounded by W Webster and W Fullerton Aves, and N Halsted St and N Kenmore Ave 362.8000 ♿

63 Sheffield Historic District Less congested and more modest than the Lincoln Park neighborhood, the Sheffield district was built in the late 19th century as a working-class area, but now rivals its eastern neighbor in popularity and price. This is the archetypal gentrified neighborhood, where young couples and families have renovated decrepit housing and converted two or three flats into luxurious single-family homes. The Sheffield Neighborhood Association sponsors a Garden Walk every July, when residents show off their spectacular landscaping. Clifton Avenue, from Armitage to Webster Avenues, has the heaviest concentration of front gardens, which provide wonderful viewing all summer long. Architecturally, the area is full of small treasures that reward the careful viewer: decorative brickwork, terra-cotta ornamentation, and carved stone lintels above doors and windows. ♦ Bounded by W Armitage and W Fullerton Aves, and N Halsted St and N Racine Ave

63 McCormick Row House District One of the loveliest, most peaceful enclaves in the city lies just beyond wrought-iron gates on West Fullerton Avenue east of the elevated train stop. The 58 private residences here were designed by **A.M.F. Colton & Son** for the **McCormick Theological Seminary,** which built them (1882-89) to generate rental income, and leased the corner houses to professors. Chalmers Place is a private street surrounding a large grassy square, anchored by **DePaul University**'s **Collegiate Gothic Commons Building** on the west and brick row houses to the north and south. It's like one of the private parks of London's residential squares, but is accessible to anyone. **DePaul** owns the green space and th institutional buildings to the east and west, but the houses were sold to private owners when the **McCormick** moved to Hyde Park in 1973. Designed in a simple, almost severe version of the popular Queen Anne style, with alternating triangular and semicircular gables the buildings have been beautifully restored, and their appearance is now monitored by a homeowners' association. The houses facing Fullerton and Belden Avenues were the first to be built, followed by those surrounding Chalmers Place. ♦ Bounded by W Belden and W Fullerton Aves, and N Halsted St and the el tracks

64 Chicago Costume Company Owner Mary Hickey occasionally outfits local theatrical productions, including some at **Victory Gardens** and **Steppenwolf.** Here she rents and sells costumes of every sort, from nun's habits to monster getups. ♦ M-F; Sa to 1PM. 1120 W Fullerton Ave (at N Racine Ave) 528.1264

65 Rose Angelis ★★$$ Tucked away in a residential corner of western Lincoln Park well off the beaten path, this fine Italian restaurant is wildly popular—and crowded to the rafters on weekends. Prime-time diners enjoy glasses of wine in the cozy, curtained storefront while they wait for tables. Go easy on the crusty, warm bread and save room for such yummy pasta entrées as ravioli Luigi (cheese-filled ravioli in sun-dried tomato sauce), *linguine frutta di mare* (with seafood) or *ravioli mezzalune al burro* (basil-pesto-filled, spinach half-moon ravioli in a brown butter sauce). Just across the street, an anne named **Verona** serves coffee and dessert; notice the lovely murals covering its walls. ♦ Italian ♦ Tu-Su dinner. No reservations accepted for parties of fewer than eight. 1314 W Wrightwood Ave (at N Lakewood Ave). 296.0081 ♿

66 Blue Parrot Yuppies flock to this upscale corner bar on weekends to shoot pool and troll for dates. Weeknights, the richly paneled wood interior and brass-trimmed bar make it a nice quiet spot to watch a game on TV or chat with buddies. ♦ Daily until 2AM. 1325 W Wrightwood Ave (at N Wayne Ave). 248.6850

67 Facets Multimedia Center The two screening rooms are dingy, cramped, and kind of depressing, but you forget about all that once the films start rolling. An eclectic schedule of foreign, art, and experimental films, plus revivals and retrospectives, provides Chicagoans with a welcome respite from the standard commercial fare. The center's programs of children's films are the nation's oldest and most extensive. Videos, film books, and film magazines are for sale in the lobby, and the basement offers video rentals of several thousand art and foreign films. ♦ Daily. 1517 W Fullerton Ave (between N Greenview and N Bosworth Aves). Recorded information 281.4114

67 Chicago Center for the Print
Representing more than a hundred artists, primarily contemporary American printmakers, this quality art gallery is a great spot for browsing; etchings, lithographs, woodcuts, silkscreens, engravings, monoprints, and French and Swiss vintage posters can be found here. ♦ Tu-Su. 1509 W Fullerton Ave (between N Greenview and N Bosworth Aves). 477.1585

68 Market Square Mall Cashing in on the Clybourn Corridor gentrification is an upscale, pastel-colored, 15-store strip mall. ♦ 2121 N Clybourn Ave (at W Dickens Ave)

Within Market Square Mall:

Treasure Island This local chain of grocery stores combines the gourmet with the everyday. You'll find imported goodies from around the world, exotic produce, the freshest meats, and a fabulous deli, along with Wonder bread, Velveeta, and high prices. This branch has a sit-down coffee shop if you need a break from pushing your cart. ♦ Daily. 880.8880. Many other locations throughout the city, including: 680 N Lake Shore Dr (between E Erie and E Huron Sts). 664.0400; 1639 N Wells St (at W North Ave). 642.1105

A Unique Presence Every item is a piece of art, literally. The work of more than 200 artists includes blown glass bowls with swirls of color, carved oak bookends, clay candle bases, hand-painted leather bags, and one-of-a-kind greeting cards. ♦ Daily. 929.4292

69 Charlie's Ale House ★$ The building, the stained-glass windows, and the massive mahogany bar date back to the 1930s. Owner Charlie Carlucci, one of the Carlucci restaurant clan, designed a room of old-fashioned wooden booths to match the bar. Pot roast dinners and other American mainstays anchor a small menu. The place is packed on weekends, doubly so when the beer garden is open. ♦ American ♦ M-F dinner; Sa-Su lunch and dinner; kitchen open to 2AM. 1224 W Webster Ave (at N Magnolia Ave). 871.1440

70 Krivoy Owner Cynthia Hadesman gave the elegant boutique her grandmother's maiden name, which in Russian means "curve." Hadesman designs almost everything you see here, including sleek dresses and hand-painted silk scarves. There's an odd but interesting assortment of contemporary hats that incorporate antique Chinese tapestries. ♦ Tu-Sa. 1145 W Webster Ave (at N Racine Ave). 248.1466

70 McShane's Exchange Junk store junkie Denise McShane Caffrey was looking for a California-style upscale consignment shop in Chicago. When she couldn't find one to her liking, she opened her own. You'll find women's designer apparel at no more than one-third of the original cost, including Ralph Lauren shirts and Maggie London silk dresses. ♦ Daily. 1141 W Webster Ave (between N Clifton and N Racine Aves). 525.0211. Also at: 815 W Armitage Ave (at Halsted St). 525.0282

71 Kangaroo Connection Owner Kathy Schubert, a frequent visitor Down Under, stocks her general store with items from Australia and New Zealand, including oilskin outback coats, Akubra hats, Aussie flags, Arnott's biscuits, boomerangs, kangaroo and koala aprons, and flyswatters in the shape of Australia. Stop by for a mail-order catalog. ♦ Tu-Sa. 1113 W Webster Ave (between N Seminary and N Clifton Aves). 248.5499

72 St. Vincent de Paul Church An enormous French Romanesque structure, the church was built by **James J. Egan** in 1895-97, when the parish consisted of a mere 75 members. A century later, the church serves a densely populated community that includes many university students. It's constructed of Bedford limestone, with ornate carving above the wide main entrance on Webster Avenue. The inside is notable, too. The high altar of white Carrara marble is inlaid with mother-of-pearl and Venetian mosaic; marble and mosaic also grace the communion rail. Jewel-colored light streams through five German Baroque stained-glass windows, designed and produced in Munich, and a rose window in the west transept, which honors St. Vincent de Paul, founder of the Vincentian order in the 17th century. A 2,800-pipe organ installed in 1901 is still playing strong. ♦ 1010 W Webster Ave (at N Sheffield Ave). 327.1113 ♿

73 McGee's On Friday and Saturday nights, the big bar inside and garden out back are hopping with yuppies. The fare: spilling-out-of-the-bun burgers and a variety of imported and domestic beers to wash them down. ♦ Daily until 2AM. 950 W Webster Ave (between N Bissell St and N Sheffield Ave). 871.4272

74 Kelly's $ This is the last of the neighborhood's old-fashioned taverns—dim, loaded with wood, and crazed during TV broadcasts of **DePaul University** basketball games. Burgers, sandwiches, snacks, and salads are available throughout the day and late into the evening. On weekends, they dish up eggs, home fries, and other breakfast basics for the bleary-eyed. The bustling beer garden is just a train token's throw below the el tracks. ♦ American ♦ M-F lunch and dinner; Sa-Su breakfast, lunch, and dinner. 949 W Webster Ave (between N Bissell St and N Sheffield Ave). 281.0656

75 Chia Women with big-time careers come here for high-fashion business suits by Chicago designers Maria Rodriguez and Peggy Martin, among others. ♦ Daily. 2202 N Halsted St (at W Webster Ave). 248.9595

76 Carlucci ★★$$$ High-quality regional Italian dishes are served in a sleek, stylish room rich with plush upholstery, wall murals, and dark woods. For openers, don't miss the three-layer vegetable terrine, or try a half portion of such inventive pasta dishes as *stracci* (rag-shaped pasta) with roasted veal and spinach. Among entrées, grilled meats and fish are standouts. Follow with one of an extensive selection of grappas and other after-dinner drinks. Light meals are served in the smaller *cantinetta* at the front of the restaurant. Try the antipasti and grilled eggplant—a thick eggplant steak served with fresh tomato-basil sauce and goat cheese. ♦ Italian ♦ Daily dinner. Reservations recommended. 2215 N Halsted St (between W Webster and W Belden Aves). 281.1220 &

76 All Our Children This is where Lincoln Park parents go to buy designer label fashions for their little darlings. A friendly staff will help you find that special party dress or layette item. Sizes run from newborn to 7. ♦ Daily. 2217 N Halsted St (between W Webster and W Belden Aves). 327.1868

77 Omiyage This gift shop is known for its one-of-a-kind earrings, most created by local artists. Glass counters are lined with pair after pair in silver, gold, platinum, plastic, glass, feathers, wood, and more. ♦ Daily. 812 W Webster (between N Halsted and N Dayton Sts). 477.1428 &

77 Glascott's Opened around the end of World War II, this Irish saloon boasts an ornately carved wooden bar from that era. Today it attracts mostly a yuppie crowd. Big windows offer views onto peaceful Webster Avenue and crowded North Halsted Street. ♦ Daily until 2AM. 2158 N Halsted St (at W Webster Ave). 281.1205

77 Saturday's Child Interesting, durable toys from around the world are crammed into this shop. They're all chosen to actively engage a child's imagination. There are kits to build and erupt your own volcano, avant-garde doll clothes, and stained-glass-window coloring books, plus more traditional stuffed animals, puzzles, tops, and yo-yos. ♦ Daily. 2146 N Halsted St (between W Dickens and W Webster Aves). 525.8697

78 Edwardo's ★$$ Here's another sunlit branch of the chain that prides itself on using all natural ingredients, including garden-fresh herbs (there's even an indoor herb garden). Spinach pizza stars; they also bake a mean stuffed pizza. ♦ Pizza ♦ Daily lunch and dinner. 2120 N Halsted St (between W Dickens and W Webster Aves). 871.3400

79 2120-26 and 2121-27 North Bissell Street Built in the 1880s, these private homes form the centerpiece of this symmetrical street, where three houses on each side share a cornice and pediment. Houses to the north and south are in pairs. Shallow rectangular bays create a continuous wall with a subtle rhythm. This street is typical of the Sheffield Historic District, although more cohesively designed than most. When the elevated train tracks were laid in 1897, the neighborhood was already completely developed, so the houses on Bissell Street lost their backyards (and residents must have lost some of their hearing). ♦ At W Dickens Ave

80 Bedside Manor, Ltd. This little store is like a cozy bedroom filled with antique-style brass and iron beds, handmade Amish quilts, imported linens, and down comforters. They will ship anywhere in the US. ♦ Daily. 2056 N Halsted St (between W Armitage and W Dickens Aves). 404.2020

80 Relish ★$$ They call the cuisine "progressive American," but the menu actually features an unusual combination of intensely flavored Native American meat and fish dishes, combined with fruits and herbs. It's interesting, to say the least. Bouquets of flowers and candles give the indoor dining room a fresh, cozy feel. In the summer, dine in the quiet, plant-filled outdoor cafe. ♦ American ♦ Daily dinner. 2044 N Halsted St (between W Armitage and W Dickens Aves). 868.9034 &

80 B. Leader & Sons, Inc. Owner Mike Leader's grandfather started the business in 1909. Today, it's the city's oldest family-owned jeweler. Glass cases mounted on old-fashioned workbenches display rings, brooches, earrings, and necklaces handcrafted in 14- and 18-karat gold and platinum inset with diamonds and precious stones. The shop sells diamonds at near-wholesale prices. Don't miss the collection of vintage timepieces from grandpa's day. ◆ Tu- Sa. 2042 N Halsted St (between W Armitage and W Dickens Aves). 549.2224

80 Cafe Ba-Ba-Reeba! ★★$$$ Crowds of beautiful people sip Spanish wines and sherries while grazing their way through ever-changing varieties of tapas, such as marinated octopus, potato-and-egg tortillas, and *pisto manchego,* a Spanish ratatouille. Entrées include a delicious seafood paella. The Iberian atmosphere carries through to the garden patio. ◆ Spanish ◆ M, Su dinner; Tu-Sa lunch and dinner. 2024 N Halsted St (between W Armitage and W Dickens Aves). 935.5000 &

81 Jennings Play the jukebox, pet the dog, or sip cappuccino while you browse through this warm, eclectic boutique. Sara Burr's men's and women's accessory store features vintage cowboy boots, artisan-designed watches, belt buckles, hats, ties, jewelry, and scarves. If you decide against a purchase, Burr will snap a photograph of you posed with the item and mount it in a card that says "you looked marvelous." ◆ Daily. 1971 N Halsted St (at W Armitage Ave). 587.7866

82 Robinson's No. 1 Ribs $$

Charlie Robinson's old family recipe took top honors in Chicago's 1982 First Annual Royko Ribfest, a half-goofy, half-serious competition that came into being when *Chicago Tribune* columnist Mike Royko and his neighbors started squabbling over who among them made the best barbecued ribs. This place barbecues ribs, chicken, hot links, pork, and beef to eat in or take out. ◆ Barbecue ◆ M-F lunch and dinner; Sa-Su dinner. 655 W Armitage Ave (at N Orchard St). 337.1399

In 1886 the British poet Robert Browning wrote that the most intelligent and thoughtful criticism of his work came from Chicago literary societies.

The late Mayor Richard J. Daley, noted for his public malapropisms, said the following at a press conference during the infamous 1968 Democratic National Convention in Chicago: "Gentlemen, get the thing straight, once and for all—the policeman isn't there to create disorder, the policeman is there to preserve disorder."

82 Art Effect

This store carries contemporary women's clothing, often with a retro flair, and scads of wonderful jewelry by local and national designers. Robin Richman's hand-knit sweaters and Christopher Phelan's elegant sterling, copper, and glass jewelry are just a few of this place's wearable goodies. There also are artist-designed functional housewares, including welded steel end tables by Michael McClatchy and ceramics by Floyd Gomph. ◆ Daily. 651-53 W Armitage Ave (between N Howe and N Orchard Sts). 664.0997

83 Lori's Designer Shoes Great women's shoes and accessories at great prices are the point here, not fancy displays. Lori Brian lines up designer shoes, boots, and bags in tidy rows and marks 10 to 50 percent off the regular retail prices. ◆ Daily. 824 W Armitage Ave (at N Halsted St). 281.5655 &

83 Charlie Trotter's ★★★★$$$$ Dubbed a "mecca of fine dining" by *Chicago* magazine, this chic restaurant in a renovated town house consistently garners rave reviews. Chef Trotter himself presides over the ever-evolving menu, which may include an appetizer of marrow-soft sea scallops stuffed with caviar; a full-flavored, but not too sweet, minted watermelon sorbet; and such entrées as sea bass fillets served with roasted garlic noodles, and smoked lobster subtly coated with apricot-infused olive oil. For a truly memorable evening, have the daily degustation or vegetable degustation, typically eight or nine small courses, each more wonderful than the last. Parties of two to four may reserve a table in the kitchen and dine while observing the staff at work, a scene that is really too noisy and bustling to be entirely enjoyable. ◆ International ◆ Tu-Sa dinner. Reservations, and jacket and tie, required. 816 W Armitage Ave (between N Halsted and N Dayton Sts). 248.6228 &

84 Celeste Turner Designer fashions— including Turner's own collection of soft suede dresses, separates, and vests— keep the regulars coming back. ◆ Daily. 859 W Armitage Ave (at N Fremont St). 549.3390

85 Turtle Creek Antiques Mary Popma carries quilts, textiles, linens, pine and wicker furniture, pottery, and glass— all antique, and all with a country feeling. ◆ Tu-Sa. 850 W Armitage Ave (between N Dayton and N Fremont Sts). 327.2630

86 Old Town School of Folk Music Founded in 1957, and at this location since 1965, the school is a local and national resource for the teaching, performance, and appreciation of folk music. It offers dozens of classes in beginning guitar, harmonica, Irish ballad singing, barn dancing, African drumming, and more. A large library/museum carries an extensive collection of recordings and vintage instruments. The well-stocked retail store carries instruments ranging from guitars to Latin percussion *afuche cabasas* and Polish *pokaleles* (ukuleles); its books and tapes cover folk music from Africa to Peru and from Pete Seeger to Chicagoan David Bromberg. Several nights a week, boisterous sing-alongs and workshops are open to the public. The school also presents a regular series of concerts by noted national artists, and the annual Festival of Latin Music. Call for a complete schedule. ♦ M-Sa. 909 W Armitage Ave (at N Fremont St). 525.7793

86 Sole Mio ★$$ This stylish trattoria sports checkered tablecloths, artsy blurred photos of the mother country, and a menu ripe with such delicious pastas as *penne con salcicci* (with homemade sausage, mozzarella, and basil in a zesty tomato-cream sauce), linguine Sole Mio (tossed with olive oil, garlic, chilies, and parsley, and topped with shaved parmesan cheese), and *pappardelle verdi con prosciutto* (large spinach noodles with tomatoes, prosciutto, lemon zest, and parmesan cheese, topped with alfredo sauce). Wonderful alternatives include stone-baked pizzas, and seafood specials such as halibut with pesto sauce. Save room for cappuccino custard for dessert. Arrive early to beat the crush. ♦ Italian ♦ Daily dinner. 917 W Armitage Ave (at N Bissell St). 477.5858

87 Active Endeavors Outfit yourself for camping, climbing, cycling, or running at this well-stocked, friendly neighborhood store. ♦ Daily. 935 W Armitage Ave (at N Bissell St). 281.8100

On 9 May, 1984, the White Sox played the longest baseball game in history against the Milwaukee Brewers. It lasted just over eight hours—34 innings—played over two days. The Sox finally won 7 to 6.

88 Espial $$ Italianate murals of ascending angels look over your shoulder as you select from a French-Italian menu that includes filet mignon, lobster, pasta, and fish. ♦ French/Italian ♦ Daily dinner. 948 W Armitage Ave (between N Bissell St and N Sheffield Ave). 871.8123

88 Second Child Among the upscale used children's clothing here you may find fancy party shoes, velvet designer dresses, Tony Lamas cowboy boots, or tiny mink coats for sizes from newborn to children's 14. Savings are generally about one-third below retail. They carry secondhand maternity clothes, cribs, and walkers too. ♦ Daily. 954 W Armitage Ave (between N Bissell St and N Sheffield Ave). 883.0880

89 Out of the West Bright and airy as a Georgia O'Keeffe sky, this boutique purveys all things Southwestern. Try on a pair of cowboy boots or admire the selection of sterling silver belt buckles and Native American jewelry, fetishes, and rugs. ♦ Daily. 1000 W Armitage Ave (at N Sheffield Ave). 404.9378 க

90 Dee's ★$$ Owners Dee and Rocky Chang serve well-prepared renditions of familiar Mandarin and Szechuan fare, from *moo shu pork* to sweet-and-sour shrimp. Choose seating in the modern dining room, outdoor patio, or sunny gardenlike atrium. ♦ Chinese ♦ M-F, Su dinner; Sa lunch and dinner. Reservations recommended Friday and Saturday. 1114 W Armitage Ave (between N Seminary and N Clifton Aves). 477.1500

91 Big John's This homey tavern, with a stuffed moose that hangs above the fireplace, caters to quiet, sports-oriented folks. The kitchen serves burgers, bratwurst, sandwiches, and other bar fare. An ivy-covered wall frames the backyard beer garden, a calm, pleasant spot to sip a pint in the summer. ♦ American ♦ Daily lunch and dinner until 2AM. 1147 W Armitage Ave (at N Racine Ave). 477.4400

92 Vertel's Many Chicago-area runners consider this *the* store for their sport, with its vast selection of shoes and gear and its well-versed staff. It's also big on racket sports, and rents tennis rackets by the day. Meet fellow runners here for a fun run at 6:30PM Monday year-round. They'll also be glad to fill you in on race information by phone, and will mail you entry forms. ♦ Daily. 2001 N Clybourn Ave (at N Racine Ave). 248.7400 &

93 Whiskey River Feelin' achy-breaky? Come on down and kick up your heels at this roadhouse-style bar. There's line dancing and two-stepping every night of the week. Hats, boots, and spurs are only for the hardcore country-western fan; most patrons come as they are. If you're unsure of your footwork, the bar offers free dance lessons from 7 to 10PM Sundays through Thursdays. Sundays from 1 to 5PM is family time, with games, toys, food, and dance lessons for the young'uns. ♦ Cover charge. M-Sa until 2AM. 1997 N Clybourn Ave (at N Racine Ave). 528.3400

94 Bossa Nova ★★$$ This converted warehouse has seen several restaurants come and go, but the current owners have hit paydirt. In 1993 *Esquire* named it one of the hottest restaurants in the country. The chefs prepare tapas (appetizer-size portions intended for sampling and sharing) from around the globe: Jamaican jerk chicken, Asian-style sesame-seed–encrusted tuna, and Middle Eastern hummus are a few of the choices. Signature drinks include the Flamenco (Absolut Citron mixed with cranberry juice, served in a martini glass Dean Martin would love) and the Caipirinha, that deliciously deadly Brazilian rum concoction. The fashionable clientele settle into quiet beige booths, while more boisterous crowds dine at large round tables. After the dinner rush, bands take the stage and the room sways to Jamaican, Brazilian, and Spanish music. ♦ International ♦ M-Sa dinner. 1960 N Clybourn Ave (south of W Cortland Ave). 248.4800 &

95 Bluebird Lounge Located on a bleak block of the Clybourn Corridor, this dark booth-lined bar attracts a mellow, artsy crowd. The kitschy 1950s lamps and objets d'art give the lounge a *Blue Velvet*–meets–*Leave it to Beaver* feel. The bartenders play CDs ranging from Jimi Hendrix to the Meat Puppets. Several imported beers are available on tap. ♦ Daily. 1637 N Clybourn Ave (at W Concord Pl). 642.3449

96 J.P.'s Eating Place ★$$$ One of several restaurants owned by Jorge Perez, this large-windowed place serves two dozen varieties of fresh seafood as well as meat dishes. Seafood may be ordered by the piece or the pound as an appetizer or in do-it-yourself combination plates. Blackened mako shark, tuna teriyaki, salmon, and scampi are just a few of the choices. There's also a good bouillabaisse and cioppino. ♦ Seafood ♦ M-Sa lunch and dinner; Su dinner. Reservations recommended. 1800 N Halsted St (at W Willow St). 664.1801

97 Vinci $$ Among the specialties at this attractive storefront restaurant are homemade pastas and fish, including a seafood mixed grill. Some say their portobello mushrooms are the best in the city. ♦ Italian ♦ Tu-Su dinner. 1732 N Halsted St (at W Willow St). 266.1199

BLUE MESA

98 Blue Mesa ★$$ Welcome to New Mexico. Tan and turquoise dining rooms, colorful artwork, and a rustic fireplace transport you far, far from North Halsted Street. The Southwestern food tends to be agreeably lighter than Mexican fare. Begin with an appetizer assortment for two, which includes blackened shrimp with tequila butter, fried jalapeño cheese, *carnitas* (grilled, skewered sirloin, marinated in a green chili sauce), empanadas stuffed with spicy meat, and guacamole. Good main courses are puffy Santa Fe pizza and crisp *chiles rellenos*. Mexican beers are available. ♦ Southwestern ♦ Daily lunch and dinner. 1729 N Halsted St (between W North Ave and W Willow St). 944.5990 &

98 Trattoria Gianni ★★$$$ Chef Giovanni De Lisi serves regional Italian cuisine in a cramped little dining room with crisp linens and black-and-white photos of Italy. The menu is small, but ever-changing. An excellent possibility is *saltimbocca sorrentino,* veal topped with mozzarella and prosciutto. The tiramisù is out of this world. ♦ Italian ♦ Tu-Su lunch and dinner. 1711 N Halsted St (between W North Ave and W Willow St). 266.1976

99 Royal-George Theatre Centre Two theaters, a cabaret, a restaurant, a piano lounge, and a wine cellar make up this entertainment complex. A number of Chicago companies rent the theaters to stage their performances. The auditorium, with balcony and box seating, seats 457, and tends to offer mainstream productions. A 60-seat gallery theater hosts experimental shows. The intimate **Ruggles Cabaret** presents occasional music or comedy acts. ♦ 1641 N Halsted St (just north of W North Ave). Box office 988.9000

99 O'Rourke's Poets, journalists, actors, and other creative types hang out at this bar late into the night beneath posters of James Joyce and Brendan Behan. ♦ Daily to 2AM. 1635 N Halsted St (at W North Ave). 335.1806

Restaurants/Clubs: Red   **Hotels:** Blue

Shops/ ♥ Outdoors: Green   **Sights/Culture:** Black

100 Crate & Barrel Outlet Store The same cool kitchenware and home accessories available at the store's other locations are here, but at amazing discounts because they're either out of season or mail-order returns. ♦ Daily. 800 W North Ave (at N Halsted St). 787.4775

100 Steppenwolf Theatre Founded in a church basement in 1976 as an ensemble group, this company has gone on to present more than a hundred productions and win national renown—for itself as well as for a number of its actors (then-unknown founding members included actor/director Gary Sinise and actors John Malkovich and Laurie Metcalf). They have been honored with 14 Jefferson Awards for Chicago Theater Excellence. Since 1982, many of the company's productions have gone on to New York, including *True West, Balm in Gilead, Orphans,* and *The Grapes of Wrath;* the latter received several Tony awards as well as the Outer Critics Circle Award for Outstanding Broadway Play. This state-of-the-art theater complex, containing a 500-seat main stage and a hundred-seat experimental theater, opened in the spring of 1991. ♦ 1650 N Halsted St (just north of W North Ave). Box office 335.1650

101 New City YMCA The North Side's most modern **Y** swarms on evenings and weekends with young professionals who sign up as fast as they can say "Goodbye, price-gouging health clubs!" The running tracks, pool, aerobics classes, weight rooms, and more are open to out-of-town **Y** members for free, and to other visitors for a nominal daily fee. ♦ Daily 6AM-11PM. 1515 N Halsted St (at N Clybourn Ave). 266.1242

On 15 April 1955, former milkshake distributor Ray Kroc opened his first McDonald's in Des Plaines, Illinois, a suburb of Chicago. When he died on 14 January 1984, more than 45 billion hamburgers had been served in 7,778 McDonald's restaurants worldwide.

Nelson Algren on Chicago: "It used to be a writer's town and it's always been a fighter's town. . . . Whether the power is in a .38, a typewriter ribbon, or a pair of six-ouncers, the place has grown great on bone-deep grudges: of writers and fighters and furtive torpedoes."

102 Golden Ox ★$$$ Dark with heavy woodwork, this German restaurant, just off the yuppie corridor, dates back to 1921, before the factories along Clybourn were turned into chic boutiques. The extensive menu includes hearty Wiener schnitzel and sauerbraten with homemade dumplings. Everything comes in giant portions, including all-you-can-eat lunch and dinner buffets. There's German beer on tap, and live zither music is played Friday and Saturday evenings. ♦ German ♦ M-Sa lunch and dinner; Su dinner. 1578 N Clybourn Ave (at W North Ave). 664.0780

103 Bub City ★$$ A revolving sign on the street announces **Bub City** on one side, Turtle Wax Car Wash on the other. From the outside, the car wash—shiny, new, and neon lit—looks better than the restaurant, an intentionally beat-up looking old roadhouse. Inside, this theme spot (another from Lettuce Entertain You Enterprises) combines a large crab house, dripping with nets and traps, with the **Club Bub**, a rocking country-western bar. The good food includes fresh-tasting crabs in garlic butter and spicy barbecued ribs. There's yummy banana pudding for dessert. ♦ American ♦ M-Sa lunch and dinner; Su dinner. Live music: Th-Sa. 901 W Weed St (at N Sheffield Ave). 266.1200 ♿

103 Mud Bug OTB This off-track betting parlor seems to have borrowed its Southern-style decor from **Bub City** next door. It's remarkably clean and cheery, a far cry from the smoke-filled OTBs of yesteryear. The spacious facility features races from local tracks (**Maywood, Balmoral, Sportsman's, Hawthorn,** and **Arlington**). Burgers, barbecue, and sandwiches are served at the bar and in the restaurant. ♦ Daily 10:30AM- 11:30PM. 901 W Weed St (at N Sheffield Ave). 787.9600

103 Crobar At this huge, alternative dance club leather-clad bikers rub epaulets with the silk-covered shoulder pads of aspiring models. Bondage-a-go-go dancers work it atop platforms that soar over the sprawling wooden dance floor, while the elite mingle upstairs in the velvet-tufted booths of the Fellini Room. A windowed skydeck overlooking the dance floor provides respite for those with throbbing eardrums. There's live music Thursdays; DJs spin dance tracks Fridays and Saturdays; on Sundays the G.L.E.E. (Gays, Lesbians—Everyone's Equal) Club convenes for dancing into the wee hours. ♦ Cover charge. W-Su to 4AM. 1543 N Kingsbury St (at W Weed St). 587.1313

04 North Beach Sand volleyball courts inside a bar? Yes, Virginia, it's a viable club concept in Chicago. During the week, leagues take over, but others can reserve court time by phone. Saturday nights after 10PM, the pits are open to one and all. Those in the know come prepared wearing shorts and T-shirts. Others just dive in, sandblasting their fine threads for the sake of a good dig. ♦ Daily to 2AM; Sa-Su from 9AM. 1551 N Sheffield Ave (at W North Ave). 266.7842

104 Arnie's Bagels Chicagoans weaned on New York bagels shed tears of joy when Arnold Fishman set up shop here in 1991. His bagels are soft inside with chewy crusts. The selection runs from the ordinary (plain, egg) to the unorthodox (cheddar and herb, spinach and blue cheese). Several varieties of cream cheese are available. Weekend mornings, the place is packed. ♦ Daily. 1001 W North Ave (at N Sheffield Ave). 944.0745. Also at: 1315 W Diversey Pkwy (at Lakewood Ave). 296.0745

Bests

Roslyn Alexander
Actress

Architecture cruise on **Chicago River** from **North Pier.** Our great designs of buildings new and old. Rejuvenation of the river side for pedestrians and leisure activities.

Terra Museum on North Michigan Avenue. The finest collection of American Impressionists.

Investigating the many small **off-Loop** storefront theaters where great work is being done artistically and innovatively. Also **Victory Gardens, Steppenwolf, Goodman,** and **Northlight** theaters.

Walk the ethnic neighborhoods: **Milwaukee Avenue** between North and Belmont Avenues (Polish); **Devon Avenue** from Broadway to Kimball (Indian/Pakistani, Jewish); **Argyle Street** from Sheridan Road to Clark (Asian); **Cermak Road** and **Wentworth** (Chinatown).

Kevin J. Bell
Director, Lincoln Park Zoological Gardens

Dining. The variety of restaurants is one of the greatest things about Chicago. Fast for at least a week before you get here (!) to make room for:

Sausage or spinach/mushroom-stuffed pizza at **Pizzeria Due.** Don't plan on being too active after you eat; you'll need all your energy just for digesting.

Steaks and, of course, cheesecake, at **Eli's.**

Margaritas—with an order of blue corn chips— at **Blue Mesa** on Halsted Street.

Sunday brunch buffet at the **Ritz-Carlton**— especially the desserts.

Out and about, any one of these will make your day:

A bike ride along the lakefront on the bike path from Foster Avenue to North Avenue.

The **Art Institute of Chicago** on Tuesday evenings, when it's open late.

The picture-perfect view from **Lincoln Park**'s **Cafe Brauer** of Chicago's famous skyline framed by the cafe's 1912-era loggias.

A **Cubs** game at **Wrigley Field** any day.

A walk along the waterfront behind the **Northwestern University** campus in Evanston.

A day at the **Kane County Flea Market** in **St. Charles,** held only the first weekend of every month. It's an antiques-hunter's delight.

Lincoln Park Zoo when the gates open first thing in the morning at 7AM.

The view at dusk, looking north down **Michigan Avenue** from the **Wabash Bridge.** On your left, the **Wrigley Building** looks like a giant wedding cake; on your right, the **Tribune Tower** appears to be a sandcastle.

Marc Schulman
President, Eli's

Experience the magic of the **Michigan Avenue** lights during the holiday season. Don't miss the lighting of the trees sponsored by the Greater North Michigan Avenue Association on the Saturday evening before Thanksgiving.

Take a walking tour of **Graceland Cemetery** to learn who built Chicago and how. Also take any of the other tours offered by the **Chicago Architectural Foundation.**

Take your children to the **Eli M. Schulman Playground** at **Seneca Park** (located just east of the historic **Water Tower**). Also walk into **Engine Company 98** of the Chicago Fire Department next door.

Take a ride through Chicago's boulevard system. Favorite stops—the **Garfield Park Conservatory,** the *Statue of the Republic* in **Jackson Park** commemorating the 1893 World's Fair, and Lorado Taft's *Fountain of Time* on the **Midway.**

Spend an afternoon at **Lincoln Park Zoo** (one of the only free zoos in the country), then walk along the park's lagoon and through the **Gold Coast** back to Michigan Avenue.

On a hot summer night, Italian ice at **Mario's Italian Lemonade** on Taylor Street.

A visit to the **Chicago Children's Museum** (at its new home at **Navy Pier**).

Bucktown/ Wicker Park

What is now Chicago's hottest new neighborhood used to be one of its scruffiest. In the 1950s, Bucktown was known primarily as the setting for novels by Nelson Algren about tough guys and losers and those who fell through the cracks. Even the name reflects its humble history: At the turn of the century, so many immigrant families kept goats in their front yards that the neigborhood was nicknamed "Bucktown." The name hasn't changed, but almost everything else has. During the course of the last 20 years, this area bordered by the **John F. Kennedy Expressway** and **Western, Chicago,** and **Fullerton Avenues** has transformed itself into a hip, artsy bohemia. Now the stomping grounds of both real and wannabe film makers, artists, actors, and rock musicians like Liz Phair and Smashing Pumpkins, Bucktown has inspired some observers to call it the "new Seattle."

In the late 1800s, many of Chicago's solid German middle-class citizens moved in to the area around Wicker Park, near the intersection of Chicago and **Damen Avenues.** As they rose in fortune and social status, prominent neighborhood residents (like retailer W.A. Wieboldt, O.W. Potter, the president of Illinois Steel, and the Uihlein family of the Schlitz brewery) built mansions in Italianate, Second Empire, and Queen Anne styles along Damen and **Hoyne, Pierce,** and **Oakley Streets.** The architecture in the area reflects the wide variety of housing built in Chicago between the Great Fire of 1871 and the turn of the century: from the small, wooden structures built by newly arrived immigrants to the stately homes erected by second- and third-generations of prosperous burghers. By 1905, factories moved in and the neighborhood underwent another significant change as many stately homes became boarding houses for immigrant Polish workers. Soon, the three-way intersection of **Milwaukee Avenue, Ashland Avenue,** and **Division Street** formed the beginning of Chicago's "Polish Downtown." Through the years, as Chicago's Polish population grew to the largest in the US, these businesses worked their way up Milwaukee Avenue (see the "Additional Highlights" chapter).

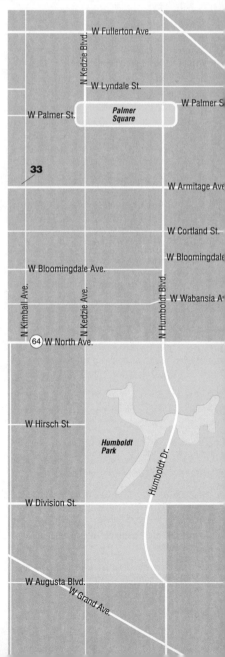

About 20 years ago, the yuppies—daunted by sky-high real-estate prices in neigborhoods like Lincoln Park/DePaul—headed west across the Kennedy Expressway, bringing gentification in their wake. Today, most of the old mansions of Wicker Park have been restored to their former elegance, and the population is a culturally diverse hodgepodge of older people who've lived here for decades, young business commuters, struggling artists, and entrepreneurs. Trendy boutiques abut old-fashioned bakeries, cool coffeehouses collide with auto parts stores, and new art galleries, jazz and rock clubs, and restaurants and cafes open every month. To the casual observer, many parts of the area still seem to be rough around the edges, but to the in crowd, this is the place to be.

1 Babaluci ★★$$ Bucktown's first Italian restaurant opened in 1991, and quickly became a neigborhood favorite. In the open kitchen chefs prepare delicious thin-crust pizzas with a variety of toppings as well as Italian standards such as spaghetti carbonara. ♦ Italian ♦ M-F lunch and dinner; Sa-Su dinner. 2152 N Damen Ave (at W Webster Ave). 486.5300 ♿

2 Frida's ★$$ Named after artist Frida Kahlo—who mixed Marxist politics and art and was married to artist Diego Rivera—this airy Mexican eatery features 25-foot murals depicting her life as well as prints of her surrealistic paintings. It's a fine atmosphere for the cactus, onion, and cheese salad followed by the *chiles rellenos* (deep-fried poblano peppers filled with cheese and covered with a lightly seasoned sauce of tomatoes and vegetables) or the chicken burritos. ♦ Mexican ♦ M-Th, Su dinner; F-Sa lunch and dinner. 2143 N Damen Ave (at W Webster Ave). 337.4327 ♿

3 St. Hedwig's Originally built to serve the Polish community in the area, this Roman Catholic church was the last building designed by German architect **Adolphus Druiding.** The cornerstone was laid in 1899 and the church was completed in 1901 at a cost of $160,000. By that time, there were 4,000 souls registered in the parish and 800 children enrolled in the school. Today, the small congregation consists of Polish and Spanish immigrant families and a growing number of young professionals who have moved into the neigborhood during the past decade. ♦ 2226 N Hoyne Ave (at W Webster Ave). 486.1660

4 Cafe du Midi ★★$$$ This popular French bistro is decorated in a simple, yet chic, style where white linens and fresh flowers abound. The menu runs to rustic and traditional fare such as steak au poivre and seed-crusted salmon; daily and seasonal specials are worth checking out, particularly the rabbit in mustard sauce. ♦ French ♦ M-F lunch and dinner; Sa-Su dinner. 2118 N Damen Ave (at W Charleston St). 235.6434

4 Savage Instincts This boutique sells some new clothes but specializes in items made from recycled goods like purses and travel journals made from old license plates and shoes made from old tires and soda bottles. Look closely at the ethnic jewelry display:

Many of the pieces have erotic undertones, like the pendant with a page from a tiny Kama Sutra. ♦ Tu-Su. 2064 N Damen Ave (at W Dickens Ave). 227.9391 ♿

4 Jean Alan The designers at this home furnishings boutique give stylish new life to vintage furniture. A pink Murano glass lamp with a trumpet-shaped base has been topped with a gorgeous new lamp shade of silk flowers. A voluptuous mohair sofa on cabriole legs has been reupholstered in a grayish-purple fabric, then accented with chartreuse cushions. There is an excellent and fun selection of hand-crafted pillows. ♦ Daily. 2062 N Damen Ave (at W Dickens Ave). 278.2345 ♿

5 Dandelion Owner Sara Cook buys, sells, and trades vintage clothing from the 1960s and 1970s for men, women, and children. The store has a generous stock of retro sequined gowns and a trove of hidden treasures— maybe you'll spot a faux leopard coat or snag an orange Tang T-shirt. ♦ Daily. 2117 N Damen Ave (between W Webster and W Dickens Aves). 862.WEED

6 Le Bouchon ★★★$$ A dozen tables in a single room decorated with French travel posters and a pressed-tin ceiling make up this intimate, stylish, authentically French restaurant. Sophisticated diners come here to try the simple yet exquisite cooking of chef Jean Claude Poilevey and the attentive ministrations of his wife, Susanne, who serves as hostess and manager. Anything-but-typical entrées include steak with shallot and sautéed rabbit hunter's style. ♦ French ♦ M-Sa dinner. Reservations recommended. 1958 N Damen Ave (between W Armitage Av and W Homer St). 862.6600

6 A'Propos Galleria of Furniture Interior designer Joseph Salvatore Tenuta operates this storefront in Bucktown and has another in Milan. The eclectic boutique has designer "juggler's chairs," replete with tassels, and other colorful designer pieces at no small price. ♦ Tu-Su. 1944 N Damen Ave (between W Armitage Ave and W Homer St). 486.9550

7 St. Mary of the Angels Dedicated in 1920 after almost nine years of construction and a cost of $400,000, this Catholic church is modeled after St. Peter's Basilica in Rome. The massive structure, which was designed by architect **Henry J. Schlacks,** takes up an entire city block. It was scheduled to shut down in the early 1990s but concerned parishioners protested and raised enough money to keep it open. ◆ 1825 N Wood St (at W Cortland St). 278.2644

8 Lydia's Cafe ★$ A dining room nearly hidden away in the back of a small grocery store serves a lively mix of traditional Mexican and Puerto Rican dishes. Owner Lydia Gonzalez dishes up *carne asada* (broiled skirt steak accompanied by rice, beans, and tortillas), *pasteles* (green-banana dough filled with seasoned pork), and *mofongo* (plaintains stuffed with shrimp or chicken). ◆ Mexican/Puerto Rican ◆ M-Sa breakfast, lunch, and dinner. 1704 N Damen Ave (at W Wabansia Ave). 235.7252

8 Portia Gallery This small glass gallery features contemporary works from artists throughout the world. Blown-glass pieces include jewelry (earrings, necklaces, and stick pins), paperweights, perfume bottles, plates and glasses, and vases. Prices range from $15 to nearly $12,000. ◆ Tu-Su. 1702 N Damen Ave (at W Wabansia Ave). 862.1700

9 Wax Trax A music store that also has its own recording label, this small shop features bootleg and rare rock recordings (mostly vinyl) as well as popular new releases (mostly CDs). ◆ Daily. 1653 N Damen Ave (at W Wabansia Ave). 862.2121

10 Club Lucky ★$$ One of the most popular hangouts in Bucktown is a Deco-style restaurant outfitted with Formica-topped tables and bar and ceiling fixtures that are exact replicas of the original fixtures in the Empire State Building. The menu features plentiful portions of real Italian home-cooking. Try *pasta e fagioli* (a macaroni-and-bean

soup) or rigatoni with veal meatballs. It's a popular place for lunch, when hearty and huge sandwiches cost only about five bucks each. ◆ Italian ◆ M-F lunch and dinner; Sa-Su dinner. 1824 W Wabansia Ave (at N Honore St). 227.2300

11 Mad Bar A pool table, backgammon and checker boards, and a laser-disc jukebox are some of the props for this hot spot, quirkily decorated with a mix of exposed brick walls, 1950s living room furniture, 1920s wall sconces, and a molded plywood bar which serves coffee drinks, beer on tap, and numerous Champagnes and single-malt scotches to an artsy, young clientele. Muffins, scones, and other snacks are available, too. ◆ Daily 8AM-2AM. 1640 N Damen Ave (at W North Ave). 227.2277

12 Gallery 1633 This storefront gallery showcases any artist who pays a small exhibit fee. ◆ Sa-Su, or by appointment. 1633 N Damen Ave (at W North Ave). 384.4441

12 Latino Chicago Theater Company/ The Firehouse Operating out of this old firehouse since 1987, the company promotes theater with Latino  themes by Latino playwrights. Works are performed in English. ◆ 1625 N Damen Ave (at W North Ave). 486.5120

13 Ziggurat This 10,000-square-foot space specializes in architectural artifacts of all periods. There's stained glass, statuary, wrought- and cast-iron details, and fireplace mantels, as well as a large selection of theatrical and religious relics. ◆ Daily. 1702 N Milwaukee Ave (at W Wabansia Ave). 227.6290

14 Ole A. Thorp House Built in 1891 by Ole Thorp, who was the proprietor of an import-export business and a real-estate developer as well, this privately owned mansion is a good example of the Romanesque architecture popular in this neighborhood at the turn of the century. Distinctive features include a rounded corner turret, an expansive front gable, and a facade of rusticated gray stone. ◆ 2156 W Caton St (at N Leavitt St)

15 Busy Bee ★$ Working-class locals and starving artists gather at this simple diner to partake of owner Sophie Madej's hearty and inexpensive Polish-American food. For a filling carbo feast, order potato pancakes and pierogi. ◆ Polish-American ◆ Daily breakfast, lunch, and dinner until 7PM. 1564 N Damen Ave (at W North Ave). 772.4433

Restaurants/Clubs: Red   **Hotels:** Blue

Shops/ ☂ Outdoors: Green   **Sights/Culture:** Black

15 Bongo Room ★$ A convenient location next to the downtown el stop makes this tiny storefront restaurant a favorite with commuters. Early birds listen to opera, sip cappuccino, and nibble on muffins or tasty egg dishes before heading off to work. ♦ Cafe ♦ Daily breakfast and lunch. 1560 N Damen Ave (at W North Ave). 489.0690

16 Cafe Absinthe ★★$$$ Don't be deceived by the looks of this place: The scruffy alley entrance leads to one of Chicago's most elegant and hippest restaurants. The kitchen prepares only a short menu, with offerings rotated regularly. A typical menu might include appetizers of grilled octopus or wild-boar salad, with entrées like quail with polenta or grilled venison loin. Upstairs is a small dance club called **Red Dog.** ♦ International ♦ Daily lunch and dinner. Reservations recommended. 1954 W North Ave (between N Damen and N Winchester Aves). 278.4488

16 Urbis Orbis Coffee House $ Coffees, teas, sandwiches, and salads are served from an open kitchen bounded by a curving counter bar. The tabletops are painted with alchemy symbols. Artsy young people hang out with a cuppa and one of the books and magazines for sale, which run the gamut from modern art to literary criticism. ♦ Coffeehouse ♦ Daily 9AM-midnight. 1934 W North Ave (at N Winchester Ave). 252.4446

17 Eat Your Hearts Out ★★$$ An eclectic hodgepodge of food and furniture, this restaurant is run by owner Debbie Sharpe, caterer to visiting celebs such as Madonna and the Rolling Stones. Crystal chandeliers hang above thrift-shop tables and chairs.

Menu choices include zingy black bean–and–jalapeño ravioli, and a tasty herb-crusted rack of free-range Australian lamb accompanied by tomato-and-zucchini ragout and roasted potatoes. ♦ International ♦ M-F dinner; Sa-Su brunch and dinner. 1835 W North Ave (at N Honore St). 235-6361 &

18 HiRicky ★$ The food at this inexpensive noodle shop draws on the flavors of Indonesia, Vietnam, Thailand, and southern China. Try the wide egg noodles with green curry, eggplant, and basil. ♦ Asian ♦ Daily lunch and dinner. 1852 W North Ave (at N Honore St). 276.8300

19 Flatiron Building Designed in 1929 by **Holabird & Root,** today this old office building houses about 25 different art galleries and artists' studios. ♦ Tu-Sa noon-5PM or by appointment. 1569-1579 N Milwaukee Ave (at W North Ave). 278.7677

20 Nick's The young, hip crowd that frequents this place drinks and shoots pool until the wee hours of the morning. ♦ Daily 4PM-4AM. 1516 N Milwaukee Ave (at N Honore St). 252.1155

21 Earwax Caffe ★$ Old circus banners line the walls of this neighborhood hangout, which serves hearty breakfast burritos, an assortment of vegetarian dishes, and a wide variety of teas and coffees. In the back is a small shop where locals rent videos and buy CDs. ♦ Vegetarian ♦ Daily lunch and dinner. 1564 N Milwaukee Ave (at Winchester Ave). 772.4019

22 Occult Bookstore This offbeat bookstore originally opened in 1915 and has moved several times since. But wherever it goes, its customers follow for books on magic, astrology, ancient Egyptian religion, psychic development, and other phenomena, as well as candles, incense, and oils. Get your palm or tarot cards read by the in-store practitioner or arrange to have your astrology chart done. ♦ M-Th 10:30AM-7PM; F 10:30AM-9PM; Su noon-6PM. 1561 N Milwaukee Ave (between N Honore St and Wolcott Ave). 292.0995

23 Hermann Weinhardt House In 1888 this mansion was built for Wicker Park politician and furniture company president, Hermann Weinhardt. Still privately owned, the structure has a mixture of traditional Victorian and Bavarian styles. Reminiscent of a mountain chalet, the house abounds with decorative elements of gingerbread and pressed metal bargeboard. ♦ 2135 W Pierce Ave (between N Hoyne Ave and N Leavitt St)

24 Hans D. Runge House Covered with intricately wrought lathe and scrollwork, this privately owned house was constructed in 1884 by the president of the Wolf Brothers Wood Milling Company. It is, however, best known as the **Paderewski House,** because of a concert given on the wide porch by the famous Polish pianist and statesman in 1930. Between World Wars I and II the house served as the Polish Consulate. ♦ 2138 W Pierce Ave (at N Hoyne Ave)

25 Adolph Borgmeier House Built in 1890 by the treasurer of the Johnson Chair Company, this privately owned home is a good example of Romanesque architecture. The facade is brick with polished granite columns and features elaborately carved stone and terra-cotta details. ♦ 1521 N Hoyne Ave (at W LeMoyne St)

26 Louis and Lena Hansen House This privately owned house is situated on one of the few remaining large lots that were once de rigueur for the ornate mansions that lined this stretch of Hoyne Avenue. Built in 1879, the redbrick-and-stone building is an excellent example of Italianate design; of particular note are the elaborately decorated door frames, window lintels, and woodwork. ♦ 1417 N Hoyne Ave (between W LeMoyne and W Schiller Sts)

27 Harris Cohen House Built in 1890 for a clothing company executive, this Romanesque mansion is distinguished by its tall, conical roof and ornate detailing that is more typical of Italianate and Second Empire designs. Framing a huge stone porch, the facade features polished granite columns and elaborate stone carvings. This is still a private residence. ♦ 1941 W Schiller St (between N Hoyne and N Damen Aves)

28 Phyllis' Musical Inn This club opened years ago as a Polish-American bar with polka music and dancing. Today the music is contemporary—jazz, blues, progressive rock—and the crowd young and energetic. There's live music of one sort or another every night. ♦ Cover charge. Daily 2PM-2AM. 1800 W Division St (at N Wood St). 486.9862

29 Bop Shop At one of the best jazz clubs in the city, owner Kate Smith has been booking a roster of exceptional jazz and blues musicians since before the neighborhood became fashionable. This is also a comfortable neighborhood bar, offering a variety of activities such as poetry readings. ♦ Cover charge. M-F, Su 7PM-2AM; Sa to 3AM. 1807 W Division St (at N Honore St). 235.1155

29 Leo's Lunchroom ★$ This grungy, tiny diner looks like it hasn't changed since the 1930s, but it offers some of the best and cheapest food in the area, making it popular with impoverished artists. Everything is tasty and the portions are generous; vegetarian chili and the breakfast burrito are the best choices. ♦ American ♦ Tu-Su breakfast, lunch, and dinner. 1809 W Division St (at N Honore St). 276.6509

30 Rainbo Club An authentic neighborhood bar that was a hangout for writers Nelson Algren and Simone de Beauvoir, it's now the domain of neighborhood regulars. Suitably dark, the beer is cheap here, and the crowd is friendly without being intrusive. ♦ M-F, Su 4PM-2AM; Sa 4PM-3AM. 1150 N Damen Ave (at W Division St). 489.5999

31 Leona's ★$ A link in a popular family-run pizza chain, this restaurant provides a homey atmosphere along with hearty Italian meals, and thin-crust, deep-dish, or stuffed pizzas with a choice of 26 toppings. ♦ Italian ♦ Daily lunch and dinner. 1936 W Augusta Blvd (at N Damen Ave). 292.4300

32 Cafe Bolero $ Run by a husband-and-wife team, this restaurant combines the owners' different ethnic backgrounds (he's Cuban, she's Serbian), producing an eclectic menu that offers Cuban sandwiches of grilled pork and cheese with fried plantains, and homemade grilled sausage with feta cheese and peppers. Whatever you order, expect hearty portions and cheap prices. ♦ Cuban/Yugoslavian ♦ Daily lunch and dinner. 2252 N Western Ave (at W Belden). 227.9000

33 Rosa's Eight blocks west of Bucktown, this club bills itself as "Chicago's friendliest blues lounge"—and it must be the truth when people come this far off the beaten track. All blues, no tourists. Free parking is available at the gas station next door. ♦ Cover charge. Daily 8PM-2AM; music starts around 9:30PM. 3420 W Armitage Ave (at N Kimball Ave). 342.0452

David Mamet won the Pulitzer Prize for drama in 1984 for the play *Glengarry Glen Ross.*

When Buffalo Bill and his Wild West Show played in Chicago the company consisted of 680 people and 700 horses.

In 1915 more than one-twelfth of Chicago's land was owned by only ten families. The Marshall Field family alone owned land worth $100 million.

Lake View/ Wrigleyville

In Lake View there's something going on every day of the week. Within the three-square-mile neighborhood, bordered by **Irving Park Road, Diversey Parkway, Lake Michigan,** and **Ashland Avenue,** you can sail, sunbathe, bike, or run at **Belmont Harbor;** dance the night away at one of the many dance clubs along **Belmont** and **Sheffield Avenues;** admire old mansions on **Hawthorne Place;** view historic gravestones at **Graceland Cemetery;** catch a play by the **Live Bait Theater** or another nearby company; congregate at **Roscoe's** cafe; browse for antiques and vintage clothing at **Flashy Trash** or one of a dozen offbeat shops along **Halsted Street;** enjoy a cocktail while you wash your clothes at **Saga's Launder-Bar and Cafe;** catch a classic flick at the **Music Box;** chow down on Japanese sashimi, Ethiopian stews, French crepes, Spanish tapas, and other ethnic eats on **Clark Street;** or root for the **Cubs** at **Wrigley Field.**

ake View began as a peaceful farming settlement for celery and greenhouse flowers. Between the 1830s and 1850s, while Chicago proper was becoming citified, Lake View was being settled by immigrants from Germany and Luxembourg who were attracted by the high ground and fertile fields. By 1854 the rapidly growing community boasted its own overnight inn, **Lake View House**, which enjoyed a panoramic view of the lake from the corner of what is now **Grace Street.** In 1857 Lake View was incorporated as a township, and plans were made to improve access to Chicago's northernmost boundary, less than a mile south at **Fullerton Avenue.** Residents pitched in to finance the paving-over of mud flats with **Lake View Plank Road.** Today, **Broadway** follows the road's original route.

Wealthy Chicagoans saw an opportunity to build spacious homes and apartment buildings along the lakefront. Meanwhile working-class immigrants continued to settle farther inland where factories proliferated. There were prosperous tool-and-die plants whose workers brought their skills from Western Europe and a brickmaking industry that supplied most of the city's bricks during the 1870s and 1880s. Row after row of balloon-frame houses that were affordable to workers were built. Next came German saloons and beer gardens, among them Schlitz Brewing Company taverns that specialized in serving the company's beer. Many of the houses and saloons from that era still stand, as do some of the original opulent gray-stone dwellings near the lake. In 1889 Lake View was annexed to the city of Chicago.

During the 1920s the expanding population sparked an apartment-house building boom, especially along **Lake Shore Drive**, where elegant structures rose to take advantage of the view. Since the 1950s, steel-and-glass high-rises have taken their places among these elegant elders. In the 1970s an influx of baby boomers in search of affordable housing led to construction of new buildings and the much-needed renovation of thousands of sturdy but dilapidated Victorian homes. Restoration continues to work its way westward, particularly in the vicinity of **Wrigley Field**, an area that real estate agents dubbed Wrigleyville. Today, a diverse population of nearly a half-million people resides in Lake View, including single young professionals, working-class families, affluent retirees, and the city's largest gay population.

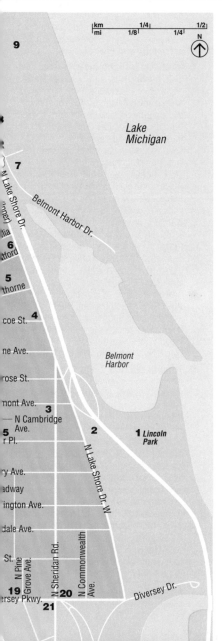

1 Lincoln Park/Belmont Harbor The park's lower boundary starts a couple of miles south in the community of the same name, and stretches northward just beyond Hollywood Avenue, hugging the lakefront the whole way; its character shifts with each neighborhood. While adjacent communities boast beaches, Lake View possesses nary a grain of sand, but plenty of concrete slabs that front the shoreline as a deterrent to erosion. Determined locals spread beach towels and picnic gear across flat-topped rocks and in nearby grassy meadows on warm summer days; more active parkgoers make the most of a soft gravel path and parallel asphalt path that traverse the park for miles. The paths attract a steady flow of runners, bicyclists, roller skaters, and—when the snowfall is right—cross-country skiers. Early birds hit the trails at dawn, starting their day with the astounding sight of the bright red sun coming up over the lake.

Look south from Diversey Harbor to one of the most dramatic views of Chicago's skyline, day or night; professional photographers are forever snapping this scene. Another great view is found about a half-mile north, at the tip of the long finger of the parkway stretching around Belmont Harbor (access is by foot from the northern edge of the harbor). Both harbors are home to hundreds of boats between April and October.

The **Belmont Yacht Club** is private but welcomes members of yacht clubs from other cities. Anyone can use the free boat-launching ramp at Diversey Harbor. (Sailboats are not recommended on Diversey Harbor, as boats must pass beneath a low bridge to reach the lake.) The **Chicago Sailing Club** (at the north end of Belmont Harbor; 871.SAIL) rents boats and also provides instruction. ♦ The park is accessible by car from several exits along N Lake Shore Dr. By foot, enter anywhere between W Diversey Pkwy and W Belmont Ave; north of Belmont, use the two underpasses along the east side of N Lake Shore Dr (Inner) (near W Roscoe and W Addison Sts), or the auto/pedestrian underpass at W Irving Park Rd

2 Briar Playlot A sturdy setup of swings, slides, monkey bars, a sandbox, and more, all shaded by trees, provides the best recreation around for many a neighborhood high-rise kid. ♦ Lincoln Park (near W Briar Pl)

3 The Belmont This fine, solid, vintage brick building with limestone trim was designed by **A.L. Himmelblau** in 1923. It has something of an elegant dowager look to it—aged, but brimming with character. For years it operated as a hotel, but in 1993 its 334 units were converted to private apartments. ♦ 3170 N Sheridan Rd (at W Belmont Ave)

Restaurants/Clubs: Red   Hotels: Blue
Shops/♥ Outdoors: Green   Sights/Culture: Black

4 3400 North Lake Shore Drive A fine example of the first generation of luxury high-rises along Chicago's lakefront, this vintage 10-story building designed by **Peter J. Weber** commanded monthly rents of $1,200 when it opened in 1922. Each 6,000 square-foot apartment featured a salon; living room; dining room; breakfast room; solarium (some of them survive); five bedrooms, each with a private bath; kitchen service, and laundry rooms; three maid's rooms with baths; and a servants' hall. A 1989 renovation by **Himmel/Bonner** divided the original 24 apartments into 51 units, which still feature high ceilings, polished oak floors, and marble fireplaces; many have French balconies and fabulous lake views. Today's tenants pay close to $4,000 per month. ♦ At W Roscoe St

5 Hawthorne Place District This quiet district (which includes Stratford Place, one block north) is one of the few remnants of residential neighborhoods dominated by single-family homes that once stretched from the Gold Coast northward to Rogers Park. The area was subdivided in 1883 and developed by the brothers Benjamin, George and John McConnell. Benjamin lived in the oldest house (1884), **568 West Hawthorne Place;** John lived at **546 West Hawthorne Place.** Many famous Chicago design firms had commissions here, including **Burnham & Root,** who designed a home for George Marshall in 1884 at **574 West Hawthorne Place; Mayo & Mayo,** who designed the house at **580 West Hawthorne Place** for Dr. Alphons Bacon; **Adler & Sullivan,** whose house for George Harvey, president of his own insurance firm, was built in 1888 at **600 West Stratford Place;** and Huehl & Schmid, who designed **606 West Stratford Place.** It remains a residential area. ♦ 529-593 W Hawthorne Pl and 600-606 W Stratford Pl (between N Lake Shore Dr and N Broadway)

6 Temple Sholom Loebl, Schlossman & Demuth were students at the **Armour Institute** (later the **Illinois Institute of Technology**) in 1921 when they teamed up with **Coolidge & Hodgdon** to design this handsome structure for the North Side's oldest Jewish reform congregation. Construction took place from 1928 to 1930. The dome and octagonal plan are reminiscent of Byzantine architecture, as are the decorative motifs on the exterior, which is faced with Wisconsin Lannon stone and trimmed with Indiana limestone. The octagonal dome rises 90 feet above the 90-by-90-foot sanctuary, which normally seats 1,350, although it can be reconfigured to seat 2,500 for High Holy Day services. ♦ 3480 N Lake Shore Dr (between W Stratford Pl and W Cornelia Ave). 525.4707 ♿

7 Totem Pole Also known as "Kwa-Ma-Rolas," this pole is a reproduction of an

original, carved at the turn of the century by the Kwakiutl Indians of British Columbia. Shaped from a single four-foot-long cedar log, the pole starts at the base with the head of a sea monster, continues with an upside-down baleen whale with a man on its back, and is topped off by a *kulos,* a member of the thunderbird family, with its wings spread. The original was acquired in 1926 by James L. Kraft, founder of the Kraft cheese company, during a collecting trip to the Pacific Northwest. Kraft donated the pole to the Chicago Park District and dedicated it to the city's schoolchildren. In the 1970s two Pacific Northwest carvers who came to Chicago to work on a project for the **Field Museum of Natural History** were shown the original totem and immediately recognized its historic value to the Kwakiutl. At their urging, the Canadian government requested the pole's return. It is now on display at the **Museum of the University of British Columbia.** This replica, carved by descendants of the original artisans, was installed in the park in 1986.
♦ Lincoln Park (at Belmont Harbor and Recreation Drs)

8 Lincoln Park Tennis Courts Ten outdoor tennis courts are available on a first-come, first-served basis. Good luck—locals seem to always get there first. ♦ Daily April through October. Lincoln Park (near W Waveland Ave)

9 Marovitz/Waveland Golf Course The only North Side lakefront site for golf was recently renamed in honor of octogenarian judge Abraham Lincoln Marovitz, but locals still call it **Waveland.** The nine-hole course is dramatically set between Lake Michigan and the Lake View skyline, which you can gaze at during the hours-long wait to tee off. You may get onto the greens quicker by joining the determined crowd that lines up at about 5:30AM or by reserving a tee-off time in advance through **Ticketmaster**—which will almost double the otherwise low greens fee. Each player must have a golf bag and five clubs to gain access to the course; all are available for rent. Caddies are not available.
♦ Daily April through November. Lincoln Park (off W Irving Park Rd, near the lake). 868.4113; Ticketmaster 559.1212

10 The Closet The name refers not only to the size of the room, but also to the process of coming out of the closet. The motorcycles out front belong to the predominantly lesbian crowd that hangs out at the bar or dances to music videos on the postage-stamp–size dance floor. ♦ Daily to 4AM; Sa to 5AM. 3325 N Broadway (at W Buckingham Pl). 477.8533

11 Windy City Fruit & Nut Company Glass cases brim with chocolates; gummy worms, bears, and fish; chunky caramels; red licorice whips; roasted and raw nuts; and dried fruits. They will create a nice gift package from your

hand-picked selections. ♦ Daily. 3308 N Broadway (at W Aldine Ave). 477.6100

12 Unabridged Bookstore Enter a rich library of polished wood shelves packed with books. Contemporary literature, gay and lesbian subjects, travel, and cooking are all well represented; there are frequently author readings. A yellow card next to a book means someone on the staff really loves it and wants you to read it too. ♦ M-F 10AM-10PM; Sa-Su 10AM-8PM. 3251 N Broadway (between W Melrose St and W Aldine Ave). 883.9119 ♿

12 He Who Eats Mud Don't be surprised if you step in for one greeting card and walk out with five. The stock includes beautiful reproductions of art masterpieces and all kinds of cards—ranging from those that amuse to one-of-a-kinds made by artists.
♦ Daily. 3247 N Broadway (between W Melrose St and W Aldine Ave). 525.0616 ♿

13 The Melrose $ The food is unremarkable coffee-shop fare—cheeseburgers, omelettes, salads—but it's available around the clock and the sidewalk patio is fun in decent weather. ♦ Coffee shop ♦ Daily 24 hours. 3233 N Broadway (at W Melrose St). 327.2060. Also at: 930 W Belmont Ave (at Wilton Ave). 404.7901

14 Reckless Records Alternative rock, a huge collection of obscure imports, plus a good supply of used records make for an inventory that runs the gamut from *Religious Industrial Sludge* to *The Best of the Lovin' Spoonful.* Bands play live in the store two Saturdays a month. ♦ M-Sa until 10PM; Su until 8PM. 3157 N Broadway (at W Belmont Ave). 404.5080

14 Annoyance Theatre Founded by **Second City** instructor Mick Napier, the resident troupe performs outrageous—and sometimes offensive—original comedies developed through improvisation. Shows have included *Dirty People on Ice* and *Coed Prison Sluts.* A long-running hit was *The Real Live Brady Bunch,* a kooky reenactment of episodes of the old TV series which toured New York and Los Angeles. Audience involvement is encouraged. ♦ 3153

N Broadway (between W Briar Pl and W Belmont Ave). 929.6200

14 Pleasure Chest It used to be almost frightening to venture into this black cavern of erotica. Take or leave a studded leather belt or two, the hard-core items have given way to sexy lingerie, greeting cards, board games, condoms, and anatomically correct candles. ♦ Daily noon-midnight. 3143 N Broadway (at W Briar Pl). 525.7151

15 Murphy's Rose Garden If you're strolling down Broadway, take a moment to detour east on Briar Place. In front of a three-flat residence on an otherwise nondescript block is a lovely rose garden. Although small, it is one of the nicest and best-maintained private rose gardens in the city. ♦ 458 W Briar Pl (at N Cambridge Ave)

16 Barbara's Bookstore While other bookstores come and go, this one, founded in the 1960s, continues to thrive. Contemporary literature and poetry fill shelves that seem to stretch into eternity. If you can't find a specific title, the staff will call the store's two other locations to try to round it up. A well-stocked drama section has everything from Molière to Mamet. Be sure to check the discount table. ♦ Daily until 10PM. 3130 N Broadway (between W Barry Ave and W Briar Pl). 477.0411. Also at: 1350 N Wells St (at W Schiller St). 642.5044; 1100 Lake St (at Marion St), Oak Park. 708/848.9140

16 Mars ★★$$ You'd be hard pressed to find a better Chinese restaurant in the city. The large dining room is airy, the tables are spaced far apart for privacy, and the service is efficient and friendly. Pot stickers and egg rolls are first-rate; the entrées are wisely limited to about 25 regional dishes, mostly Szechuan. Everything is well prepared (without MSG) and well presented. ♦ Chinese ♦ Daily lunch and dinner. 3124 N Broadway (between W Barry Ave and W Briar Pl). 404.1600 ♿

17 House of Fine Chocolates Willie Rahmig opened his candy shop in 1945 and, two generations later, his family still makes chocolates and fillings from scratch in the kitchen in back. Try a hand-dipped chocolate filled with amaretto, or nibble a white chocolate swan. ♦ Tu-Su. 3109 N Broadway (at W Barry Ave). 525.8338

22 January 1930 marked Chicago's coldest day on record—32 degrees below zero. The hottest day was 117 degrees on 14 July 1954.

SPARE PARTS

18 Spare Parts Striking fashion accessories for men and women are imported from around the world. The soft leather briefcases, handbags, wallets, and daily business planners from South America, Italy, and Spain are real beauties. ♦ Daily. 2947 N Broadway (at W Oakdale Ave). 525.4242 ♿

Nancy's

18 Nancy's Original Stuffed Pizza $ Deep-dish pizza is a Chicago original, and several pizza joints compete ferociously for tourist bucks by claiming to be the best, first, or healthiest. This pizzeria offers an excellent pie (deep-dish, heaped with ingredients, then topped with a crust and an extra layer of tomato sauce) without all the hype. The restaurant is dimly lit and decorated like a 1970s basement rec room but, for the quality of pizza and the lack of crowds, it's worth it. There's takeout too. ♦ Pizza ♦ Daily lunch and dinner. 2930 N Broadway (at W Surf St). 883.1616

19 Brewster Apartments Originally known as the **Lincoln Park Palace,** this eight-story structure was commissioned in 1893 by B. Edwards, publisher of *American Contractor* magazine, who wanted a building of small, elegant apartments. Designed by **E.H. Turnoch** and renovated in 1972 by **Mieki Hayano,** it has been designated a Chicago landmark for its excellent early application on a residential building of the principles of metal-frame construction, in which the use of iron or steel as a frame made it possible to build to greater heights. The exterior is faced in rusticated stone; the upper stories are banded by a large terra-cotta frieze with details in the style of **Louis Sullivan,** and the terra-cotta cornice features lion heads. The entryway on North Pine Grove Avenue, originally the ladies' entrance, is flanked by four polished jasper colonettes inset with windows. Make a friend in the building so that you can see the interior, one of the most fabulous remaining 19th-century atriums in the city. Patterns of intertwined tendrils and oak leaves adorn the lobby moldings, and open-case elevators, staircases, and bridges are all woven in extraordinary cast-iron latticework. ♦ 2800 N Pine Grove Ave (at W Diversey Pkwy)

19 Chicky's Choice One flight up a little stone staircase, Rita "Chicky" Sudak and daughter

Julie Rembert offer a splashy selection of women's clothing and accessories. Artsy and casual, these pieces all have that one-of-a-kind look. ♦ Tu-Su. 516 W Diversey Pkwy (between N Pine Grove and N Cambridge Aves). 348.8877 &

20 330 and 340 West Diversey Parkway Designed as the **Commonwealth Promenade** by **Mies van der Rohe** in 1957, these residential high-rises are refined and well detailed, especially at the corners. The precise placement of the towers on their lot and their glassy curtain walls create units that are brightly and naturally lit, and have fabulous views too. ♦ At N Sheridan Rd

21 Pars Cove ★$$ The scene at this Persian restaurant is exotic and romantic, with its semisubterranean setting, stone floors, ceiling fans, and pianist playing smooth jazz. *Koubideh,* kabobs of ground lamb and beef, are traditional favorites. Don't miss melt-in-your-mouth *fesen jan,* chicken simmered in rich pomegranate-and-walnut sauce. ♦ Persian ♦ Daily lunch and dinner. 435 W Diversey Pkwy (between N Lakeview and N Pine Grove Aves). 549.1515

22 Comfort Inn $ Clean, simple, and sufficient, this 75-room motel is part of a sprawling chain, but nonetheless feels friendly and intimate. The real beauty of staying here is that you're within walking distance of the park, the lakefront, and the main thoroughfares of Diversey Parkway, Clark Street, and Broadway. There is no restaurant, but there is free parking—like manna from heaven in this part of town. ♦ 601 W Diversey Pkwy (between N Lehmann Ct and N Clark St). 348.2810, 800/221.2222; fax 348.1912 &

23 Hanig's Slipper Box The city's largest collection of Birkenstock sandals, as well as classic shoe styles, can be found at this busy corner store. Keep an eye open for frequent sidewalk sales with terrific buys on good name brand men's and women's shoes. ♦ Daily. 2754 N Clark St (at W Diversey Pkwy). 248.1977 &

23 Sherwyn's Take one step backward into the 1960s and two steps forward into the New Age in Chicago's biggest and busiest health food store. Friendly Birkenstock-shod clerks direct you through rows of organic produce; bulk nuts, grains, and herbs; 20 kinds of honey and olive oil; macrobiotic seaweeds; natural cosmetics; juicers; and self-help books and tapes. ♦ Daily. 645 W Diversey Pkwy (near N Clark St). 477.1934

Barnes & Noble
Booksellers Since 1873

23 Barnes & Noble A large selection of books, a trendy coffee bar, visiting authors, talks on every imaginable subject, and great music in the background makes this a fun place to shop any night of the week. It's a great place to hang out, and a lot of singles in the neighborhood do just that. ♦ Daily until 11PM. 659 W Diversey Pkwy (between N Clark and N Orchard Sts). 871.9004; fax 871.5893 &

24 Century Mall This six-story, 50-store mall rose from the innards of a former movie palace dating from the 1930s. The facade, much of it preserved from the original structure, is a study in grandiose terra-cotta detailing. Inside, many of the original features remain—sans red-velvet seats, of course. All the stores are accessible by elevator or by a curving concrete ramp that lends the mall a distinct nautical look. A small food court downstairs serves burgers, pizza, and sushi. ♦ Daily. 2828 N Clark St (at W Diversey Pkwy). 929.8100 &

Within Century Mall:

Les Parfums Scents from around the world for men and women, along with a beautiful collection of crystal and multicolored glass perfume bottles, are sold here. ♦ Ground floor. 525.9077 &

Cignal Contemporary clothing and accessories attract a young, hip crowd of men and women. Moderately priced avant-garde clothing and leather are featured. ♦ Third floor. 281.6635 &

Gamers Paradise Parcheesi, Monopoly, playing cards—you name the game, they've got it. Don't miss the extensive collection of chess sets, from ancient marble to high-tech steel. ♦ Fifth floor. 549.1833 &

25 Borders In addition to buying books, you can often hear free music, poetry, and interesting speakers at this mega chain bookstore. The environment manages to be pleasant as well as stimulating, and there is the requisite in-store cafe. ♦ M-Th, Su until 11PM; F-Sa until midnight. 2817 N Clark (at W Diversey Pkwy). 935.3909 &

25 La Creperie ★$ Chicago's only creperie resembles a French bistro out of a 1960s movie. Create your own entrée, starting with buckwheat crepes and adding your choices of fillings like broccoli, cheese, chicken, and mushrooms. Dessert crepes with butter and sugar are delectable—and it's all quite inexpensive. Great for a first date if you're young and not rich. ♦ Crepes ♦ Tu-Su lunch and dinner. 2845 N Clark St (near W Diversey Pkwy). 528.9050 &

26 SuperCrown In addition to offering heavy discounts on hardcover and paperback books, this large chain bookstore also has an extensive magazine and periodicals selection. It may not have all the extras of the nearby **Barnes & Noble** and **Borders**, but you can't beat the prices. ◆ Daily until 11PM. 801 W Diversey Pkwy (at N Halsted St). 327.1551

27 Gaslight Corner ★$ Located next door to Sarantos Studios and just across from the **Touchstone** and the **Shattered Globe Theatres**, this neighborhood tavern tends to draw a mixed crowd of locals, blue-collar workers, actors, and theatergoers. Some come to drink and socialize, but many come to eat. As bar grub goes, the hamburgers, pizza, bratwurst, and onion rings are top-notch and dirt cheap. There's a beer garden in back. ◆ American ◆ Daily lunch and dinner. 2858 N Halsted St (at W George St). 348.2288

28 Touchstone Theatre The company moved to the city from the suburbs in 1991, first producing shows at the **Theatre Building** (see below) before settling into the space that the renowned **Steppenwolf Theatre** had occupied for years. Ina Marlowe's company produces several shows a year—from original works to the classics. In November and December, the troupe performs its traditional holiday play, a charming adaptation of *The Little Prince.* ◆ 2851 N Halsted St (between W Wolfram and W George Sts). 404.4700 ♿

29 La Paella ★★$$$ Spanish music sighs in the background and brass chandeliers gleam overhead at this romantic hideaway. Graze on a wide variety of tapas—baby clams flambéed with brandy, lamb sweetbreads, and puffy potato tortillas, among them—or order entrées such as clams with cod, duck in a heady mango sauce, and, of course, paella. Don't miss the garlic soup. ◆ Spanish ◆ Tu-Su dinner. Reservations recommended. 2920 N Clark St (at W Oakdale Ave). 528.0757

30 Wild Thing Men's and women's retro fashions from the 1940s to the 1970s fill this funky shop. Specialty: vintage bridal dresses. ◆ Daily. 2933 N Clark St (at W Oakdale Ave). 549.7787

30 Deni's Den $$ Moussaka, stuffed grape leaves, and other Greek stalwarts, all so-so, are served at tables laid out cabaret-style around a small stage and dance floor. A bigger draw than the food is soulful Greek singer Vasilios Gaitanos, who rouses everybody to sing and dance to Greek music until closing time. ◆ Greek ◆ W-Su dinner until 4AM. Music starts at 8:30PM. Reservations recommended. 2941 N Clark St (between W Oakdale and W Wellington Aves). 348.8888

31 Ivanhoe Theater This building, with its faux castle facade, was constructed as a dinner-theater in the 1940s. After jousting with lagging popularity for years, it stood empty in the 1980s. It found a new life when, after extensive renovations (including building a thrust stage for much-improved sightlines), it reopened in 1990 with a production of *Shirley Valentine* starring Ellen Burstyn. Since then it has presented a number of other dramas, including a successful run of David Mamet's *Oleanna.* ◆ 750 W Wellington Ave (at N Clark St). Box office 975.7171 ♿

BRIAR STREET THEATRE

32 Briar Street Theatre Built in 1901 as a stable for Marshall Field and Company's delivery horses and carriages, the building was purchased in 1930 by Martin H. Kennelly (who later became mayor) and turned into a warehouse for his moving and storage company. In the 1970s Swell Pictures, a video and film production company, converted it into a soundstage. Since 1985 it has served as a rental space for theater, dance, and music. Thanks to the building's origins as a stable, there are no columns—and excellent sightlines. Recent productions have included John Leguizamo's one-man comedy *Spic-o-rama*, staged in conjunction with the **Goodman Theatre**, and the road company of *Having Our Say.* ◆ 3133 N Halsted St (at W Briar Pl). Box office 348.4000 ♿

33 The Helmand ★★$$ Dinner at the only Afghani restaurant in town is both exotic and surprisingly economical. The serene room is decorated with plants and traditional costumes and brassware. The menu, though limited, offers something for the adventurous as well as the timid. An appetizer of baked baby pumpkin served with yogurt and spicy meat sauce is a must, and the lamb entrées are excellent; try *kabuli,* tender lamb baked atop rice strewn with raisins and lightly candied julienne carrots. Finish with baklava made with ground pistachios. ◆ Afghani ◆ Daily dinner. Reservations recommended Friday and Saturday. 3201 N Halsted St (at W Belmont Ave). 935.2447

34 Yoshi's Cafe ★★★$$$$ Japanese-born chef Yoshi Katsumara ingeniously and deliciously pairs classical French technique with Japanese and American accents. The menu changes regularly, but look for a starter of California goat cheese and bell pepper in melt-away pastry swathed in red bell pepper cream sauce, and a

YOSHI'S

entrée of veal medaillons with candied ginger and lemon zest. Fresh seafood selections may include tuna in a light basil, garlic, and tomato oil, or strips of salmon and Dover sole. The wine list is adequate. Tables for a total of 50 diners are tucked closely together and graced with fresh flowers. ♦ French ♦ Tu-Su dinner. Reservations recommended. 3257 N Halsted St (at W Aldine Ave). 248.6160

35 Oo-La-La ★$$ This French-Italian bistro draws an eclectic, nightclubby crowd. The hip decor is quite theatrical, with gilded red fabric walls. Pastas predominate on the menu, but the food plays a supporting role to the scene. ♦ Italian/French ♦ M-Sa dinner; Su brunch and dinner. 3335 N Halsted St (at W Buckingham Pl). 935.7708

35 Silver Moon Would-be Fred Astaires and Ginger Rogerses will find all the right vintage clothes here, including tailcoats, top hats, 1920s silk dresses with long trains, and red velvet capes. The inventory also includes vintage housewares, bridal dresses, and some furniture. Do some serious digging in the racks to make sure you've spotted all the good stuff. ♦ Tu-Su. 3337 N Halsted St (between W Buckingham Pl and W Roscoe St). 883.0222

35 Gallimaufry Gallery *Gallimaufry* means "hodgepodge" or "stew" in Elizabethan English and translates here into a beautiful assortment of hand-crafted gifts. The display of musical instruments from around the world includes African drums and gamelans, traditional percussion instruments from Indonesia. Kaleidoscopes come in two dozen styles, some of which use art-glass marbles to create their hypnotic images. ♦ Tu-Su. 3345 N Halsted St (at W Roscoe St). 348.8090 &

36 Roscoe's The bar and the adjacent cafe (see below) once were an old-fashioned corner grocery store, vestiges of which remain in the tin ceiling and mahogany woodwork. While the bar—its crowd primarily gay males—appears small from the front, it actually stretches back to two additional bars and a dance floor located in what used to be a coach house. The whole shebang has come a long way from its staid origins. ♦ Daily to 2AM; Sa to 3AM. 3356 N Halsted St (at W Roscoe St). 281.3355

36 Roscoe's Cafe Fiasco $ Offering respite from the wild scene next door at **Roscoe's** bar, the cafe serves alcoholic drinks, juices, coffee, and light fare such as chicken-salad sandwiches and broccoli quiche at a half-dozen tables. ♦ American ♦ Daily lunch and dinner to 1AM. 3354 N Halsted St (at W Roscoe St). 281.3355

37 Caffe Pergolesi $ A beatnik-style coffeehouse that's been in the neighborhood since the 1970s, it's dark, dim, and full of beat-up furniture, old newspapers, and the scent of a million cups of coffee. Proprietor David Weinberg serves vegetarian dishes, including a hearty black-bean soup and tasty vegetable stews that contain *nuksia,* an imitation meat-from-wheat that he invented. Young punks and old hippies rub elbows and smoke cigarettes here. ♦ Vegetarian ♦ Daily lunch and dinner. 3404 N Halsted St (at W Roscoe St). 472.8602

37 99th Floor Shoppers virtually crawl over one another in the tight aisles here to get at the fashions on the racks. It's hard to see exactly what's there until your eyes adjust to the dark: Almost everything is black, with an occasional white skull or gold crucifix accent, including crushed velvet baby-doll dresses, men's topcoats, studded leather collars, and motorcycle caps. The shoes are stunning, from pointy-toed purple velvet cowboy boots to Doc Martens lace-up boots and women's thigh-high red vinyl boots. ♦ Tu-Su. 3406 N Halsted St (between W Roscoe St and W Newport Ave). 348.7781

37 Beatnix Vintage duds from the 1960s and funky discowear from the 1970s are where it's at in this eclectic boutique. You can find anything from a shiny suit to a Jackie O leopard pillbox hat. ♦ Daily. 3436 N Halsted St (at W Newport Ave). 935.1188

FLASHY TRASH

38 Flashy Trash One of the premier vintage shops on Halsted Street carries clothes from the turn of the century through the 1960s. Owner Harold Mandel has costumed a number of movies, films, and TV series shot in Chicago, among them *The Untouchables.* Everything in his store's two rooms is arranged so neatly that it looks almost new. (Actually, about three-quarters of the merchandise is new-old—stored unused for years.) Standouts are a rack of Dobie Gillis–type knitted men's sweaters from the 1950s, beaded cocktail gowns from the Roaring Twenties, and a section of black skirts, shirts, dresses, and suits. Prices range from under $1 to hundreds of dollars. ♦ Daily. 3524 N Halsted St (at W Brompton Ave). 327.6900

39 Angelina Ristorante ★★$$ Sylvester Stallone look-alike Nunzio Fresta named this trattoria after his Sicilian grandmother. He and partners Callin Fortis and Ken Smith (they also own **Oo-La-La** on Halsted Street; see above) serve tender veal marsala, pasta carbonara, and other Italian favorites in a room made romantic with gauzy curtains, old wine bottles, candles, and flowers. ♦ Italian ♦ Daily dinner. 3561 N Broadway (at W Addison St). 935.5933

40 Brown Elephant This veritable warehouse of a resale shop carries housewares, books, records, and clothing. Most clothes are in good condition and even fashionable—and they're cheap: Men's dress shirts go for $1.50, and women's sweaters start at $3. Some of the shoppers trying on women's clothes, by the way, are men. All profits go to Chicago's Howard Brown Memorial Clinic, a treatment center for AIDS patients. ♦ Daily noon-6PM. 3641 N Halsted St (at W Addison St). 549.5943 &

41 Anna Maria Pizzeria $ This small take-out–oriented restaurant serves delicious thin-crust pizzas with unorthodox toppings like salmon and squash. ♦ Pizza ♦ Daily lunch and dinner. 3920 N Broadway (between W Sheridan Rd and W Dakin St). 348.4840

42 Alta Vista Terrace Forty row houses built in various styles between 1900 and 1904 line this blocklong street, developed by S.E. Gross. The detailed facades of these private residences, many in Georgian or Classic Revival style, are more reminiscent of London or Edinburgh than of the surrounding Chicago streets. The architect is unknown. ♦ 3800 block of N Alta Vista Terr (at W Grace St)

43 Graceland Cemetery Chicago's 19th-century movers and shakers, as well as famous architects **Louis Sullivan, Daniel Burnham, John Wellborn Root,** and **Ludwig Mies van der Rohe,** are buried here. Established in 1860, this is Chicago's most significant burial ground, architecturally and otherwise. Landscape architect H.W.S. Cleveland created early designs for the cemetery, with paths and plots sodded to produce a uniform surface. Park designer and landscape architect Ossian Simonds, consulting designer for **Lincoln Park,** created a naturalistic landscape of native plants. The cemetery's buildings were all designed by **Holabird & Roche.**

In death, as in life, waterfront property has cachet. Look for some of Chicago's most prominent names at lakeside. Bertha and Potter Palmer lie here in a tomb suggestive of a Greek temple. Marshall Field is nearby, beneath the stone memorial *Memory* by sculptor Daniel Chester French. One of the more interesting monuments is that of George

Pullman, inventor of the Pullman sleeping car and founder of the company town of Pullman on the city's South Side. A tall Corinthian column marks his grave. But beneath that, Pullman's coffin is sunk in a room-size concrete block, the top overlaid with railroad ties and more concrete, precautions taken by Pullman's family to protect the body from railroad workers angry over the bitter Pullman strike of 1894. Next to the Pinkerton family's plot are plots for the original Pinkerton employees. Kate Warn, the first woman detective, is buried here.

The most famous monument architecturally is the **Carrie Eliza Getty Tomb,** built in 1890. The delicately carved blocks of gray Bedford limestone and the bronze gates are some of architect **Louis Sullivan**'s finest decorative work. **Sullivan,** who died in poverty, lies not far away under a simple marker designed by his former employee **George Grant Elmslie.** ♦ Daily. Entrance on N Clark St (off W Irving Park Rd)

44 Live Bait Theater The theater is the home of the **Live Bait Theatrical Company,** founded in 1988 by actor, artist, and playwright Sharon Evans and her husband, playwright John Ragir. The company mostly performs original comedies, but has also mounted such 20th-century classics as *Anna Christie*. The **City Lit Theater Company** rents the theater for its own productions, and other companies present shows Fridays and Saturdays at 11:15PM. ♦ 3914 N Clark St (at W Byron St). 871.1212

44 Mashed Potato Club ★$ This homey, yet wildly eclectic restaurant and bar serves spuds roasted, baked, and mashed with garlic and cream cheese, as well as sweet potatoes, all with your choice of 104 toppings. They also serve a mean pot roast with gravy and, of course, potatoes. ♦ Cafe ♦ Daily dinner. 3912 N Clark St (between W Grace and W Byron Sts). 871.4062

45 "Nuts on Clark" A 30,000-square-foot warehouse is chock-full of bags, boxes, and barrels of chocolates, licorice, party mints, dried fruit, cognac cordials, macadamia nuts, and cinnamon drops, plus pastas, gourmet coffees, and wine. Most candies and nuts are already weighed and packaged in clear plastic with price labels slapped on. Coffee beans are weighed and freshly ground for you. They ship everywhere. ♦ M-Sa. 3830 N Clark St (between W Grace and W Byron Sts). 549.6622

46 Gingerman Tavern The same customers have been hanging out at this worn-around-the-edges tavern for 15 years—drinking beer, listening to classical music tapes, and shooting a little pool. Those aging hippies have been joined here by younger compatriots who appreciate an unpretentious neighborhood bar. ♦ Daily until 2AM. 3740 N Clark St (between W Waveland Ave and W Grace St). 549.2050

46 Metro/Smart Bar/Clubhouse Arguably the best concert hall in the city—and possibly the whole Midwest—in which to see live rock music, **Metro** hosts such national and international bands as the Meat Puppets, the Pixies, and the Mekons, as well as top local acts. There's plenty of room to dance, or watch from seats behind the stage or in the balcony. For postconcert dancing and people watching, head downstairs to the jam-packed **Smart Bar.** The decor and dress are black, the crowd is punk and artsy. **Clubhouse,** the adjacent coffeehouse, serves java, tea, and alcohol-free drinks in a cramped space filled with alternative rock memorabilia. ♦ Cover charge. Daily. 3730 N Clark St (between W Waveland Ave and W Grace St). Metro 549.0203, Smart Bar 549.4140, Clubhouse 549.2325

46 Raw Bar $ The bar is black lacquer; the barstools, tables, and chairs are black; the bartender has slicked-back black hair; and the menu includes raw oysters, smothered alligator, and papaya and blueberry daiquiris, all resulting in a strange sort of chic. ♦ Seafood ♦ Daily dinner until 2AM. 3720 N Clark St (at W Waveland Ave). 348.7291

Bill Veeck, the maverick White Sox owner, actually got his baseball start working for the Cubs, where his father was general manager. In his teen years, Bill Jr. worked at Wrigley Field as a vendor and later helped plant the trademark ivy that still grows along the ballpark's outfield wall.

Tradition has it that after every Cubs game at Wrigley Field, a flag is flown atop the scoreboard. A white flag with a blue W indicates a win; a blue flag with a white L denotes a loss.

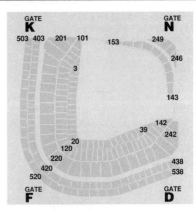

47 Wrigley Field Built in 1914, this field (seating plan above) was originally named **Weeghman Park,** after Charles Henry Weeghman, owner of the Federal League's **Chicago Whales.** When the league folded after two years, Weeghman purchased the **Cubs** and moved them to his new ballfield. A live bear cub was present at the park when the team played its first game here on 20 April 1916. The park was given its present name in 1926, after William Wrigley Jr. purchased the **Cubs.** It was designed by **Zachary Taylor Davis,** who also built the original **Comiskey Park,** home of the **White Sox** on the South Side. (That field was torn down in 1992 and replaced by a modern stadium near the original site.)

Street parking is restricted during day games, and even more so during night games, when cars must display official resident stickers. Some neighborhood entrepreneurs set up makeshift lots in their yards. The **CTA** also has designated parking lots in outlying areas, from which you can catch a shuttle bus to the park. Taking the el is really a better bet than driving; the stadium was placed at this site because of its proximity to the **Howard/Dan Ryan** line Addison Street stop. ♦ 1060 W Addison St (at N Clark St). 404.2827, CTA information 836.7000

48 Cubby Bear Lounge Stretching around the corner directly across the street from **Wrigley Field,** the lounge is a sports bar by day and an eclectic music club by night. Acts have included Queen Ida's Cajun zydeco band. There are four pool tables on the upper deck and a beer garden. ♦ Cover charge Wednesday through Saturday nights. Daily. 1059 W Addison St (at N Clark St). 327.1662

49 Wild Hare & Singing Armadillo Frog Sanctuary An award-winning renovation transformed this once dingy and broken-down bar into a clean, comfortable bilevel nightclub. Reggae bands perform every night, attracting folks from all walks of life. Despite the spacious layout, the club gets crowded on weekends, so arrive early and stake out a spot before the band starts. ♦ Cover charge. Daily 8:30PM-2AM; Sa to 3AM; from 4PM for Cubs day games. 3530 N Clark St (at W Cornelia Ave). 327.4273

50 Addis Ababa ★$$ Ethiopian food is the specialty, including good kabobs and meat and seafood stews, both mild and spicy. Accompany your meal with the traditional *tej,* a sweet honey wine. ♦ Ethiopian ♦ Daily dinner. 3521 N Clark St (at W Cornelia Ave). 929.9383

50 Jezebel ★★$$$ This elegant pastel-colored restaurant claims that "Those Who Know Us, Love Us." Whether or not that's true, the menu offers inventive dishes like stuffed breast of duck with venison sausage, goat cheese, and mushrooms topped with a red-wine–and–dried-cranberry sauce; and grilled beef tenderloin with fusilli, caramelized onion, and gorgonzola, in scarlet-brandy-cream sauce. For appetizers try the rolled eggplant stuffed with ricotta, mozzarella, and goat cheese in a tomato-basil sauce. ♦ Italian ♦ M-Sa dinner; Su brunch and dinner. 3517 N Clark St (at W Cornelia). 929.4000

51 Matsuya ★★$ One of the best choices for sushi on Clark Street, with two well-lit rooms with blond wood tables and booths, and a long sushi bar where you can see your food being prepared. Seaweed-rolled *makimono,* molded *oshi-sushi,* and other raw fish dishes are available individually or in combinations—all at remarkably reasonable prices. Also recommended are the noodle soups and top-notch appetizers such as grilled squid in ginger sauce and *sunomono* (marinated cucumbers and crabmeat). They prepare cooked fish well, too, offering delicately broiled red snapper, butterfish, and others each day. ♦ Japanese ♦ Daily dinner. Reservations recommended Friday and Saturday. 3469 N Clark St (between W Newport and W Cornelia Aves). 248.2677

52 Flashback Collectibles A Day-Glo explosion of knickknacks from the 1960s and 1970s, this is the place to find that "Brady Bunch" lunch box you've been dreaming of. Authentic pop-culture collectibles share shelf space with whoopee cushions and schlocky Farrah Fawcett posters, so serious collectors rub shoulders with kitsch-hungry slackers. A great source for fun T-shirts emblazoned with logos from 1970s TV shows and old advertising campaigns. ♦ Daily from noon. 3450 N Clark St (between W Newport and W Cornelia Aves). 929.5060 ♿

52 Strange Cargo Palm trees and leather trunks in the front window suggest a tropical theme. True, you'll find lots of Hawaiian shirts, muumuus, even grass skirts, but it's really a vintage general store carrying all sorts of items from the 1940s through 1970s. Everything is arranged by type—hats, shoes, shirts, dresses—in two rooms. Impulse purchases are encouraged at the cash register with a tempting display of tacky plastic earrings at el cheapo prices. ♦ Daily from noon. 3448 N Clark St (between W Newport and W Cornelia Aves). 327.8090

The Outpost

52 The Outpost ★★$$ "Life's short, eat well," is the motto of this Australian-themed eatery and bar. While service is sometimes abrupt, the food is consistently good. Entrées include stone-crab–filled red pepper ravioli with lobster cream tomato sauce; grilled venison with sweet potato hash and juniper berry wine sauce; and grilled filet mignon with mushroom, pecan, and double-bacon compote. ♦ International ♦ Tu-Sa dinner; Su brunch and dinner. 3438 N Clark St (at W Newport and N Sheffield Aves). 244.1166

53 El Jardin Cafe ★$ Operated by Gus Quinones of the family that owns the nearby restaurant of the same name (see below), this airy, informal cafe serves simple, tasty Mexican fare. The collegiate crowd that lines up on the sidewalk on weekends is not there for the food. They come for Gus's deadly margaritas. Beware. ♦ Mexican ♦ Daily breakfast, lunch, and dinner. 3401 N Clark St (at W Roscoe St). 935.8133

54 Star Market, Inc. This is one of the largest Japanese grocery stores in the city. Owners Paul Oda and Ryuji Hashimoto import much of their inventory directly from Japan. One refrigerator case is stuffed with different varieties of seaweed in plastic packages; another is filled with eel, tuna, and other fish, much of it flown in fresh twice a week. The produce section has rows of exotic greens, and the shelves are lined with dozens of varieties of soy sauce, cooking oils, curly noodles, rice cakes, and brightly colored rice-based confections. ♦ Daily. 3349 N Clark St (at W Roscoe St). 472.0599

54 P.S. Bangkok ★$$ Owner Suradet Yongsawaii prepared take-out food in a Bangkok market before emigrating to the US. Although always busy, his storefront restaurant maintains a calm atmosphere, with linen tablecloths and dinner candles. The extensive menu starts with 33 appetizers. Curry entrées prepared with coconut milk are special standouts. You will find the noodle dishes unlike those at other Thai restaurants; the sauce on *pad thai,* for example, is almost caramelized. ♦ Thai ♦ Tu-Su lunch and dinner. Reservations recommended Friday and Saturday. 3345 N Clark St (between W Buckingham Pl and W Roscoe St). 871.7777

54 El Jardin $$ This was once a quaint Mexican restaurant with terrific food, but the quality slipped when it expanded to accommodate demand, and you can still expect a wait. It's always packed with young professionals downing fizzy margaritas and platters of *bistec à la Mexicana* (steak) and *enchiladas verdes* (with spicy green sauce). Brunch features fruit, soups, tamales, and meat and fish entrées. The main dining room resembles a plaza, with redbrick floors, whitewashed walls, and big windows. In warm weather, sit out on the peaceful patio, which is shielded from the busy street by tall stucco walls. ♦ Mexican ♦ M-Sa lunch and dinner; Su brunch and dinner. 3335 N Clark St (at W Buckingham Pl). 528.6775

55 Happi Sushi ★$$ The chefs at the sushi bar greet you in Japanese as you enter this small, casual storefront restaurant. The menu is long on sushi and sashimi, and all the seafood—abalone, clam, tuna, salmon—is fresh and tender. The preparations are as satisfying to look at as to eat. The rumbling you hear is the el passing practically overhead. ♦ Japanese ♦ Daily lunch and dinner. 3346 N Clark St (at W Roscoe St). 528.1225

55 Hubba-Hubba Mother and daughter Ellen Freedman and Julie Schneider have put together a playful collection of men's and women's vintage clothing and jewelry. Everything is well displayed and in excellent condition. Look for their colorful crinoline skirts and flouncy party dresses. ♦ Daily. 3338 N Clark St (between W Buckingham Pl and W Roscoe St). 477.1414 &

Harry Caray, sportscaster for the Chicago Cubs, won the Ford Frick Award for meritorious contributions to broadcasting in 1989.

Despite fame and success during his lifetime, architect Louis Sullivan died poor, sick, and alone. Five years after his death, a group of architects financed a headstone for him in Graceland Cemetery.

55 Thai Classic ★$ They serve tasty chicken with basil leaves and coconut-milk curries, along with other customary dishes, but they're best at seafood specials such as shrimp with garlic, basil leaves, and peppers. The seasoning is milder than at other Thai restaurants. Seating is either American style or Asian style on pillows at low tables with sunken wells for your legs. ♦ Thai ♦ Daily lunch and dinner. 3332 N Clark St (at W Buckingham Pl). 404.2000 &

56 Coffee Chicago $ Light and airy, this spot has two walls of floor-to-ceiling windows and plenty of room to stretch out between tables. An open kitchen in back serves coffee, espresso, fresh juices, pastries, good homemade pasta salads, quiche, and other light meals. It opens early and closes late—a good spot for an after-theater snack. ♦ Coffeehouse ♦ Daily. 3323 N Clark St (between W Aldine Ave and W Buckingham Pl). 477.3323. Also at: 2922 N Clark St (at W Oakdale Ave). 327.3228

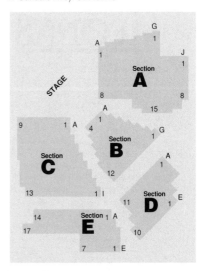

56 Organic Theatre Established in 1969, the company has produced plays ranging from Homer's *Odyssey* to David Mamet's *Sexual Perversity in Chicago* to the long-running spoof of **Cubs** fans, *Bleacher Bums.* In addition to featuring the company's own productions, the 400-seat **Mainstage** (see the plan pictured above) and the 90-seat **Greenhouse Theater** are rented out for productions such as the popular "Stories on Stage" readings. ♦ 3319 N Clark St (between W Aldine Ave and W Buckingham Pl). 327.5588

56 Bar San Miguel Old movies play on overhead TVs at this comfortable after-theater hangout, where local actors mingle with the postdinner crowd from next door. Mexican food, sandwiches, and desserts are available. On a warm night, move to the backyard patio.

♦ Daily to 2AM. 3313 N Clark St (between W Aldine Ave and W Buckingham Pl). 871.0896

56 Mia Francesca ★$ Chef and owner Scott Harris puts together an interesting, ever-changing menu that features six daily pastas, three fresh fish choices, and an occasional beef or veal dish. All of the desserts are made in-house; they include tiramisù and lemon mascarpone mousse. Expect a crowd, even on weeknights; good food and reasonable prices make this one of the neighborhood's most popular eateries. The wine bar is a great spot to enjoy an appetizer and a drink while waiting for a table. ♦ Italian ♦ Daily dinner. 3311 N Clark St (between W Aldine Ave and W Buckingham Pl). 281.3310

56 Toshiro New owners Janet and John Moran showcase women's contemporary clothing as well as antiques, gifts, housewares and home accessories in a high-tech Japanese decor. ♦ Daily. 3309 N Clark St (at W Aldine Ave). 248.1487

⚚ LEONA'S ⚚

57 Leona's ★$$ The late Leona Szemla opened her first restaurant in 1950. Today, the Toya family—Leona's grandchildren—runs five of them. The dinner line starts forming on the sidewalk by 6PM, but a free glass of wine helps you wait patiently. There are two bustling floors plus a deck filled with checkered-cloth–covered tables. Peruse the long Italian menu, but don't miss the flaky thin-crust whole-wheat pizza with a choice of 28 toppings, from artichokes to zucchini. ♦ Italian/Pizza ♦ Daily lunch and dinner. 3215 N Sheffield Ave (between W Belmont Ave and W School St). 327.8861. Also at: 1936 W Augusta Blvd (at Winchester Ave). 292.4300; 6935 N Sheridan Rd (at Morse Ave). 764.5757; 1419 W Taylor St (at Loomis Pl). 850.2222; 7443 W Irving Park Rd (at Harlem Ave). 625.3636

58 Sheffield's Wine and Beer Garden Once a quiet corner tavern where actors and their hangers-on hung out, the club has gentrified along with the neighborhood, but without losing too much of its artsy charm. Jeremy Turner's disturbing artwork still holds pride of place in the front room, and the cat is still curled up by the fireplace in the back. The bar is well stocked with microbrews from around the country, as well as several decent wines. Pamphlets with thorough descriptions of potable selections are available for serious beer-heads. In summertime, the adjacent beer garden (complete with shaded pool table) is packed to the fences. ♦ M-F, Su to 2AM; Sa to 3AM. 3258 N Sheffield Ave (at W School St). 281.4989

59 Chicago Comics The guys behind the counter look like they're playing hooky from high school—or could it be that sitting around reading comic books keeps a person forever young? They stock all the usual superheroes—Superman, Batman, Wonder Woman—plus Dick Tracy, Teenage Mutant Ninja Turtles, posters, and T-shirts. You can also pick up hard-to-find Marvel and DC editions from the "Silver Age" (early 1960s). ♦ Daily. 3244 N Clark St (between W Belmont Ave and W School St). 528.1983

60 Cafe Voltaire This combination cafe/theater has squishy old velour couches and a revolving art show on the walls to lend atmosphere, as well as picnic benches plopped onto white gravel to constitute a backyard patio. Upstairs, a cafe serves mediocre vegetarian fare (falafel, black-bean burritos) to crowds who don't seem to care. The underground performance space presents an odd assortment of shows. The cult gay play *Party* debuted here, as did a long-running production of Dylan Thomas's *Under Milkwood*. Check the bulletin boards for plays, concerts, and poetry readings around town. ♦ Daily; F-Sa until 3AM. 3231 N Clark St (between W Belmont Ave and W School St). 528.3136

61 Architectural Revolution Plaster casts of gargoyles, John Lennon, Mozart, Greek gods, and the like—much of it pretty kitschy, needless to say—are for sale here. But you'll also find impressive Roman columns suitable as table bases and decorative stands. ♦ Daily. 856 W Belmont Ave (at N Clark St). 752.7837 ♿

62 Berlin The crowd, largely gay and lesbian, gyrates to DJ tapes, music videos, and occasional live acts. The exhibitionistic do their dancing atop go-go platforms. The decor's theme changes monthly, and special events include a pet costume contest, "drag" races, and a monthly 1970s disco night. ♦ Cover charge. Daily to 4AM. 954 W Belmont Ave (at N Sheffield Ave). 348.4975

63 B.L.U.E.S. Etc. The Big Time Sarah Blues Band, Son Seals, and a slew of other famed blues figures might as well be in your living room when they play here. Though newer and bigger than its sister club on Halsted Street, this spinoff gets smoky and sweaty as the night progresses, just as a real blues bar should. ♦ Cover charge. Daily; music from 9:30PM. 1124 W Belmont Ave (at N Clifton Ave). 525.8989

64 People Like Us Books In addition to books, this store devoted to gay and lesbian literature carries magazines, videos, greeting cards, and gay newspapers from around the country, and acts as an informal clearinghouse of information about Chicago's gay community. ♦ Daily until 9PM. 1115 W Belmont (between N Seminary and N Clifton Aves). 248.6363 ♿

65 Theatre Building Over the years, the two stages here have been home to hundreds of non-Equity theater companies, including the **Northlight Theatre Co.**'s *Bubbe Meises* and **Hartzell Production**'s *Vampire Lesbians of Sodom.* ♦ 1225 W Belmont Ave (at N Racine Ave). 327.5252

66 Jeanny's ★$ It may look like a standard Chinese restaurant, but the food is far from standard. Dishes are uniformly good and reasonably priced, and the service is pleasant. Some of the more popular dishes are Mandarin chicken (crunchy chicken pieces sautéed with minced hot peppers in a sweet/hot suace with fresh broccoli) and Mongolian beef (sliced beef sautéed with green onions and bamboo shoots, topped with crispy rice noodles). Eat in or order to go. ♦ Chinese ♦ M-Sa lunch and dinner; Su dinner. 1053 W Belmont Ave (at N Kenmore Ave). 248.1133

67 Moti Mahal ★$ This small Indian restaurant is renowned for its delicious *nan* bread. The tear-shaped loaves are served hot from a clay oven, soft, chewy, and dripping with butter. Dip them into the lively curry sauces that accompany such entrées as spicy *chicken vindaloo* or *saag paneer* (spinach with Indian cheese). The restaurant offers many vegetarian dishes, and its weekday lunch buffet is made for budget-conscious folks with huge appetites. It's especially crowded on weekends, when the seating area expands into the adjacent market to accommodate the crush. Bring your own alcohol. ♦ Indian ♦ Daily lunch and dinner. 1031 W Belmont Ave (at N Kenmore Ave). 348.4392

67 The Stars Our Destination Partners Alice Bentley, who used to work in particle physics, and Greg Ketter stock just about every sci-fi, fantasy, and horror book or magazine known to earthlings. ♦ Daily. 1021 W Belmont Ave (between N Sheffield and N Kenmore Aves). 871.2722

67 Bella Vista ★★$$$ When this stunning restaurant opened in a renovated former bank in 1992, people wondered whether the food could measure up to the surroundings. It's hardly a fair question, because the two-level dining area that fronts an open kitchen is such a feast for the eyes that it must be seen to be believed. While the pasta, pizzas, and seafood can't compete with the decor, they're consistently inventive and tasty. ♦ Italian ♦ M-Sa lunch and dinner; Su dinner. Reservations recommended. 1001 W Belmont Ave (at N Sheffield Ave). 404.0111

68 The Vic/Brew & View This faded theater has a split personality. **The Vic,** one of the city's most popular live concert venues, hosts performers across the pop-rock spectrum: Jackson Brown, Diamanda Galas, Skinny Puppy, and Sepultura have all appeared here. When no concerts are scheduled, it becomes a second-run movie theater known as the **Brew & View,** which sells beer during the flicks and permits smoking. The crowds can get boisterous (weeknight screenings are tamer). The theater's screen is one of the largest in the city, and the price is right— $2.50 for a double feature. ♦ Daily. 3145 N Sheffield Ave (at W Belmont Ave). 618.8439, Ticketmaster 559.1212

69 Ann Sather ★★$ In 1946 the owner for whom this eatery is named spent her life savings to buy the **Swedish Diner;** 10 years later she moved down the block to this larger location. Although Ann is no longer around, the menu—course after course of such Swedish mainstays as meatballs, dumplings, and overcooked vegetables—remains the same. On weekends, crowds line up for breakfasts of Swedish pancakes with lingonberries, Swedish potato sausage, cinnamon rolls, and limpa bread. The upstairs banquet room is a frequent meeting place for community groups. ♦ Swedish/American ♦ Daily breakfast, lunch, and dinner. 929 W Belmont Ave (at N Wilton Ave). 348.2378. Also at: 5207 N Clark (just north of Foster). 271.6677

69 Standard India ★$ The dim lighting and worn furnishings are a bit depressing, but the food compensates. Try *saag paneer,* spicy spinach with chunks of Indian cheese, and the delicate *chicken makhani* with tomato and parsley. A good way to sample many entrées is the inexpensive prix-fixe buffet Monday through Thursday evenings. ♦ Indian ♦ M, W-Su lunch and dinner; Tu dinner. 917 W Belmont Ave (at N Wilton Ave). 929.1123

70 J. Toguri Mercantile Co. This Japanese department store carries a full range of kimonos, china, and various imports from the Orient. The long aisles are lined with ceramic soup bowls and spoons, bamboo bird cages, paper lanterns, and Japanese-language books, magazines, and cassette tapes. ♦ M-Sa. 851 W Belmont Ave (at N Clark St). 929.3500

71 Scenes Coffee House and Dramatist Bookstore $ Chicago actor Jamie Ashe owns this place but usually stays in the wings, letting playwright friends run the show. Tables and chairs for about 35 are snugly tucked between shelves of books for the theatrically inclined, mostly scripts and film criticism.

Patrons drink coffee and nibble pastries, smoking and gazing out the window onto Clark Street, obeying signs that say books from the shelves are not to be browsed at the tables. ♦ Coffeehouse ♦ M-Th, Su until 11:30PM; F-Sa until 2:30AM. 3168 N Clark St (between W Fletcher St and W Belmont Ave). 525.1007

72 Pops for Champagne One of the city's most elegant jazz clubs features well-known local combos. Plush booths, Art Deco sconces, a semicircular bar, and a gleaming black grand piano atop an elevated stage set the scene. Taittinger Blanc de Blanc 1981, Dom Pérignon 1982, and more than a hundred other Champagnes are available, many by the glass, along with some 20 other sparkling wines. Light appetizers and dessert are served, too. The brick outdoor patio is lovely in the summer, although the music can't be heard there. ♦ Cover charge and minimum. Daily; Su brunch. 2934 N Sheffield Ave (at W Oakdale Ave). 472.1000

Chicago Theater: Second to None

The **Steppenwolf Theatre Company** may have put Chicago on the international theater map, but the award-winning ensemble is hardly the only show in town. Other stellar theaters in the city include the **Goodman, Victory Gardens,** and **Court** theaters, where new works and new interpretations of old works are often premiered. **Second City** invented improvisational theater almost 40 years ago and the craft continues there today, as well as at the **Improv Olympic** and the **Players Workshop.**

Unlike any other theater community in the country, Chicago is known for developing risk-taking new works. There is a thriving off-Loop theater scene, where more than a dozen Equity companies and scores of non-Equity troupes tread the boards. Small companies like **Roadworks, Touchstone,** and **Straw Dog** are establishing their own reputations, and even more alternative fare is being produced by such daring young groups as the **Annoyance Theater, Live Bait Theater,** and **Neo-Futurariums.**

The Joseph Jefferson Awards Committee honors excellence in local professional theater. The 40-member panel judges more than a hundred productions each year, bestowing "Jeff" Awards for superior work in Equity shows and noncompetitive citations for outstanding work in non-Equity productions.

In the recent past, however, some of Chicago's nonprofit and experimental theaters have fallen by the wayside, unable to compete with the big commercial productions coming out of London and New York. The **Shubert** and **Auditorium** theaters host blockbusters like the current revival of *Showboat* and the ongoing *Miss Saigon.* There is also talk that the Disney corporation is planning to acquire the **Chicago Theater** for its production of *Beauty and the Beast.*

For up-to-the minute information, consult publications such as the *Reader, Chicago Tribune,* and *Chicago* magazine. To charge theater tickets by phone, call the **Ticketmaster Arts Line** (902.1500). **HOT TIX** booths, which are owned and operated by the League of Chicago Theatres, offer half-price and discounted day-of-performance tickets, as well as full-price tickets to **Ticketmaster** events. All **HOT TIX** sales must be made in person; booths are found at the following locations:

The Loop: 108 N State St (between Washington and Randolph Sts); M-F 10AM-7PM, Sa 10AM-6PM, Su noon-5PM

Magnificent Mile: Chicago Place, 6th floor, 700 N Michigan Ave (at E Huron St); M-F 10AM-7PM, Sa 10AM-6PM, Su noon-5PM

Evanston: 1616 Sherman Ave (between Davis and Church Sts); W-Th 11AM-3PM, F-Sa 10AM-4PM, Su noon-4PM

73 Terracotta Row Five buildings were constructed on Oakdale Avenue in the 1880s by the Northwestern Terra Cotta Company, which became a national leader in the terra-cotta industry. Three still stand in good condition: **1059, 1057,** and **1048 West Oakdale Avenue.** The last (the most elaborate) was the home of Henry Rokham, the company's president. It features gables with prominent corner pieces, an Italianate sunburst and flower finial, a gabled roof, a corbelled chimney, and extensive trim. On the building's west side is a terra-cotta relief of a woman in a skirt and bonnet seated at a spinning wheel. The houses are all private residences. ♦ On W Oakdale Ave (between N Sheffield and N Seminary Aves)

74 Cue Club Pool is cool, as evidenced by the hordes of young professionals who descend nightly to play and spectate at the 10 Brunswick Gold Crown III tables in this polished setting of pine woodwork and dramatic lighting. There's a 40-foot bar with overhead TVs blaring sports programs. The club recently expanded into a back room, where rock bands perform on weekends. A small menu prepared with no special flair includes nachos and signature sandwiches called—what else?—Cue Clubs. ♦ Music cover. Daily. 2833 N Sheffield Ave (at W Wolfram St). 477.3661

75 Lawry's Tavern ★$ This restaurant (not to be confused with the prime rib restaurant downtown) was a neighborhood institution decades before jazz clubs and fern bars moved in. Back then it was owned by the father of the current owner, Lawrence Price. It looks like any other saloon, but three nights a week tables are covered with checkered tablecloths and families line up for a fried-chicken feast (Wednesdays and Saturdays) and an all-you-can-eat fish fry (Fridays). The bargain prices are one of the city's best-kept secrets; regulars would like it to stay that way. ♦ American ♦ M-Sa lunch and dinner to 2AM; Sunday lunch and dinner during football season. 1028 W Diversey Pkwy (at N Kenmore Ave). 348.9711

76 Cozy Cafe ★$ From the outside, it looks like a place you'd think twice about before entering. Inside, this noisy little joint is the quintessential greasy spoon, with a menu of eggs, pork chops, ham, biscuits, and gravy. Most of the employees seem to be starting up a rock band or already in one, and they keep the fine jukebox on high volume. In warm weather, some people gravitate toward a patio in back. The smart money says to stay inside. ♦ Coffee shop ♦ Daily 7AM-3PM. 2819 N Lincoln Ave (at W Diversey Pkwy and N Racine Ave). 549.9374

77 Powell's Bookstore Arguably the best used bookstore in the city, this shop stocks about 100,000 books spread out through three rooms in a neat, organized fashion. The subject range is vast: The large literature collection ranges from yellowing leather-bound volumes of classics to contemporary paperbacks; there's a good selection of children's books; and you will find beautiful art books on everything from Renaissance painters to photography. Best of all, the prices are consistently lower than at similar stores—there's even a bin of free books for true literary scavengers! ♦ Daily. 2850 N Lincoln Ave (at W Diversey Pkwy). 248.1444. Also at: 1501 E 57th St (at S Blackstone Ave). 955.7780; 828 S Wabash Ave (at E Eighth St). 341.0748

78 Elbo Room Once a factory, this two-story space is now a performance venue for jazz orchestras, poets, rock and country bands, and comedy troupes. Barrett Deems and his band play every Tuesday night. The stage is downstairs, cozily surrounded by tables, but the coolest seats in the house are the booths recessed off the main room and located directly below the sidewalks. The club takes its name from the building's triangular shape. ♦ Cover charge. Daily 8PM-2AM; Sa to 3AM. 2871 N Lincoln Ave (at W George St). 549.5549

79 St. Alphonsus Church A monumental Gothic church built for a German congregation, this is a neighborhood landmark not only because it juts out above all the surrounding structures, but also because of its imposing siting at this six-cornered intersection. It was built from 1889 to 1897 by **Adam Boos** and **Josef Bettinghofer,** then **Schrader & Conradi.** ♦ 2950 N Southport Ave (at N Lincoln Ave)

80 Chicago Antique Mall This warehouse of an antiques store comprises some 25 different dealers' stalls, all overseen by proprietor Sue Kress. The selection is strong on Art Deco pieces and Victorian furniture. **Cavalier Antiques** has a striking display of 19th-century chandeliers, which are dripping with crystals and completely wired for the 20th century, and there's an impressive collection of maps and globes dating back to the 16th century. Most of the dealers here will pack and ship your purchases. ♦ Daily. 3045 N Lincoln Ave (at W Wellington Ave). 929.0200 &

81 Little Bucharest ★★$ Reds and browns dominate both the decor and the food in one of the few Romanian restaurants in the city. The veal paprikash, chicken à la Bucharest with liver and white-wine stuffing, and other dishes are terrific, but their low prices are even more notable. Rich homemade chocolate tortes will do you in if dinner doesn't. Watch for summertime outdoor feasts, when the

---

estaurants/Clubs: Red   **Hotels:** Blue

hops/ ♥ Outdoors: Green   **Sights/Culture:** Black

restaurant takes over a block of Wellington Avenue for a festive pig and lamb roast. ◆ Romanian ◆ Daily lunch and dinner. Reservations recommended Friday and Saturday. 3001 N Ashland Ave (at W Wellington Ave). 929.8640

82 Feliz Cakes $ The glass cases in this sunny, whitewashed shop display such Filipino treats as *ube* (cake made from purple yams and sporting purple frosting), *mamon* (sponge cake), and *ensaymada* (sweet rolls), plus a few American cookies and cakes, all baked on the premises. Take items out or eat inside at one of the half-dozen tables. Tuna sandwiches, steamed rolls with pork, and other snacks are also available. ◆ Filipino ◆ Tu-Sa. 3056 N Lincoln Ave (at W Barry Ave). 549.4188

83 Da Nicola ★★★$$ This comfy and totally untrendy neighborhood Italian restaurant features a menu of Northern and Southern Italian dishes served by an attentive and knowledgeable wait staff. The menu includes an impressive array of pastas and sauces, seafood, steak, and chicken, along with an extensive wine list. Try the lunch special for only $4.95. ◆ Italian ◆ Daily lunch and dinner. 3114 N Lincoln Ave (between W Barry and N Ashland Aves). 935.8000

84 Beat Kitchen Opened in 1991 by Alan Baer, who for years operated **Orphans** in Lincoln Park, this rock 'n' roll bar quickly earned a reputation as one of the best small venues in the city. It generally draws good bands, including local faves like the Elvis Brothers and Alluring Strangers. The kitchen's fare—pizza, gumbo, blackened chicken—is a pleasant surprise. ◆ Cover charge for shows. M-Sa to 1AM; music from about 9:30PM. 2100 W Belmont Ave (at N Lincoln Ave). 281.4444

85 Schuba's Tavern $ This Neo-Gothic building was constructed in the early 1900s by the Schlitz Brewing Company, one of several taverns the company built in Chicago to serve its beer (the facade still sports the Schlitz logo in terra-cotta). In the late 1980s brothers Chris and Michael Schuba purchased and breathed new life into the tavern, with its green tin ceiling, 30-foot-long mahogany bar, and great jukebox loaded with oldies. The restaurant in the back serves all-too-ordinary cheeseburgers, BLTs, chili, and such. Local rock and blues bands play on a stage in the back Wednesday through Saturday nights. ◆ American ◆ Cover charge for music. Daily breakfast, lunch, and dinner. 3159 N Southport Ave (at W Belmont Ave). 525.2508

86 Uncle Fun Rubber hot dogs, statuettes of "Star Trek" characters, Dr. Seuss T-shirts, and various odds and ends abound in this cramped toy store. Artists flock to the shop to pick through the dozens of drawers full of junk—lighters, tiny plastic baby heads, and other seemingly useless raw material. Collectors snap up vintage valentines or Beatles dolls, and slackers spend hours browsing for weird toys from the 1950s. ◆ W-Su. 1338 W Belmont Ave (between N Lakewood and N Southport Aves). 477.8223

87 Southport Lanes Like **Schuba's Tavern** down the street (see above), this bowling alley/pool hall is housed in an old Schlitz tavern, and the old-fashioned charm still comes through. It's the only bowling alley in the city that still employs pin-boys to manually reset the pins. There are just four lanes and they fill up fast; call first to make sure someone hasn't rented them out for a private party. The bar has beautiful wood and stained glass, and a spacious back room boasts six pool tables. In warm weather, the sidewalk cafe makes for great people watching. Food includes burgers, salads, wings, nachos, and the like. ◆ Daily to 2AM. 3325 N Southport Ave (at W School St). 472.1601

88 Sweet Pea The pickings at this pint-size store consist of quality toys from around the world: books, dolls, art supplies, and crafts and games designed to stimulate creativity in children. ◆ Tu-Su. 3338 N Southport Ave (between W Henderson and W Roscoe Sts). 281.4426

89 Chair The name says it all. This small boutique offers a wide selection of one-person seats (in other words, chairs) from Chippendale to Charles Eames. Services include custom upholstery, vintage fabrics, painted finishes, and a finder's service. ◆ W-Su. 3402 N Southport Ave (at W Roscoe St). 348.USIT

90 Viennese Kaffee Haus Brandt ★$ The atmosphere here is authentically Viennese, complete with classical music and rich European desserts. Although the kitchen whips up breakfast, lunch, and dinner offerings, you can feel comfortable relaxing with just a cup of coffee. ◆ Coffeehouse ◆ Daily breakfast, lunch, and dinner. 3423 N Southport Ave (between W Roscoe St and W Newport Ave). 528.2220

91 Saga's Launder-Bar & Cafe $ It's "Loads of fun" at this unique operation, which is a combo laundromat, restaurant, and bar. The 66-washer, 48-dryer laundromat is decorated with old washboards, soap ads, and other antique laundry gear. Customers (most of them in their 20s and 30s) load their clothes into washers, then head through a doorway to the bar and restaurant for chicken soup and turkey-salad sandwiches. The bar serves drinks with names like the "Triple-Loader" and "Polyester Blend." A lightboard hooked up to each of the washers blinks to let diners know when it's time to move clothes to the dryer. ♦ American ♦ Daily breakfast, lunch, and dinner. 3435 N Southport Ave (at W Newport Ave). 929.WASH

91 Fourth World Artisans This small shop features unique handcrafted decorative accessories, art, and clothing from artists and craftspeople around the world. ♦ Tu-Su. 3453 N Southport (between W Newport and W Cornelia Aves). 404.5200

92 Wild Onion ★$$ Three dining rooms with high beamed ceilings, polished wooden floors, exposed brick walls hung with colorful contemporary paintings, and rows of low-slung banquettes make this a chic people watching place. The restaurant's name is taken from the presumed translation of the Illini tribe's word *Che-cau-gou,* from which the city gets its name. The regional cooking includes a tasty curried Iowa lamb stew, enchiladas filled with Indiana duck, and a tasty grilled shark sandwich. ♦ American ♦ M-Sa lunch and dinner. 3500 N Lincoln Ave (at W Cornelia Ave). 871.5113 &

92 Paulina Market A virtual meat museum, this sprawling family-owned butcher's shop sells specialty cuts of beef, lamb, pork, and veal, as well as an array of smoked meats. A zillion varieties of homemade sausages line one wall, forming an eye-popping display. Hot oven-roasted chicken, turkey breast, loin of pork, and fresh ham are also available. Friendly counter help will provide advice and recipes if asked. ♦ M-Sa. 3501 N Lincoln Ave (at W Cornelia Ave). 248.6272 &

93 Music Box Theater Built in 1929, this movie palace showed some of the early talkies, then closed down, opening intermittently over the years to show porno, Spanish, and Arabic films. After a major renovation in 1983, it reopened as Chicago's only locally owned first-run movie house, and now shows art, foreign, and vintage films. It boasts great vintage details: the lobby's multicolored tile floor, squishy old chairs, and a ceiling that twinkles with tiny lights set amid painted clouds. The sign out front is the last working neon and incandescent marquee in the city. In 1992 it added a tiny multiplex-style screening room next to the main room. Phone ahead to make sure that the movie you want to see is playing on the big screen. ♦ 3733 N Southport Ave (at W Grace St). 871.6604

94 New World Resource Center At this independent, nonsectarian, left-wing bookstore, you'll find books, cassettes, and periodicals on everything from the US labor movement to liberation theology. ♦ Tu-Th 3PM-9PM; F-Su noon-7PM. 1476 W Irving Park Rd (between N Southport and N Ashland Aves). 348.3370 &

94 Gone to Pot Potter Marcy Glick works in a dusty studio in the back of her store, in which she features her own handmade colored inlaid clay as well as a revolving gallery of works by about 60 other craftspeople. The selection may include blown glass, masks, weavings, watercolors, wood carvings, candlesticks, and clothing (even hand-painted bicycle shorts). Ask her to show you around the studio; she might craft a piece while you watch. ♦ M-Sa by appointment. 1432 W Irving Park Rd (between N Southport and N Ashland Aves). 472.2274

Bests

Kenan Heise
Author/historian

The dust of Chicago's greatness can be found in **Graceland Cemetery.** It is very tourable. The front office has a brochure and guide booklet to help you. A young architectural student I took there stood with his feet a foot off the ground in front of the grave marker for **Louis Sullivan,** the architect who helped free his art from the slavery of foreign entanglements.

Also there is the grave of another inspirer, John Peter Altgeld, former governor of Illinois, whom poet Vachel Lindsay described as "the eagle forgotten." He did brave things for prisoners, immigrants, the poor, and the politically disenfranchised. He was hero to both Clarence Darrow and President John F. Kennedy.

Be sure to see the grave of George F. Pullman, who gave his name to the sleeper car and the company town, now part of Chicago's far South Side. You will wish you had X-ray vision so you could see the mass of rails and cement used to protect his coffin from a paranoid fear that his former employees would desecrate his remains.

Chicago society queen, Bertha Palmer, and husband, Potter, upstaged almost everyone else in the place with their elegant Greek-pillared monument.

The founder of the National Baseball League, William A. Hurlbert, and former heavyweight boxing champion, Jack Johnson, both, to use a euphemism, rest here.

I recommend the island in **Lake Willomere** for the grave of **Daniel Burnham,** the Lorado Taft sculpture for the Graves family grave marker, the pyramid mausoleum, and, most of all, the **Getty Tomb,** designed by **Louis Sullivan** and called a "requiem in architecture."

Enjoy the place.

Hyde Park/ Kenwood

Middle-class, liberal-minded, and more racially integrated than any other part of the city, Hyde Park is an urban oasis of smarts and savvy. Bordered by **47th Street**, the **Midway Plaisance** along **60th Street, Cottage Grove Avenue**, and **Lake Michigan**, it is home to the 175-acre **University of Chicago**. Vast parklands provide public recreation as well as homes for the beloved **Museum of Science and Industry** in **Jackson Park** and the distinguished **Du Sable Museum of African-American History** in **Washington Park**. Popular restaurants, alluring shops, and some of the city's best bookstores make up the main shopping districts along **53rd, 55th**, and **57th Streets**. The imposing architecture ranges from **I.M. Pei**'s **University Town Houses** on 55th Street to rows of 19th-century mansions along **Kenwood** and **Kimbark Avenues** between 47th and **49th Streets**, from **Frank Lloyd Wright**'s Prairie-style **Robie House** to the Gothic **Rockefeller Chapel**, both on the **University of Chicago** campus.

Hyde Park was created in 1852 when Chicago lawyer Paul Cornell purchased 300 acres of lakefront property and promoted it among affluent Chicagoans as a suburb and summer-home site, giving it a name with appropriately upper-class connotations. Success was assured when he deeded property to the **Illinois Central Railroad** in return for regular commuter train service to the Loop, and prosperous Chicagoans began to build their homes here. Adding to the attraction was the development of bordering parks designed by famous landscape architect Frederick Law Olmsted.

Kenwood, north of **Hyde Park Boulevard**, was founded in 1856 when Chicago dentist John A. Kennicott built an estate there and named the community after his mother's ancestral home in Scotland. Close to both the commuter train and the bustling **Union Stockyards,** about three miles north, Kenwood attracted meatpacking king Augustus Swift, as well as Sears, Roebuck & Company mogul Julius Rosenwald, and numerous others whose mansions matched their status as business giants. The construction of nearby workers' cottages to house their servants simultaneously created a large Irish community.

Both areas escaped the 1871 Chicago Fire, leaving them with some of the city's oldest homes and spurring a housing boom. Rapid growth prompted annexation to Chicago in 1889, despite protests by middle-class residents who preferred suburban status. Four years later, the World's Columbian Exposition, commemorating the 400th anniversary of Columbus's arrival in America, was held here in **Jackson Park,** causing a further boom of hotels, apartment buildings, and stores. The exposition's legacy also lives on throughout **Jackson Park; the Museum of Science and Industry**, for example, is situated in what had been the fair's **Palace of Fine Arts.**

In 1892, just a year before the fair, the **University of Chicago** was founded by John D. Rockefeller on Hyde Park land donated by retailer Marshall Field. Faculty, staff, and students moved in and transformed what had been a largely conservative, commerce-minded community into a liberal and intellectual one. By the 1920s, Hyde Park had become something of a resort community, with luxurious lakefront hotels attracting visitors from throughout the city and beyond. After World War I and again after World War II, increasing numbers of African-Americans began to settle here. To diminish racial conflict, neighbors formed block clubs that encouraged integration.

Throughout the 1940s and 1950s, however, both Kenwood and Hyde Park faced serious downturns. Affluent residents left Kenwood in droves, and the neighborhood declined in socioeconomic status, spurred by odoriferous downwind drafts from the stockyards. While Hyde Park supported a bohemian community of artists, writers, and a satirical group called the **Compass Players**, founded by Mike Nichols and Elaine May and later to become **Second City**, it was turning into a rundown and crime-ridden community. In the late 1950s a long and controversial process of urban renewal commenced. While some buildings were preserved and restored, whole blocks were torn down to make way for new construction. Hyde Park has since stabilized, portions of Kenwood have undergone restoration, and gentrification is now on a steady course toward the community's western border.

A proper visit to Hyde Park and Kenwood is best as a daylong event, perhaps concluded by an evening concert or play at the university, or dinner at one of the many fine restaurants.

1 Jackson Park This park was originally developed as the site of the World's Columbian Exposition of 1893, which celebrated the 400th anniversary of Columbus's arrival in the New World and was attended by more than 27 million visitors. The Exposition's designer-in-chief was famed visionary **Daniel Burnham.** Frederick Law Olmsted, who created New York City's Central Park, designed the landscaping; artists Augustus Saint-Gaudens, Daniel Chester French, and Lorado Taft contributed statues; and the major buildings were designed by a dozen architects from around the country, among them **Louis Sullivan,** who created the **Transportation Building.** The result was a "White City" of gleaming temporary buildings housing exhibits from around the world that ranged from a demonstration of gold mining in South Africa to a miniature replica of Des Moines, Iowa. The South Pond contained a reproduction of Christopher Columbus's *Santa Maria.* Gondoliers in 15th-century costume plied the lagoons.

Today **Jackson Park** retains some features of the Exposition, while tennis courts, baseball diamonds, and an 18-hole golf course have been added. The ponds have become harbors, home to the **Jackson Park Yacht Club** (a private club, but open to members of yacht clubs elsewhere in the country). The **Wooded Island** is a kind of nature retreat with many varieties of trees, wildlife, and 300 species of birds. At its northern end is the **Japanese Garden,** a re-creation of the Exposition's Japanese Pavilion tea garden. The only building remaining from the fair is the **Palace of Fine Arts,** home to the **Museum of Science and Industry** on 57th Street. ◆ Bounded by E 56th and E 66th Sts, and Lake Michigan and S Stony Island Ave. 493.7058 &

2 Museum of Science and Industry
The building most often visited by tourists in Chicago was originally the **Palace of Fine Arts,** which was designed by **Charles B. Atwood** and built for the 1893 World's Columbian Exposition. Most of the Exposition's buildings were little more than set decorations of timber and plaster and did not survive long, but the **Palace of Fine Arts,** designed to safeguard important artwork, was made of brick. It was the most overtly Classical of the Exposition's buildings. **Atwood** was inspired by two cultures: The colonnaded porches and caryatids (the 13-foot-tall maidens supporting the porch pediments) are of Greek origin; the dome is Roman. The Greek elements are derived from many of the buildings on the Acropolis in Athens, including the Parthenon and the Erechtheion.

After the Exposition closed, the building was used by the **Field Museum** (now at Burnham Harbor) until 1920, and then was renovated to house the new science and technology museum funded largely by philanthropist

and Sears mogul Julius Rosenwald. The renovation took place from 1929 to 1940. The exterior was designed by **Graham, Anderson, Probst & White; Shaw, Naess & Murphy** were responsible for the interior. Until 1991, when it began charging admission, the museum was the second most visited in the country (after the Air and Space Museum in Washington, DC), hosting 4.5 million visitors each year. The traffic took its toll on the physical plant, and the museum has embarked on an ambitious capital improvement and exhibit redesign program called MSI 2000 to contemporize the facility for the next century.

MUSEUM OF SCIENCE AND INDUSTRY

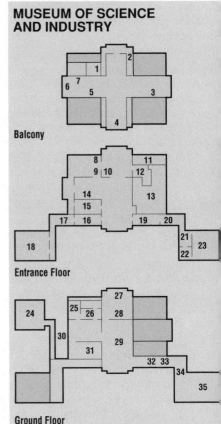

Balcony

Entrance Floor

Ground Floor

1 Kungsholm Puppets	19 Omnicom
2 Regensteln Hall of Chemistry	20 Whispering Gallery
3 Grainger Hall of Basic Science	21 Imaging
4 Human Body	22 Virtual Reality
5 Flight Observation Deck	23 Auditorium
6 Civilization Through Tools	24 Henry Crown Space Center/ Omnimax Theater
7 Historic Aircraft	25 Plumbing
8 Yesterday's Main Street	26 Energy Lab
9 Wheels of Change	27 Fairy Castle
10 Coal Mine	28 Science Theater
11 Earth Trek	29 Gas Energy
12 Architecture	30 U-505 Submarine
13 Movie Magic & Monsters	31 Idea Factory
14 Historic Locomotives	32 Ships Through the Ages
15 Food for Life	33 Racing Cars
16 Museum Shop	34 Dolls
17 Spaceport	35 Little Theater
18 Navy: Technology at Sea	

The museum's 14 acres (see floor plan on page 164) are a whirl of sound, light, and activity as visitors push buttons, operate computers, turn cranks, watch videos, hear recordings, and otherwise engage in the more than 2,000 wide-ranging interactive exhibits. Special attractions include a captured World War II German submarine; a high-tech exhibit unlocking the mysteries of the human brain; a replica of a Southern Illinois coal mine, complete with a coal train and a hoist down a mine shaft; cross sections of a human cadaver (employees call him "Deli-Man"); a simulated space-shuttle ride; a walk along a turn-of-the-century cobblestone street; *Colleen Moore's Fairy Castle*, an enchanting dwelling furnished with more than a thousand miniature treasures; and the annual Christmas Around the World festival. In 1986 an addition designed by **Hammel, Green & Abrahamson** was built to accommodate the futuristic **Henry Crown Space Center,** which houses the *Apollo 8* and *Aurora 7 Mercury* spacecrafts and chronicles our galactic adventures.

Within the center, the domed **Omnimax Theater,** with a five-story, 76-foot-wide screen and 72-speaker sound system, presents outstanding films several times a day. Numerous gift shops throughout the museum carry a wide variety of science toys, books, postcards, and other souvenirs. Food services sell sandwiches, pizza, salads, and so forth. A better bet is to get your fill of museum sights, then venture into the neighborhood to satiate your appetite. ♦ Admission. Additional charge for Omnimax. Daily. Free parking. E 57th St and S Lake Shore Dr. 684.1414

3 Midway Plaisance This block-wide, mile-long strip of land just west of the main fairgrounds was home to the World's Columbian Exposition's **Bazaar of Nations.** Among the exhibits were replicas of a German village, an Irish market town, a Chinese teahouse, a Hawaiian volcano, the Swiss Alps, and the streets of Cairo, where the undulations of a belly dancer named Little Egypt scandalized visitors. The world's first Ferris wheel took compartments the size of streetcars up for a bird's-eye view at 250 feet. The **Midway**'s festive atmosphere has had a lasting legacy: To this day, fairs and carnivals everywhere have their own "midways," avenues of concessions and amusements.

Fronted by the Gothic structures of the **University of Chicago** campus, the **Midway** has become a recreational site where students and neighbors play football and soccer, toss Frisbees, jog, and, during the winter, ice skate or cross-country ski. Two sculptures mark its western and eastern ends. On the west, the monumental *Fountain of Time,* created by Lorado Taft in 1922, depicts humanity passing before the figure of Time. On the eastern end is a statue of Thomas Masaryk, president and liberator of Czechoslovakia, sculpted by Albin Polasek in 1949. ♦ Bounded by E 59th and E 60th Sts, and S Cottage Grove and S Stony Island Aves

Within the Midway Plaisance:

Midway Studios The former studios of sculptor Lorado Taft are now a National Historic Landmark and house the university's art and design department. Visitors are welcome. ♦ Free. M-F. 6016 S Ingleside Ave (at E 60th St). 667.9126

4 University of Chicago Founded in 1892 by John D. Rockefeller, with an initial enrollment of 594, the prestigious private university today has more than 10,000 students attending undergraduate programs and graduate schools of law, medicine, business, and theology, among others. More than 60 Nobel Prize winners have been associated with the university as students or faculty. The campus, spanning 175 acres, is composed of stately Gothic architecture laid out by **Henry Ives Cobb.** Some 70 other architects have since contributed buildings; the best way to see the architecture and sculpture is to take a guided tour. ♦ Free tours M-Sa at 10AM; tours leave from the Visitor Center (Ida Noyes Hall, 1212 E 59th St), where metered parking is also available. Bounded approximately by E 55th and E 59th Sts, and S Dorchester and S Cottage Grove Aves. 702.1234, tours 702.8370

4 University of Chicago Main Quadrangle In 1891 architect **Henry Ives Cobb** chose Late English Gothic as the predominant style for the campus to establish a tone somewhat similiar to Oxford and Cambridge. It also gave an air of instant permanence to the university, which had sprung up almost overnight from swampy property next to the site of the World's Columbian Exposition. The **Main Quad** covers four blocks and contains 35 buildings that break down into six smaller courtyards. Gray Bedford limestone is used throughout. The choice of Gothic, a style with much variety, has proven wise, as it blends well with modern motifs. Most of the remainder of the campus shows how architects of the past 50 years have reinterpreted it. **Cobb Hall,** in the middle of the western edge of the **Quad, Cobb Gate,** and **Hull Court** were all designed by **Cobb.** Over the years other buildings were designed by **Shepley, Rutan & Coolidge; Holabird & Roche; Dwight H. Perkins;** and others. Explore the quadrangle by entering through **Cobb Gate** across from the **Regenstein Library** (see below)on 57th Street. Look up on the tunnel-like entranceway to see the most incredible profusion of gargoyles since Notre Dame Cathedral. ♦ Between E 57th and E 59th Sts, and S University and S Ellis Aves

5 Tower Group Plopped down in the middle of this group of classroom buildings on the quad without knowing where you are, you'd think you were in England. Built in the late 1890s, the Gothic Revival architecture here is stunning. ♦ Bounded by E 57th and E 58th Sts, and S University and S Ellis Aves.

Within the Tower Group are:

Hutchinson Commons $ A formal, dark-wood-paneled, men's-club atmosphere, with portraits of university presidents and trustees watching from the walls, is the setting for casual self-serve fare. There are sandwiches and such in the **Deli,** while the adjacent **C Shop** sells ice cream and sweets. ♦ Cafeteria ♦ Daily. 493.2808

Reynolds Club Some surprisingly good performances are mounted here by the school's **University Theater,** especially considering that pre-med students and English grads are putting on the show (the university has no drama major). The bill is mostly classics such as *Romeo and Juliet* and *The Glass Menagerie.* ♦ 702.8787

Mandel Hall In 1904 the **Chicago Symphony Orchestra** gave its premier performance here, in the university's assembly hall. In 1976, under the direction of **Skidmore, Owings & Merrill,** the hall's proscenium stage and guts were modernized and the Victorian-era detailing was restored. Plays, lectures, and concerts are presented here, among them performances by the **Chamber Orchestra of Lincoln Center,** the university's **Contemporary Chamber Players,** and the annual University of Chicago Folk Festival. ♦ 702.8068 &

6 Joseph Regenstein Library It looks like concrete, but the building's facing is actually a roughly textured, grooved limestone that was chosen to blend with the cladding of the surrounding buildings. Built in 1970, the seven-story "Reg" was designed as the **Graduate Research Library.** Each floor is dedicated to a particular discipline—business, geography, military science, film, and music, to name a few—and is divided into stacks, offices, reading areas, and faculty studies. **Walter A. Netsch, Jr.** of **Skidmore, Owings & Merrill** also designed the libraries at **Northwestern University** and the **University of Illinois at Chicago.** Of special interest are the fourth-floor **Center for Children's Books,** and the sub-basement-level **Map Collection,** which includes atlases, gazetteers, travel guides, and 350,000 maps and aerial-view photos for most regions of the world. An exhibit area on the first floor is open to the general public; access to the rest of the library is restricted. ♦ M-F until 4:30PM; Sa until noon. 1100 E 57th St (between S Greenwood and S Ellis Aves). 702.8731 &

7 Nuclear Energy Sculpture A dramatic bronze by Henry Moore commemorates the site of the world's first self-sustained nuclear chain reaction, carried out during World War II by Enrico Fermi and his scientific team under the stands of the now-demolished **Stagg Field.** Moore described the piece as evoking the human skull, a mushroom cloud, and cathedral architecture. ♦ S Ellis Ave (between E 56th and E 57th Sts)

8 John Crerar Library Built in 1984 by **Stubbins Associates** and **Loebl Schlossman & Hackl,** this is just one of the university's seven libraries, which have combined holdings of some five million books, seven million manuscripts and archival pieces, and 350,000 maps. The **Crerar** has one of the most extensive science collections in the world—a million volumes in pure and applied sciences, from agriculture to zoology. Nonstudents are welcome to browse the first of its three floors, where they may read periodicals and use reference materials and computer search services. On request, the circulation desk will page materials from elsewhere in the library, but nonstudents may not check books out. Don't miss the *Crystara,* a sculpture in aluminum and Waterford crystal by John Mooney, which is suspended from the central skylit atrium. ♦ M-Sa. 5730 S Ellis Ave (at E 57th St). 702.7409

9 University of Chicago Bookstore More than a bookstore—an experience. Academic and general-interest titles range from medical texts to children's books. The second floor is your source for **University of Chicago** T-shirts, sweatsuits, baby booties, and other memorabilia. ♦ M-Sa. 970 E 58th St (at S Ellis Ave). General books 702.7712, textbooks 702.8729 &

10 Jones Laboratory The human-made element plutonium was first isolated and weighed in Room 405 in 1942. The building, designed by **Coolidge & Hodgdon** in 1929, is now a National Historic Landmark. ♦ 5747 S Ellis Ave (at E 57th St)

The Manhattan Project's first controlled nuclear reaction occurred in 1942 in a squash-court laboratory under the football field at the University of Chicago.

University of Chicago professor Mortimer Adler collaborated with university president Robert Maynard Hutchins to start the Great Books program in 1952.

For three years in a row, the Nobel Prize for Economics was won by University of Chicago professors—1990: business professor Merton Miller; 1991: law professor Ronald Coase; 1992: economics professor Gary Becker.

11 Renaissance Society In addition to classrooms, **Cobb Hall** contains an art gallery with an illustrious history. Founded in 1915, the Society quickly developed a reputation for providing a forum for art's avant-garde, hosting groundbreaking exhibits of works by Picasso, Braque, Miró, Matisse, and Klee, among others. A recent exhibition examined time and the concept of time. ◆ Free. Tu-Su until 4PM. Cobb Hall, 5811 S Ellis Ave (at E 58th St), Fourth floor. 702.8670

12 School of Social Service Administration Building This 1965 **Mies van der Rohe** building includes most of his favorite design elements—a steel frame, large expanses of glass, and an open plan. The lobby is one of his best. ◆ 969 E 60th St (at S Ellis Ave)

13 Laird Bell Law Quadrangle This quad is one of Chicago's few projects by **Eero Saarinen,** the famous architect of the TWA Terminal at JFK Airport in New York and the St. Louis Gateway Arch. The library, built in 1960, is sheathed in angled panels of dark glass that appear pleated; to the east is the auditorium. In 1987 **Cooper-Lecky** built an addition to the back of the building. The sculpture outside, *Construction in Space in Third and Fourth Dimensions,* is by Antoine Pevsner. ◆ 1111 E 60th St (at S University Ave)

14 Rockefeller Memorial Chapel University **of Chicago** founder John D. Rockefeller donated the **University Chapel,** which was built by **Bertram G. Goodhue** in 1928. It was renamed in Rockefeller's honor in 1937 after his death; by the terms of his bequest, it is always to be the tallest building on campus. Perhaps the grandest Gothic house of worship in Chicago, the chapel is 265 feet long and 207 feet high, with masonry walls up to eight feet thick; steel is used only in the beams supporting the roof, which weighs 800 tons. The interior is richly decorated but delicately colored. Be sure to look up at the tiled vaulted ceiling. Also noteworthy are the sculptures of saints and Old Testament prophets, and the magnificent organ. Concerts on the chapel's 72-bell carillon, named after Laura Spellman Rockefeller (JDR's mother), are performed throughout the year; call for the schedule. For a tour of the carillon, meet 30 minutes before a concert at the chapel door. The chapel also hosts three orchestral concerts each year, including Handel's *Messiah.* ◆ 1156-80 E 59th St (at S Woodlawn Ave). 702.2100 ♿

15 5855 South University Avenue This 1894 **Henry Ives Cobb** building is the private home of the university's president (now Hugo Sonnenschein). Until 1993 the house was inhabited by Hanna Holborn Gray, the first woman president of any major private American university. ◆ Between E 58th and E 59th Sts

Rockefeller Memorial Chapel

16 Oriental Institute This university organization has supported research and archaeological excavations in the Near East since 1919. It found a permanent home in 1931 in a building designed by **Mayers, Murray & Phillips.** Most of the artifacts in its world-class collection—only a fraction of which are actually displayed in the expansive museum—are treasures from those digs in Iraq, Iran, Turkey, Syria, and Palestine. The pieces date from 9000 BC to AD 900. A number of other museums refer to this collection to date their own pieces. Ancient life from the everyday to the otherworldly is represented in clay tablets, papyrus scrolls, well-preserved mummies, a gargantuan statue of King Tut, a monumental winged bull from Iraq, and literally tons of other fascinating objects. Free films on topics related to the Near East are shown Sundays at 2PM. The **Suq** (Arabic for "market") museum store carries authentic reproduction jewelry, gifts, and crafts sought out in Near East *suqs,* along with postcards, and books such as *How to Write Your Name in Hieroglyphics.* ♦ Free. Tu-Su; W until 8:30PM. Guided group tours available with advance reservations. 1155 E 58th St (at S University Ave). 702.9520

17 Seminary Co-op Bookstore Ensconced within the university's **Chicago Theological Seminary,** which was built in 1923 by **Herbert Riddle,** this semisubterranean bookstore carries roughly 100,000 titles in academic and general subjects, from the *Neurobiology of Cognition* to the complete works of Charles Dickens. The store is especially strong in social sciences, religion, philosophy, and fiction, and also provides mail-order service. A second location with more general offerings is **57th Street Books** (see below). ♦ Daily. 5757 S University Ave (at E 58th St). 752.4381

Two famous alumna of Chicago's Hyde Park High School are singer Mel Torme and comedian Steve Allen.

18 Frederick C. Robie House Robie, a bicycle and automobile parts manufacturer, hired **Frank Lloyd Wright** to build him a house with lots of sunlight, no curtains, and rooms that flowed into one another. He got all that in this bold Prairie Style house (pictured on page 169) that made his name famous when it was finished in 1909. The interlocking masses are complex, yet the house is full of repose, with strong horizontal lines in the sweeping eaves, the bands of beautifully leaded casement windows, and the limestone sills. **Wright** had for some years been designing homes where the entrance was not immediately apparent; here it's at the back of the house and very private.

Wright also designed the furniture, lamps, and rugs. The magnificent dining room set is part of the collection of the nearby **Smart Museum of Art** (see page 172). Refuting **Wright**'s reputation as an arrogant architect with little concern for client needs or budget, Robie late in his life lauded **Wright** for sticking to the original budget of $60,000 and called the commission "the cleanest business deal I ever made."

The house has been renovated and restored several times; a National Historic Landmark, it is currently owned by the **University of Chicago.** ♦ Fee. Tours daily at noon, or for groups by prior arrangement. 5757 S Woodlawn Ave (at E 58th St). 702.2150, group reservations 702.8374

19 57th Street Books Before the birth of the superstore, the Midwest's greatest concentration of books lay on this block and the next. The shops here still boast the greatest selection. At this one, help yourself to a cup of coffee brewing in the reading area and linger in front of the fireplace for as long as you like, working your way through the wide-ranging general-interest titles. A separate kids' reading area with toys supplements the substantial children's book collection. The store's complete collection of Penguin Classics titles is a standout. ♦ M-Sa until 10PM; Su until 8PM. 1301 E 57th St (at S Kimbark Ave). 684.1300

19 Edwardo's of Hyde Park ★$$ This restaurant makes some of the city's tastiest deep-dish pizzas, using natural ingredients and herbs grown on the premises. ♦ Pizza ♦ Daily lunch and dinner. 1321 E 57th St (between S Kimbark and S Kenwood Aves). 241.7960. Also at: Numerous locations throughout the city

19 Medici on 57th ★$$ Deep-dish pizza, burgers, and many varieties of rich, strong coffee are specialties at this neighborhood hangout. Dim lighting and rough wooden booths covered with graffiti qualify it as a true collegiate coffeehouse. ♦ Pizza/Coffeehouse ♦ Daily breakfast, lunch, and dinner until midnight. 1327 E 57th St (between S Kenwood and S Kimbark Aves). 667.7394

Frederick C. Robie House

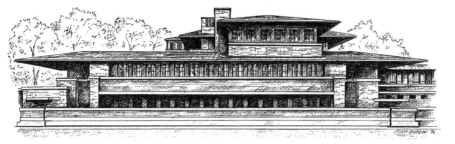

19 Ann Sather ★$ This Swedish diner opened here in 1989 after much success on the city's North Side. Fanciful wall murals by Scandinavian artist Sigmund Arseth add warmth to the spare diner decor left over from a previous tenant. Salads and lighter fare supplement the hearty meat-and-dumplings menu that has been an **Ann Sather** tradition for decades. A cut-rate ($5) student special available to anyone after 8:30PM includes soup, sandwich, beverage, and cinnamon roll. ♦ Swedish/American ♦ Daily breakfast, lunch, and dinner until 10PM. 1329 E 57th St (at S Kenwood Ave). 947.9323. Also at: 929 W Belmont Ave (at N Sheffield Ave). 348.2378; 5207 N Clark St (at W Foster Ave). 271.6677

20 O'Gara & Wilson, Ltd. Chicago's oldest bookstore, which was established in 1882 and has operated under other names, is furnished with old-fashioned ladders on tracks and a blue-gray Persian cat named Hanna Gray in honor of the University of Chicago's president emeritus. The store's 200,000 used and out-of-print titles include a comprehensive art section and what may be the city's best array of British and American literary criticism. Newly acquired books are put out every Friday night. ♦ Daily until 10PM. 1448 E 57th St (between S Harper and S Blackstone Aves). 363.0993 &

21 Powell's Bookstore
Used books on all topics fill the store from floor to ceiling. While specializing in academic remainders, it also stocks antiquarian books and has a substantial and not-often-found selection of used children's books. There are cheap paperbacks galore and—better yet—occasional freebies. ♦ Daily until 11PM. 1501 E 57th St (at S Harper Ave). 955.7780. Also at: 828 S Wabash Ave (at Eighth St). 341.0748; 2850 N Lincoln Ave (at W Diversey Pkwy). 248.1444

22 Windermere House Designed by **Rapp & Rapp** in 1924, this was once one of Hyde Park's grandest hotels, playing host to such celebrated guests as John D. Rockefeller, Edna Ferber, and Thomas Mann, who started writing *Dr. Faustus* here while visiting his daughter, a student at the university. It has since been converted to rental apartments. ♦ 1642 E 56th St (at S Hyde Park Blvd)

Within Windermere House:

Piccolo Mondo ★$ Authentic Italian food is served at this gourmet grocery store and simply appointed restaurant, a good choice for lunch during a visit to the **Museum of Science and Industry.** In fair weather you may dine alfresco on the terrace overlooking **Jackson Park.** Salads, sauces, and pastas such as *rotolo*—layered dough, Italian cheeses, ham, and spinach topped with *besciamella* (cream) sauce—are all made on the premises. ♦ Italian ♦ M-Sa lunch and dinner; Su dinner. 643.1106

23 Promontory Point A pretty, landscaped park jutting out into Lake Michigan at 55th Street was created from landfill in the 1920s. "The Point" is a pleasant place for a warm-weather picnic or Frisbee toss, not to mention a perfect vantage point for a dramatic view of the city skyline to the north and the hazy shores of Indiana southward. Swimming is forbidden because the waters are quite deep and dangerous, but a bit farther south is the 57th Street Beach, a spacious and safe place to swim or catch a few rays. ♦ At the lakefront (just north of E 55th St)

Celluloid Heroes

Chicago is a deservedly popular location for movie production. Flicks filmed or set in the city include:

Adventures in Babysitting (1988) Elizabeth Shue plays a baby-sitter who takes her two charges to downtown Chicago, where various mishaps ensue.

The Babe (1992) John Goodman plays Babe Ruth in a sentimental biography of the Yankee slugger.

Backdraft (1991) Robert De Niro and Kurt Russell star in Ron Howard's story about two firefighting brothers at odds with each other. You can count on spectacular fire scenes in this flick.

Blink (1993) Madeline Stowe plays a blind woman caught up in a murder investigation.

The Breakfast Club (1985) Judd Nelson, Molly Ringwald, and Ally Sheedy star in this teen movie about five students sitting out a school detention, coining the term "The Brat Pack" in the process.

Child's Play (1989) and *Child's Play II* (1991) Chucky, the murderous doll, comes to life in this sometimes tongue-in-cheek horror thriller and its sequel.

Dennis the Menace (1993) The comic strip character's adventures, starring Nick Castle and Walter Matthau.

Eight Men Out (1988) Director John Sayles retells the story of baseball's most corrupt incident, when the 1919 Chicago **White Sox** accepted bribes and threw the World Series.

Flatliners (1990) Medical students Kiefer Sutherland, Julia Roberts, Kevin Bacon, and William Baldwin experiment with life after death.

The Fugitive (1993) Harrison Ford stars as Dr. Richard Kimble in this runaway hit based on the television series. Best Chicago moment—the St. Patrick's Day Parade.

Groundhog Day (1992) Bill Murray and Andie McDowell relive the day over and over and over again.

Henry: Portrait of a Serial Killer (1986) John McNaughton's disturbing story of the life of a Texas mass murderer, with Michael Rooker and Tracy Arnold.

Home Alone (1991) and *Home Alone 2* (1992) Macaulay Culkin fends off two bumbling burglars after his parents accidentally leave him behind.

Mad Dog and Glory (1992) Robert De Niro, Uma Thurman, and Bill Murray star in another John McNaughton crime story.

Malcolm X (1992) Spike Lee's retelling of the life of the Black Muslim leader, who spent his early years in and around the Chicago area.

North by Northwest (1959) Alfred Hitchcock's suspense masterpiece may be best remembered for its Mount Rushmore conclusion, but many of the interior shots were filmed in the **Omni Ambassador East.**

Only the Lonely (1991) Cop John Candy's Irish mother, played by Maureen O'Hara, resists his romance with Italian girlfriend, Ally Sheedy.

The Package (1990) Gene Hackman plays an Army sergeant rooked into a Russian/American conspiracy plot.

Primal Fear (1996) A tale of corruption in the Catholic church and Chicago politics, starring Richard Gere as an arrogant attorney who defends an altar boy accused of murdering the Archbishop.

Risky Business (1984) Shy teenager Tom Cruise lets loose when his parents leave him home alone.

Sixteen Candles (1984) Molly Ringwald turns 16 in John Hughes's comic coming-of-age story.

Sleepless in Seattle (1992) Long-distance romance between Chicago resident Meg Ryan and Seattle resident Tom Hanks reaches its high point in New York City.

Uncle Buck (1990) In this John Hughes comedy actor John Candy's character is left to take care of his brother's kids for a few days.

The Untouchables (1987) Brian DePalma and David Mamet teamed up to bring the popular TV series to the big screen, with help from Kevin Costner, Sean Connery, and Robert De Niro. The banquet (or baseball bat) scene was filmed in the **Blackstone Hotel.**

When Harry Met Sally (1990) Meg Ryan and Billy Crystal play friends who could never, ever be lovers—or could they? They begin their journey to New York from the **University of Chicago** campus in **Hyde Park.**

While You Were Sleeping (1994) **CTA** token clerk Sandra Bullock poses as the fiancée of one brother while falling in love with the other.

24 Promontory Apartments The continuing shortage of steel after World War II dictated that **Mies van der Rohe** use reinforced concrete to build this 1949 high-rise apartment building, his first such structure. The visible expression of underlying structure for which **Mies** is famous is seen here, as the columns are stepped back at the sixth, 11th, and 16th stories, emphasizing the fact that the load lightens as the building rises. ◆ 5530 S Shore Dr (at E 55th St)

24 T.J.'s in the Park ★$$ It's somewhat formal for the neighborhood, but cozy, with a fireplace and piano bar, and all the tables overlook **Jackson Park** and Promontory Point across the drive. The food is French and the chef has a special way with fish. ◆ French ◆ Daily lunch and dinner. 5500 S Shore Dr (at E 55th St). 752.6191 ♿

25 Orly's ★$$ The next several restaurants along this stretch are fast, cheap, and popular with students; this one is dark and more relaxed. There's an array of Tex-Mex appetizers, an interesting black bean soup, and such heart-healthy main dishes as honey-garlic roasted chicken, vegetarian *abbondanza* (abundance), and Chinese chicken salad. The ice-cream cake is special. ◆ Tex-Mex ◆ Daily lunch and dinner. 1660 E 55th St (at S Hyde Park Blvd). 643.5500

25 La Brioche Bakery This lovely little shop serves freshly baked breads, pastries, cookies, cakes, croissants, and the namesake brioche at a half-dozen marble-topped tables. ◆ Tu-Su. 1658 E 55th St (between S Hyde Park Blvd and S Cornell Ave). 493.3900

26 Snail $ A light and cozy place that college students love simply because there's nothing on the menu that costs more than $6.99. The Thai curry sauce can be ordered on seafood, chicken, beef, or pork and is one of the most popular dishes here, along with Bangkok chicken, which is marinated, breaded, deep-fried, then stir-fried. ◆ Thai ◆ Daily lunch and dinner. 1649 E 55th St (at S Hyde Park Blvd). 667.5423

26 Siam $ This storefront cafe offers traditional Thai cuisine at reasonable prices. The most popular dishes here include Bangkok chicken, which is breaded and stir-fried with bell peppers and cashews; and *pad ped talay* (shrimps, scallops, and squid stir-fried with vegetables in a red curry sauce). Delivery is available. ◆ Thai ◆ Daily lunch and dinner. 1639 E 55th St (at S Cornell Ave). 324.9296

27 Morry's Deli ★$ Kosher hot dogs, corned beef, pastrami, and the like are available at this New York–style deli. For breakfast, there's Egg McMorry, a bagel with cheese, egg, salami, and pastrami. ◆ Deli ◆ Daily breakfast, lunch, and dinner. 5500 S Cornell Ave (at E 55th St). 363.3800

27 Nile $ A clean spot with Middle Eastern cuisine at prices students can afford. In addition to falafel and hummus, there's chicken *shawarma* (boneless chicken which is marinated, then rotisseried and sliced thin), and shish kebabs of lamb, beef, or chicken. ◆ Middle Eastern ◆ Daily lunch and dinner. 1609 E 55th St (between S Cornell and S Lake Park Aves). 324.9499

27 Thai 55th $ One of three Thai joints in a one-block stretch, this one also caters to student appetites and budgets. Bangkok chicken is again a favorite, but here it's served with almonds, bell peppers, onions, and scallions. ◆ Thai ◆ Daily lunch and dinner. 1607 E 55th St (between S Cornell and S Lake Park Aves). 363.7119

28 Hyde Park Historical Society Housed in a restored 1893 cable-car station, the museum documents Hyde Park history, culture, art, and architecture. ◆ Free. Sa-Su 2-4PM. Lectures and tours of the neighborhood available by prearrangement. 5529 S Lake Park Ave (between E 55th and E 56th Sts). 493.1893

29 Hyde Park Shopping Center No longer recognizable as an **I.M. Pei** design, this urban renewal project sprang up in 1959 to replace demolished structures. It has undergone some renewal itself and contains new shops selling shoes, sporting goods, children's clothes, and the like. Among the old-time businesses are the **Hyde Park Cooperative Society Grocery Store,** the oldest single-store cooperative in the country, founded in 1932. (You need not be a co-op member to shop here.) A post office and credit union are in its basement. ◆ Daily. E 55th St and S Lake Park Ave. 667.1444

30 University Apartments In 1955 buildings along this entire stretch of 55th Street were demolished as part of a grand plan of urban renewal for Hyde Park. These "traffic island apartments," built between 1959 and 1962 by **I.M. Pei, Harry Weese & Associates,** and **Loewenberg & Loewenberg,** were a cornerstone of the plan. A little swimming pool is hidden at their western edge. ◆ 1400-1450 E 55th St (between S Blackstone and S Dorchester Aves)

31 Ex Libris Used and out-of-print theology and religion books are the specialties in this shop, which is especially strong in church history, philosophy of religion, and biblical studies. ◆ M-Sa noon-5PM. 1340 E 55th St (at S Kenwood Ave). 955.3456 ♿

32 Jimmy's Woodlawn Tap Chicago Bears fans cheering football games on the TV, debating academicians, and literary and dramatic types all feel at home at this sallow-walled, sagging-floored, longtime **University of Chicago** hangout. Musicians and improvisational comedians perform every Thursday at 8PM. ◆ Daily until 2AM. 1172 E 55th St (at S Woodlawn Ave). 643.5516

33 5551 South University Avenue George Fred Keck designed the startlingly modern **House of Tomorrow** at the 1933 Century of Progress World's Fair, but he had few commissions during the Depression. This one, designed with his brother, **William Keck,** was built in 1937. Decades ahead of its time, the three-unit cooperative apartment building is a study in simplicity, practicality, and fine detailing. The metal louvers act as blinds, providing privacy and regulating heat gain through the windows. Both architects occupied units in the building at one time. ◆ Between E 55th and E 56th Sts

34 David and Alfred Smart Museum of Art Founded by the **University of Chicago** in 1974 to house its substantial art holdings, the museum has a large permanent collection ranging from Christian and Byzantine artifacts to furniture by **Frank Lloyd Wright** and contemporary paintings by Mark Rothko. The adjacent courtyard holds four sculptures: *Reclining Figure* by Henry Moore; *Grande Radar* by Arnaldo Pomodoro; *Why?* by Richard Hunt; and *Truncated Pyramid* by Jene Highstein, a memorial to a university student who was brutally murdered in 1990. Adjoining the museum is the **Cochrane-Woods Art Center,** which houses the art history department. Both buildings were designed by New Yorker **Edward Larrabee Barnes,** who also designed the Walker Art Center in Minneapolis. ◆ Free. Tu-Su. 5550 S Greenwood Ave (between E 55th and E 56th Sts). 702.0200 ♿

35 Court Theatre Designed in 1981 by **Harry Weese,** this is one of the city's premier professional theaters, presenting innovative renditions of classics with an occasional foray into more modern works. Typical offerings have included Oscar Wilde's sparkling *The Importance of Being Earnest* and Donna Blue Lachman's *Frida: The Last Portrait,* about Frida Kahlo. The well-designed proscenium stage and theater provide good sightlines from every one of the 250 seats. ◆ 5535 S Ellis Ave (between E 55th and E 56th Sts). 753.4472 ♿

36 DuSable Museum of African-American History Named in honor of Chicago's first permanent settler, Jean Baptiste-Pointe duSable, a Haitian of mixed African and European parentage, the museum's extensive artifacts, photos, and paintings trace the black experience in America. There are permanent exhibits such as *Up From Slavery,* which vividly depicts the life of African-Americans from pre-Civil War days to the civil rights movement, and *Illinois Black History Makers.* The Works Progress Administration period and the 1960s black arts movement are particularly well represented. The gift shop carries jewelry, fabrics, and other arts and crafts by African-American, Egyptian, Haitian, and African artists. The museum building has an unusually institutional look because it was previously a park administration building and then a police lockup. The front steps descend to the beautiful lawns of **Washington Park,** designed by famed landscape architect Frederick Law Olmsted. Beyond the brick terrace, imagine the race course that filled the park a century ago with city swells. ◆ Admission. Daily. E 57th St and S Cottage Grove Ave. 947.0600 ♿

37 5300 Block of University Avenue This street is the perfect spot for a spring or summer stroll. Home to many university professors, the block has a neighborhood-wide reputation for its resplendent flower gardens. ◆ Between E 53rd and E 54th Sts

38 Boyajian's Bazaar Handicrafts and gifts from the Near East, Asia, and Africa cram this tiny storefront. Best of all are the boxes and boxes of beads in myriad colors, patterns, and materials: Freshwater pearls, Baltic amber, old Bohemian crystals, African trade beads, hand-glazed Chinese porcelain, Indian camel bone, and Jamaican wood are just a few. ◆ Daily. 1305 E 53rd St (at S Kimbark Ave). 324.2020

39 Freehling Pot & Pan Co. Everything for the kitchen is here, all of very high quality—from long-lasting All-Clad and Scanpan cookware, shimmering baking tins for muffins and scones, and 19-quart boiling pots, to ceramic Thanksgiving turkey platters. ◆ M-Sa 1365 E 53rd St (at S Kenwood Ave). 643.8080

39 2nd Hand Tunes Lincoln Park's excellent used-record empire has an outlet here, as well as locations in Evanston and Oak Park. ◆ Daily. 1375 E 53rd St (at S Kenwood Ave). 684.3375. Also at: 2550 N Clark St (at W Deming Pl). 281.8813; 2604 N Clark St (at W Wrightwood Ave). 929.6325

40 Scholars' Books Everything you ever wanted to know about Asia is available here in Chinese, Korean, and English. Books range from scholarly political tomes to Chinese fairy tales. ◆ Daily. 1379 E 53rd St (between S Dorchester and S Kenwood Aves). 288.6565

40 Ribs 'N' Bibs $ Smell that hickory smoke? Here's where die-hard Hyde Park rib fans come for yummy full- and half-slabs and rib tips. ◆ Barbecue ◆ Daily lunch and dinner until midnight. 5300 S Dorchester Ave (at E 53rd St). 493.0400

41 Art Werk Gallery Joe Clark, the owner of this unpretentious gallery devoted to African-American art, prides himself on introducing art to people who might otherwise have been unable to afford or appreciate it. Among the offerings are paintings and enamels by Fred Jones, and a large collection of pieces by Works Progress Administration artists, among them William Carter, who continues to paint into his 80s. ◆ Daily. 5300 S Blackstone Ave (at E 53rd St). 684.5300

42 Bonne Sante University communities are usually full of health food shops; this one in Hyde Park mainly carries healthful, organic groceries, but it also has a wonderful juice bar that makes fabulous protein shakes. ◆ Daily. 1457 E 53rd St (at S Harper Ave). 667.5700

43 Harper Court When artists elsewhere in Hyde Park were displaced by urban renewal, this two-story structure was built by supporters of the arts as cheap gallery space. These days, the tenants are commercial—it's a shopping center, spread over four buildings, smack dab in the middle of a parking lot. Surprisingly, an artsy air persists. ◆ Daily. S Harper Ave (between E 52nd and E 53rd Sts)

Within Harper Court:

Sunflower Seed Hyde Park appears to be the only neighborhood in the city able to support two health food stores within a stone's throw of each other. This one is well stocked with vitamins, teas, and other necessities of healthy living. ◆ Daily. 363.1600

Dr. Wax If you can't peddle those old Bee Gees albums around the corner at **2nd Hand Tunes,** try here before using them as Frisbees. ◆ Daily. 493.8696. Also at: 2529 N Clark St (at W Deming Pl). 549.3377

Artisans 21 Gallery Among the members' work showcased at this cooperative gallery are unusual hand-painted pottery and woven garments in rich hues. ◆ Tu-Su. 288.7450

Freedom Found Books Proprietors Robert Vaughters and Jeff Boysaw specialize in books by and about African-Americans, from fiction by Toni Morrison to essays on self-esteem by J.A. Rogers. Sociology, politics, and jazz are well covered. A good selection of books for kids includes African folk tales. They also sell T-shirts, jewelry, and African crowns. ◆ M-Sa unitl 8PM; Su. 288.2837

Window To Africa Owner Patrick Woodtor brings authentic fabrics, baskets, jewelry, and other crafts and art back from trips to his native West Africa. ◆ Daily. 955.7742

Court Grill $$ Windows overlooking a courtyard make for a nice business lunch or a romantic dinner setting at this eclectic American restaurant. Order a juicy hamburger or a grilled portobello mushroom sandwich. ◆ American ◆ M-Sa lunch and dinner; Su brunch and dinner. 667.4745

44 Mellow Yellow ★$ The prizewinning chili is served five ways, from the usual bowlful to over spaghetti and topped with cheese, onions, and sour cream. Some prefer the fresh croissants and good coffee at breakfast at this bright, friendly spot with a big yellow awning out front. ◆ American ◆ Daily breakfast, lunch, and dinner. 1508 E 53rd St (at S Harper Ave). 667.2000

44 Valois ★$ Named in a *Chicago Tribune* list of "top greasy spoons," this spot with the slogan "See Your Food" has been dishing out wholesome and cheap cafeteria fare for nearly 70 years. At lunchtime four or five guys behind the little counter hustle to deliver corn on the cob, hot beef sandwiches, roast pork, overcooked vegetables, and cheap sides of coleslaw. The biscuits and gravy are tops, and the breakfasts are good. Customers cover the socioeconomic gamut. In 1991, its patrons were the subject of the highly lauded book *Slim's Table*, by **U of C** grad student Michael Dunier. ◆ Cafeteria ◆ Daily breakfast, lunch, and dinner. 1518 E 53rd St (between S Lake Park and S Harper Aves). 667.0647

estaurants/Clubs: Red   Hotels: Blue
hops/ ⚑ Outdoors: Green   **Sights/Culture: Black**

173

cedars of Lebanon

45 Cedars of Lebanon ★$ Restaurants in Hyde Park generally cater to either of two kinds of patrons: pairs of students, usually on a date, or crowds that mix faculty and students and visitors—often all engaged in one discussion. This place attracts both with spinach pie, made while you wait, fresh hummus, and tasty lamb. ◆ Middle Eastern ◆ Daily lunch and dinner. 1618 E 53rd St (at S Cornell Ave). 324.6227

46 Cornell Village Gospel singer Mahalia Jackson lived in this middle-income, mixed-race housing development until the end of her life. ◆ 5201 S Cornell Ave (at E 52nd St)

47 Hyde Park Art Center A community art school and the **Ruth Horwich Gallery,** set in the ballroom of the former **Del Prado Hotel** (now an apartment building), carry on the legacy of what used to be the **57th Street Artists Colony.** The gallery has played an important part in the careers of emerging artists, debuting the work of Ed Paschke, among others. On your way in, note the painted terra-cotta Indians in headdresses decorating the lobby ceiling. ◆ Tu-Sa. 5307 S Hyde Park Blvd (at E 53rd St). 324.5520 &

48 Eastview Park Yes, those really are green, squawking parrots flapping around in this tiny park with view of the lake. Native to the South American Andes, the Adam and Eve of the flock were probably pet store escapees. Today their 50-or-so offspring live a liberated lifestyle year-round in giant stick nests they've constructed in an ash tree. The tree is just across the street from the entrance to the **Hampton House Condominiums,** where, by the way, Chicago's late mayor Harold Washington lived. ◆ Bounded by E 53rd and E 56th Sts, Lake Michigan, and S Shore Dr and S Hyde Park Blvd

49 Regents Park Between the twin towers of this luxury apartment building complex is the 1.3-acre **Bergen Garden.** Designed by landscape architect Phil Shipley, it sports a small waterfall, fountains, and lagoons and is home to numerous species of birds, plants, and trees. It may be toured only by prearrangement. Shipley also designed the **Regents Club** health club, open to members only. Gourmet groceries and take-out meals are available at the **Market in the Park.** ◆ 5050 S Lake Shore Dr (at E 50th St). Tour reservations 288.5050, market 734.3687

50 Isidore H. Heller House Frank Lloyd Wright was working his way toward the Prairie Style in this 1897 project (pictured below), which features the exaggeratedly horizontal Roman brick, widely projecting eaves, and geometric forms of that slightly later style. This is a city house—narrow but deep, just like the lot, with a more closed facade at ground level. A beautiful third-floor frieze of molded plaster is by sculptor Richard Bock, a frequent collaborator. It's a private residence. ◆ 5132 S Woodlawn Ave (between E 52nd St and E Hyde Park Blvd)

51 K.A.M. Isaiah Israel Temple The oldest Jewish congregation in the Midwest, **Kahilath Anshe Ma'ariv,** founded in 1847, merged with the **Isaiah Israel** congregation and made their home in one of Chicago's most magnificent houses of worship. The brick and limestone temple, designed in 1924 by **Alfred S. Alschuler,** uses Byzantine style in its octagon form and arch-and-dome construction. A minaret rising behind the dome is actually a smokestack. The ornamentation is derived from that of a second-century synagogue in Tiberias in Palestine. The temple houses the **Morton B. Weiss Museum of Judaica,** which has a small but valuable collection of Jewish artifacts. ◆ 1100 E Hyde Park Blvd (at S Greenwood Ave). 924.1234 &

Isidore H. Heller House

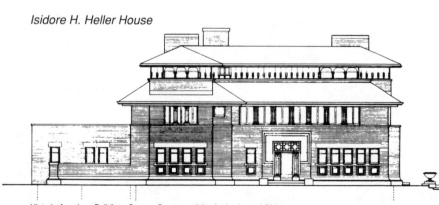

Historic American Buildings Survey. Courtesy of the Art Institute of Chicago

52 Julius Rosenwald House Rosenwald was head of Sears, Roebuck & Company and a famous philanthropist. His 42-room mansion was designed in 1903 by **Nimmons & Fellows**, the architects of many Sears facilities. The Roman-brick house with Prairie School elements is oriented to the south and originally looked out over elaborate gardens. Unfortunately, this private residence is no longer spectacular. ♦ 4901 S Ellis Ave (at E 49th St)

53 Ernest J. Magerstadt House Characteristic of Prairie School architect **George W. Maher**'s work is the use of Roman brick, elaborately detailed column capitals, and a light color palette. Maher's "rhythm-motif" theory of architecture called for the repeated application of a single decorative element throughout. In this 1908 house (still a private residence), the decorative element is the poppy, rendered especially well in the leaded glass windows. ♦ 4930 S Greenwood Ave (between E 49th and E 50th Sts)

54 4944 South Woodlawn Avenue Heavyweight boxing champion Muhammad Ali used to punch around in this place, his massive brick mansion of a home, built in 1916 for $40,000. It now belongs to the Islamic Foundation and is not open to the public. ♦ Between E 49th and E 50th Sts

55 4855 South Woodlawn Avenue The late Black Muslim leader Elijah Muhammad lived in this Moorish home. It is now privately owned by minister Louis Farrakhan, controversial head of the Nation of Islam. ♦ Between E 48th and E 49th Sts

56 George Blossom House In this 1892 **Frank Lloyd Wright** project, the round-headed Palladian windows and Ionic capitals give no hint that the 25-year-old designer would develop into a revolutionary American architect. But the Roman brick foundation and deep eaves of this private residence anticipate his later Prairie School designs. ♦ 4858 S Kenwood Ave (between E 48th and E 49th Sts)

56 Warren McArthur House Like the **Blossom House** next door, this house was a bootlegged commission, a job done on the side by **Frank Lloyd Wright** in 1892 while he was still employed by **Louis Sullivan.** The large gambrel roof that dominates this privately owned house sits atop symmetrical octagonal bays with leaded windows. ♦ 4852 S Kenwood Ave (between E 48th and E 49th Sts)

57 Ramada Inn Lakeshore $$ There are panoramas of Lake Michigan and the city skyline from many of the 300 rooms and 15 suites, so be sure to ask for a room with a view. The tone here is comfortably low-key. Amenities include an outdoor swimming pool, access to a nearby health club, business/conference facilities, and a free shuttle bus to downtown and local restaurants and sights. ♦ 4900 S Lake Shore Dr (near E 49th St, on Lake Michigan). 288.5800, 800/237.4933; fax 288.5745 ♿

Bests

Wilbert R. Hasbrouck, FAIA
Architect, Hasbrouck Peterson Zimoch Sirirattumrong

An architect in Chicago is like a kid in a candy store. Downtown Chicago is literally a three-dimensional encyclopedia of modern architecture. Even with limited time, one can still enjoy Chicago's buildings.

The best starting point is the **Chicago River** at **Dearborn Street.** The panorama to the south is simply breathtaking, but the walk down Dearborn Street is even more so.

Just north of the river are the **Marina City Towers, Bertram Goldberg**'s monument to modernity. As one walks south other modern structures by **Cesar Pelli, Jack Brownson, Mies van der Rohe, Skidmore Owings & Merrill,** as well as a host of others quickly become apparent. The **Loop**'s oldest office building, the **Delaware** (1871-72), still stands, beautifully restored at Dearborn and Randolph. Further on, one passes the **Marquette, Monadnock, Fisher, Manhattan,** and **Pontiac** buildings, all giving eloquent testimony to the 19th-century Chicago School of Architecture.

Dearborn Street ends, dramatically, at **Dearborn Street Station** (1882), now restored and adapted for shopping. A half-block north is the **Prairie Avenue Bookshop,** an architect's paradise, where virtually every current book on architecture can be found in splendid surroundings.

And this is only the beginning.

Barbara Gaines
Artistic Director, Shakespeare Repertory

Walking my golden retriever, Fanny, along the beach at 6AM—especially in the winter.

Sitting in the bleachers at **Wrigley Field.**

Coming home late at night from a tech rehearsal and finding a parking space right in front of my building.

Picking up just-out-of-the-oven chocolate chip bagels from **Arnie's Bagels.**

Listening to bands and looking at the Chagall mosaic outside **First National Plaza** in the summer.

Seeing the skyline from the lake.

Walking down **Michigan Avenue,** crossing the **Chicago River,** and realizing that I'm not in New York.

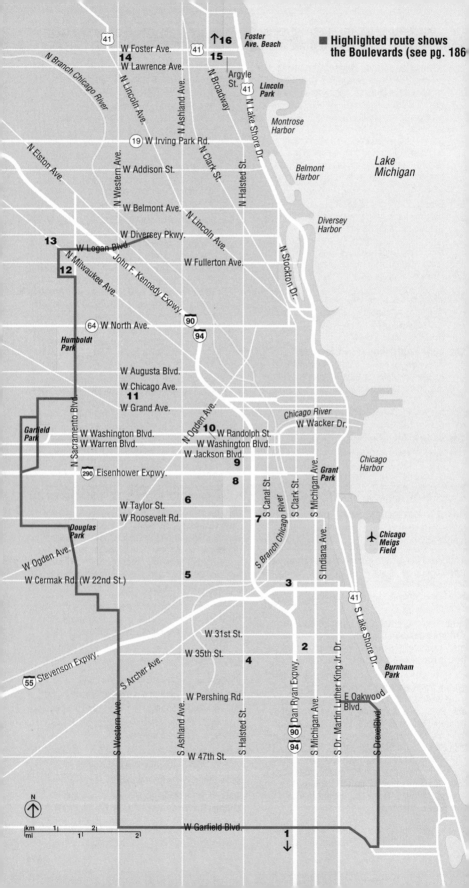

Highlighted route shows the Boulevards (see pg. 186)

↑**16**
Foster Ave. Beach

15
Argyle St.

Lincoln Park

W Foster Ave.
14
W Lawrence Ave.

41

41

N Branch Chicago River

N Elston Ave.

N Lincoln Ave.

N Western Ave.

N Ashland Ave.

N Broadway

N Clark St.

N Halsted St.

N Lake Shore Dr.

Montrose Harbor

Belmont Harbor

Lake Michigan

19 W Irving Park Rd.

W Addison St.

W Belmont Ave.

N Lincoln Ave.

W Diversey Pkwy.

Diversey Harbor

13

W Logan Blvd.

12

N Milwaukee Ave.

John F. Kennedy Expwy.

W Fullerton Ave.

N Stockton Dr.

64 W North Ave.

90
94

Humboldt Park

W Augusta Blvd.

W Chicago Ave.

11

W Grand Ave.

N Ogden Ave.

Chicago River

W Wacker Dr.

N Sacramento Blvd.

Garfield Park

W Washington Blvd.

W Warren Blvd.

10 W Randolph St.

W Washington Blvd.

W Jackson Blvd.

9

Grant Park

Chicago Harbor

290 Eisenhower Expwy.

8

6

W Taylor St.

W Roosevelt Rd.

S Canal St.

S Branch Chicago River

S Clark St.

S Michigan Ave.

7

S Indiana Ave.

✈ Chicago Meigs Field

5

Douglas Park

W Ogden Ave.

W Cermak Rd. (W 22nd St.)

3

41 S Lake Shore Dr.

Stevenson Expwy.

55

S Western Ave.

S Archer Ave.

W 31st St.

W 35th St.

2

Dan Ryan Expwy.

S Michigan Ave.

S Dr. Martin Luther King Jr. Dr.

Burnham Park

4

S Ashland Ave.

S Halsted St.

W Pershing Rd.

90
94

E Oakwood Blvd.

W 47th St.

S Drexel Blvd.

N

km   1   2
mi   1   2

W Garfield Blvd.

1
↓

Additional Highlights

There's more to Chicago than the bustling Loop, the elegant Gold Coast, and the affluent North Side. If you wander off the beaten tourist trails, you will find areas of rich ethnic diversity that offer plenty of interesting eats, good shopping, and enjoyable entertainment. South of the city is the historic town of **Pullman** (built by the infamous railroad magnate of the same name for his workers), the Hispanic neighborhoods of **Pilsen** and **Little Village,** as well as **Chinatown, Greektown,** and **Little Italy.** North of downtown is teeming **Argyle Street,** where you can still buy live fish in the custom of southeast Asian shoppers, and **Lincoln Square,** where Mayor Daley can often be seen dining on hearty German fare with his friends.

1 Pullman Chicago industrialist George M. Pullman, manufacturer of the Pullman Sleeping Car, built this quaint "model town" on the city's Far South Side for his factory workers. Designed in the 1880s by architect **Solon S. Beman** and landscape architect Nathan F. Barrett, the 1,800-building community was intended not so much to make workers happy as to increase productivity by providing clean and pleasant surroundings. The town was said to be patterned after Saltaire in Northern England, built by textile manufacturer Sir Titus Salt.

Pullman's workers, whom he called his "children," were required to live here, paying rent and utilities at rates that earned him a six-percent annual profit. In 1893 the company fired thousands of employees and cut the wages of remaining workers by an average of 25 percent. Pullman did not, however, reduce their rent, leading to the near-starvation of many during the winter of 1893-94. That spring, the workers went on strike, and in the summer, member unions of the American Railway Union, led by Eugene V. Debs—who later founded the Socialist Party—staged sympathy strikes. When violence erupted, President Grover Cleveland sent in federal troops. Debs was sentenced to six months in prison. Although the workers lost the strike, Pullman drew little sympathy. Upon his death in 1897, he was buried beneath several protective tons of steel rails and concrete in Graceland Cemetery, as his family feared enemies would rob his grave.

In 1907 the town was sold to its residents, who still form a very tightly knit community. Pullman was declared a national landmark in 1971, and since then many efforts have been made to restore and revitalize the area. More than 80 percent of the original buildings still stand. A walk through the area is a visit to a small 19th-century town of handsome brick row houses and common buildings. The structures are Victorian in style, with plain Italianate town houses, lavish Queen Anne residences, and many examples of Romanesque arches, one of the architect's signature design elements.

♦ To reach Pullman, take the Dan Ryan Expressway (I-90/94) to 111th Street. Go west just a few blocks and turn left on Forrestville Avenue, and you'll be right in front of the Hotel Florence.

Highlights of the town include the following:

Hotel Florence In 1881 **Beman** made this turreted and gabled fantasy in the Queen Anne style. Named after Pullman's daughter, the hotel was the grandest structure in the town. It contained the only bar in Pullman, which was open only to guests. This National Historic Landmark is no longer renting rooms, but you can eat in the **Hotel Florence Restaurant** which serves breakfast and lunch, but is most famous for its Sunday brunch. The hotel is now a museum operated by the **Historic Pullman Foundation;** you can view George Pullman's private suite and other rooms restored to turn-of-the-century style. Town maps and related information are available in the lobby. ♦ Free. Museum: M-F 11AM-2PM. 11111 S Forrestville Ave (at E 111th St). 785.8181

Administration Building and Clock Tower Architect **Solon S. Beman** favored rounded Romanesque arches for this 1880 three-story building, which housed offices of the Pullman Palace Car Company. The 120-foot **Clock Tower** tops the building. Cottage Grove Avenue now runs right through the former site of Lake Vista, a three-acre artificial lake that once fronted the building. The state of Illinois is working to turn the area into a historical park with exhibits on 19th-century industrialization. An urban transit car company also plans to locate a new factory here. ♦ 11011 S Cottage Grove Ave (at E 111th St)

Pullman United Methodist Church Built in 1882 as **Greenstone Church,** this was the only religious structure in the original company town. Pullman had intended all workers to worship together in a community church, but in the end each religious group chose its own minister. Even the church had to pay rent to the Pullman Company, although none of the separate congregations could afford to on their own. The Methodists bought the church in 1907 and changed its name. **Solon S. Beman**'s green serpentine limestone walls contrast sharply with the brick buildings in the rest of the town. ♦ 11211 S St. Lawrence Ave (at E 112th St)

Pullman Stables The carved horses' heads above the entrance mark the only place in Pullman where the residents could keep their horses. Carriages were also available for rent here. ♦ 11201 S Cottage Grove Ave (at E 112th St)

Historic Pullman Foundation Visitor Center Across the street from the stables is a nondescript building that now houses the foundation's **Visitor Center.** A video presentation introduces visitors to the area, and guided tours are available from the center on selected Sundays from spring to fall. ♦ Sa 11AM-2PM; Su noon-3PM; M-F for special events or by appointment for groups of 20 or more. 11141 S Cottage Grove Ave (at E 112th St). 785.8181

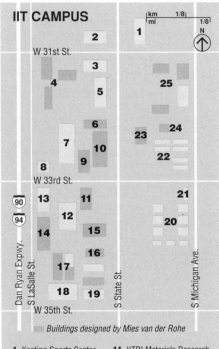

IIT CAMPUS

Buildings designed by Mies van der Rohe

1 Keating Sports Center
2 Stuart Building
3 Life Sciences Building
4 Association of America Railroads Complex
5 Engineering 1 Building
6 Alumni Memorial Hall
7 Grover M. Hermann Hall
8 Machinery Hall
9 Wishnick Hall
10 Perlstein Hall
11 Siegel Hall
12 Paul V. Galvin Library
13 Main Building
14 IITRI Materials Research
15 S. R. Crown Hall
16 Institute of Gas Technology Complex
17 IIT Research Institute
18 Chemistry Research Building
19 IITRI Tower
20 Fraternity Complex
21 Farr Hall
22 Residence Halls
23 Commons Building
24 St. Savior Chapel
25 Apartment Buildings

2 Illinois Institute of Technology (IIT)

In 1938 German architect **Mies van der Rohe** was recruited by Chicago architect **John A. Holabird** to head the architecture department at the **Armour Institute of Technology.** When **Armour** merged with the **Lewis Institute** in 1940 to become **IIT, Mies** was asked to design a campus for the new school, a task that occupied him until his retirement from the faculty in 1958. His goal was a visually unified campus, with a rational master plan and a repetitive module on which each building's design would be based. The Chicago grid street plan inspired the uncompromisingly rectilinear campus layout (see the plan at left), arranged to define but not enclose the open spaces between buildings.

The most famous aphorism attributed to **Mies** is "less is more," an apt description of his clean, uncluttered designs. Another of his sayings, equally applicable to his work, is "God is in the details." The progression of **Mies**'s design is revealed in subtle developments from one building to the next, and the campus provides an unusual opportunity to see his philosophy develop. In 1976 the American Institute of Architects recognized the **IIT** campus as one of the 200 most significant works of architecture in the US.

While **IIT** itself is safe, the housing projects to the south can be very dangerous, especial at night. Use your judgment on whether to drive, take a cab, or ride on the **Englewood** or **Dan Ryan** els (both stop at **35th Street**). Free visitor parking is available in a lot at the southeast corner of 33rd and State Streets. Group tours are available on request. ♦ S State St (between 35th and 31st Sts)

Among the campus's most notable buildings are the following:

Main Building The only remaining structure from the institutions that preceded **IIT** provides the sharpest possible contrast with **Mies**'s vision: Designed in 1891 by **Patton & Fisher,** this brick and terra-cotta structure was the main classroom building for the old **Armour Institute,** founded by Phil Armour, one of Chicago's most prominent meatpackers. Characteristic of Romanesque designs of this time, it features rusticated masonry at the first level, with smooth brick above and two series of roundheaded windows. 3300 S Federal St (at W 33rd St)

Alumni Memorial Hall With **Perlstein** and **Wishnick Halls,** this 1946 building form **Mies**'s first completed open quadrangle. The skin consists of buff-colored brick panels, steel, and panes of glass, which for the first time in the architect's work fill the entire bay. **Mies** devoted much thought to how a buildin turns a corner; here, the corners are graceful serrated. **Holabird & Root** served as associa architects on the project. 3201 S Dearborn St (at W 32nd St)

Perlstein Hall Also designed by **Mies** in 1946 in association with **Holabird & Root,** this steel-framed building has a light court that was designed by **Walter A. Netsch, Jr.** of **Skidmore, Owings & Merrill.** ♦ 10 W 33rd St (at S State St)

S.R. Crown Hall The most famous building on campus and a world-renowned masterpiece of structural Expressionism, this hall consists of an elegant and spare skin of steel and glass stretched over a column-free space 220 feet by 120 feet. No fireproofing materials obscure the view of the structure, which features a roof hung from four steel-plate girders. The 18-foot interior height and minimal partitions create an unusual spatial experience. Students in architecture, planning, and urban design work in a space that sharply contrasts with the typical design-school studio, which is often carved into small cubbyholes. Here, the openness promotes interaction and learning from other students, as well as from the faculty. In keeping with students' long hours, the building is usually open early and late Mondays through Saturdays during the school year. ♦ 3360 S State St (between 35th and 33rd Sts)

Robert F. Carr Memorial St. Savior Chapel Known as the "God box," the chapel was designed by **Mies** in 1952 with the same stark vocabulary as **Crown Hall** and the campus boiler plant. **Mies** originally intended the entire building to be of steel construction; because of the cost, however, only the roof was made of steel. The brick walls create a private enclosed space—unlike the typical college chapel, but well suited to contemplation. ♦ 65 E 32nd St (at S State St)

Paul V. Galvin Library Architects after **Mies** continued to be inspired by his vision for the campus. **Walter A. Netsch, Jr.** at **Skidmore, Owings & Merrill** carefully studied **Crown Hall** before designing this library in 1962; from the front, you can compare and contrast the two buildings. ♦ 35 W 33rd St (between S Dearborn and S Federal Sts)

3 Chinatown Chicago's first Chinese immigrants, who began to arrive in the 1870s, originally settled in the South Loop. At the turn of the century, those connected with the On Leong fraternal organization founded an official Chinatown on the city's South Side near Cermak Road. Only a few blocks square, the community has a dense population of about 10,000. The main streets—whose names appear on street signs in Chinese characters as well as in English—are Wentworth Avenue, Cermak Road (22nd Street), and Archer Avenue. These boundaries have extended farther north to 18th Street with **Chinatown Square,** a shopping mall and

600-unit apartment complex built on former railroad yards in 1993. In the 1970s a smaller Chinatown sprang up on the North Side along Argyle Street, but the neighborhood has evolved into Little Saigon, with more of a Southeast Asian than a Chinese community between Broadway and Sheridan Road. While Chicago's Chinese populace is spread throughout the city and suburbs, these neighborhoods are wonderful microcosms of Asian culture, from the exotic grocery stores to the Chinese New Year parades held in both communities each February, complete with fire-breathing dragons and dancing, firecracker-tossing lions. ♦ Bounded by Wentworth Ave, 18th St, 23rd St, and Archer Ave

Among the treats to be found in Chinatown are the following:

Hong Min ★★$ Just about anything on the extensive menu at this bare-bones double storefront will satisfy. Start with a big bowl of shrimp dumplings in broth. Seafood comes in vast variety: Choose from clams, crabs, cuttlefish, snails, steamed fish with black-bean-and-garlic sauce, squid, oysters, and more. The seafood-stuffed vegetables are especially delightful. Beef-eaters will be pleased with the tasty meat dishes. ♦ Chinese ♦ Daily 10AM-2AM. 221 W Cermak Rd (at S Wentworth Ave). 842.5026

Three Happiness ★$$ Skip the regular menu, which pales by comparison to the dim sum, a seemingly endless array of steamed dumplings, deep-fried pastries, and other exotica. ♦ Chinese ♦ Daily. 2130 S Wentworth Ave (at W Cermak Rd). 791.1228

On Leong Merchants Association Constructed in the 1920s, the ornamental building with its twin-pagoda roof long served as a kind of Chinese City Hall, with a courtroom where disputes among community members were settled. Today, except for a couple of retail stores on the ground level, the building is vacant, having been seized by the federal government in 1988 after a raid on a gambling operation inside. The fraternal organization now meets at 218 West 22nd Place (842.0807); it has become much more circumspect about its activities. ♦ 2214 S Wentworth Ave (at W Cermak Rd)

Chiu Quon Bakery Steamed buns stuffed with pork or lotus-seed paste, sesame balls, watermelon cake, and almond cookies are just a few of the fresh-baked treats here. You can order to take out or sit down and eat in the little tearoom in back. ♦ Daily 7AM-10PM. 2229 S Wentworth Ave (between W 23rd St and W Cermak Rd). 225.6608

Restaurants/Clubs: Red   **Hotels:** Blue
Shops/ 🍴 Outdoors: Green   **Sights/Culture:** Black

Frida's

Frida's Bakery Right across the street from **Chiu Quon**, this cross-cultural bakery offers a good selection of American and French specialities as well as the familiar Chinese baked goods. This and several other Western-style bakeries along the street are a reminder that there's still a significant Italian population in the residential area west of Wentworth. ♦ Daily 7AM-10PM. 2228 S Wentworth Ave (between W 23rd St and W Cermak Rd). 808.1113

Woks 'n' Things You'll be able to open your own Chinese restaurant after a visit here. The small but well-stocked shop carries woks in a dozen sizes, the largest fit for an emperor at 30 inches across. ♦ Daily. 2234 S Wentworth Ave (between W 23rd St and W Cermak Rd). 842.0701

Emperor's Choice ★★$$ Chef Ron Moy's distinctive cuisine is showcased in this contemporary and bright restaurant. Seafood shines, especially plump oysters or fresh sole lightly seasoned with ginger, cilantro, and black beans. Order the outstanding Peking duck a day in advance. ♦ Chinese ♦ Daily lunch and dinner. 2238 S Wentworth Ave (between W 23rd St and W Cermak Rd). 225.8800

The original nicknames for the Bridgeport neighborhood were "Hardscrabble" and "Cabbage Patch."

In 1980 a one-mile stretch of 43rd Street on the Southwest Side was named Pope John Paul II Drive to commemorate the pontiff's visit to Chicago the previous year. In the first six months after the renaming, 23 street signs were stolen.

The American Communist Party was founded in Chicago in 1919 at the Merchants Hall (113 S Ashland Ave). In a scene dramatized in the Warren Beatty movie *Reds,* John Reed and others walked out of a Socialist Labor Party meeting to form the new political party.

Ten Ren Tea A tea lover's delight, featuring about 50 varieties of teas—loose, boxed, and tinned—including ordinary black tea, Oriental Beauty tea, Iron Goddess of Mercy tea, and $118-per-pound Ten Wu tea grown on the highest-altitude tea plantation in Taipei expressly for this Taiwanese tea conglomerate. The red-clay teapots are one of a kind. ♦ Daily. 2247 S Wentworth Ave (between 23rd St and W Cermak Rd). 842.1171

Mandar Inn ★$$ Somewhat more elegant than its neighbors, this restaurant is popular with suburbanites. A pleasant ambience and helpful wait staff combine to offer a comfortable experience for the uninitiated; ask for advice on what to order. Possible choices include eggplant in hot sauce with pork or vegetables, filet mignon in black pepper sauce, and Szechuan string beans. Next door is a gift shop with a spectacular array of Chinese knickknacks. ♦ Chinese ♦ Daily lunch and dinner. 2249 S Wentworth Ave (between W 23rd St and W Cermak Rd). 842.4014

Dong Kee Company A one-stop shop for china, woks, kitchen gadgets, gifts, teas, and even fresh-made almond cookies. ♦ Daily 9AM-9PM. 2252 S Wentworth Ave (between W 23rd St and W Cermak Rd). 225.6340

Chee King ★$$ Good food in substantial portions is offered at reasonable prices. Try delectably crunchy potato nests filled with colorful vegetables and seafood, or stir-fried shrimp. Skip the spicy Hunan and Szechuan dishes, but count on crispy chicken to be deftly seasoned with a five-spice powder. ♦ Chinese ♦ Daily lunch and dinner. 216 W 22nd Pl (at S Wentworth Ave). 842.7777

Sixty-Five ★★$ Try this place if your wallet is a bit thin. Live crabs, lobsters, and fish swim around in tanks in the front window; eventually they'll be steamed or stir-fried with ginger and green onions, or slathered with black-bean sauce. ♦ Chinese ♦ Daily lunch and dinner. 2409 S Wentworth Ave (at W 24th St). 842.6500

4 Bridgeport The 11th Ward is historically the center of Chicago politics, and Bridgeport serves as its county seat. Until the current mayor, Richard M. Daley, moved to Dearborn Park in the South Loop in 1993, he lived here, as did his father, the late Richard J. Daley. This ward also produced the legendary Ed Kelly, who served from 1933 to 1947, when his overt corruption prompted Democratic machine leaders to install a figurehead reformer, Martin Kenelly, also from Bridgeport, in his place. Known for its corner churches and corner bars, Bridgeport is a quiet Irish Catholic neighborhood mostly of tidy little bungalows with perfectly manicured lawns. ♦ Bounded by S State St and S Ashland Ave, and W Pershing Rd and S Archer Ave

Among the Bridgeport sights are the following:

Schaller's Pump Directly across the street from the 11th Ward Regular Democratic Organization headquarters, this is a neighborhood tavern where beer and politics mix famously, as long as you've got the right point of view. Don't speak kindly of the late Harold Washington, Jane Byrne, or the Republican party. ♦ M-F 11AM-2AM; Sa 5:30PM-3AM; Su 3:3PM-9PM. 3714 S Halsted St (at W 37th St). No phone

Bubbly Creek The south fork of the south branch of the Chicago River runs through the Bridgeport and Canaryville neighborhoods four blocks west of Halsted Street. Used as a sewer by meatpacking houses, Bubbly Creek got its name from the natural fermentation of animal carcasses that took place in it. Yes, it still bubbles. ♦ W 35th St (at the Chicago River)

City Center When you stand at this intersection, 12 blocks west of the house at 3602 South Lowe Avenue where Mayor Richard M. Daley grew up, you are at the exact geographical center of the city. ♦ W 37th St and S Honore St

Old Stone Gate This triple-arched gate, which was designed most likely by **John Wellborn Root,** marked the entrance to the

Union Stock Yards. A wooden gate built in 1875 stood on this spot, but was replaced circa 1879 by this one, now a national landmark. It heralds the entrance to an industrial park once filled with acres and acres of animal pens. ♦ W Exchange Ave and S Peoria St

International Amphitheatre Once one of the largest and busiest convention and exhibit halls in the country (and the site of the infamous Democratic Convention of 1968), this huge building has been used infrequently since **McCormick Place** was built. Today it hosts the occasional rodeo, boxing match, and bargain clothing sale. ♦ 4220 S Halsted St (at W 42nd St)

St. Gabriel's Church Constructed from 1887 to 1888, this is the only Catholic church in Chicago built by **Burnham & Root. Daniel Burnham** was the son-in-law of John Sherman, president of the Union Stock Yard & Transit Company. **John Wellborn Root** designed the church, which, with its massive brick structure and spacious interior, is reminiscent of the firm's **Rookery Building** and evokes Carl Sandburg's metaphor of big shoulders. Although a section of the 160-foot-tall tower was removed, the church still looms over the neighborhood, serving as a tribute to Rev. Maurice J. Dorney, the founder of the parish, who was known as "The King of the Yards." ♦ 4501 S Lowe Ave (at W 45th St)

St. Gabriel's Church

Comiskey Park

Comiskey Park Home of the **Chicago White Sox,** this state-of-the-art stadium opened in 1991. It was built with public funds after ball club president Jerry M. Reinsdorf threatened to move the team out of town. It's located on 35th Street, across from the site of the original **Comiskey Park.** Built in 1910 and demolished in 1992, it was the nation's oldest ballpark. Now a parking lot, there's a plaque where home plate once stood. Street parking around **Comiskey** is virtually nonexistent, so you'll have to park in one of the official lots, which are a nightmare to get in and out of, or in a private lot to the west. The **CTA's Red Line** from the Loop runs along the Dan Ryan Expressway two blocks east. Southeast of the park are Stateway Gardens and Robert Taylor Homes, two of the city's most decaying, crime-ridden public housing complexes. ♦ W 35th St and S Shields Ave. 924.1000

5 Pilsen/Little Village These neighborhoods on the West Side were the port of entry for European immigrants from the 1870s through 1950s. Today they are home primarily to Mexican immigrants. The main streets—18th and 26th Streets, and Halsted, Ashland, and Blue Island Avenues—are a jumble of brightly colored stores, bakeries, and restaurants. In fact, 26th Street is also known as Avenida Mexico. Regular events celebrate the community's Mexican heritage, including the annual Fiesta Del Sol held in late July; also in summer, Mexican rodeos, or *charreadas* are held. Both take place at **Plaza Garibaldi** (W 26th St and California Ave; 847.0990). A fascinating

spectacle takes place every Good Friday, when residents reenact the Passion of Christ staged over an eight-block stretch of 18th Street, culminating in a simulated crucifixion at Plaza Garibaldi.

An artists' community has sprung up on the eastern border of Pilsen, along Halsted and 18th Streets, attracting residents ranging from computer artists from the **University of Illinois** to hair stylists from Oak Street. Wander around on a Saturday afternoon and follow those who appear to be in the know into the often hidden shops and galleries. Among the highlights is **Prospectus Gallery** (1210 W 18th St, between S Racine Ave and S Allport St, 733.6132), which features contemporary North American and Latin American art. Another local find is the **Blue Rider Theater,** where buoyant personality Donna Blue Lachman performs one-woman shows, including portrayals of Frida Kahlo and Rosa Luxemburg (1822 S Halsted St, between W 19th and W 18th Sts, 733.4668).

The best time to visit the area is Saturday afternoon, when the streets teem with locals out shopping. **CTA** service to the area is slow and not the safest; take a cab or drive. As the area can be a bit seedy—especially at night—stick to main thoroughfares. ♦ Bounded by S Halsted St and S Western Ave/Blvd, and W 18th and W 43rd Sts

A sampling of sights at Pilsen/Little Village:

Casa Aztlan The murals on the front of this social service center were contributed by numerous artists from the area. They depict Benito Juárez and other Mexican heroes, as well as the evolution of the neighborhood. ◆ 1831 S Racine Ave (between W 19th and W 18th Sts). 666.5508

Mexican Fine Arts Center Opened in 1987, the first Mexican cultural center in the Midwest remains the largest and busiest, with regularly changing exhibitions. Live multilingual shows are presented in the theater. The **Tzintzuntzan** gift shop sells outstanding Mexican arts and crafts. ◆ Free. Tu-Su. 1852 W 19th St (at S Damen Ave). 738.1503 &

Nuevo Leon ★$ Authentic Mexican dishes draw locals and visitors alike. Though preparations tend to be heavy on lard, at least they don't taste like the fare at chain restaurants. For something different, order the breaded fried brains. ◆ Mexican ◆ Daily breakfast, lunch, and dinner until midnight; F-Sa to 5AM. 1515 W 18th St (between S Laflin St and S Ashland Ave). 421.1517. Also at: 3657 W 26th St (at S Lawndale Ave). 522.1515

Nuevo Leon Bakery An authentic Mexican *panaderia* tempts you with warm *bobolillos* (a type of bread) and an assortment of sugar-laden deep-fried or baked pastries. Hand pick your selections with a pair of tongs and a paper plate. ◆ Daily 6AM-9PM. 1634 W 18th St (between S Ashland Ave and S Paulina St). 243.5977

Sabas Vega Carniceria The glass cases are laden with Mexican *chorizo* (sausage), steaks, and a variety of delicious freshly made specialties such as cactus salad to take out. ◆ Daily. 1808 S Ashland Ave (at W 18th St). 666.5180

Bishop's Chili ★★$ According to those in the know, the search for the best chili in Chicago begins and ends here. ◆ Chili ◆ M-F 11AM-6PM; Sa to 2PM. 1958 W 18th St (at S Damen Ave). 829.6345

6 Little Italy This neighborhood stretches primarily along Taylor Street west from Morgan Street. Access is a bit tricky, due to some non-through streets. To get here, take a cab or drive west from the Loop on Harrison Street, turn south on Halsted Street, proceed four blocks to Taylor Street, and head west. Between Racine Avenue and Loomis Street, just east of Ashland Avenue, is a relatively well-maintained low-rise public housing project; east of it is **Arrigo Park,** which includes a statue of Christopher Columbus. Across the park along Lexington Street are a few blocks of restored Victorian houses; now home both to neighborhood Italian families and **University of Illinois** faculty, these were built as the city's Irish Gold Coast. (It's quite safe to wander through here during the day.) ◆ W Taylor St, between S Morgan St and S Ashland Ave

A few places to see in Little Italy:

Tuscany

Tuscany ★★$$$ From the splashy neon sign over the entrance to the dining room with glass doors that open in the summer to create a gardenlike atmosphere, this place is stylish. The kitchen's rotisseries produce superb whole chicken, among them *paillard di pollo al palio* (grilled chicken breast marinated in herbs and topped with fresh mozzarella and tomatoes). The daily specials are often the best choice. ◆ Italian ◆ M-F lunch and dinner; Sa-Su dinner. Reservations required. 1014 W Taylor St (between S Morgan and S Miller Sts). 829.1990 &

Mario's Italian Lemonade This little wooden sidewalk stand, brightly painted green, white, and red, is famous for the old-fashioned Italian treat it serves. Choose from more than a dozen syrup flavors, poured over cones of shaved ice. ◆ Daily May through October. 1070 W Taylor St (between S Morgan and S Aberdeen Sts). No phone

Trattoria Roma Terza ★$$ A cosmopolitan dining room has a Roman-ruins decor like its sister restaurant in Old Town. Pizza and cold antipasti are good starters, but the daily-changing menu suffers from inconsistency. Pasta is generally the best bet. ◆ Italian ◆ M-F lunch and dinner; Sa-Su dinner. Reservations recommended. 1119 W Taylor St (between S Aberdeen St and S Racine Ave). 226.6800

Conte di Savoia This international gourmet grocery store is stocked with homemade Italian pastas, sauces, and sausages; mozzarella made fresh daily; imported olive oils and tomatoes; and Italian chocolates and baked goods. There's also an espresso and cappuccino bar. They will ship anywhere in the world. ◆ Daily. 1438 W Taylor St (at S Bishop St). 666.3471

Rosebud ★★$$$ Even with reservations, you'll stand in line to get seated at this enormously popular place. The food is sometimes worth the wait. For starters, try the fried zucchini or the delightful escarole soup with Italian sausage. Though pastas tend to be overcooked, the portions are big enough for two (there's a surcharge if you split them). Chicken Vesuvio, hard to do right, is good and garlicky here. Spumoni is a must for dessert. ◆ Italian ◆ M-F lunch and dinner; Sa-Su dinner. Reservations recommended. 1500 W Taylor St (at S Laflin St). 942.1117

BAR & GRILL

Hawkeye's Bar & Grill $$ An authentic Chicago experience, this place attracts rowdy fans attending **Bulls** and **Blackhawk** games at the nearby **United Center**. Many come here first for lunch or dinner, then board a bus to the game, leaving their car in the restaurant's parking lot. Diehards return afterward to celebrate or mourn. The food tends to things that go well with beer, like the build-your-own burger, double-baked chili (served in a bowl of bread with lots of cheese), and chicken in various presentations. ◆ American ◆ Daily lunch and dinner. Reservations recommended. 1458 W Taylor St (between S Bishop and S Laflin Sts). 226.3951

7 Roosevelt Road A bustling wholesale district before World War II, especially for clothing jobbers, Roosevelt Road east of the Dan Ryan Expressway still boasts a number of stores—some warehouse-size, others tiny—offering good retail prices amid a wheeler-dealer atmosphere. (West of the Dan Ryan Expressway, Roosevelt Road steadily deteriorates and becomes one of the city's grimiest, and most dangerous, thoroughfares.) The infamous **Maxwell Street Market** has been removed in order to accommodate expansion of the **University of Illinois at Chicago.** ◆ Between Canal St and the Dan Ryan Expressway

A sampling of stops along Roosevelt Road follows:

Kale Uniforms Since Chicago police, firefighters, US postal workers, and other official servicepeople are this store's priority customers, don't expect much in the way of service. But ordinary citizens can buy many of the goods here, including mail carriers' walk-for-miles shoes, flameproof rubber hip boots, and bulletproof vests. A mail-order catalog is available. ◆ M-Sa. 555 W Roosevelt Rd (in River West Plaza). 563.0022

Eppel's $ Start your day with breakfast before the sun comes up with folks from the neighborhood. Omelettes are immense, the hash browns are crispy, and the coffee is good and hot. Best of all, the prices can't be beat. ◆ Coffee shop ◆ Daily 4AM-3PM. 554 W Roosevelt Rd (between S Clinton and S Jefferson Sts). 922.2206

Leather Makers This shop offers leather attire at prices about 20 percent below regular retail. ◆ Daily. 560 W Roosevelt Rd (between S Clinton and S Jefferson Sts). 427.3567

Chernin's Shoes In this gigantic emporium brand-name men's and women's shoes are sold at prices 20 to 40 percent off suggested retail. ◆ Daily. 606 W Roosevelt Rd (at S Jefferson St). 922.4545

Manny's ★$ This large two-room cafeteria doling out huge helpings of comfort food from steam tables boasts that it has been serving "Chicago's best corned beef since 1942." According to a June 1994 article in *Gourmet*, "if Damon Runyon had written about Chicago, **Manny's** would have been his favorite setting." ◆ American ◆ M-Sa breakfast and lunch, from 5AM until 4PM. 1141 S Jefferson St (at W Roosevelt Rd). 939.2855

8 University of Illinois at Chicago (UIC) Architect **Walter A. Netsch Jr.** of **Skidmore, Owings & Merrill** was the chief designer for the campus, which also features buildings by **C.F. Murphy Associates, A. Epstein & Sons, Harry Weese & Associates,** and **Solomon Cordwell Buenz & Associates,** among others. The majority of the buildings were constructed between 1965 and 1971. **Netsch** had a vision of bold architectural geometry that he described as "field theory," in which squares were overlaid and rotated. His buildings are easy to pick out on campus. The **Art and Architecture Laboratories** (845 W Harrison St) is geometrically logical in plan but difficult to navigate internally. The **Behavioral Sciences Building** (1007 W Harrison St) is even more complex in plan and was designed with offices along the many-faceted exterior walls and laboratories in the large, windowless interior section. **University Hall** (601 S Morgan St), the 28-story administration building, was of great interest at the time of its construction because it is 20 feet wider at the top than at the bottom.

A new era of building was ushered in with the 1988 construction of the **Student Residence and Commons,** designed by **Solomon Cordwell Buenz & Associates. UIC**'s first student residence, the three-building complex forms a defined campus boundary at the corner of Halsted and Harrison Streets and offers pleasant common areas.

Change continues with the ongoing reconstruction of the central campus. Though **Netsch**'s original plans had intellectual purity (the sound of one hand clapping, a critic has said), they had little aesthetic appeal for students or faculty. Nor did they work very well for their intended purpose. The bilevel walkways, the top levels of which were never used and the bottoms of which soon began to leak, are being done away with in a refreshing alteration by **Daniel P. Coffey & Associates.** ♦ Bounded by S Halsted and S Morgan Sts, and W Roosevelt Rd and W Harrison St

In the UIC campus:

Jane Addams Hull House Museum

In 1889 Jane Addams and Ellen Gates Starr opened the doors of America's first settlement house. Here thousands of needy neighbors—mostly immigrants from the surrounding slums—received education, political support, and cultural edification. Addams and her compatriots—mostly college-educated women—proved instrumental in abolishing child labor, establishing labor unions, and improving public health, among numerous other accomplishments. Programs continued to grow to meet varied needs of the community, which necessitated a remodeling of the house and the addition of several new structures; in its heyday, **Hull House** occupied a 13-building complex. It continued to play a significant part in the neighborhood's life until the 1950s. Several social service organizations under the organization's umbrella are now scattered throughout the city, but this original location has been converted to a museum owned by the **University of Illinois.** In 1963 the additions were demolished and the house restored to resemble the country estate it was when it was built in 1856 by an unknown architect. It contains fascinating exhibits that document the history of the neighborhood. ♦ Free. M-F, Su. 800 S Halsted St (at W Polk St). 413.5353

9 Greektown Greek immigrants began to settle in Chicago's Near West Side in the late 1800s. At one time, so many resided in one triangle-shaped community that it became known as the Delta, after the triangular Greek letter. A number of Greek restaurants still do a brisk lunchtime and dinner business in the neighborhood, which is a quick cab ride from the Loop. ♦ S Halsted St (between W Van Buren and W Monroe Sts)

Highlights of Greektown include:

Santorini ★★$$ Seafood stars at this romantic stucco-walled villa complete with a crackling fireplace. As a starter, try the charcoal-grilled octopus. Fresh fish entrées range from Norwegian salmon with dill sauce to terrific crisp-fried *baccalo* (cod filet), which comes with a potent potato-garlic puree. There's a nice list of Greek wines and beers. ♦ Greek ♦ Daily lunch and dinner. Reservations recommended weekends. 138 S Halsted St (between W Adams and W Monroe Sts). 829.8820 &

Greek Islands $ The crowd is boisterous, the waiters bustle, and the muraled, polished-wood environs are bright and airy. Though the food can sometimes be disappointing, portions are large and Greek wines are available. ♦ Greek ♦ Daily lunch and dinner. Reservations recommended for parties of five or more. 200 S Halsted St (at W Adams St). 782.9855 &

10 Museum of Holography This small museum is filled with astonishing holographic images—an enormous Tyrannosaurus Rex, Dracula, and Michael Jordan, to name three of the most popular. There's a medical exhibit, where you can experience the interior of a heart. While walking through other rooms, a pitchfork may lunge at you out of the darkness or you may see a prisoner pacing behind bars, but it's all an illusion. Holographic jewelry, watches, and bookmarks are for sale in the gift shop. ♦ Admission. W-Su 12:30-5PM. 1134 W Washington Blvd (at N May St). 226.1007; fax 829.9636

11 Ukrainian Village For more than a century, this neighborhood and similar enclaves to the north have been destinations for immigrants from Germany, Poland, and other Eastern European countries. These communities have also recently attracted urban pioneers from elsewhere in the city in search of sturdy housing in relatively stable neighborhoods, but the European flavor still lingers. This may be the city's quietest and cleanest neighborhood. ♦ Bounded by N Damen and N Western Aves, and W Grand and W Chicago Aves

Among the Village's highlights:

Ukrainian National Museum Ukrainian pottery, weaving, intricately decorated Easter eggs, and photos from the old country are among the exhibits in this small museum set in an old house. Tours that include talks on Ukrainian culture and history are given spontaneously by enthusiastic guides. ♦ Nominal admission. Th-Su 11AM-4PM, or by appointment. 2453 W Chicago Ave (between N Western and N Campbell Aves). 421.8020

Galans ★$$ The Eastern European home cooking includes a great marinated herring appetizer. As for entrées, go for the "Kozak feast": borscht, house salad, *holubtsi* (cabbage rolls), *barenyky* (filled dumplings), kielbasa, *kapusta* (sauerkraut), *kozak spys* (chunks of beef tenderloin and pork on a skewer), *carto planyk* (country-style potato pancakes), and coffee à la Galans (spiked with several potent mystery liqueurs) and homemade apple strudel. Live Ukrainian music plays Friday and Saturday evenings. ♦ Ukrainian ♦ Tu-Su lunch and dinner. 2212 W Chicago Ave (between N Leavitt St and N Bell Ave). 292.1000

Restaurants/Clubs: Red **Hotels:** Blue
Shops/ 🍸 Outdoors: Green **Sights/Culture:** Black

Wishbone ★$ People in the know fill two cramped rooms to partake of great Southern home cooking that includes grits, beans and rice, and homemade biscuits smothered in gravy thick with bits of ham and sausage. ♦ Southern ♦ Tu-F breakfast, lunch, and dinner; Sa-Su brunch. 1800 W Grand Ave (at N Wood St). 829.3597. Also at: 1001 W Washington St (at N Morgan St). 850.2663

12 The Boulevards For a comprehensive view of residential Chicago in all its social and architectural grandeur and grimness, nothing beats an afternoon drive along the city's Boulevard system (the route is highlighted on the map on page 177). Conceived by landscape architect Frederick Law Olmsted in 1869, the Boulevards were intended to create a network of parks linked by grassy thoroughfares that would encircle the city. Olmsted himself created much of the design, along with architects **William Le Baron Jenney** and **Jens Jensen**.

Starting at Logan Boulevard and Diversey Parkway on the North Side and concluding on Oakwood Boulevard on the South Side, the system is 28 miles long and links six squares and seven parks. Along the way, you'll see stunning mansions and churches—some in mint condition, others completely dilapidated—and, of course, people of all ethnic and socioeconomic persuasions. You'll pass **Logan Square, Humboldt Park, Garfield Park** (while you're here, consider a stop at the **Garfield Conservatory,** which dwarfs the one in Lincoln Park), **Douglas Park,** Cook County Jail, and the **University of Chicago.**

A word of caution: Unless you are *very* streetwise, you'd be smart not to get out of your car and wander in any section of the Boulevards south of Chicago Avenue until you reach Hyde Park. ♦ From W Logan Blvd and W Diversey Pkwy to E Oakwood Blvd and S Dr. Martin Luther King Jr. Dr

13 Milwaukee Avenue Chicago's Polish population is the largest in the world outside of Warsaw. The full length of this avenue and the neighboring streets were predominantly Polish from about 1867 until the middle of the 20th century. A drive along this strip reveals plenty of Polish delicatessens, restaurants, and stores labeled with signs in that language, but they are increasingly interspersed with enterprises of different ethnic origins. ♦ Between W Augusta Blvd and Harlem Ave

Make sure you don't miss the following:

Polish Museum of America Nicolaus Copernicus, Marie Curie, Lech Walesa, and Pope John Paul II are among the notables of Polish descent honored at this museum. Pianist and statesman Ignacy Paderewski rates an entire room. The complete Polish culture exhibition from the 1939 World's Fair was moved here from New York City. ♦ Donation

requested. Daily 11AM-4PM. 984 N Milwaukee Ave (at W Augusta Blvd). 384.3352

Mareva's ★★$$$ From the thickly upholstered dining room with its marvelous etched-glass mural of Copernicus and other Polish luminaries to the baby grand piano, this elegant Polish restaurant offers such authentic dishes as veal Casmir, sautéed and glazed with butter and sherry, and poached salmon in raspberry sauce. Save room for the rich homemade cheesecake. ♦ Polish ♦ Tu-S dinner. Reservations recommended. 1250 N Milwaukee Ave (between N Ashland Ave and N Paulina St). 227.4000

Logan Square In the center of Logan Square stands the **Illinois Centennial Monument,** designed by **Henry Bacon** in 1918 to commemorate Illinois's first hundred years of statehood. Teens who hang out here call this monument "the turkey," even though it's actually an eagle. Named after Civil War general John A. Logan, this area between Bloomingdale and Diversey Streets is slowly but steadily rebuilding from a period of neglect; it has been known for decades for its ethnic diversity. ♦ Milwaukee Ave, at N Kedzie Blvd

Abril ★$ This bright, friendly Mexican restaurant offers a great vantage point for watching the hustle and bustle on the square. It also serves good margaritas and enchiladas. ♦ Mexican ♦ Daily lunch and dinner. 2607 N Milwaukee Ave (at N Kedzie Ave). 227.7252

Tania's ★$$ Set in a spacious, high-ceilinged hacienda, one of Chicago's few Cuban/Spanish restaurants has an extensive menu of such exotic treats as monkfish seviche, and New Zealand mussels with a spicy garlic sauce. A perfect finish is Caribbean coffee with Kahlua or flambéed rum. Live music is featured Wednesday through Saturday evenings. ♦ Cuban/Spanish ♦ Daily lunch and dinner to 4AM. Reservations required Friday and Saturday nights. 2659 N Milwaukee Ave (between N Kedzie and N Kimball Aves). 235.7120

Polonia Book Store One of the largest Polish bookstores in the country, this shop carries books (in English and in Polish) by

Polish authors as well as Polish translations of American potboilers. ♦ M-Sa. 2886 N Milwaukee Ave (at N Drake Ave). 489.2554

Home Bakery and Restaurant ★$ The dining room alongside this bakery/grocery store serves a full dinner at super cheap prices. Soups stand out, as do such hearty favorites as plump pierogi (stuffed with meat, cheese, potato, or sauerkraut), smothered pork chops, and crisp potato pancakes with dollops of sour cream and applesauce. Calorific pastries sometimes come fresh from the oven; at other times they seem to have been waiting for weeks. ♦ Polish ♦ Daily breakfast, lunch, and early dinner. No credit cards accepted. 2931 N Milwaukee Ave (at N Central Park Ave). 252.3708

Andy's Deli Some 65 kinds of sausages and meats, plus cheeses, pierogi, and other Polish delicacies fill the glass cases and shelves in this delicatessen. ♦ Daily. 3055 N Milwaukee Ave (at N Hamlin Ave). 486.8160. Also at: 1737 W Division St (at N Wood St). 486.8870; 5438 N Milwaukee Ave (at W Bryn Mawr Ave). 631.7304

Czerwone Jabluszko/Red Apple Restaurant ★$ The all-you-can-eat buffet—a mere $5.50 for lunch and $6.50 for dinner on weekdays, $6.95 on Saturdays and Sundays—draws crowds to this bright room with a basket of apples on every table. Load up on roast chicken or turkey, pierogi, pig's trotters, and boiled potatoes. Finish with cheese-filled crepes, fresh fruits, or a torte. ♦ Polish ♦ Daily lunch and dinner. 3123 N Milwaukee Ave (at W Belmont Ave). 588.5781. Also at: 6474 N Milwaukee Ave (at W Devon Ave). 763.3407

14 Ravenswood/Lincoln Square Once a predominantly German neighborhood, Ravenswood is now home to Greeks, Koreans, Thais, and a burgeoning group of professional people seeking moderately priced housing. An intriguing mix of Old World–style European shops, delicatessens, pastry shops, and all sorts of ethnic restaurants line the mall. ♦ Bounded by N Ashland Ave and N Kedzie Aves, and W Montrose and W Foster Aves

Highlights of the neighborhood include:

Bando ★$$ If you've never sampled Korean cuisine, this is a good place to start. The tables are outfitted with grills so diners can barbecue an array of meats—from chicken and beef to tripe and tongue. Or let the kitchen do the cooking and order from a menu that includes broiled salmon, octopus in red sauce, and chicken teriyaki. A wide assortment of interesting appetizers will keep you entertained—and guessing. ♦ Korean ♦ Daily lunch and dinner. 2200 W Lawrence Ave (at N Leavitt St). 728.0100

Grecian Taverna ★$$ Charming and casual, this tavern combines Mediterranean style with a sense of solid American neighborhood comfort. Try the flaming cheese appetizer followed by roast leg of lamb. The thick Greek coffee is an excellent way to end the meal. ♦ Greek ♦ Daily lunch and dinner. 4761 N Lincoln Ave (south of W Lawrence Ave). 728.1600

Timeless Toys This small shop offers a grand stock of wooden doll houses and castles imported from Europe, puppets from all over the world, and a nice sampling of childrens' books. ♦ Daily. 4740 N Lincoln Ave (south of W Lawrence Ave). 334.4445

Chicago Brauhaus ★★$$ A traditional Austrian band holds forth in this old-fashioned German restaurant. Robust fare such as sauerbraten and sausage are offered; more unusual dishes like roasted rabbit are also on the menu. Whatever you order, be sure to accompany your meal with a frosty mug of German beer. ♦ German ♦ M, W-Su lunch and dinner. 4732 N Lincoln Ave (south of W Lawrence Ave). 784.4444

Merz Apothecary The pharmacists here fill regular prescriptions, but they'll also advise you about homeopathic remedies. The turn-of-the-century interior is packed with pure plant extracts, herbs, aromatherapy oils, and European toiletries. ♦ M-Sa. 4716 N Lincoln Ave (south of Lawrence Ave). 989.0900

Kelmscott Gallery This spectacular building with the Art Nouveau facade was built in 1920 as the **Krause Music Store;** it was the last commissioned work of architect **Louis Sullivan.** Restored by **Michael J. Pado,** it now houses a gallery that specializes in **Frank Lloyd Wright** artifacts, drawings, and furniture. ♦ Tu-Sa. 4611 N Lincoln Ave (between W Montrose Ave and W Lawrence Ave). 784.2559.

Lutz Continental Cafe and Pastry Shop ★★$ Possibly Chicago's best German pastry shop, it offers napoleons, Linzer tortes, coffee cakes bursting with almonds, homemade ice cream, and good coffee served on pretty china in a dining room with pink tablecloths or on a plant-filled outdoor patio. Soups, crepes, and sandwiches are also served. ♦ Bakery/Cafe ♦ Tu-Su 7AM-10PM; cafe from 11AM. 2458 W Montrose Ave (between N Artesian and N Campbell Aves). 478.7785

Thai Touch ★★$ About eight blocks west of Lincoln Square, on the eastern boundary of Albany Park, this corner restaurant makes it well worth going the extra mile. The menu has inexpensive traditional Thai dishes such as basil chicken and lemongrass beef, but it's the little touches—friendly service, adept spicing, and presentation—that make the difference. ♦ Thai ♦ M-Sa lunch and dinner. 3200 W Lawrence Ave (at N Kedzie Ave). 539.5700

Arun's ★★★$$$ This is a palace for Thai connoisseurs, who come prepared to empty their wallets. Openers include crab spring rolls and diced grilled pork with lemongrass, chilies, and mint. Among the mainstays are prawns in garlic lime sauce, and *panang* beef curry with roasted spices. The Singha beer has never tasted so good or cost so much. Save room for an interesting variety of Thai custards. ◆ Thai ◆ Tu-Sa dinner; Su brunch and dinner. 4156 N Kedzie Ave (at W Berteau Ave). 539.1909

15 Argyle Street Although smaller than the older Chinatown, this Asian enclave is worth a visit for delicious Vietnamese food and a stroll through interesting shops. ◆ Between N Sheridan Rd and N Broadway

In and around Argyle Street:

Viet Hoa Market The scent of pungent spices hits you as you walk through the door of this Vietnamese grocery store, which has an especially nice selection of unusual teas and produce. ◆ Daily. 1051 W Argyle St (between N Sheridan Rd and N Broadway). 334.1028

Trung-Viet This grocery store doubles as a pharmacy. Proprietor Quoc Tran and his colleague Van Troung, who ran a medicine shop in Saigon for more than 35 years, will concoct a special medicine for whatever ails you from such traditional ingredients as powdered tiger bones and Chinese tree bark. ◆ Daily. 4942 N Sheridan Rd (at W Argyle St). 561.0042

Vietnam Museum The war America would like to forget is movingly recalled in photos, maps, military uniforms and gear, medals, and other memorabilia. The museum was founded in the 1970s by a Vietnam vet. ◆ Free. Sa-Su 11AM-4PM. 954 W Carmen Ave (at N Sheridan Rd). 728.6111 &

Hua Giang ★★$ An amazing variety of delicious Vietnamese food is offered at very low prices. Try the do-it-yourself appetizer: grilled shrimp or beef, rice noodles, and vegetables, which you tuck and roll into rounds of rice paper. As a main course, the traditional catfish in caramelized sauce cooked in a clay pot is superb. Finish with refreshing Vietnamese iced coffee. ◆ Vietnamese ◆ M-W, F-Su lunch and dinner. 1104-06 W Argyle St (between N Sheridan Rd and N Broadway). 275.8691

Pasteur ★★$$ This popular Vietnamese restaurant located in a former greasy spoon offers an array of delicious dishes. Some tend toward the unusual and decidedly upscale, such as marinated clams with ginger sauce. ◆ Vietnamese ◆ Daily lunch and dinner. 4759 N Sheridan Rd (at W Lawrence Ave). 271.6673. Also at: 45 E Chicago Ave (between N Rush St and N Wabash Ave). 587.9992

Nhu Hoa Cafe ★$ A bright pink awning signals the entrance to this Laotian/ Vietnamese restaurant. The expansive menu has Polaroid photos of the more popular dishes. Try Laotian *keng phet kay*, delicately yet devilishly spiced curried chicken with peas, bamboo shoots, and coconut milk, served with a steaming pot of rice. ◆ Vietnamese/Laotian ◆ Tu-Su lunch and dinner. 1020 W Argyle St (at N Sheridan Rd). 878.0618

16 Rogers Park Rogers Park was originally a north suburban community of single-family homes. In the 1920s apartment buildings went up and the area began to attract a diversity of ethnic groups, including large numbers of Irish Catholics and Jews. While they no longer predominate, their influence is still seen in such institutions as **Loyola University**, numerous synagogues, and kosher delis along Devon Avenue. A visit to Rogers Park offers a glimpse of handsome houses, exposure to bits of curious culture, and the opportunity to go to the beach, since the community's eastern edge runs right along Lake Michigan. ◆ Bounded by N Sheridan Rd and N Kedzie Ave, and W Devon Ave and W Howard St

A few sights not to miss:

Loyola University Founded as **St. Ignatius** in 1870, the school received its charter as **Loyola Academy for Boys** in 1909. It became a coeducational university in 1914. The tiny lakefront campus is a surprisingly peaceful oasis of densely packed classroom buildings and residence halls. The main building of **Mundelein** (6363 N Sheridan Rd), a Catholic women's college now part of **Loyola,** is a dramatic limestone Art Deco skyscraper on Devon Avenue. ◆ 6525 N Sheridan Rd (between W Devon and W Loyola Aves). 274.3000

In 1889 social worker Jane Addams founded Hull House, the nation's first settlement house. In 1931 she became the first American woman to be awarded the Nobel Peace Prize.

America's movie industry started in 1907 at Essanay Studios, which was on Chicago's North Side, on Argyle Street near Racine Avenue. Charlie Chaplin made his only Chicago film, *His New Job,* here before California's milder climate lured the industry westward.

Lakefront A broad, sandy beach starts at North Shore Avenue and stretches several blocks northward. Backed by grassy parkland, it's perfect for a picnic. Along with the usual suntan set are neighborhood families, many of them recent émigrés chatting away in anything from Spanish to Russian. There are other beaches along the city shoreline, including Foster Avenue Beach. Beyond that, the next closest beach is in Evanston, but that suburb charges a fee to swim off its sands. ◆ From W North Shore Ave to W Touhy Ave

Heartland Cafe $ This lively restaurant with a broad wooden deck out front serves hearty but bland health food such as gigantic salads brimming with sprouts and thick sandwiches to ex-hippies and other left-leaning types. It's one of several businesses along Glenwood Avenue between Pratt Boulevard and Lunt Avenue that hark back to the age of Aquarius, among them the **No Exit Cafe, Isis Rising** bookstore, and shops selling incense and tie-dyed T-shirts. ◆ Health food ◆ Daily breakfast, lunch, and dinner. 7000 N Glenwood Ave (at W Lunt Ave). 465.8005

16 Devon Avenue Russian and Urdu are the languages you'll most likely hear on Devon between Western and Francisco Avenues. A mainly Jewish community until the 1970s, it's now heavily Indian and Pakistani, with a more recent influx of Russian immigrants. Russian delis, Greek fruit markets, and Indian jewelers mix in profusion. Highlights include **Chicago Hebrew Bookstore** (2942 W Devon Ave, at N Richmond St, 973.6636) and **Russia Books** (2746 W Devon Ave, at N California Ave, 761.3233). **Jai Hind Foods and Video** (2658 W Devon Ave, at N Washtenaw Ave, 973.3400) has a marvelous, neatly arranged array of both, plus a restaurant and a jewelry store. **Sari Niketan** (2613 W Devon Ave, at N Rockwell Ave, 338.9399) and some 15 other stores sell exquisite fabrics in six-yard lengths for traditional wraparound saris. If you have an appetite for a spicy meal, you'll find plenty of opportunities to satisfy it. Among the choices are the upscale **Viceroy of India** (2518 W Devon Ave, between N Campbell and N Maplewood Aves, 743.4100) and the less fancy **Gandhi India** (2601 W Devon Ave, at Rockwell Ave, 761.8714).

Bests

udy Markey
yndicated columnist, Chicago Sun Times; Talk how host, WGN Radio

est hotel lobbies for late-afternoon drinks—the **our Seasons** and **Inter-Continental,** both located n Michigan Avenue. The first one is drop-dead orgeous, the second has bunches of free food nd a lovely yesteryear feeling.

est lunch place when spring is almost here and you ave to beat the lake—**Rocky's Fish Shack,** slightly outh of **Navy Pier.**

est ladies' room in the city—the **Drake Hotel.** lakes you feel as if you belong to a country club. osh, private, relaxing.

est secret windswept place for winter kissing—he dock for **Wendella** boat rides during the off-eason. Located down the stairs from the **Wrigley uilding.** Desolate, great view, romantic, but I have rst dibs.

lost real mix-it-up place with fabulous Greek lamb hops and no shortage of Damon Runyon types—**liller's Pub,** on Wabash Avenue, right next to the almer House.

good hidden, romantic restaurant that's jammed r lunch but not for dinner—**Trattoria No. 10** on orth Dearborn Street. Great lighting for women ver 40; fabulous food; not an annoying people-atching sideshow spot.

est crab cakes, Caesar salad, and seafood in eneral—**Blue Crab Lounge** at **Shaw's Crab ouse,** on Hubbard. It never misses.

Sara N. Paretsky
Mystery writer

My personal favorite restaurant in Chicago is a noisy, crowded bistro—**Le Bouchon,** run by Jean-Claude Poilevy. It is an unpretentious, friendly, and uniformly charming place.

For fine dining, my personal favorite elegant restaurant is **Printer's Row.**

For old style Italian cooking, take a cab to 26th and Oakley on the **Near South Side** of the city and sample any of the restaurants in that short two-block strip, the remnants of **Little Tuscany.**

While Chicago touts deep-dish pizza, my own personal favorite is the thin-crust, beautifully light pizza at **Cafe Spiaggia.** I've never had better pizza.

Mike Royko
Columnist, Chicago Tribune

The lakefront. Walk it, bike it, enjoy it all year. Spring smelt fishing. Summer chess games at **North Avenue.** Fall leaves. Winter ice formations.

CTA. You can get anywhere on public transportation. (It's sometimes an adventure in human nature.)

Grant Park blues, jazz, and gospel fests.

The "Oprah" and "Jenny Jones" shows. Lots of laughs. Write ahead for tickets.

The Pump Room. When I want to feel pampered, on birthdays, anniversaries, Guy Fawkes Day. Great bar, great food, great ambience.

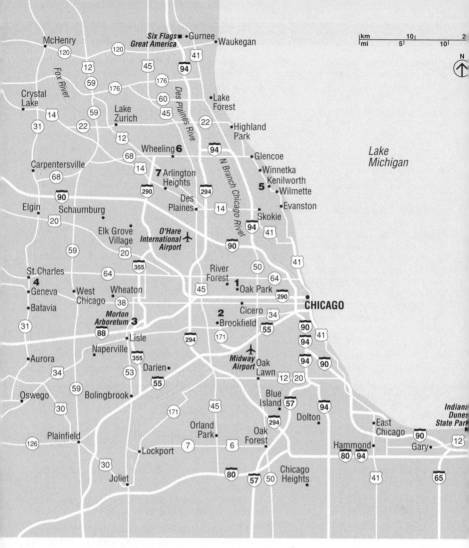

Environs

Some of Chicago's finest attractions aren't in Chicago at all. The surrounding suburbs are home to a variety of fascinating sites: There's the wealth of **Frank Lloyd Wright** buildings in **Oak Park**, the **Baha'i House of Worship** in **Wilmette**, and the **Chicago Botanic Garden** in **Glencoe** to name a few. You'll even find what many consider Chicago's best restaurant—the five-star French restaurant **Le Francais**—in the suburb of **Wheeling**. For more information on Chicago's environs, call the **Illinois Tourist Information Office** at 800/223.0121.

1 Oak Park/River Forest The neighborhood of Oak Park richly deserves its reputation as a mecca for architecture buffs, for it was here that **Frank Lloyd Wright** created what is now known as the Prairie School of Architecture. **Wright** lived in Oak Park from 1889 until 1909. Twenty-five of his buildings still stand in the village, and another six survive in the adjoining suburb of River Forest. Prairie School designs are characterized by sweeping horizontal lines, wide eaves, and decorative details. Significant works in the two villages by other noted Prairie School architects such as **William Drummond, Tallmadge & Watson, George Maher, John Van Bergen, Purcell & Elmslie, E.E. Roberts,** and **Robert Spencer** number in the hundreds.

As if the architectural heritage were not enough, Oak Park is also the birthplace of Ernest Hemingway. His boyhood homes still stand, as does **Oak Park and River Forest High School,** where young Ernest edited the school newspaper, *Trapeze,* and was memorialized in the yearbook with the tagline, "There are none so clever as Ernie." A leisurely visit might include a stop at one of Oak Park's many eating establishments. If you come by car, stop in at the **Oak Park Bakery** right off the **Eisenhower Expressway** (904 S Oak Park Ave, 708/383.1712) for world-class *kolachkes* (sweet yeast buns), cinnamon crisps, almond crescents, and other baked goods. **Philander's** (1120 W Pleasant St, in the Carleton Hotel, 708/848.4250), named after turn-of-the-century photographer Philander Barclay, serves delicious seafood and boasts a gallery of photos of old Oak Park. **Petersen Ice Cream** (1100 W Chicago Ave, 708/386.6131), one block west of the **Frank Lloyd Wright Home and Studio** (see below), is perfect for a simple meal of sandwiches, salads, and delicious baked goods after a tour; it's famous throughout the Chicago area for its own terrifically rich ice cream. Downtown Oak Park along **Lake Street** has several other restaurants.

Guided tours of Oak Park are available almost every day of the week (for information, call the Oak Park Visitors' Center, 708/848.1500). A highlight, though, is the annual **Wright Plus** tour on the third Saturday of May; it offers rare viewings of the interiors of privately owned homes designed by **Wright** and several other local architects. ◆ Oak Park is nine miles west of the Loop and is easily reached by the Metra West Line train from Northwestern Station or the Green Line CTA. The 23 Washington express bus is another option. By car, take the Eisenhower Expressway (I-290) west to the Harlem Avenue exit.

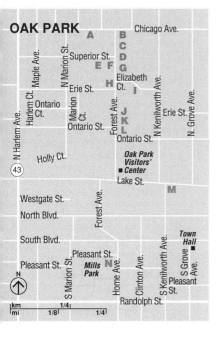

OAK PARK

The following is a suggested walking tour of Oak Park's Forest Avenue area (the letters preceding each entry refer to the map at lower left):

A Thomas H. Gale House, Robert P. Parker House, Walter H. Gale House Built in 1892, 1892, and 1893, respectively, these are three of **Frank Lloyd Wright**'s so-called bootlegged houses, designed while he was still working for **Adler & Sullivan.** They are large Victorian cottages that barely hint at the radical departure **Wright** was soon to make from this vertical, turreted style. The closely spaced spindles and the band of leaded glass windows on the **Walter H. Gale House** are the only clues to the direction **Wright**'s work would take. All three are private residences. ◆ Thomas H. Gale House, 1027 Chicago Ave; Robert P. Parker House, 1019 Chicago Ave; Walter H. Gale House, 1031 Chicago Ave, Oak Park

B Frank Lloyd Wright Home and Studio More than any of his other works, **Wright**'s own home and studio show the development of his style, serving as "architectural laboratories." This small cottage facing Forest Avenue was the first home **Wright** created for himself, and he worked on it from 1889 to 1911.

It began as a shingled cottage, built low to the ground and graced with diamond-paned leaded windows. A spectacular barrel-vaulted playroom was added in 1895 to accommodate his family of four sons and two daughters. In 1897 he added the attached studio, which he remodeled almost continuously during the years he lived here. Inside are **Wright**'s office, a library, and a double-height drafting room featuring a balcony suspended by a complex and graceful system of chains.

Wright separated from his wife and left Oak Park in 1909, but his family remained in the house. He remodeled the complex in 1911, adding living space in the studio and rental units to the home to provide some income. The house has been restored by the **Frank Lloyd Wright Home and Studio Foundation** to appear as it did in 1909. ◆ Admission. Tours: M-F 11AM, 1PM, and 3PM; Sa-Su every 15 minutes from 11AM to 4PM. 951 Chicago Ave (at Forest Ave), Oak Park. 708/848.1976 &

C A.J. Redmond House Oak Park resident E.E. Roberts was a popular architect for houses, stores, schools, and churches in Chicago and the western suburbs. This solid brick and stone house, built in 1901, is a more expensive version of the classic Oak Park house—rectilinear, 2.5 stories, hip-roofed, with a broad front porch and wide eaves. Roberts was extremely talented with decorative details, a gift visible here in the leaded, colored-glass windows. It's a private residence. ◆ 422 Forest Ave (off Chicago Ave), Oak Park

D **W.M. Harman House** Originally a grandly scaled, low-roofed Italianate house by an unknown architect, this home had already received a hipped roof when **Frank Lloyd Wright** was commissioned to remodel it in 1908. Most of **Wright**'s work is inside; the geometric wood mullions in the windows are about the only exterior evidence of his involvement. The house remains a private home. ◆ 400 Forest Ave (at Superior St), Oak Park

E **E.E. Roberts House** E.E. Roberts opened his own office in Oak Park in 1893 and was working in the Queen Anne style when this house was built in 1896. An extensive remodeling courtesy of the architect in 1911 changed the home to incorporate more of the Prairie School details—wide eaves and leaded glass windows in particular—that **Roberts** was using at the time. It's a private residence. ◆ 1019 Superior St (between Forest Ave and N Marion St), Oak Park

F **Nathan Moore House** Frank Lloyd Wright experimented with many styles in the 1890s and mastered more than a few. The first house he built on this site in 1895 was a 2.5-story Tudor mansion, complete with decorative half-timbering at the second and third levels. The coach house at the west end of the lot gives some idea of the style of the original commission. Moore's house burned in 1922, and **Wright** rebuilt it in an eclectic style with decided Tudor overtones. Terra-cotta embellishments include rows of balls with Sullivanesque "organic" ornament and window detailing. Orienting the house toward the yard rather than the street increased the amount of light and privacy; it also faced a house later remodeled for Moore's daughter Mary (see below). This is a private residence. ◆ 333 Forest Ave (at Superior St), Oak Park

Throughout the years unconventional recommendations have been made to city officials concerning the use of Chicago's tunnel system. In his book *Forty Feet Below: The Story of Chicago's Freight Tunnels,* author Bruce Moffat recounts proposals that have ranged from the commonplace to the downright peculiar. Converting the system into an underground mushroom farm, bomb shelters against a nuclear attack, a steam-heat conduit network, and a downtown people mover were a few of the ideas entertained by those searching for practical uses for the tunnels. According to Moffat, "Probably the most bizarre suggestion came from then Cook County Sheriff Joseph I. Woods in 1968. He opined that the tunnels would be an ideal place to detain the many demonstrators who converged upon the city for the Democratic National Convention that year."

G **Arthur B. Heurtley House** Designed by **Frank Lloyd Wright** in 1902, this is a classic example of his Prairie house—low, solid, with exaggeratedly wide eaves and a delightfully mysterious entry behind a half-hidden round brick arch. The main living area is on the second floor, providing lovely treetop views of Forest Avenue from the living and dining rooms. The roof visually floats above the bands of leaded casement windows, especially in the evening when the lights are on. This house remains a private home. ◆ 318 Forest Ave (between Elizabeth Ct and Chicago Ave), Oak Park

H **Edward R. Hills/DeCaro House** Nathan Moore hired **Frank Lloyd Wright** in 1905 to remodel an 1886 Stick-style home for his daughter Mary and her husband. He turned it 90 degrees on the lot and practically rebuilt it, inside and out. During an extensive restoration in 1976, the house was virtually destroyed by fire and then rebuilt by the DeCaro family, who had it designed as closely as possible to Wright's original plan. Note the carefully detailed roof, which shows the layering of shingles to emphasize the horizontal line, a detail common to many Prairie School homes at the time of construction, but rarely retained in subsequent reroofings. This is a private residence. ◆ 313 Forest Ave (at Erie St), Oak Park

I **Mrs. Thomas H. Gale House** The widow of **Frank Lloyd Wright**'s client for his "bootlegged" house on Chicago Avenue (see above) commissioned **Wright** for this residence in 1909. It was one of his last in Oak Park. The dramatically cantilevered balconies show the beginning of the design direction **Wright** would take in the 1930s, particularly in works such as Fallingwater, the great house he designed for Edgar Kaufman in Pennsylvania. Strongly horizontal, even to the flat roof, the house is more starkly modern than the neighboring **Wright** houses on Forest Avenue. It remains a private residence. ◆ 6 Elizabeth Ct (between Forest and N Kenilworth Aves), Oak Park

J **Peter A. Beachy House** It is thought that **Frank Lloyd Wright**'s talented employee **Walter Burley Griffin** influenced the look of this brick and stucco house, designed by **Wright** in 1906. Compared with most of his works from this era, the house is more massive and blocky. **Wright** was originally commissioned to remodel and add to a small wooden Gothic cottage on the site; no trace of this original structure is visible. The house is built to the scale of the site, deep and with a room-size side porch that takes advantage of the width of the lot. Wood mullions rather than lead cames define the windows. The great gable across the front is echoed by three smaller gables that roll down the sides of this immense home. The house is still a private residence. ♦ 238 Forest Ave (between Ontario St and Elizabeth Ct), Oak Park

K J.D. Everett House This 1888 home by **Wilson, Marble & Lamson** is a fine example of an exuberant Queen Anne house executed in wood, characteristic of the style popular in Oak Park homes when the young **Frank Lloyd Wright** arrived in the village. Variety of form, especially in window shapes and gables, and a many-angled roof were important attributes of this style. The architects practiced together only briefly, but as individuals and in other partnerships designed many homes and public buildings throughout the 1880s. This is a private residence. ♦ 228 Forest Ave (between Ontario St and Elizabeth Ct), Oak Park

L Frank W. Thomas House Built in 1901, this is **Frank Lloyd Wright**'s first true Prairie School house (pictured below) in Oak Park. The ground level contains only utility rooms. A mysterious yet compelling roundheaded doorway leads to stairs, hidden from the street view, that take the visitor up to the full-length leaded-glass front door. The living rooms are elevated, providing some privacy from pedestrians and motorists on Ontario Street and lovely views over Forest Avenue to **Austin Gardens,** formerly the Henry Austin estate. The leaded glass is perhaps the most spectacular element of the house and is best appreciated in the early evening. It's a private residence. ♦ 210 Forest Ave (at Ontario St), Oak Park

M Unity Temple A National Historic Landmark, built from 1905 to 1908, **Unity Temple** is deservedly one of **Frank Lloyd Wright**'s most famous buildings. Economic concerns and the architect's interest in the material led to the choice of reinforced concrete, a sharp contrast with the stone and brick churches that began to line Lake Street in the 19th century. The choice of material dictated simple forms, which in **Wright**'s hands became a complex set of interlocking rectangles embellished with simple geometric decoration on the piers between the high windows. Although it can appear gloomy from outside, the inside is beautifully lit by a skylight and clerestory windows. The golden glass of the skylight panes ensures that even on overcast days the quality of light is pleasing. ♦ Admission. Cassette tours daily 1PM-4PM; guided tours daily 1PM, 2PM, and 3PM. 875 Lake St (at N Kenilworth Ave), Oak Park. 708/383.8873

N Pleasant Home The investment banker John Farson commissioned architect **George W. Maher** to design this home in 1899, and named it for the intersection where it stands. It is one of **Maher**'s great early designs and shows a debt to **Wright**'s **Winslow House** in River Forest (see below).

The house exhibits **Maher**'s preferred palette, which was lighter than that of his Prairie School colleagues; vanilla Roman brick and cream-colored trim were favored here. **Maher** used several motifs that are repeated throughout the house and on some of the furnishings. The "Roman tray," a rectangle with an extra dollop on each end resembling the bottom of a shallow triangle, appears in the fence, in the medallions on either side of the front porch, in the magnificent windows by the front door, and on many of the door plates and drawer pulls.

Frank W. Thomas House

A lion's head can be seen on the third-floor dormer, on the front of the house near the foundations, and on some of the furniture. The interior has elements of Victorian as well as Prairie styles and offers a fascinating example of a house at the turning point of the designer's developing style. Much of the interior detailing and some of the furniture remains. The home is open for tours and also houses the **Historical Society of Oak Park and River Forest,** a museum with a small Hemingway display as well as other mementos of early Oak Park. ♦ Admission. Th-Su 1PM-4PM; tours at 1PM, 2PM, and 3PM. 217 Home Ave (at Pleasant St), Oak Park. 708/383.2654

In nearby River Forest:

William H. Winslow House Frank Lloyd **Wright**'s first great commission after leaving **Adler & Sullivan** was a groundbreaking design. The **Winslow House** is strikingly simple and modern for 1893. Set low to the ground with no visible basement, the house is firmly anchored visually by its foundation and by the low, hipped roof with its extremely deep eaves. The color palette is fresh and warm, and the broad band of geometric ornament at the second-floor level enriches the simplicity of the forms. Look through the porte cochere on the north to see the stables, also designed by **Wright.** This is a private residence. ♦ 515 Auvergne Pl (off Lake St), River Forest

William Drummond House Architect **William Drummond** went to work for **Frank Lloyd Wright** in his Oak Park studio in 1899 and remained on his staff until the studio closed in 1909. This home, built in 1910, especially reflects the influence of an unbuilt project **Wright** designed for *The Ladies Home Journal* in 1905, "A Fireproof House for $5,000." **Drummond**'s work typically has less decorative embellishment than that of his Prairie School colleagues, but is noteworthy for his mastery of proportion and warm, livable interiors. The porch of this private residence was originally open and had several large trees growing through it. ♦ 559 Edgewood Pl (off Lake St), River Forest

Isabel Roberts House Frank Lloyd Wright designed this house in 1908 for his secretary and bookkeeper. The plan is cruciform and the interior is spacious, with a two-story living room in front. Originally built in stucco, the house was later covered with brick. It's another private residence. ♦ 603 Edgewood Pl (off Lake St), River Forest

2 Brookfield Zoo A sprawling suburban zoo (see the map on page 195) 14 miles west of the Loop spans 204 acres of naturalistic habitats and gardens that are home to more than 2,000 animals representing 425 different species. Among the highlights are **Tropic**

World of Apes and Monkeys, the world's largest indoor zoo exhibit, which simulates rain forest regions of Asia, Africa, and South America. The **Seven Seas Panorama** includes an arena for viewing dolphins (there's a nominal ticket charge in addition to general admission) as they perform acrobatics and demonstrate echolocation, their form of sonar communication. The **Children's Zoo,** open to visitors of all ages, presents baby animals and pettable goats, lambs, and horses. **Backstage at the Zoo** offers, for an extra charge, in-depth tours of selected animal exhibits for kids ages seven and over. The **Zoo Shop** is well stocked with attractive animal-theme gifts and souvenirs, plus more than 4,500 books on animals and nature. Several fast-food restaurants are on the premises. ♦ Admission and parking fees; half-price admission on Tuesday and Thursday. Daily. First Ave and 31st St, Brookfield. By car, take I-55, I-290, or I-294 to the Brookfield Zoo exits. By commuter train from Union Station, take the Burlington line to the Metra Zoo stop at the Hollywood Station. 708/485.0263

3 Morton Arboretum The 1,500-acre refuge for woody plants from around the world was created in 1922 by Joy Morton, founder of the Morton Salt Company, on the grounds of his estate in what is now the western suburb of Lisle. (Apparently the whole family was fond of trees; Morton's father was J. Sterling Morton, a Nebraska statesman who originated Arbor Day.) This peaceful spot is walker's delight, with grassy slopes in every direction, trees and shrubs both familiar and unusual, and six lakes. There are numerous display gardens, among them **Hedge Gardens,** with more than a hundred formally laid-out hedges, and the **Fragrance Garden,** abloom with fragrant flowers and foliage. There's an indoor visitors' center, but the big attractions are outdoors, so dress for the weather. An introductory program, including a tour by foot or open-air bus, will show you around. You can tour the grounds in your own car along an eight-mile route, or set off on hiking trails. The arboretum is packed on weekends during April and May, when magnolias and other flowering trees go into bloom, and in mid- to late October, when fall colors reach their peak. Visit on a weekday instead if you can. Eats are available at a fast food restaurant, as well as in the full-menu

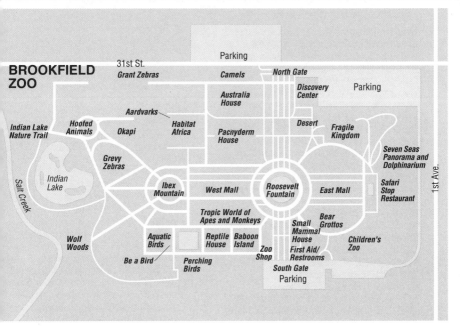

BROOKFIELD ZOO

31st St.
Grant Zebras
Camels
North Gate
Parking
Discovery Center
Parking
Australia House
Aardvarks
Habitat Africa
Desert
Fragile Kingdom
Indian Lake Nature Trail
Hoofed Animals
Okapi
Pacnyderm House
Grevy Zebras
Seven Seas Panorama and Dolphinarium
Indian Lake
Ibex Mountain
West Mall
Roosevelt Fountain
East Mall
Safari Stop Restaurant
1st Ave.
Salt Creek
Tropic World of Apes and Monkeys
Bear Grottos
Small Mammal House
Wolf Woods
Aquatic Birds
Reptile House
Baboon Island
Zoo Shop
First Aid/ Restrooms
Children's Zoo
Be a Bird
Perching Birds
South Gate
Parking

Gingko (708/719.2467) restaurant overlooking Meadow Lake. ♦ Admission. Daily. Rte 53, just off I-88, Lisle. Group tour reservations 708/719.2465 ♿

4 Geneva/St. Charles/Batavia Drive the roaring Eisenhower Expressway (I-90), then take Interstate 88 westward from the Loop for about an hour, and you end up in these three lovely towns along the Fox River. An antiques-lover's heaven, they boast hundreds of dealers along with numerous shops selling arts and crafts. On the first weekend of every month, the **Kane County Flea Market** (on Randall Rd, just west of Geneva) shows the wares of up to a thousand dealers. Many 19th-century Victorian homes and other landmark buildings throughout all three towns have been preserved and are open to the public. Special museums include the **Garfield Farm Museum** (admission; open Wednesday and Sunday 1PM-4PM, June through September; Garfield Rd, at Rte 38, five miles west of Geneva, 708/584.8485 ♿), which spans 212 acres and depicts farm life in the mid-19th century; the museum is open only Wednesdays and Sundays from 1 until 4PM. Recreational opportunities include bicycling along riverfront trails, canoeing, fishing, golfing at nearby courses, and cross-country skiing. Third Street is one of the Chicago area's most charming places to shop; dozens of antiques and gift stores line this street of 19th-century brick and wooden houses. Restaurants abound, particularly in Geneva, which was established in the same year as Chicago: The **Mill Race Inn** (4 E State St, at the Fox River, 708/232.2030 ♿) is a special treat for dinner, as is **302 West** (302 W State St, at Third St, 708/232.9302). ♦ Take I-290 and I-88 west from the Loop, exit on Rte 31, and head north through Batavia and Geneva to St. Charles. For more information, call the St. Charles Visitor's Bureau 800/777.4373, the St. Charles Chamber of Commerce 708/584.8384, the Geneva Chamber of Commerce 708/232.6060, or the Batavia Chamber of Commerce 708/879.7141

5 North Shore A journey northward along Lake Michigan through Evanston, Wilmette, Kenilworth, Winnetka, Glencoe, and Highland Park—some of the city's most affluent suburbs—makes a pleasant day trip, whether it's nature scenes, gigantic mansions, or other sights you're interested in. Sheridan Road meanders through the entire area. ♦ From the Loop, take Lake Shore Drive north to its natural end at Hollywood Avenue, where it turns into Sheridan Road, and continue north through Rogers Park and out of the city to Evanston. You may also reach a number of these areas by **CTA**'s **Red Line** or **Evanston Express,** also called the **Purple Line; Metra** trains go there, too. For information on public transportation, call 836.7000

Oak Park resident Edgar Rice Burroughs created the literary figure, Tarzan.

The Chicago Cubs have played in and lost the World Series a total of eight times. They won the World Series in 1907 and 1908.

Restaurants/Clubs: Red   **Hotels:** Blue
Shops/ 🍴 Outdoors: Green   **Sights/Culture:** Black

Highlights of the North Shore include:

Evanston Home to the 160-building campus of **Northwestern University,** Evanston has a small-town, yet cultured, feeling. Numerous art galleries, interesting shopping (primarily along Chicago, Sherman, and Orrington Aves), fine restaurants, and a pretty lakefront make it a pleasant place to visit. One highlight is the 113-foot-tall 19th-century **Grosse Point Lighthouse** (admission; tours Sa-Su 2PM, 3PM, 4PM June-Sept; no children under 5; 2535 Sheridan Rd, at Central St, 847/328.6961). On the grounds of **Northwestern University**'s Evanston campus is the **Mary & Leigh Block Gallery.** This fine arts museum contains an outdoor sculpture garden and a permanent collection of works by 20th-century artists (free; Tu-Su; 1967 Sheridan Rd, 847/491.4000). The **Evanston Historical Society/Dawes House** is a national landmark mansion (admission; M-Tu, Th-Sa 1-5PM; 225 Greenwood St, at Lake Michigan, 847/475.3410). Among the eateries, **Va Pensiero** (1566 Oak St, at Davis St, 847/475.7779) is the most elegant, **Bistro 1800** (1800 Sherman Ave, at Clark St, 847/492.3450) the most convenient, and **Lucky Platter** (514 Main St, between Hinman and Chicago Aves, 847/869.4064) the most whimsical in decor and healthy in menu (it's vegetarian). The Evanston Lakefront is a beautiful spot, and you can walk its entire length from Main Street to the **Northwestern** campus.

Wilmette Sheridan Road takes you right by the breathtaking **Baha'i House of Worship** (100 Linden Ave, at Sheridan Rd, 847/853.2300). On the National Register of Historic Places, this is the first house of worship erected in the United States for the Baha'i faith, which originated in Iran and has followers throughout the world. It was constructed under the direction of architect **Louis J. Bourgeois** from 1920 to 1953. Farther along Sheridan Road you will come to **Plaza del Lago,** an upscale shopping center that includes a **Crate & Barrel** furniture store. Wilmette is also home to the **Kohl Children's Museum,** which features numerous hands-on displays, plus puppet shows, sing-alongs, and other special events (admission; Tu-Su; 165 Green Bay Rd, at Linden Ave, 847/256.6056). It also has the area's most beautiful beach, Great Gillson Beach (off Sheridan Rd), where sailboats can be rented as well; for beach and boat-rental information, call 847/256.9660.

Glencoe The **Chicago Botanic Garden,** where plants, trees, and flowers from around the world are cultivated on 300 acres of landscaped hills and islands, makes its home here. The park is interspersed with lakes, naturalistic wooded areas, and nature and prairie trails (free; parking fee; daily 8AM-

sunset; Lake Cook Rd, east of Edens Expressway, 847/835.5440). Spring and autumn, of course, are particularly beautiful times. The garden's **Education Center** houses the **Museum of Floral Arts,** the **Plant Information Service,** a gift shop, and the **Food for Thought Cafe**. You may also bring along a picnic lunch and eat at one of several designated areas in the garden. Two architecturally notable buildings in Glencoe are the **Glasner House** (850 N Sheridan Rd), private residence built in 1904 by **Frank Lloyd Wright,** and the reinforced concrete **Temple of North Shore Congregation Israel** (1185 N Sheridan Rd), which was designed in 1963 by **Minoru Yamasaki** and completed in 1983 by **Hammond, Beeby & Babka.**

Highland Park Continuing your drive along Sheridan Road, you will pass the **Ward W. Willits House** (1445 N Sheridan Rd), a Prairie School house built in 1902 by **Frank Lloyd Wright** that is still a private residence. Also while in town, don't miss **Carlos** for exquisitely prepared nouvelle cuisine (daily dinner; reservations required; 429 Temple Ave, between Green Bay Rd and Highwood Ave, 847/432.0770). Another Highland Park highlight is the Ravinia Festival, which hosts evening performances in a parklike setting from June through September (312/728.464 in season, 847/433.8800 year-round). The high-powered performers range from Joan Baez to the **Chicago Symphony Orchestra,** as well as dance companies and chamber orchestras. You can reserve seats in the roofed arena, but most concertgoers bring a blanket, a bottle of wine, and a picnic, and settle on the grassy lawns beneath the stars. ♦ Enter the park from Sheridan, Green Bay, or Lake Cook Roads.

6 Le Francais ★★★★$$$$ The suburb of Wheeling is home to what some say is the best restaurant in Chicago. Expect not only meticulously prepared French food, but an 80-page wine list. ♦ French ♦ Tu-F lunch and dinner; Sa dinner. Reservations required. 269 S Milwaukee Ave (two blocks east of Dundee Rd), Wheeling, 847/541.7470 ৬

7 Arlington Heights Flower-filled **Le Titi de Paris** serves French classics and more daring specials (Tu-F lunch and dinner; Sa dinner; reservations recommended; 1015 W Dundee Rd, at Kenicott St, 847/506.0222) This is also the town for a day at the races; the ponies run on Monday, and Wednesday through Sunday, May through October at the **Arlington International Racecourse** (at Eucl. and Wilkie Aves, 847/255.4300).

Western Avenue is the longest street in the city, measuring 23.5 miles.

Architectural Highlights

Chicago is the world's largest outdoor museum of modern architecture. Turn almost any corner in the Loop and you'll discover a building that marks structural, technical, or aesthetic achievement. This is the birthplace of the skyscraper and home to three of the world's tallest buildings, including the record-holding **Sears Tower.** Not all of the landmarks are a hundred stories tall, however. Chicago's architectural heritage encompasses many styles and movements; some are world-famous and some are only now gaining the appreciation they deserve. But all have contributed to a vibrant cityscape that continues to inspire visitors and residents alike.

After Chicago's Great Fire of 1871 destroyed four square miles of the central city, architects, engineers, and artisans arrived in great numbers to take part in the massive rebuilding effort. The rapidly increasing land values in the central business district motivated developers to build as high as they possibly could. The invention of the elevator, along with technological advances in foundation laying and wind-bracing metal framing, made it possible to construct buildings taller than five stories. Most important was the discovery of how to protect the metal structure from fire by cladding it in terra-cotta. (The cast-iron columns and beams of Chicago's supposedly fireproof earlier buildings had melted in the intense heat of the blaze.) With this knowledge, the only remaining limitation was the weight of the building itself.

William Le Baron Jenney is frequently called the father of the skyscraper, as much for his role in training a new generation of Chicago architects as for his own considerable achievements. **Jenney**'s structural innovations included designing the first buildings that were supported entirely by their metal frameworks, such as the **Manhattan Building** in the Loop. Even the exterior walls did not support their own weight; they were hung on the steel structure like drapery (today they are known as curtain walls).

Many architects believed that the new structural technology should be reflected in equally innovative exterior forms. The powerful designs of these early buildings led historians to refer to them collectively as the Chicago School of Architecture, the first truly modern architecture. The chief characteristic of this style is the straightforward expression of structure, with a masonry grid overlaying the steel framework and the spaces between them filled with large panes of glass. Ornamentation became subordinate to expression of the framework; ornamentation was most often used on the bottom and top floors to create a three-part facade composition resembling the base-shaft-capital design of Classical columns. Projecting bay windows created a lively rhythm while admitting abundant daylight, increasing rentable square footage, and improving cross-ventilation. A key feature is the Chicago window, a three-part window (illustrated at right) with a large fixed pane flanked by a pair of smaller sash windows.

The Chicago Window

The three outstanding Chicago School firms were **Adler & Sullivan, Holabird & Roche,** and **Burnham & Root.** And architect **Louis Sullivan** is revered today not only for his buildings but for the unique style of ornamentation he developed, the **Carson Pirie Scott** store in the Loop providing the most spectacular example. **Holabird & Roche** is the firm most closely associated with the Chicago School, having established a style of solid, straightforward structures with the **Pontiac** and **Marquette Buildings** (in the South Loop and Loop, respectively).

Burnham & Root created the masterpieces of the **Rookery** and **Monadnock Buildings** in the Loop; after the early death of **John Wellborn Root** in 1891, the firm's work became increasingly Classical. **Root**'s successor as chief designer, **Charles Atwood,** completed work on the **Reliance Building** in the Loop, a tour de force that combines lush ornamentation with a clear display of structure, proving that the two were not incompatible.

Daniel Burnham became increasingly influential as a city planner. His 1909 Plan of Chicago was the country's first all-encompassing urban plan. He is also known as the design chief for the 1893 World's Columbian Exposition. However, much to the consternation of his fellow Chicago architects (particularly **Louis Sullivan**), he let East Coast architects dominate the fair stylistically. The resulting Neo-Classical "White City" helped shift local taste away from buildings that displayed their structure to those that disguised it in historical garb. The formal Beaux Arts style was deemed especially suitable for the city's growing cultural institutions; prominent examples include the **Art Institute** and the **Cultural Center,** which were designed in the 1890s by the Boston firm **Shepley, Rutan & Coolidge.**

In the early 1900s **Frank Lloyd Wright** and his contemporaries were developing a modern style now known as the Prairie School. The houses designed in this style generally have low, ground-hugging forms, hovering roofs with deep eaves, and bands of casement windows. The interiors feature broad, centrally located hearths, natural woodwork, earth colors, and rooms tied together by open floor plans and uniform wall treatments. The break from the historically inspired Victorian styles began in the 1890s with designs such as the **Charnley House** in the Gold Coast and the **Winslow House** in River Forest, both by **Wright.** The largest groups of Prairie Houses are in the suburbs, especially in Oak Park, where Forest Avenue and surrounding streets are lined with houses by **Wright** and members of his Oak Park studio. The **Madlener House** in the Gold Coast, by **Hugh M.G. Garden** and **Richard E. Schmidt,** and the houses on Hutchinson Street by **George W. Maher** exemplify the rectilinear, horizontal, and beautiful detailing characteristics of this style. **Wright**'s **Robie House** in Hyde Park is the most famous Prairie School house, a National Historic Landmark and an American masterpiece.

The prosperity of the 1920s created a building boom, and the 1920 construction of the **Michigan Avenue Bridge** pushed development north of the river. Three of the four buildings at this prominent river crossing are wonderful examples of the fanciful borrowings from European sources that characterized architecture at the time: the **Wrigley Building**, the **Tribune Tower**, and **360 North Michigan Avenue.**

The **Tribune Tower** was the result of a 1922 design competition—a competition that is famous for the lasting influence of its many losing entries. For example, **Eliel Saarinen**'s second-place design was adapted by **Holabird & Root** in 1928 for the building just across the river at **333 North Michigan Avenue,** Chicago's first Art Deco skyscraper. This successor firm to **Holabird & Roche,** whose name changed in 1927 when **John Root Jr.** became a partner, designed most of Chicago's Art Deco masterpieces, including the **Board of Trade.** The decade's other prolific firm was **Graham, Anderson, Probst & White,** which carried on **Daniel Burnham**'s practice.

The Depression brought an abrupt halt to construction, and in the next two decades the city's architects received few commissions. In the late 1930s Nazi persecution spurred the immigration of several German architects; many of them settled in Chicago, including **Ludwig Mies van der Rohe.** In the 1940s **Mies** designed the campus of the **Illinois Institute of Technology,** where he taught architecture. When the postwar economic recovery arrived, **Mies** began to receive commissions for apartment buildings, and the steel-and-glass towers he designed at **860-880 North Lake Shore Drive** in 1952 ushered in a new era of skyscraper design.

Mies was as concerned with structural expression and exploitation of new technology as the architects of the 1880s had been, and the "glass box" era that he began is often called the Second Chicago School. The firm of **Skidmore, Owings & Merrill (SOM)** furthered the global dominance of Modernism from the 1950s through the 1970s. **SOM** architect **Bruce Graham** and engineer Fazlur Khan together designed some of the tallest buildings in the world. The **John Hancock Center** of 1969 flaunts its unusual structure, with giant wind-bracing Xs marching up its four sides. The **Sears Tower** is much less demonstrative, utilizing a "bundled tube" structural system that is far from obvious to the casual observer.

Just when this style seemed to have become formulaic, the inevitable rebellion began. Postmodernism, a catchall term for anything

outside the strict canon of the Modernist style, landed in the heart of the city with such buildings as **Kohn Pedersen Fox**'s **333 Wacker Drive,** a wedge of green glass bowed to follow the river, and **A. Epstein & Sons**' **150 North Michigan Avenue,** with its bisected triangular towers and sloping glass roof. **SOM** itself has now officially abandoned Modernism, creating such period pieces as **Adrian Smith**'s Art Deco **NBC Tower.** And **Thomas Beeby**'s award-winning design for the **Harold Washington Library Center,** the most recent great building in Chicago, is a fusion of historical references that pays tribute to the city's Classical architecture.

The pluralism of the 1980s has inspired greater scrutiny of the orthodox Modernist view of Chicago's architectural history, and caused critics to take a second look at works previously dismissed as eclectic. Much credit for this revisionism goes to early rebels such as **Ben** and **Harry Weese, Stanley Tigerman, Larry Booth,** and **Jack Hartray.** Perhaps the most important development is that architects and a growing number of concerned citizens now rigorously fight the destruction of the city's historical buildings to ensure that Chicago's rich architectural heritage will remain one of its chief glories.

Wrigley Building

KAHLER/MORROW

History

The land that today is Chicago lay below the ocean 400 million years ago. A series of gigantic glaciers created the lakes, rivers, and trails used by the native Potawatomi, Wea, Miami, and Illinois tribes, and later traveled by European explorers.

1682 French explorer René-Robert Cavelier Sieur de La Salle first refers to the area as *Che-cau-gou,* an Indian name with several possible meanings, including "wild onion" and "strong and great."

1763 The French, having claimed the land, bequeath it to the English as part of their settlement in the Seven Years' War.

1783 The British hand over the land to the newly independent United States of America.

1784 Jean Baptiste-Pointe duSable becomes the area's first non-Indian settler when he builds a house and trading post at the intersection of **Lake Michigan** and the **Chicago River,** the Chicago portage.

1795 Native Americans surrender a six-square-mile piece of land at the mouth of the Chicago River, which empties into the southwest end of Lake Michigan, clearing the way for the establishment of what is now downtown Chicago.

1803 To protect the growing European community from Native Americans and to provide a strategic United States military site, **Fort Dearborn** is built south of the Chicago River, where the **Michigan Avenue Bridge** is today.

1812 When the British declare war on the United States, **Fort Dearborn** occupants evacuate their haven and are massacred by the Indians.

1816 A second **Fort Dearborn** is constructed. It stands until 1856.

1827 The federal government issues a land grant for the building of a canal between Lake Michigan and the Mississippi River. Construction begins in 1836, and the first boats travel it in 1846.

1829 The city's first meatpacking plant is constructed by Archibald Clybourne, one of Chicago's earliest butchers.

1832 The first street (unnamed) is surveyed, running from the east end of **Water Street** (now **Wacker Drive**) to Lake Michigan.

1833 The **Village of Chicago,** covering an area of one square mile, is officially chartered with a population of 340. A group of 76 Indian chiefs signs a treaty surrendering more land, and they begin moving their tribes to reservations.

1836 Shopkeepers Caroline and Henry Clarke build a two-story white frame house in what is then the suburbs. More than a century and a half later, the **Clarke House** is Chicago's oldest surviving building, located in the **Prairie Avenue Historic District.**

1837 Chicago is incorporated as a city and has a population of 4,170.

1839 William Stuart founds the *Daily American,* the city's first daily newspaper.

1847 The *Chicago Tribune* newspaper is founded.

1848 The Chicago Board of Trade is created.

1849 Chicago's first beer is brewed by German immigrant Adolph Mueller.

1850 Chicago's population reaches 29,963.

1851 The **Illinois Central Railroad,** the country's first land-grant railroad, is chartered.

Allan Pinkerton is hired as Chicago's first detective.

1853 The city's population tops 60,000.

Chicago now has seven daily newspapers.

1854 A paid city fire department is established. (Four years later it is discovered that a blaze that destroyed a lumberyard was set by firefighter "Beast" Brown after the lumberyard owner refused to buy tickets to the Fireman's Ball.)

1855 A riot breaks out when police try to stop Germans from drinking beer, as ordered by Mayor Levi Boone, who considers the practice "foreign and anti-American."

1857 The **State Street** area becomes a retail center when the 32-stall **Market Hall** is constructed.

The city's first steel-rolling mill, the **North Chicago Rolling Mill,** opens.

1858 Illinois adopted son Abraham Lincoln makes his first Senate campaign speech. Later in the year, he debates the subject of slavery with rival Stephen A. Douglas on the balcony of the **Tremont House Hotel.**

Chicago has become the country's chief railroad shipper, with 20 million bushels of produce transported each year.

1859 Chicago's first horse-drawn railways go into operation.

The **University of Chicago** opens; in 1886 it closes due to a lack of funds and internal problems. A second, unrelated **University of Chicago** opens successfully in 1892.

1860 The Republican National Convention, held downtown, nominates Lincoln for president.

The city's population approaches 110,000, half of whom are foreign-born.

1863 Chicago overtakes Cincinnati as the country's pork-packing center.

1864 George Pullman builds the *Pioneer,* the first specially constructed railway sleeping car.

1865 The **Union Stock Yards,** the largest in the world, begin operation on Christmas Day.

1866 Construction of **Lincoln Park** begins on land that had previously served as the city cemetery.

1867 Real estate mogul Potter Palmer becomes the city's first millionaire.

Philip D. Armour opens a meatpacking plant.

1869 Burlesque makes its United States debut at **Crosby's Opera House** with Lydia Thompson and her British Blondes.

1871 The Great Chicago Fire, which presumably started in Mrs. Kate O'Leary's barn, rages through the city for three days, destroys millions of dollars in property, and leaves one-third of the population homeless.

1872 The City Council passes an ordinance outlawing wooden buildings downtown.

1873 The Bread Riot starts when starving workers marching to the Relief and Aid Society are driven into the **La Salle Street Tunnel** at Randolph Street by Chicago police and clubbed to death.

1874 The *Chicago Daily News* is founded and quickly becomes the city's largest newspaper.

1877 Federal troops are called in to end the railroad workers' strike.

1879 Carter H. Harrison is elected mayor for the first of five straight terms.

1880 The city's population reaches a half-million.

1882 The **Chicago Stock Exchange** is established.

Charles T. Yerkes builds the city's first cable car line.

1886 The Haymarket Massacre occurs when a bomb explodes in the midst of a group of policemen who had been sent in to control the crowd assembled for a labor rally at **Haymarket Square.** In retaliation, the police fire upon the crowd. A monument to the dead police officers is built; in the 1960s it is blown up, and in 1972 it is relocated to police headquarters.

1887 **Fort Sheridan** is constructed on the lakefront north of the city and is run by United States Army troops to protect Chicagoans against anarchists. Although there is no evidence that any of the seven anarchists being held by the police made or threw the bomb that killed seven police officers during the Haymarket rally, four labor leaders—George Engel, Adolph Fischer, A.R. Parsons, and August Spies— are convicted and executed by hanging. A fifth, Louis Lingg, is found in his cell with his head blown off.

1892 Telephone communications are established between Chicago, New York, and Boston.

1893 The World's Columbian Exposition opens in **Hyde Park**. Mayor Carter H. Harrison is assassinated on the last day of the fair.

Governor John Peter Altgeld pardons three Haymarket rioters, a decision that will prevent his re-election.

1896 The Municipal Voters' League accuses 26 of the city's 34 aldermen of being crooks.

1897 The $2-million **Chicago Public Library** opens on the lakefront. The **Loop** rapid transit system, which encircles the downtown area, is constructed.

1900 Chicago's booming population approaches 1.7 million.

Ada and Minna Everleigh open the **Everleigh Club,** the Midwest's most elegant and expensive brothel.

1903 A fire at the **Iroquois Theater** kills 603 people.

Essanay Studio, one of the country's first movie studios, opens. It later moves to California.

1905 **Orchestra Hall** opens.

The Industrial Workers of the World (IWW) labor union is organized.

1906 Upton Sinclair's *The Jungle* is published, exposing inhumane working conditions in the Chicago stockyards.

1912 Prostitution is made illegal, and all the bordellos on **Michigan Avenue** are closed.

1914 Tens of thousands of African-Americans migrate from the South in search of industrial work.

William Hale "Big Bill" Thompson, future pal of gangster Al Capone, is elected mayor.

1915 The excursion steamer *Eastland* capsizes in the Chicago River, killing 835 people.

1919 Race riots break out when a black man enters a segregated South Side beach; 15 whites and 25 blacks die.

1920 Chicago's population reaches 2.7 million, a third of whom are Catholic.

Prohibition begins and bloody gang wars erupt over the control of bootlegging.

1922 Chicago sends a letter to other American cities urging a constitutional amendment that would legalize the sale of wine and beer.

1929 Seven of Al Capone's rivals are machine-gunned to death in a North Side garage in the St. Valentine's Day Massacre.

1931 Al Capone is found guilty of tax evasion and sentenced to 10 years in prison.

1933 Mayor Anton J. Cermak, the first Czechoslovakian elected to such an office in the US, is shot to death in Miami by an assassin who was trying to kill President Franklin D. Roosevelt.

1942 The first atomic chain reaction is set off in a nuclear reactor at the **University of Chicago** under the direction of Enrico Fermi.

1949 The **Midwest Stock Exchange** is formed as a result of a merger between the Chicago Stock

Exchange and exchanges in Cleveland, St. Louis, and Minneapolis/St. Paul.

1950 Chicago's population reaches 3,621,000.

1955 Richard J. Daley is elected mayor, a post he holds for six terms, spanning 21 years.

1957 *Life* magazine reports that the Chicago police department is the most corrupt in the nation.

1959 The **Chicago White Sox** win the American League pennant. Air raid sirens, turned on in celebration, set off a citywide panic.

1960 Investigations reveal that corrupt Chicago cops are working with a gang of burglars.

Orlando Wilson, chair of the criminology department at the **University of California,** is appointed police commissioner.

1968 Riots break out in African-American neighborhoods in reaction to the assassination of Martin Luther King Jr. Mayor Daley issues police a "shoot-on-sight" order to try to halt the violence in which seven people are killed and 500 injured.

During the Democratic National Convention, fighting ensues between police and anti–Vietnam War demonstrators.

1969 The Chicago Eight, including Abbie Hoffman, go on trial, accused of inciting riots during the convention.

Black Panthers Fred Hampton and Mark Clark are slain when Chicago police, working with a floor plan provided by the FBI, raid Hampton's apartment at dawn, firing a hundred shots.

1971 The **Union Stock Yards** close. The Reverend Jesse Jackson founds Operation PUSH (People United to Save Humanity) to serve the city's poor.

1975 The **Water Tower Place** high-rise shopping mall opens on **North Michigan Avenue.**

Chicago Mob chieftain Sam "Momo" Giancana is shot seven times in the head while cooking sausages in his **Oak Park** basement. He dies.

1978 Chicago aldermen vote themselves a 60-percent pay hike soon after President Jimmy Carter asks Americans to limit wage increases to seven percent.

State Street is turned into a pedestrian-only mall.

1979 Jane Byrne replaces ex-mayor Michael Bilandic, whose failure to get the city back on its feet after a four-foot snowstorm infuriated Chicagoans. She hires her husband, Jay McMullen, as her $52,000-a-year political advisor.

1980 The population, though decreasing, still stands at an impressive 2,969,570.

1981 The Chicago Mob puts out a $100,000 contract on Mayor Byrne when she fails to support casino gambling in the city. No one takes up the offer.

1983 Chicago elects its first African-American mayor, Harold Washington, setting off council wars as the old guard fights to maintain control of the city.

1984 The **Chicago Cubs** win the Eastern Division Title, but lose the National Pennant to the San Diego Padres.

1986 The **Chicago Bears** win the Super Bowl, making coach Mike Ditka the city's newest hero and restaurateur. When he is fired in 1992, his restaurant, no longer trading on his celebrity, closes.

1987 Mayor Washington dies of a heart attack. Chaos ensues as aides and aldermen vie for control.

1989 Richard M. Daley, son of the late Richard J., is elected mayor.

1990 The United States Census Bureau counts 2,725,979 people living in Chicago; it becomes the third- rather than second-largest city (after New York and Los Angeles). The metropolitan area numbers over seven million.

After long controversy, lights are installed in **Wrigley Field,** and the **Chicago Cubs** begin playing night games.

1992 A section of the freight tunnel under the Chicago River caves in, causing flooding that paralyzes the Loop for two weeks.

1993 The **Bulls** win the National Basketball Association championship for the third consecutive year. The team's star guard, Michael Jordan, Chicago's most famous resident, retires.

1994 Chicago lawyer Dawn Clark Netsch wins the Democratic nomination for governor; her running mate is also a woman, making this the nation's first all-female gubernatorial ticket.

For the first time in history, the President of the Cook County Board is not a white, male Democrat. African-American John Stroger, the Democratic party's nominee, defeats Joe Morris, a white Republican.

1995 Mayor Richard M. Daley is reelected for a third term. Michael Jordan comes out of retirement to rejoin the **Bulls.**

1996 With 72 victories, the **Bulls** set an NBA record for the most wins ever in a single season. They go on to win the NBA championship.

The Chicago-based Playboy Enterprises has a reference library with over 8,000 magazines, including a collection of Playboy magazines in Braille.

Index

Index

Index

Index

Restaurants

Only restaurants with star ratings are listed below. All restaurants are listed alphabetically in the main (preceding) index. Always call in advance to ensure a restaurant has not closed, changed its hours, or booked its tables for a private party. The restaurant price ratings are based on the average cost of an entrée for one person, excluding tax and tip.

★★★★ An Extraordinary Experience
  ★★★ Excellent
    ★★ Very Good
      ★ Good

$$$$ Big Bucks ($20 and up)
 $$$ Expensive ($15-$20)
  $$ Reasonable ($10-$15)
   $ The Price Is Right (less than $10)

Hotels

The hotels listed below are grouped according to their price ratings; they are also listed in the main index. The hotel price ratings reflect the base price of a standard room for two people for one night during the peak season.

$$$$ Big Bucks ($250 and up)
$$$ Expensive ($175-$250)
$$ Reasonable ($100-$175)
$ The Price Is Right (less than $100)

$$$$

$$$

Page	Entry #	Notes

Credits

Writer and Researcher
Marilyn Soltis

Writers and Researchers (Previous Edition)
**Connie Goddard
Kate Campion
Nell Goddard**

ACCESS®PRESS

Editorial Director
Lois Spritzer

Managing Editor
Laura L. Brengelman

Senior Editors
**Mary Callahan
Beth Schlau**

Associate Editors
**Patricia Canole
Gene Gold
Susan McClung**

Map Coordinator
Jonathan Goodnough

Editorial Assistant
Susan Cutter Snyder

Contributing Editor
Kathryn Clark

Senior Art Director
C. Linda Dingler

Design Supervisor
Joy O'Meara

Designer
Elizabeth Paige Streit

Map Designer
Patricia Keelin

Associate Director of Production
Dianne Pinkowitz

Director, Electronic Publishing
John R. Day

Cover Photo©
StockFood America/Sandmann

Special Thanks
**Laurie McGovern Petersen,
  Architectural Consultant
Anne Spiselman, Restaurant Consultant**

The publisher and authors assume no legal responsibility
for the completeness or accuracy of the contents of this
book, nor any legal responsibility for the appreciation or
depreciation in the value of any premises, commercial
or otherwise, by reason of inclusion in or exclusion
from this book. All contents are based on information
available at the time of publication. Some of the maps
are diagrammatic and may be selective of street inclusion.

ACCESS®PRESS does not solicit individuals,
organizations, or businesses for inclusion in our books,
nor do we accept payment for inclusion. We welcome,
however, information from our readers, including
comments, criticisms, and suggestions for new
listings. Send all correspondence to: **ACCESS®**PRESS,
10 East 53rd Street, 18th Floor, New York, NY 10022

Art Institute of Chicago

PRINTED IN HONG KONG

ACCESS® Guides

Order by phone, toll-free: 1-800-331-3761

Name _____ Phone _____

Address _____

City _____ State _____ Zip _____

Please send me the following ACCESS® Guides:

☐ **ATLANTA** ACCESS® $18.50
0-06-277156-6

☐ **BARCELONA** ACCESS® $17.00
0-06-277000-4

☐ **BOSTON** ACCESS® $18.50
0-06-277143-4

☐ **BUDGET EUROPE** ACCESS® $18.50
0-06-277171-X

☐ **CAPE COD** ACCESS® $18.50
0-06-277159-0

☐ **CARIBBEAN** ACCESS® $18.50
0-06-277128-0

☐ **CHICAGO** ACCESS® $18.50
0-06-277144-2

☐ **FLORENCE/VENICE/MILAN** ACCESS® $18.50
0-06-277170-1

☐ **HAWAII** ACCESS® $18.50
0-06-277142-6

☐ **LAS VEGAS** ACCESS® $18.50
0-06-277177-9

☐ **LONDON** ACCESS® $18.50
0-06-277161-2

☐ **LOS ANGELES** ACCESS® $18.50
0-06-277131-0

☐ **MEXICO** ACCESS® $18.50
0-06-277127-2

☐ **MIAMI & SOUTH FLORIDA** ACCESS® $18.50
0-06-277178-7

☐ **MONTREAL & QUEBEC** ACCESS® $18.50
0-06-277160-4

☐ **NEW ORLEANS** ACCESS® $18.50
0-06-277176-0

☐ **NEW YORK CITY** ACCESS® $18.50
0-06-277162-0

☐ **NEW YORK CITY RESTAURANT** ACCESS®
$13.00
0-06-277191-4

☐ **ORLANDO & CENTRAL FLORIDA** ACCESS®
$18.50
0-06-277175-2

☐ **PARIS** ACCESS® $18.50
0-06-277163-9

☐ **PHILADELPHIA** ACCESS® $18.50
0-06-277155-8

☐ **ROME** ACCESS® $18.50
0-06-277150-7

☐ **SAN DIEGO** ACCESS® $18.50
0-06-277185-X

☐ **SAN FRANCISCO** ACCESS® $18.50
0-06-277121-3

☐ **SAN FRANCISCO RESTAURANT** ACCESS®
$13.00
0-06-277192-2

☐ **SANTA FE/TAOS/ALBUQUERQUE** ACCESS®
$18.50
0-06-277148-5

☐ **SEATTLE** ACCESS® $18.50
0-06-277149-3

☐ **SKI COUNTRY** ACCESS®
Eastern United States $18.50
0-06-277125-6

☐ **SKI COUNTRY** ACCESS®
Western United States $18.50
0-06-277174-4

☐ **WASHINGTON DC** ACCESS® $18.50
0-06-277158-2

☐ **WINE COUNTRY** ACCESS®
France $18.50
0-06-277151-5

☐ **WINE COUNTRY** ACCESS®
Northern California $18.50
0-06-277164-7

Prices subject to change without notice.

Total for **ACCESS®** Guides:	$
Please add applicable sales tax:	
Add $4.00 for first book S&H, $1.00 per additional book:	
Total payment:	$

☐ Check or Money Order enclosed. Offer valid in the United States only.
Please make payable to HarperCollins*Publishers*.

☐ Charge my credit card　☐ American Express　☐ Visa　☐ MasterCard

Card no. _____ Exp. date _____

Signature _____

Send orders to:　HarperCollins*Publishers*
P.O. Box 588
Dunmore, PA 18512-0588

ACCESS®
The Neighborhood Guide